The inside story behind the de[sign,]

architecture, and future of Mic[rosoft's]

next generation operating system

I N S I D E

WINDOWS NT™

INSIDE
WINDOWS
NT™

 **Microsoft** PRESS

HELEN CUSTER
FOREWORD BY DAVID N. CUTLER

PUBLISHED BY
Microsoft Press
A Division of Microsoft Corporation
One Microsoft Way
Redmond, Washington 98052-6399

Library of Congress Cataloging-in-Publication Data
Custer, Helen, 1961–
    Inside windows NT / Helen Custer.
       p. cm.
    Includes bibliographical references and index.
    ISBN 1-55615-481-X
    1. Operating systems (Computers)   2. Windows NT. I. Title.
  QA76.76.063C89 1992
  005.4'469--dc20   92-26231
                                          CIP

Printed and bound in the United States of America.

1 2 3 4 5 6 7 8 9 AGAG 8 7 6 5 4 3

Distributed to the book trade in Canada by Macmillan of Canada, a division
of Canada Publishing Corporation.

Distributed to the book trade outside the United States and Canada by
Penguin Books Ltd.

Penguin Books Ltd., Harmondsworth, Middlesex, England
Penguin Books Australia Ltd., Ringwood, Victoria, Australia
Penguin Books N.Z. Ltd., 182–190 Wairau Road, Auckland 10, New Zealand

British Cataloging-in-Publication Data available.

3Com is a registered trademark of 3Com Corporation. Apple and Macintosh are
registered trademarks of Apple Computer, Inc. Banyan and VINES are registered trademarks of Banyan Systems, Inc. DEC, PDP-II, VAX, and VMS are registered trademarks
and DECnet and MicroVAX are trademarks of Digital Equipment Corporation. Intel is
a registered trademark and Intel386 and Intel486 are trademarks of Intel Corporation.
Microsoft, MS-DOS, and XENIX are registered trademarks and Windows, and Windows
NT are trademarks of Microsoft Corporation. OS/2 is a registered trademark licensed
to Microsoft Corporation. NetWare and Novell are registered trademarks of Novell, Inc.
Sun, Sun Microsystems, and Sun Workstation are registered trademarks of Sun Microsystems,
Incorporated. UNIX is a registered trademark of UNIX Systems Laboratories.

Acquisitions Editor: Dean Holmes
Manuscript Editor: Nancy Siadek
Project Editors: Nancy Siadek and Deborah Long
Technical Editor: Jeff Carey

This book is dedicated to the members of the Windows NT team,

many of whom have made considerable personal sacrifices

to design and construct this operating system.

Long may she run.

Contents Summary

Table of Contents

CHAPTER FIVE

WINDOWS AND THE PROTECTED SUBSYSTEMS **115**

CHAPTER EIGHT

CHAPTER NINE

FOREWORD

In 1965, I graduated from college with a B.A. in mathematics, a minor in physics, and an overwhelming desire to be an engineer and to build things. So I took a job with DuPont in Wilmington, Delaware, as a materials testing engineer. After about a year of absolute boredom, I was lent to the mathematics and statistics group and assigned to construct a computer simulation model for a new foam-making process that the Scott Paper Company was developing. Working with machines that never did what I meant them to was humiliating, but within six months I was hooked, and what I had shunned coming out of school—computers—turned into my life's vocation.

Soon after, I transferred to DuPont's engineering department, where I could program full time. DuPont had a small group that built online computer system applications. My real motivation for joining this group was to get closer to computers, and in fact, I wanted to work on implementing an operating system. While in this group, I had the good fortune to work on several stand-alone real-time systems where the project involved writing the central control program that scheduled the various tasks and monitored system activity as well as writing the actual application code.

It soon became apparent that the only way I was going to get the opportunity to work on implementing a real operating system was to join a company that made computers its business. And so in 1971 I left DuPont for a job in Maynard, Massachusetts, with Digital Equipment Corporation. As it turned out, this put me in the operating system business for quite some time to come. Little did I know that I would be fortunate enough to develop several operating systems in my lifetime; developing one is a rare opportunity for anyone.

My first operating system project was to build a real-time system called RSX-11M that ran on Digital's PDP-11 16-bit series of minicomputers. At the time, our goals seemed very ambitious. We were asked to build a multitasking operating system that would run in 32 KB of memory with a hierarchical file system, application swapping, real-time scheduling, and a set of development utilities. The operating system and utilities were to run on the entire line of PDP-11 platforms, from the very small systems up through the PDP-11/70, which had memory-mapping hardware and supported up to 4 MB of memory.

I have many fond memories of how RSX-11M took shape. I had a rubber stamp made that proclaimed ''Size Is the Goal'' and proceeded to stamp every last bit of project correspondence to make sure that all the programmers and product managers understood how important it was to achieve our goals. We also learned the power of conditional assembly (high-level language use in operating systems was in its infancy at this time), and whenever someone added a feature, we just made it a system-generation option.

While developing RSX-11M, we spent most of our time engineering solutions to memory problems. Because the system had to run in 32 KB, we generated a memory budget that divided available memory equally between the operating system and the utility programs. That left a mere 16 KB for utility programs and led to long hours tuning overlay structures to achieve acceptable performance for many of the RSX-11M system programs.

Although RSX-11M had some very stringent size and performance constraints, of the systems I've worked on it was probably the easiest one to develop. It involved re-implementing an existing system but allowed us the freedom to change and subset the programming interfaces as long as applications could be reassembled or recompiled with minimal source-code changes. RSX-11M was introduced in 1973, 18 months after we had started building it. It proved to be very successful and helped make the PDP-11 the most popular 16-bit minicomputer of its time.

The PDP-11 provided better price/performance than mainframes, was affordable at the departmental level, and along with other popular minicomputers of the same era, led to the first wave of "downsizing" in the computer industry. Downsizing was an attempt to "bring down" mainframe applications to the minicomputer systems. Many of the mainframe programs were larger than the PDP-11 could easily accommodate, and almost immediately Digital was up against what Gordon Bell has deemed the single most important reason that computer architectures become obsolete: the lack of enough address bits.

Out of this need, the VAX architecture was born, and it became one of the most popular architectures of the late '70s and remained popular throughout the '80s. The VAX architecture provided 32 bits of virtual address space and eliminated the need to wrestle programs into what seemed to be an ever-decreasing amount of virtual address space.

My second opportunity to develop an operating system arrived with the VAX. I was very fortunate to be chosen to lead the operating system effort for the VAX-11 architecture, the result of which was the VMS operating system.

VMS was Digital's second general-purpose time-sharing system, developed specifically for the VAX architecture. Because the VAX architecture had grown out of the tremendous success of the PDP-11, however, this time it was mandatory to provide more than source-level compatibility for applications.

Thus, the VAX-11 architecture included a PDP-11 compatibility mode in which PDP-11 instructions were executed directly by hardware. At that time, it was inconceivable that a single operating system could support more than one "compatibility" environment. Although it wasn't the best known of the PDP-11 operating systems (amazingly, Digital had no fewer than 10 PDP-11 operating systems at one time or another!), RSX-11M was chosen as the operating system interface that would be emulated in PDP-11 compatibility mode on the VAX. This decision probably didn't make sense to a number of people outside the company, but RSX-11M had the largest number of application development tools, had the most general-purpose operating system features, supported multitasking, and had a file system structure that could be compatibly extended. Ultimately, the VAX-11 system ran RSX-11M binaries right off the distribution kit; it allowed RSX-11M volumes to be directly mounted and their files to be accessed and shared between RSX-11M compatibility-mode programs and native VMS programs.

From a technical perspective, the biggest mistake we made in VMS was not writing it in a high-level language. At the time, we had a group of very accomplished assembly language programmers, some stringent size constraints, and no compiler with the appropriate quality for operating system development. So, to ensure that we would ship the system in a marketable time frame, we wrote it in assembly language. Looking back on what happened, it would still be hard to make the decision to write VMS in a high-level language. (Moral: The right thing to do technically isn't always the best thing to do financially.)

Early in the '80s, while minicomputers were busy absorbing mainframe and other new applications, two important technologies were emerging: the personal computer (PC) and workstations. After the VMS project, I spent a few years developing compilers and then led a group that built Digital's first MicroVAX workstation—the MicroVAX I.

Workstations like the MicroVAX provided individual, high-performance computing for applications such as computer-aided design (CAD), whereas PCs supported business applications aimed at personal productivity, such as spreadsheets and word processors—two very successful early PC products. Although workstations were relatively pricey, personal computers had to be affordable to small businesses.

In order to meet price objectives, the original PCs were built with 8-bit, and later with 16-bit, microprocessors. They were constrained in much the same way RSX-11M had been and required considerable effort on the part of programmers and operating system designers to accommodate their limitations. Hardware resources were so scarce that operating systems existed mainly to handle a few low-level hardware functions and to provide a set of file system libraries. But the personal computer offered something that minicomputers did not—a market in which independent software developers could sell their programs at a high volume. As a result, the breadth and variety of applications that run on PCs and exploit their capabilities is truly amazing.

In the mid-'80s, microprocessors gained 32-bit addressing, and workstations were quick to take advantage of this capability. However, because of the very large installed base of personal computers and their applications, it was not easy to simply roll in another computer and then recompile and relink all the application software. End users of PCs simply didn't have the source code for their programs, and they demanded binary compatibility.

In the summer of 1988, I received an interesting call from Bill Gates at Microsoft. He asked whether I'd like to come over and talk about building a new operating system at Microsoft for personal computers. At the time, I wasn't too interested in working on personal computers, but I thought this would be a good opportunity to meet Bill and discuss what he had in mind. What Bill had to offer was the opportunity to build another operating system, one that was portable and addressed some of the concerns people had about using personal computers to run mission-critical applications. For me, it meant the chance to build another operating system!

Bill finally convinced me that this was an opportunity I couldn't pass up, and in October of 1988, I came to Microsoft and started to build the team that would build the new operating system. I didn't realize it at the time, but this would be the most ambitious operating system project on which I had ever embarked.

Our goals for the system included portability, security, POSIX compliance, compatibility, scalable performance (multiprocessor support), extensibility, and ease of internationalization. Of all these goals, by far the one that was hardest to achieve and that had the most profound effect on the structure of the system was compatibility. Hundreds of thousands of PDP-11 systems had been sold, but tens of millions of personal computers were in operation! As if that weren't enough, we needed to compatibly support three separate 16-bit operating environments and add new 32-bit capabilities to free personal computer applications from the same kind of virtual address constraints that had existed for the PDP-11. To top it off, we wanted to support the UNIX standard interface specification called POSIX.

Now, almost four years later, we are on the brink of bringing this system, Windows NT, to market. Helen Custer started work on this book when the operating system design began. As our design has matured, the book has undergone continual change to track the operating system architecture. This has been an arduous task—keeping up-to-date and writing and rewriting the various chapters of the book as the design evolved. Although it is our design, Helen is the one who has captured the essence of that design and made it understandable to more than just serious operating system implementers. For this, we owe Helen a great debt.

It is impossible to acknowledge all the people who contributed to the design of Windows NT. I must say that I did not design Windows NT—I was merely one of the contributors to the design of the system. As you read this book, you will be introduced to some, but not all, of the other contributors. This has been a team effort and has involved several hundred person-years of effort. Perhaps the most important contribution of all was that made by the people who have tested and stressed the system. Without their effort, Windows NT could not have achieved the level of quality that it has achieved.

I hope you enjoy this book about Windows NT as much as we enjoyed designing the system.

Dave Cutler
Director, Windows NT Development

PREFACE

It has been a long road from 1989, when I began writing this book, to now. Nothing could have prepared me for the all-consuming immersion in operating system theory, design, implementation, and lore that began when I accepted this challenge. Before starting, I reread Tracy Kidder's *Soul of a New Machine* for inspiration and for a sense of kinship with at least one other person who had traveled a path similar to the one I was about to travel. In many respects, the construction of Windows NT was a software version of the hardware construction documented in Kidder's book, and my experience, I suspect, bore some resemblance to his.

Creating an operating system, like creating a computer, is an opportunity few engineers ever get. Most operating system engineers spend their entire careers enhancing or modifying existing operating systems or designing new ones that are never built or are never marketed. Computer companies fail regularly or undergo financial or managerial difficulties that require them to cancel projects before they are completed. Those systems that are completed often don't catch on in the marketplace or are largely irrelevant because existing applications require the old systems to be supported throughout eternity. Even fewer writers get the opportunity to write a book such as this one, which documents the design of a significant new operating system. It has been an unusual privilege to do so.

The background information in this book is not new. Most of it has been written before in many forms and often with more eloquence than I have mustered in these pages. However, my goal was not to write a book that teaches operating system principles better presented in other books, but to place Windows NT within the context of existing systems. Although I have not belabored the often complex reasoning behind implementation decisions, I have tried to provide glimpses into some of the operating system history and research that have influenced Windows NT's final form.

This book is not written for operating system designers, who are likely to want more detail about the inner workings of Windows NT than this forum can provide. Rather, it is for the rest of us, those who know something about computers and who want to understand the internal design of this system in order to write better applications or to simply demystify that black box called an operating system.

Inside Windows NT was completed several months before the final snapshot of Windows NT was taken. Therefore, some of the features described in this book might not ultimately appear in the first release; some might be postponed until subsequent releases, and others might be dropped entirely. I attempted, however, to provide a long-term vision of Windows NT without resorting to too much "pie-in-the-sky" and without relying too heavily on implementation details that are likely to change. Everything described herein either is already in the system or exists but might be withheld until it can be tested further or until the proper mix of software products exists to complement it. Some topics are necessarily omitted, either because they were introduced into the system late in its development or because they are likely to be documented elsewhere. Other topics, such as security and the internal design of each subsystem, are abbreviated. A notable example is the Win32 subsystem, which is described in Chapter 5, "Windows and the Protected Subsystems," but whose internal details would fill another volume. Rather than documenting the Win32 API, which other authors have already begun to do, this book focuses on the design of Windows NT and on how the Win32 and other API environments "plug into" the NT executive.

It is not necessary to read the book from cover to cover; it is constructed so that you can read the first two chapters and then jump into whatever topic you prefer. Terminology and theory tend to build upon themselves, however, so reading the book from front to back will increase your comprehension in certain areas.

Over the last three years, I have talked to, cajoled, listened to, and argued with many people, all of whom deserve my thanks. My greatest thanks go to Dave Cutler for wanting this book to be written and for giving me the unprecedented opportunity to write it. His technical and editorial comments were also extremely valuable to me.

I also owe great thanks to Lou Perazzoli, the only person who read every draft of everything I wrote along the way, even when his impossible schedule made this a difficult endeavor. This book would not exist without Lou's assistance and support.

Special thanks go to Ron Burk and Gary Kimura for suggesting appropriate frameworks within which I could organize the enormous amount of information I collected as this project progressed. Finding an editorial framework and squeezing such a multifaceted system into it was one of the toughest hurdles in writing this book.

Thanks also to the software engineers who allowed me to freely borrow text from their technical specifications and who were patient as I tried to reflect their views from a perspective that was not theirs. Although it might not be written exactly as they would have written it, this book is really their book; it chronicles the source of their joy, anxiety, frustration, and inspiration for four years. It has been a privilege and a challenge to work with them and to share this unique experience. In addition to those listed above, special thanks for technical, editorial, or moral support go to Darryl Havens, Steve Wood, Mark Lucovsky, Jim Kelly, Scott Ludwig, Matthew Felton, Mark Zbikowsky, Chandan Chauhan, Chuck Lenzmeier, Mary Hutton, Asmus Freytag, Dave Thompson, Larry Osterman, Sanjay Jejurikar, David Gilman, Robert Reichel, Chad Schwitters, Bryan Willman, Eric Kutter, Lee Smith, Steve Rowe, Paul Leach, Bruce Hale, Roberta Leibovitz, Gregory Wilson, David Treadwell, Sudeep Bharati, Chuck Chan, Manny Weiser, Leif Pederson, Dan Hinsley, Bob Rinne, David McBride, Richard Barth, John Balciunas, Rick Rashid, Therese Stowell, Dave Hart, Matthew Bradburn, Cliff Van Dyke, David Thacher, Jane Howell, Lorelei Seifert, Bob Muglia, and Paul Maritz.

My personal thanks to Callie Wilson for handling the internal distribution of the book and to Carl Stork for running interference for me as news of the manuscript's existence leaked out. It was also a great pleasure to work with Microsoft Press staff, including Nancy Siadek, Jeff Carey, Deborah Long, Judith Bloch, Connie Little, Katherine Erickson, Peggy Herman, Jean Trenary, Barb Runyan, Kim Eggleston, Wallis Bolz, and Dean Holmes. Thanks to them for meeting a challenging publication schedule and handling with aplomb the intricacies of this large and detailed book.

I extend my gratitude to the Microsoft library staff for acquiring all the articles and many of the books that I used as background and reference material. They never let me down when I submitted esoteric requests, and they never yelled at me for keeping anything too long. I also owe a belated thanks to Daniel Cañas, my operating systems instructor at the University of Kansas, who sparked my interest in operating systems and who taught me the value of research.

Throughout this book, you will see the names of designers and implementers of Windows NT. Many names are omitted, but the omissions are random, reflecting only that certain parts of the operating system are not described in this book or that there were too many contributors to a particular component to mention everyone. And although this text cites him primarily as the developer of the NT kernel, Dave Cutler, the chief architect of Windows NT and one of its most prolific coders, provided code or at least direction for nearly every part of the operating system.

There is a certain beauty in well-designed operating systems, an understandable order beneath the seemingly endless details its implementation comprises. My goal in writing this book was to examine this very large body of software and peel away enough of the details to reveal its inner order. The paradox of that difficult venture is perhaps best revealed in a brief anecdote:

I sat in Lou Perazzoli's office one afternoon while he described to me the ins and outs (almost literally) of working-set trimming, a component of the virtual memory system. As he explained, I listened intently and formed in my mind an abstraction of his description, one that would fit within the scope of this book. When he finished, I summarized what he had said from my point of view and then asked, "Is that right?" He responded earnestly, "Yes, that's *exactly* what we sort of do."

This book represents a balancing act between detailed truth and ordered beauty. As a result, it documents "exactly" what the developers "sort of" did. I owe them my thanks for sharing with me the contents of their heads. Any errors in transcribing those contents are mine.

Helen K. Custer
September 1992

CHAPTER ONE

THE MISSION

In the world of operating systems, the wheels of progress turn slowly. Operating systems take years to develop. Once complete, they remain lifeless until applications are written to exploit their capabilities. Even after applications exist, people must learn how to use them through documentation, training, and experience. This, coupled with the delays common in developing applications for operating systems, means that ordinary users often own and use 10- or 20-year-old operating system technology.

While operating systems await acceptance, hardware technology marches forward. Computers with faster processors, more memory, and even multiple processors become commonplace, while operating system developers scurry to extend their existing systems to take advantage of the new features.

The Intel 80386 and 80486 chips, along with many other popular processors, are known as *complex instruction set computers* (CISC). Their chief characteristic is a large number of machine instructions, each of which is elaborate and powerful. In the last few years, Intel has made major advances in the speed and power of its processors, and other manufacturers have developed multiprocessor machines based on the Intel CISC technology.

In the mid-1980s, the hardware industry created another type of processor architecture called *reduced instruction set computers* (RISC). RISC chips differ from CISC chips primarily in the small number of simple machine instructions RISC chips provide. Because of the simplicity of their instruction sets, the RISC processors run at increased clock speeds and achieve very fast execution times.

In both the CISC and RISC arenas, promising processor technologies have emerged rapidly. Microsoft saw that in order to exploit these and other hardware advances, it needed to produce an operating system for the 1990s—one that was portable and able to move easily from one hardware platform to another. Although Microsoft and IBM created the OS/2 operating system in the 1980s, Microsoft recognized that the system had many shortcomings, the most obvious being that OS/2 is not portable. It was written in assembly language to run on single-processor, Intel 80286 computers. Rather than try to overhaul the OS/2 system software, Microsoft decided to build a new, portable operating system from the ground up.

1.1   An Operating System for the 1990s

In the fall of 1988, Microsoft hired David N. Cutler ("Dave") to lead a new software development effort: to create Microsoft's operating system for the 1990s. Dave, a well-known architect of minicomputer systems,[1] quickly assembled a team of engineers to design Microsoft's new technology (NT) operating system. Early in 1989, Bill Gates and key Microsoft strategists met to review the operating system specifications Dave Cutler's group had defined. Their plans identified these primary market requirements for the new operating system:

Portability Hardware advancements occur quickly and often unpredictably. RISC processors represent a great departure from traditional CISC technology, for example. Writing NT in a portable language would allow it to move freely from one processor architecture to another.

Multiprocessing and Scalability Applications should be able to take advantage of the broad range of computers available today. For example, computers with more than one processor appear on the market regularly, but few existing operating systems can fully employ them. Making NT a scalable, multiprocessing operating system would allow a user to run the same application on single-processor and multiprocessor computers. At the high end, the user could run several applications simultaneously at full speed, and compute-intensive applications could deliver improved performance by dividing their work among several processors.

---

1. Prior to his work at Microsoft, Dave Cutler was a senior corporate consultant at Digital Equipment Corporation and had spent 17 years there developing a number of operating systems and compilers, including the VAX/VMS operating system, the MicroVAX I workstation and operating system, the RSX-11M operating system running on DEC's PDP-11 machine, and the VAX PL/1 and VAX C language compilers.

Distributed Computing With the increasing availability of personal computers in the 1980s, the nature of computing was irrevocably altered. Where once a single, large mainframe computer served an entire company, smaller and cheaper microcomputers proliferated and are now standard issue for rank-and-file employees. Enhanced networking capabilities allow the smaller computers to communicate with one another, often sharing hardware resources such as disk space or processing power (in the form of file servers, print servers, or compute servers). To accommodate this change, developers of the NT system would build networking capabilities directly into the operating system and would provide the means for applications to distribute their work across multiple computer systems.

POSIX Compliance In the mid-to-late 1980s, U.S. government agencies began specifying POSIX as a procurement standard for government computing contracts. POSIX, an acronym rather loosely defined as "a portable operating system interface based on UNIX," refers to a collection of international standards for UNIX-style operating system interfaces. The POSIX standard (IEEE Standard 1003.1–1988) encourages vendors implementing UNIX-style interfaces to make them compatible so that programmers can move their applications easily from one system to another. To meet the government's POSIX procurement requirements, NT would be designed to provide an optional POSIX application execution environment.

Government-Certifiable Security In addition to POSIX compliance, the U.S. government also specifies computer security guidelines for government applications. Achieving a government-approved security rating allows an operating system to compete in that arena. Of course, many of these required capabilities are advantageous features for any multiuser system. The security guidelines specify required capabilities such as protecting one user's resources from another's and establishing resource quotas to prevent one user from garnering all the system resources (such as memory).

The initial target for NT security is the so-called Class C2 level, defined by the U.S. Department of Defense as providing "discretionary (need-to-know) protection and, through the inclusion of audit capabilities, for accountability of subjects and the actions they initiate."[2] This means that the owner of a system resource has the right to decide who can access it and that the operating

---

2. *Department of Defense Trusted Computer System Evaluation Criteria,* DoD 5200.28–STD, December 1985.

system can detect when data is accessed and by whom. U.S. government security levels extend from level D (least stringent) to level A (most stringent), with levels B and C each containing several sublevels. Although NT would initially be written to support the C2 security level, enhancements in future releases could meet the more stringent requirements of higher security levels.

With these market requirements in place, the NT development team had its mission: to create Microsoft's operating system for the 1990s. Originally, the plan also called for NT to have an OS/2-style user interface and to provide the OS/2 *application programming interface* (API) as its primary programming interface. Midway through the development of the system, however, Microsoft Windows version 3.0 hit the market and was an instant success, in contrast to OS/2, which had not caught on with large numbers of users.

Recognizing this marketplace mandate and the complexities involved in enhancing and supporting two incompatible operating systems, Microsoft decided to alter its course and direct its energies toward a single, coherent operating system strategy. The strategy is to produce a family of Windows-based operating systems that spans computers from the smallest notebooks to the largest multiprocessor workstations. Windows NT, as the next-generation Windows system is named, takes its place at the high end of the Windows family. It sports a Windows graphical user interface and is Microsoft's first Windows-based operating system to supply the *Win32 API*, a 32-bit programming interface for new application development. The Win32 API makes advanced operating system capabilities available to applications through features such as multithreaded processes, synchronization, security, I/O, and object management.

Windows NT does not exist in a vacuum. It can interoperate with other Microsoft systems, with the Apple Macintosh, and with UNIX-based operating systems on a Microsoft LAN Manager or other network. A sample configuration appears in Figure 1-1.

The servers in this configuration can provide operating system facilities, such as file services, print services, or system management functions, or they can provide application facilities, such as database services. An application might even interact with the server on a user's behalf without the user's knowledge. When configured as a server, Windows NT works as a multiuser operating system, servicing the needs of numerous users on a network. Each workstation can support one interactive user and multiple remote users, with each user (or application) required to log on before accessing the system.

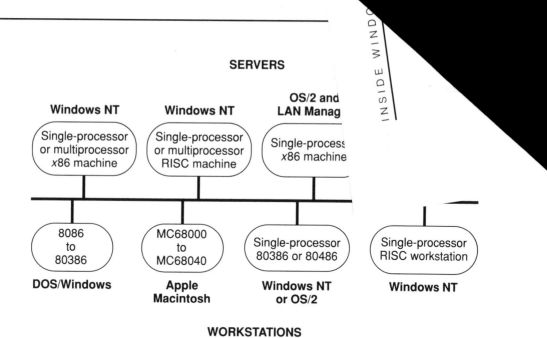

SERVERS

WORKSTATIONS

Figure 1-1. Connecting Multiple Systems

1.2 Design Goals

The software design of Windows NT required some serious thinking. In order for the system to fulfill its market requirements, it was crucial that complex features such as POSIX compliance and security be incorporated from the beginning.

Before they began writing the several hundred thousand lines of code that Windows NT would eventually comprise, the system's designers carefully constructed a set of software design goals. Such design goals facilitate making the thousands of ancillary decisions that determine the internal structure of a large software project. When two proposed design options conflict, the design goals help establish which is best. The following are the Windows NT design goals:

- Extensibility. The code must be written to comfortably grow and change as market requirements change.

- Portability. As dictated by market goals, the code must move easily from one processor to another.

- Reliability and robustness. The system should protect itself from both internal malfunction and external tampering. It should behave predictably at all times, and applications should not be able to harm the operating system or its functioning.

5

■ Compatibility. Although Windows NT should extend existing technology, its user interface and APIs should be compatible with existing Microsoft systems.

■ Performance. Within the constraints of the other design goals, the system should be as fast and responsive as possible on each hardware platform.

The following sections discuss the Windows NT design goals in more detail and describe their effect on the final form of the operating system.

1.2.1 Extensibility

Operating systems invariably change over time. The changes usually present themselves incrementally in the form of new features: for example, support for a new hardware device, such as a CD-ROM reader; the ability to communicate over a new type of network; or support for up-and-coming software technologies, such as graphical user interfaces or object-oriented programming environments.

Ensuring the integrity of the Windows NT code as the operating system changes over time was a primary design goal. For the Mach operating system developed at Carnegie-Mellon University, Dr. Richard Rashid and his colleagues took a unique approach to this problem by creating an operating system base that provides primitive operating system capabilities. Application programs called servers[3] provide additional operating system capabilities, including full-featured APIs. The base portion of the system remains stable, while the servers are enhanced or new ones are created as requirements change.

Windows NT borrows from this design and consists of a privileged *executive* and a set of nonprivileged servers called *protected subsystems*. The term *privileged* refers to a processor's modes of operation. Most processors have a privileged mode (or perhaps several), in which all machine instructions are allowed and system memory is accessible, and a nonprivileged mode, in which certain instructions are disallowed and system memory is inaccessible. In Windows NT terminology, the privileged processor mode is called *kernel mode* and the nonprivileged processor mode is called *user mode*.

Usually an operating system executes only in kernel mode, and application programs execute only in user mode except when they call operating

---

3. This type of server refers to a process on a local computer and should not be confused with separate computers on a network that provide file services or network services. See Chapter 2 for more information.

system services. Windows NT's design is unique, however, because its protected subsystems execute in user mode like applications do. This structure allows protected subsystems to be modified or added without affecting the integrity of the executive. (See Chapter 5, "Windows and the Protected Subsystems," for more information.)

In addition to protected subsystems, Windows NT includes numerous other features to ensure its extensibility:

- A modular structure. The executive comprises a discrete set of individual components that interact with one another only through functional interfaces. New components can be added to the executive in a modular way, accomplishing their work by calling the interfaces supplied by existing components.

- The use of objects to represent system resources. *Objects*, abstract data types that are manipulated only by a special set of object services, allow system resources to be managed uniformly. Adding new objects does not undermine existing objects or require existing code to change. (See Chapter 3, "The Object Manager and Object Security," for more information.)

- Loadable drivers. The Windows NT I/O system supports drivers that can be added to the system as it runs. New file systems, devices, and networks can be supported by writing a device driver, file system driver, or transport driver and loading it into the system. (See Chapter 8, "The I/O System," and Chapter 9, "Networking," for more information.)

- A *remote procedure call* (RPC) facility, which allows an application to call remote services without regard to their locations on the network. New services can be added to any machine on the network and can be immediately available to applications on other machines on the network. (See Chapter 9, "Networking," for more information.)

1.2.2 Portability

The second design goal, code portability, is closely related to extensibility. Extensibility allows an operating system to be easily enhanced, whereas portability enables the entire operating system to move to a machine based on a different processor or configuration, with as little recoding as possible. Although operating systems are often described as either "portable" or "nonportable," portability is not a binary state, but a matter of degree. The crucial question is not whether software will port (most will, eventually), but how difficult it is to port.

Writing an operating system that is easy to port is similar to writing any portable code—you must follow certain guidelines. First, as much of the code as possible must be written in a language that is available on all machines to which you want to port. Usually this means that you must write your code in a high-level language, preferably one that has been standardized. Assembly language code is inherently nonportable, unless you plan to port only to machines with upwardly compatible machine instructions (such as moving from the Intel 80386 to the Intel 80486, for example).

Second, you should consider to which physical environments you want to port your software. Different hardware imposes different constraints on an operating system. For example, an operating system built on 32-bit addresses could not be ported (except with enormous difficulty) to a machine with 16-bit addresses.

Third, it's important to minimize, or eliminate wherever possible, the amount of code that interacts directly with the hardware. Hardware dependencies can take many forms. Some obvious dependencies include directly manipulating registers and other hardware structures or assuming a particular hardware configuration or capacity.

Fourth, whenever hardware-dependent code cannot be avoided, it should be isolated to a few easy-to-locate modules. Hardware-dependent code should not be spread throughout the operating system. These last two guidelines work hand in hand. For example, you can hide a hardware-dependent structure within a software-defined, abstract data type. Other modules of the system manipulate the data type rather than the hardware by using a set of generic routines. When the operating system is ported, only the data type and the generic routines that manipulate it must be changed.

Windows NT was designed for easy porting. Some of its features include the following:

- Portable C. Windows NT is written primarily in the C language,[4] with extensions for Windows NT's structured exception handling architecture. The developers selected C because it is standardized and because C compilers and software development tools are widely available. In addition to C, small portions of the system were written

---

4. ANSI Standard X3.159–1989.

in C++, including the graphics component of the Windows environment and portions of the networking user interface. Assembly language is used only for parts of the system that must communicate directly with the hardware (the trap handler, for example) and for components that require optimum speed (such as multiple precision integer arithmetic). However, nonportable code is carefully isolated within the components that use it.

■ Processor isolation. Certain low-level portions of the operating system must access processor-dependent data structures and registers. However, the code that does so is contained in small modules that can be replaced by analogous modules for other processors.

■ Platform isolation. Windows NT encapsulates platform-dependent code inside a dynamic-link library known as the *hardware abstraction layer* (HAL). Platform dependencies are those that vary between two vendors' workstations built around the same processor—for example, the MIPS R4000. The HAL abstracts hardware, such as caches and I/O interrupt controllers, with a layer of low-level software so that higher-level code need not change when moving from one platform to another.

Windows NT was written for ease of porting to machines that use 32-bit linear addresses and provide virtual memory capabilities. It can move to other machines as well, but at a greater cost.

1.2.3 Reliability

Reliability was a third design goal for the Windows NT code. Reliability refers to two different but related ideas. First, an operating system should be robust, responding predictably to error conditions, even those caused by hardware failures. Second, the operating system should actively protect itself and its users from accidental or deliberate damage by user programs.

Structured exception handling is a method for capturing error conditions and responding to them uniformly. It is Windows NT's primary defense against errors in software or hardware. Either the operating system or the processor issues an exception whenever an abnormal event occurs; exception handling code, which exists throughout the system, is automatically invoked in response to the condition, ensuring that no undetected error wreaks havoc on user programs or on the system itself. (See Chapter 2, "System Overview," for more information.)

Robustness is further enhanced by other features of the operating system:

- A modular design that divides the executive into a series of orderly packages. The individual system components interact with one another through carefully specified programming interfaces. A component such as the memory manager, for example, could be removed in one piece and replaced by a new memory manager that implements the same interfaces. (See Chapter 2, "System Overview," for more information.)

- A new file system designed for Windows NT, called the *NT file system* (NTFS). NTFS can recover from all types of disk errors, including errors that occur in critical disk sectors. It uses redundant storage and a transaction-based scheme for storing data to ensure recoverability.

The following features of Windows NT protect it from external assault:

- A U.S. government-certifiable security architecture, which provides a variety of security mechanisms, such as user logon, resource quotas, and object protection. (See Chapter 5, "Windows and the Protected Subsystems," for more information.)

- *Virtual memory*, which furnishes every program with a large set of addresses that it can use. When a program accesses these virtual addresses, the memory manager maps, or translates, them into actual memory locations. Because it controls the placement of every program in memory, the operating system prevents one user from reading or modifying memory occupied by another user, unless the two users explicitly share memory. (See Chapter 6, "The Virtual Memory Manager," for more information.)

1.2.4 Compatibility

Software compatibility, the fourth design goal for Windows NT code, is a complicated subject. In general, compatibility refers to an operating system's ability to execute programs written for other operating systems or for earlier versions of the same system. For Windows NT, the compatibility theme takes several forms.

Defining this theme is the issue of binary compatibility versus source-level compatibility of applications. Binary compatibility is achieved when you can take an executable program and run it successfully on a different operating system. Source-level compatibility requires you to recompile your program before you can run it on the new system.

Whether a new operating system is binary compatible or source-code compatible with an existing system depends on several things. Foremost among them is the architecture of the new system's processor. If the processor uses the same instruction set (with extensions, perhaps) and the same size memory addresses as the old, then binary compatibility can be achieved.

Binary compatibility is not as easy between processors based on different architectures. Each processor architecture ordinarily carries with it a unique machine language. This means that cross-architecture, binary compatibility can be achieved only if an emulation program is provided to convert one set of machine instructions to another. Without an emulator, all applications moving from the old architecture to the new must be recompiled and relinked (and likely debugged).

Through use of protected subsystems, Windows NT provides execution environments for applications other than its primary programming interface—the Win32 API. When running on Intel processors, Windows NT's protected subsystems supply binary compatibility with existing Microsoft applications, including MS-DOS, 16-bit Windows, OS/2, and LAN Manager. On the MIPS RISC processors, binary-level compatibility is achieved for MS-DOS, 16-bit Windows, and LAN Manager applications (using an emulator). Windows NT also provides source-level compatibility with POSIX applications that adhere to the POSIX operating system interfaces defined in IEEE Standard 1003.1.

In addition to compatibility with programming interfaces, Windows NT supports existing file systems, including the MS-DOS file system (FAT), the OS/2 *high-performance file system* (HPFS), the *CD-ROM file system* (CDFS), and the new, recoverable NT file system (NTFS).

1.2.5 Performance

Windows NT's final design goal was to achieve great performance. Compute-intensive applications such as graphics packages, simulation packages, and financial analysis packages require rapid processing in order to give the user good response times. Fast hardware is not enough to achieve good performance, however. The operating system must also be fast and efficient.

Ensuring good performance was a goal throughout Windows NT's development. The following process helped achieve that goal:

- Each component of Windows NT was designed with an eye toward performance. Performance testing and modeling were done for the parts of the system that are critical to performance. System calls, page faults, and other crucial execution paths were carefully optimized to ensure the fastest possible processing speeds. (See Chapter 6, "The Virtual Memory Manager," and Chapter 7, "The Kernel," for more information.)

- The protected subsystems (servers) that perform operating system functions must frequently communicate with one another and with client applications. To guarantee that this communication does not hinder the servers' performance, a high-speed message-passing mechanism called the *local procedure call* (LPC) facility was included as an integral part of the operating system. (See Chapter 4, "Processes and Threads," for more information.)

- Each protected subsystem that provides an operating system environment (*environment subsystem*) was carefully designed to maximize the speed of frequently used system services. (See Chapter 5, "Windows and the Protected Subsystems," for more information.)

- Crucial components of Windows NT's networking software were built into the privileged portion of the operating system to achieve the best possible performance. Although they are built-in, these components can also be loaded and unloaded from the system dynamically. (See Chapter 9, "Networking," for more information.)

1.3   The Team

At one time, it was possible for a handful of people to lock themselves away, emerging with an operating system in a few frenzied months. But times have changed.

Modern operating systems must satisfy a myriad of new hardware requirements, such as supporting multiple network protocols, multiple processors, multiple file systems, and an ever-increasing number of I/O devices. In addition to these new demands, a system is considered unusable unless it arrives with a multitude of software, including libraries, a graphical user interface, tools, and applications—not to mention documentation.

The group that designed the NT executive and its first protected subsystems was rather small—about 10 people at the beginning, growing to perhaps 40 or 50 later in the project. This book will introduce some of the operating system's designers and implementers. These individuals, although key to the project, could never have succeeded without many others. The contributors to Windows NT tools, applications, and device drivers, those responsible for porting Windows NT, and a host of software testers, program managers, marketing personnel, and support staff comprise a group of over 200 people. Ultimately, the creation of Windows NT was an enormous, multigroup effort.

1.4   The Rest of the Book

The next chapter begins with a grand overview of Windows NT and the models on which it is based and a summary of its components. Each successive chapter looks at an individual operating system component, its important characteristics, the salient features of its design, and its interactions with other components. The discussion of the system proceeds in a "middle-out" fashion: It begins in the middle with processes and objects, moves toward the top to discuss protected subsystems and API environments, and then zigzags its way to the bottom toward memory management, the kernel, the I/O system, and networking.

CHAPTER TWO

SYSTEM OVERVIEW

An operating system is a computer program that provides an environment in which other computer programs can run, allowing them to easily take advantage of the processor and of I/O devices such as disks. Although a great convenience, an operating system is not strictly necessary for using computer hardware. In the early days of computing, technicians loaded programs into memory using antiquated input devices such as buttons and switches or paper tape. Then they manually entered a program's starting address and directed the computer to jump to it and begin executing. Modern computer users, however, have become accustomed to more sophisticated facilities.

Today's operating systems provide two fundamental services for users. First, they make the computer hardware easier to use. They create a "virtual" machine that differs markedly from the real machine. Indeed, the computer revolution of the last two decades is due, in part, to the success that operating systems have achieved in shielding users from the obscurities of computer hardware. In addition, programmers no longer need to rewrite an application for every computer they want to run it on.

Second, an operating system shares hardware resources among its users. One of the most important resources is the processor. A *multitasking* operating system, such as Windows NT, divides the work that needs to be done among *processes,* giving each process memory, system resources, and at least one *thread of execution,* an executable unit within a process. The operating system runs one thread for a short time and then switches to another, running each thread in turn. Even on a single-user system, multitasking is extremely helpful because it enables the computer to perform two tasks at once. For example, a user can edit a document while another document is printing in the background or while a compiler compiles a large program. Each process gets its work done, and to the user all the programs appear to run simultaneously.

In addition to sharing the processor, the operating system divvies up memory and regulates access to files and devices. Every operating system differs in the way it presents its virtual machine to users and in how it divides resources among them. The way in which Windows NT accomplishes this is the subject of the rest of this book.

The first section of this chapter examines the models that influenced the operating system's form. The second section takes a glimpse under the hood of the system, revealing its interior structure. The third section describes two additional system-wide architectures: internationalization and structured exception handling.

2.1 Windows NT Models

An operating system is a complex program, a layering of detail upon detail. Indeed, orchestrating these details, these bits and bytes, into a cohesive form is one of the most important tasks in creating a new operating system. A unifying model is required to ensure that the system can accommodate its required features without compromising its design goals.

What is an operating system model? The dictionary defines *model* as "a tentative description of a system or theory that accounts for all its known properties."[1] An operating system model is a broad framework that unifies the many features and services the system provides and the tasks it performs.

The Windows NT design was guided by a combination of several models. Windows NT uses a *client/server model* to provide multiple operating system environments (initially, Windows, MS-DOS, OS/2, and POSIX) to its users, and it uses an *object model* to uniformly manage operating system resources and dispense them to users. A third model, *symmetric multiprocessing* (SMP), allows Windows NT to achieve maximum performance from multiprocessor computers.

2.1.1 Client/Server Model

Operating system code can be structured in a number of different ways. One approach, particularly common in smaller operating systems such as MS-DOS, organizes the operating system as a set of procedures and allows any procedure to call any other. This monolithic structure does not enforce data hiding in the operating system, and it embeds assumptions about how the system fits together throughout the operating system code. Extending such a system can be difficult work because modifying a procedure can introduce bugs in seemingly unrelated parts of the system.

In all but the simplest monolithic operating systems, applications are separated from the operating system itself. That is, the operating system code

---

1. *American Heritage Dictionary,* 2d ed. (Boston: Houghton Mifflin Company, 1985).

runs in a privileged processor mode (referred to as *kernel mode* in this book), with access to system data and to the hardware; applications run in a nonprivileged processor mode (called *user mode*), with a limited set of interfaces available and with limited access to system data. When a user-mode program calls a system service, the processor traps the call and then switches the calling thread to kernel mode. When the system service completes, the operating system switches the thread back to user mode and allows the caller to continue. The monolithic operating system structure with separate user and kernel processor modes is shown in Figure 2-1.

A different structuring approach divides the operating system into modules and layers them one on top of the other. Each module provides a set of functions that other modules can call. Code in any particular layer calls code only in lower layers. On some systems, such as VAX/VMS or the old Multics operating system, hardware even enforces the layering (using multiple, hierarchical processor modes). Figure 2-2 on the next page illustrates one possible layered structure.

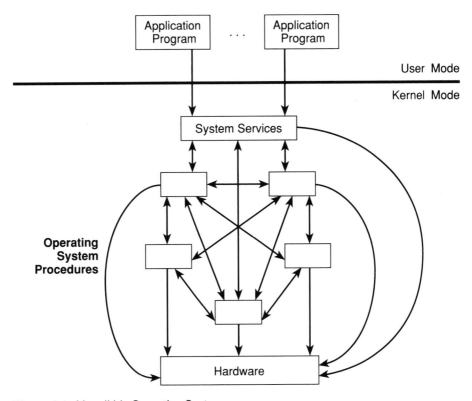

Figure 2-1. Monolithic Operating System

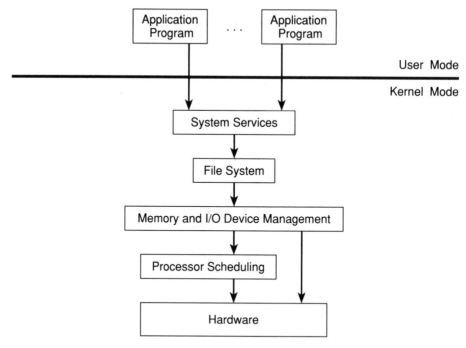

Figure 2-2. Layered Operating System

One advantage of a layered operating system structure is that each layer of code is given access to only the lower-level interfaces (and data structures) it requires, thus limiting the amount of code that wields unlimited power. This structure also allows the operating system to be debugged starting at the lowest layer, adding one layer at a time until the whole system works correctly. Layering also makes it easier to enhance the operating system; one entire layer can be replaced without affecting other parts of the system.

A third approach to structuring an operating system is the client/server model. The idea is to divide the operating system into several processes, each of which implements a single set of services—for example, memory services, process creation services, or processor scheduling services. Each *server* runs in user mode, executing a loop that checks whether a client has requested one of its services.[2] The *client*, which can be either another operating system component or an application program, requests a service by sending a message to the server. An operating system kernel (or microkernel) running in

---

2. Some operating systems, such as Clouds and BiiN (see bibliography), operate differently, using the caller's thread to execute server code but switching address spaces prior to execution.

kernel mode delivers the message to the server; the server performs the operation; and the kernel returns the results to the client in another message, as illustrated in Figure 2-3.

The client/server approach results in an operating system whose components are small and self-contained. Because each server runs in a separate user-mode process, a single server can fail (and perhaps be restarted) without crashing or corrupting the rest of the operating system. Furthermore, different servers can run on different processors in a multiprocessor computer or even on different computers, making the operating system suitable for distributed computing environments.

The theoretical model shown in Figure 2-3 is an idealized depiction of a client/server system in which the kernel consists of only a message-passing facility. In reality, client/server systems fall within a spectrum, some doing very little work in kernel mode and others doing more. For instance, the Mach operating system, a contemporary example of the client/server architecture, implements a minimal kernel that comprises thread scheduling, message passing, virtual memory, and device drivers. Everything else, including various application programming interfaces (APIs), file systems, and networking, runs in user mode.

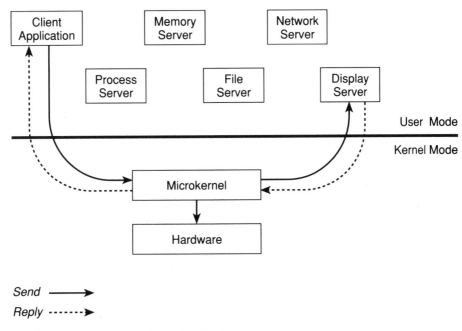

Figure 2-3. Client/Server Operating System

The structure of Windows NT borrows from both the layered model and the client/server model. The kernel-mode portion of Windows NT is called the *NT executive*. It comprises a series of components that implement virtual memory management, object (resource) management, I/O and file systems (including network drivers), interprocess communication, and portions of the security system. For the most part, these components interact with one another in a modular, rather than a layered, fashion. Each component calls the others through a set of carefully specified internal routines.

However, the layered operating system model comes into play in the NT executive's I/O system, described shortly, and in the bottommost portions of the NT executive: the *NT kernel* and the *hardware abstraction layer* (HAL). All other components of the NT executive are layered on these two components. The NT kernel performs low-level operating system functions, much like those found in microkernel, client/server operating systems—for example, thread scheduling, interrupt and exception dispatching, and multiprocessor synchronization. It also provides a set of routines and basic objects that the rest of the executive uses to implement higher-level constructs. Below the kernel is the HAL *dynamic-link library* (DLL), a layer of code that protects the kernel and the rest of the NT executive from platform-specific hardware differences. The HAL manipulates hardware directly.

As Figure 2-4 illustrates, Windows NT uses the client/server model primarily to provide APIs and the facilities that one ordinarily regards as an operating system environment. Although the Win32 protected subsystem (server) provides the user interface and is fundamental to the system's operation, the other servers "plug into" the executive and can be loaded on a mix-and-match basis, with several in operation at a time if desired. The servers communicate with application processes through a message-passing facility provided in the NT executive.

Using the client/server model has several benefits:

- It simplifies the base operating system, the NT executive. One goal for Windows NT is to provide Win32, MS-DOS, 16-bit Windows, POSIX, and OS/2 APIs. Moving each API into a separate server removes conflicts and duplications from the executive and allows new APIs to be added easily.

- It improves reliability. Each server runs in a separate process, partitioned into its own memory, and is thus protected from other processes. Furthermore, because the servers run in user mode, they cannot directly access hardware or modify memory in which the executive is stored.

■ It lends itself well to a distributed computing model. Because networked computers are based on a client/server model and use messages to communicate, local servers can easily send messages to remote machines on behalf of client applications. Clients need not know whether certain requests are being serviced locally or remotely.

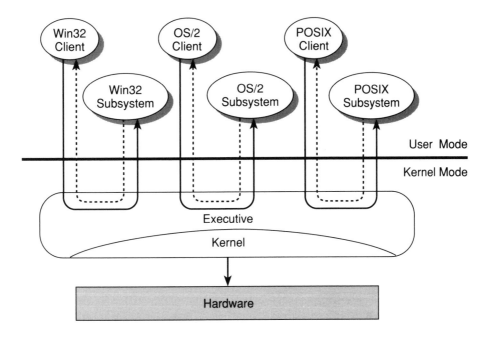

Send ⟶

Reply ┈┈┈▶

Figure 2-4. Windows NT's Client/Server Structure

2.1.2 Object Model

Bertrand Meyer, in his book *Object-oriented Software Construction,* characterizes operating systems as programs that "have no top."[3] As with other large software systems, it is difficult to identify a single "main program" that drives an operating system. Therefore, instead of attempting to design such a system from the top down, object-oriented methodology focuses initially on the data

---

3. Bertrand Meyer, *Object-oriented Software Construction* (Hertfordshire, United Kingdom: Prentice-Hall International, 1988), 47.

that the software must manipulate to do its job. For an operating system, such data takes the form of system resources—files, processes, blocks of memory, and so on.

The primary goal of designing a system around data is to create software that is easy (and cheap) to change. The importance of modifiability becomes evident when you consider the often-quoted statistic that 70 percent of software cost is attributable to maintenance. Software maintenance includes changes such as adding new features, modifying data formats, fixing bugs, and accommodating new hardware.

One way in which object-oriented software minimizes change is by hiding the physical representation of data within objects. An *object* is a data structure whose physical format is hidden behind a type definition. It embodies a set of formal properties (called *attributes*) and is manipulated by a set of services.

Although not strictly an object-oriented system (as Meyer defines it), Windows NT uses objects to represent system resources. Any system resource that can be shared by more than one process—including files, shared memory, and physical devices—is implemented as an object and manipulated by using object services. This approach lessens the impact of changes that will be made in the system over time. If a hardware change, for example, forces a change in the operating system, only the object that represents the hardware resource and the services that operate on the object must change; code that merely uses the object remains the same. Likewise, when the system needs to support new resources, a new object is created and added to the system without disturbing the existing code.

In addition to limiting the effects of change, building an operating system based on objects has some distinct advantages:

- The operating system accesses and manipulates its resources uniformly. It creates, deletes, and refers to an event object in the same way it does a process object: by using object handles. And because each resource is an object, tracking resource usage is done simply by monitoring the creation and use of objects.

- Security is simplified because all objects are protected in the same way. When someone tries to access an object, the security system intervenes and validates the operation, regardless of whether the object is a process, a section of shared memory, or a communication port.

■ Objects provide a convenient and uniform paradigm for sharing resources between two or more processes. Object handles are used to manipulate all types of objects. Two processes share an object when they each open a handle to it. The operating system can track how many handles are open to an object to determine whether the object is still in use. The operating system can then delete the object when it is no longer in use.

Chapter 3, "The Object Manager and Object Security," describes the object manager, the NT executive component that implements and manages Windows NT objects.

2.1.3 Symmetric Multiprocessing

Multitasking is the operating system technique for sharing a single processor among multiple threads of execution. However, when a computer has more than one processor, the multitasking model must be upgraded to a *multiprocessing* model. A computer that has two processors can execute two threads simultaneously. Thus, whereas a multitasking operating system appears to execute multiple threads at the same time, a multiprocessing operating system actually does it, executing one thread on each of its processors.

Multiprocessing operating systems fall into one of two categories, supporting either asymmetric or symmetric processing, as illustrated in Figure 2-5.

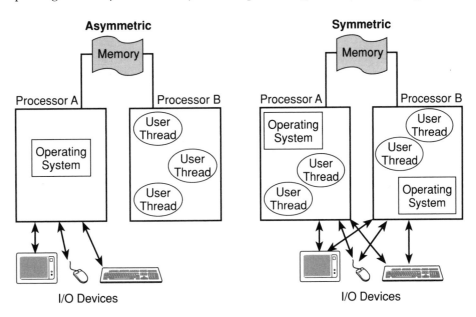

Figure 2-5. Asymmetric and Symmetric Multiprocessing

Asymmetric multiprocessing (ASMP) operating systems typically select the same processor (A, for example) to execute operating system code while other processors run only user jobs. Because operating system code runs on a single processor, ASMP operating systems are relatively easy to create by extending existing single-processor operating systems. ASMP operating systems are especially well suited to running on asymmetric hardware, such as a processor with an attached coprocessor or two processors that don't share all available memory. However, it's difficult to make ASMP operating systems portable. Hardware from different vendors (and even different versions of hardware from the same vendor) tends to vary in its type and degree of asymmetry. Either the hardware vendors must target their hardware for specific operating systems or the operating system must be substantially rewritten for each hardware platform.

Symmetric multiprocessing (SMP) systems, including Windows NT, allow the operating system to run on any free processor or on all processors simultaneously, sharing memory among them. This approach better exploits the power of multiple processors because the operating system itself can use a significant percentage of a computer's processing time, depending on the applications it is running. Executing the operating system on only one processor can tax that processor, leave others idle, and decrease the system's throughput; as the number of processors on the system increases, operating system activities are more likely to become a bottleneck. In addition to balancing the system load, SMP systems reduce downtime because operating system code can execute on other processors if one processor fails. Finally, because symmetric hardware is implemented similarly from vendor to vendor, it is possible to create a portable SMP operating system.

Unlike ASMP systems, SMP systems are usually designed and written from the ground up because they must adhere to strict coding guidelines to ensure correct operation. Resource contention and other performance issues are more complicated in multiprocessing systems than in ordinary operating systems and must be accounted for in the system's design.

Windows NT incorporates several features that are crucial to its success as a multiprocessing operating system:

■ The ability to run operating system code on any available processor and on multiple processors at one time. With the exception of its kernel component, which handles thread scheduling and interrupts, all operating system code can be preempted (forced to give up a processor) when a higher-priority thread needs attention.

■ Multiple threads of execution within a single process. Threads allow one process to execute different parts of its program on different processors simultaneously.[4]

■ Server processes that use multiple threads to process requests from more than one client simultaneously.

■ Convenient mechanisms for sharing objects between processes and flexible interprocess communication capabilities, including shared memory and an optimized message-passing facility.

Processes and threads are described in Chapter 4, "Processes and Threads," and Windows NT servers are described in Chapter 5, "Windows and the Protected Subsystems."

2.2 Windows NT Structure

The structure of Windows NT can be divided into two parts: the user-mode portion of the system (the Windows NT protected subsystems) and the kernel-mode portion (the NT executive). A detailed illustration of Windows NT is shown in Figure 2-6 on the next page.

Windows NT servers are called *protected subsystems* because each one resides in a separate process whose memory is protected from other processes by the NT executive's virtual memory system. Because the subsystems do not automatically share memory, they communicate by passing messages. The solid lines in Figure 2-6 represent paths that messages can take between clients and servers or between two servers. All messages pass through the executive, but for simplicity's sake, those paths are not shown in the figure.

As mentioned previously, the NT executive is an operating system engine capable of supporting any number of server processes. The servers give the NT executive its user and programming interfaces and provide execution environments for various types of applications. The following two sections take a closer look at the Windows NT structure.

2.2.1 Protected Subsystems

As the term "server" implies, each protected subsystem provides an API that programs can call. When an application (or another server) calls an API

---

4. Note that in writing about multithreaded processes, it is often easier to state "a process executes" rather than "a thread within a process executes." Therefore, this text occasionally refers to a process as requesting memory or generating an exception, but you should understand that in Windows NT, the actual agent of execution is always a thread within the process.

routine, a message is sent to the server that implements the API routine via the NT executive's *local procedure call* (LPC) facility, a locally optimized message-passing mechanism. The server replies by sending a message back to the caller.

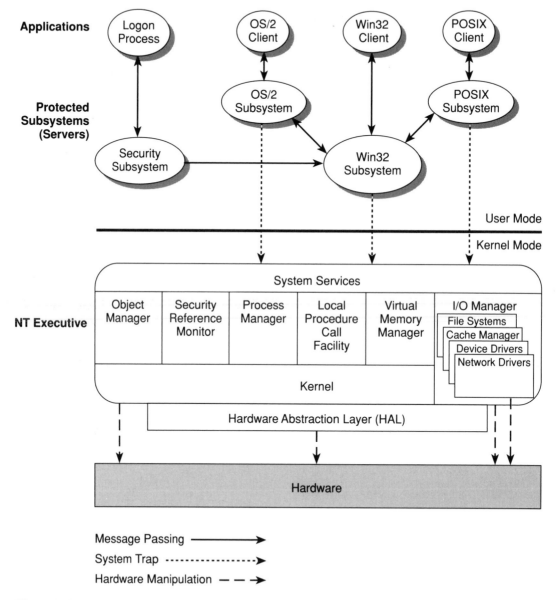

Figure 2-6. Windows NT Block Diagram

Windows NT has two types of protected subsystems: *environment subsystems* and *integral subsystems.* An environment subsystem is a user-mode server that provides an API specific to an operating system. When an application calls an API routine, the call is delivered through the LPC facility to the environment subsystem. The environment subsystem executes the API routine and returns the result to the application process by sending another LPC.

Windows NT's most important environment subsystem is the Win32 subsystem, which makes Microsoft's 32-bit Windows API available to application programs. In addition, the Win32 environment subsystem provides Windows NT's graphical user interface and controls all user input and application output. Windows NT also supplies a POSIX environment subsystem, an OS/2 environment subsystem, a 16-bit Windows subsystem, and an MS-DOS subsystem. (The latter two are not shown in Figure 2-6.) These subsystems provide APIs but use the Win32 subsystem to receive user input and to display output.

The remaining protected subsystems—the integral subsystems—are servers that perform important operating system functions. Several integral subsystems have come and gone during Windows NT's development, but one has remained throughout: the security subsystem. The security subsystem runs in user mode and records the security policies in effect on the local computer. For example, it keeps track of which user accounts have special privileges, which system resources are audited for access, and whether audit alarms or audit messages should be generated. In addition, the security subsystem maintains a database of information about user accounts, including account names, passwords, any groups the user belongs to for security purposes, and any special privileges the user owns. It also accepts user logon information and initiates logon authentication.

Several components of the Windows NT networking software are also implemented as integral subsystems. Two are worth mentioning here: the workstation service and the server service. Each of these *services,* as networking subsystems are often called, is a user-mode process that implements an API to access and manage the LAN Manager network redirector and server, respectively. The redirector is the network component responsible for sending (redirecting) I/O requests across a network when the file or device to be accessed is not local. The server sits on the remote machine and receives such remote requests. Both the LAN Manager redirector and the LAN Manager server are implemented as file system drivers—that is, as part of the NT I/O system, described shortly.

2.2.2 Executive

The NT executive is the kernel-mode portion of Windows NT and, except for a user interface, is a complete operating system unto itself. The executive consists of a series of components, each of which implements two sets of functions: system services, which environment subsystems and other executive components can call, and internal routines, which are available only to components within the executive. The interfaces are illustrated in Figure 2-7.

Although the executive provides API-like system services, it is fundamentally different from the environment subsystems. It does not run continually in a process of its own but instead runs in the context of an existing process by taking over an executing thread when important system events occur. For example, when a thread calls a system service and is trapped by the processor or when an external device interrupts the processor, the NT kernel gains control of the thread that was running. The kernel calls the appropriate system code to handle the event, executes it, and then returns control to the code that was executing before the interruption.

Executive components maintain independence from one another, each creating and manipulating the system data structures it requires. Because the interfaces between components are carefully controlled, it is possible to completely remove a component from the operating system and replace it with one that operates differently. As long as the new version implements all the system services and internal interfaces correctly, the operating system runs as before. Maintaining the operating system is also an easier task because the NT executive components interact in predictable ways.

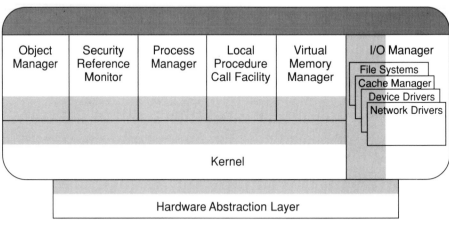

Figure 2-7. System Interfaces

The responsibilities of the executive components are listed here:

- Object manager. Creates, manages, and deletes NT executive objects, abstract data types that are used to represent operating system resources.

- Security reference monitor. Enforces security policies on the local computer. It guards operating system resources, performing run-time object protection and auditing.

- Process manager. Creates and terminates processes and threads. It also suspends and resumes the execution of threads and stores and retrieves information about NT processes and threads.

- Local procedure call (LPC) facility. Passes messages between a client process and a server process on the same computer. LPC is a flexible, optimized version of *remote procedure call* (RPC), an industry-standard communication facility for client and server processes across a network. (See Chapter 9, ''Networking,'' for more information.)

- Virtual memory (VM) manager. Implements *virtual memory*, a memory management scheme that provides a large, private address space for each process and protects each process's address space from other processes. When memory usage is too high, the VM manager transfers selected memory contents to disk and reloads the contents when they are used again, a practice known as *paging*.

- Kernel. Responds to interrupts and exceptions, schedules threads for execution, synchronizes the activities of multiple processors, and supplies a set of elemental objects and interfaces that the rest of the NT executive uses to implement higher-level objects.

- I/O system. Comprises a group of components responsible for processing input from and delivering output to a variety of devices. The I/O system includes the following subcomponents:

  □ I/O manager. Implements device-independent input/output facilities and establishes a model for NT executive I/O.

  □ File systems. NT drivers that accept file-oriented I/O requests and translate them into I/O requests bound for a particular device.

  □ *Network redirector* and *network server*. File system drivers that transmit remote I/O requests to a machine on the network and receive such requests, respectively.

□ NT executive device drivers. Low-level drivers that directly manipulate hardware to write output to or retrieve input from a physical device or network.

□ *Cache manager*. Improves the performance of file-based I/O by storing the most recently read disk information in system memory. The cache manager uses the VM manager's paging facility to automatically write modifications to the disk in the background.

■ Hardware abstraction layer (HAL). Places a layer of code between the NT executive and the hardware platform on which **Windows NT** is running. It hides hardware-dependent details such as I/O interfaces, interrupt controllers, and multiprocessor communication mechanisms. Rather than access hardware directly, NT executive components maintain maximum portability by calling the HAL routines when they need platform-dependent information.

Windows NT is a portable operating system, designed to limit the amount of code that relies on a particular hardware architecture. Some processor-specific code (for instance, Intel 486 or MIPS R4000) is required, however, and is located in the lowest layers of the NT kernel, with smaller portions located in the VM manager. These components, particularly the NT kernel, hide processor differences from the rest of the operating system.

Platform-dependent code—that is, code that relies on a particular manufacturer's implementation of a MIPS R4000 computer, for example—is located in the HAL and is provided by individual computer manufacturers. Device drivers contain device-specific code, of course, but they avoid processor-dependent and platform-dependent code by calling NT kernel routines and HAL routines.

2.2.3 A Brief Tour

With minor exceptions, Windows NT does not appear to be a unique new operating system from a user's point of view. It looks like Windows and runs Windows-based programs. Underneath its user interface, however, it is radically different. The following sections provide a whirlwind tour of how the various pieces of Windows NT fit together, beginning at its user interface and working downward into the NT executive.

2.2.3.1 Logon Session

Windows NT is a secure operating system that requires each user to establish an account and to log onto that account before access to the system is granted.

Each user account has associated with it a security profile, which is a collection of security-related information stored in a system database. The security subsystem employs this information to verify that users are who they claim to be. The system components involved in logon are highlighted in Figure 2-8.

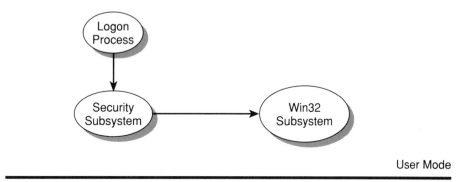

User Mode

Local Procedure Call (LPC) ⟶

Figure 2-8. Logging On

A security system process, called a *logon process,* sits waiting for user input. Several logon processes can be active, each one monitoring a separate class of logon devices—for example, a keyboard/mouse combination or a network connection. A thread in the process detects when a user attempts to access the system and prompts the user for an account name and a password.

From there the logon process passes the user's information to the security subsystem, which checks the information against a security database. If the logon is authentic, the subsystem creates an object that uniquely identifies this user in all subsequent transactions. The object, called an *access token,* is the key to security in Windows NT: It determines which system resources the user's threads may access.

After the user's identity is established, the security subsystem creates a process, attaches the user's access token to it, and then passes the process to the Win32 subsystem, which runs the Win32 Program Manager in the process's address space. With that, the user has established a logon session. Windows NT supports both local and remote logons, and a server machine running Windows NT is likely to have numerous logon sessions active at the same time.

As soon as an interactive user successfully logs onto Windows NT, the Win32 subsystem takes control of the screen. In its first release, Windows NT looks like, and is compatible with, Windows 3.1, as depicted in Figure 2-9. With

Windows NT, users can transparently run Win32 programs and 16-bit Windows programs, as well as MS-DOS, OS/2, and POSIX programs.

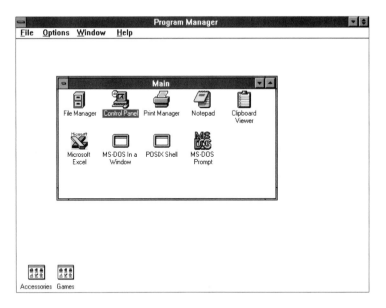

Figure 2-9. Windows NT's User Interface

2.2.3.2 Environment Subsystems

The Win32 environment subsystem provides Windows NT's user interface. It controls not only the video display but also the keyboard, the mouse, and other input devices attached to the machine. In addition, it is a server for Win32 applications, implementing the Win32 API.

Not all applications are Win32 applications, and the Win32 subsystem does not control the execution of non-Win32 applications. When the user runs an application that the Win32 subsystem does not recognize, the subsystem determines what type of application it is and then either calls another subsystem to run the application or calls code to initialize an MS-DOS environment in which to run the application. (See Figure 2-10.)

Each of the environment subsystems supplies an API that its client applications use. For example, the Win32 subsystem supplies 32-bit Windows API routines, and the OS/2 subsystem supplies OS/2 API routines. Applications cannot mix and match API routines from different subsystems because each environment subsystem operates differently. A file handle created by the Win32 subsystem does not translate to the POSIX subsystem, for example. Furthermore, such hybrid applications would not run on MS-DOS/Windows, POSIX, or OS/2 operating systems.

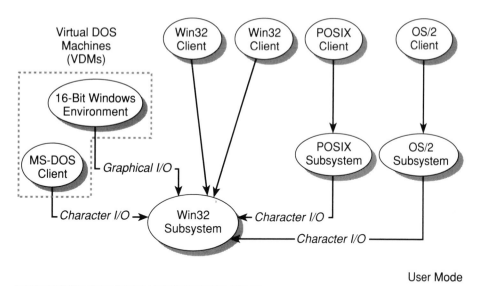

Kernel Mode

Local Procedure Call (LPC) ——————▶

Figure 2-10. Environment Subsystems and Client Applications

MS-DOS and 16-bit Windows emulation are supplied by an environment subsystem called a *virtual DOS machine* (VDM), which provides a complete MS-DOS machine environment. MS-DOS and 16-bit Windows applications run within the context of VDM processes, which are unlike other environment subsystems in that multiple VDM processes can be running at one time. (See Chapter 5, "Windows and the Protected Subsystems," for more information.)

Because the Win32 subsystem handles all video output, the other environment subsystems must direct the output of their applications to the Win32 subsystem for display. The VDM running 16-bit Windows applications translates the applications' output calls into Win32 calls and sends them in a message to the Win32 subsystem for display. The OS/2 and POSIX subsystems, as well as any VDMs running MS-DOS applications, direct their applications' character-mode output to the Win32 subsystem, which displays the output in character-mode windows, called *consoles.*

An environment subsystem can support many client applications. Each subsystem keeps track of its clients and maintains any global information that all the client applications share. Although several subsystems and VDMs might be running, Win32 is the only environment subsystem that makes itself visible. To the user, it appears that Windows runs all the applications.

2.2.3.3 Native Services

Environment subsystems implement their API routines by calling *NT native services,* the system services provided by individual components of the NT executive. The VM manager supplies memory allocation and deallocation services, for example, whereas the process manager provides services to create and terminate processes and threads. As Figure 2-11 illustrates, when a subsystem calls an NT native service, hardware detects the call and transfers control to the NT executive. The service then runs in kernel mode.

Because the native services are used by different environment subsystems, they must be general—even primitive. They must be flexible, without unnecessary built-in constraints. And they must not generate side effects that might conflict with the diverse needs of the environment subsystems.

One way in which the native services are flexible is in their ability to act on any process the caller specifies. The caller supplies a handle to a process,

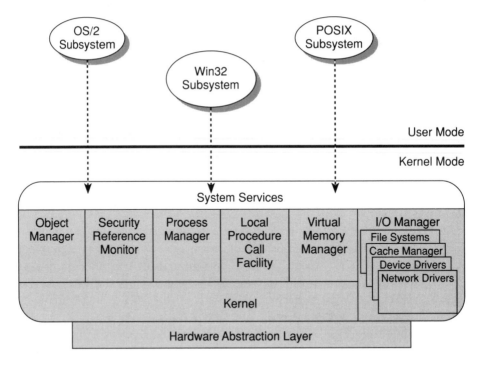

Figure 2-11. Native System Service Call

and the service operates on that process. For example, a subsystem can call a native service to create a thread or allocate memory for one of its client processes. Of course, most normal processes cannot perform such operations on other processes. Environment subsystems have powerful access tokens that grant them control over their clients.

Protected subsystems, DLLs, and components of the NT executive are the primary users of NT native services. Applications that run on Windows NT are written to Win32, MS-DOS, 16-bit Windows, POSIX, and OS/2 programming interfaces, which are supplied by environment subsystems.

2.2.3.4 Objects

Many, perhaps most, NT native services are object services. That is, they perform some action on an object in the NT executive. A thread opens a handle to an object and then uses that handle when calling services to operate on the object.

Shareable resources, including processes, threads, files, and shared memory, are implemented as objects in the NT executive. This allows the operating system to take advantage of the similarities among resources and to use common code wherever possible in order to manage them. The NT object system is a focal point for several types of resource management tasks, such as resource naming, placing limits (called *quotas*) on the amount of resources each process can use, sharing resources between two processes, and securing resources against unauthorized access.

Environment subsystems frequently call object services to create, open a handle to, manipulate, or delete objects. For example, if the user starts a Win32 application—Microsoft Excel, for instance—the Win32 subsystem calls the NT process manager to create a process (the process in which Excel will run) and open a handle to it. The process manager, in turn, calls the object manager to create a process object and a thread object. Similarly, if the user saves a new Excel spreadsheet, the Win32 subsystem calls the NT I/O manager to create a file object that represents the file in which the spreadsheet is stored and to open a handle to the object. The I/O manager calls the object manager to do the job. Figure 2-12 on the next page illustrates.

Much of NT's resource management takes place when some process creates an object and/or opens a handle to an object. For example, when a process (in this case, the Win32 subsystem) creates an object, it can optionally give the object a name. Giving an object a name makes that object available for sharing by other processes. A process that wants to share the object simply retrieves the object's name by calling the NT object manager and then opens a handle to that object.

Objects are allocated from operating system memory. To keep any one process from using too much system memory, processes are charged a set amount of their quota each time one of their threads opens a handle to a particular type of object. If a process exhausts its quota, the object manager does not allow it to open any more object handles.

In addition to managing resources and facilitating resource sharing, the NT object system serves as a focal point for resource security. When a process opens a handle to an NT object, the NT security subsystem is activated. Each object has attached to it a little database, called an *access control list* (ACL), containing information regarding which processes can access the object and what they can do to it. When a process opens a handle to an object, it specifies the operations it wants to perform. For example, it might open a file for read access. The security system checks whether the process is allowed read access to the file object in question, and if so, the object manager returns an object handle containing read access. The caller can then use the handle to read from that particular file. If the caller also needs write access to the file, it can request both read and write access when it opens the first handle or it can open a second handle for write access. Because a process must open a handle

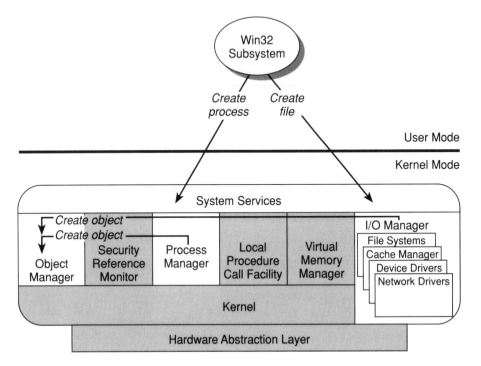

Figure 2-12. Creating NT Objects

to an object before it can do anything to it and because opening a handle invokes the security system, no process can bypass NT security.

2.2.3.5 Virtual Memory

Operating systems adopt different views of physical memory and require their programs to access memory in specified ways. In Windows NT, application programs run in an operating system environment that behaves like Windows, MS-DOS, POSIX, or OS/2. The challenge is to allow all the different types of applications to run without being rewritten and without bumping into each other in memory.

Each of Windows NT's environment subsystems provides a view of memory that corresponds to what its applications expect. Underneath the environment subsystems, the NT executive has its own memory structure, which the environment subsystems access by calling NT native services.

The NT memory architecture is a virtual memory system based on 32-bit addresses in a flat (linear) address space. A process's *virtual address space* is the set of addresses available for the process's threads to use. At runtime, the VM manager, with assistance from hardware, translates, or *maps*, the virtual addresses into physical addresses, where the data is actually stored. By controlling the mapping, the operating system can ensure that individual processes don't bump into one another or overwrite the operating system.

Each process's virtual address space is 4 gigabytes (2^{32} bytes), with 2 gigabytes reserved for program storage and 2 gigabytes reserved for system storage. Four gigabytes (or even 2) is much larger than the amount of physical memory likely to be available on ordinary machines. When physical memory becomes full, the VM manager transfers, or pages, some of the memory contents to disk. Paging data to disk frees physical memory so that it can be used for other things. When a thread accesses a virtual address that has been paged to disk, the VM manager loads the information back into memory from disk. Virtual memory is described in greater detail in Chapter 6, "The Virtual Memory Manager."

In Windows NT, the operating system resides in high virtual memory and the user's code and data reside in low virtual memory, as shown in Figure 2-13 on the next page. A user-mode thread cannot read or write to system memory directly.

A portion of the system memory, called *nonpaged pool*, is never paged to disk and is used to store some NT objects and other important data structures. Another portion of system memory, called *paged pool*, is paged to disk. All of user memory can be paged. (See Chapter 6, "The Virtual Memory Manager," for more information.)

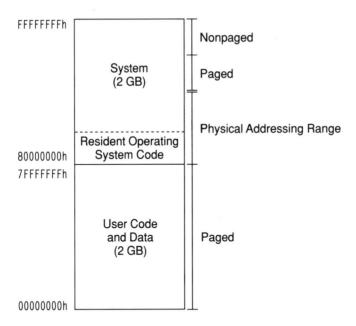

Figure 2-13. NT Address Space Layout

2.2.3.6 I/O and File Systems

As with memory, environment subsystems provide whatever I/O facilities their applications expect. They implement those individual facilities by calling native NT I/O services.

The native I/O system uses an asynchronous I/O model, but it provides system services that allow environment subsystems to use either a synchronous or an asynchronous model. *Asynchronous I/O* allows a caller to request an I/O operation and then do other work while the device finishes transferring the data. The I/O system automatically notifies the caller when the I/O is complete so that the caller can do subsequent processing. Because I/O devices are generally much slower than processors, a program that does a lot of I/O can often improve its performance by using asynchronous I/O.

Windows NT supports multiple file systems, including the *file allocation table* (FAT) file system, the *high-performance file system* (HPFS), and a new file system called the *NT file system* (NTFS). NTFS extends the capabilities present in both the FAT file system and the HPFS to add the following new features:

- File system recovery that allows for quick restoration of disk-based data after a system failure.

- The ability to handle (ridiculously) large storage media—up to 2^{64} bytes, or approximately 17 billion gigabytes, in size.

- Security features, including execute-only files.

- Unicode filenames, which allow documents to be transferred from one computer to another internationally, without garbling filenames and pathnames. (See Section 2.3.1.)

- Support for the POSIX operating system environment, including hard links, case-sensitive names, and information about when a file was last opened.

- Features for future extensibility, such as transaction-based operations to support fault tolerant applications, user-controlled version numbers for files, multiple data streams per file, flexible options for file naming and file attributes, and support for popular file servers.

The I/O manager allows device drivers and file systems (which it views as "device" drivers) to be loaded dynamically into and out of the system, based on the needs of the user. Drivers are modular and can be layered one on top of another, which, for example, allows different file systems to call the same floppy disk driver or hard disk driver to access files, as shown in Figure 2-14.

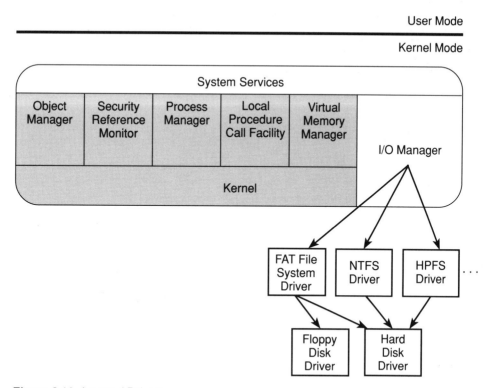

Figure 2-14. Layered Drivers

The layered driver model also provides the ability to insert additional drivers in the hierarchy. For example, logical file system drivers or fault tolerant drivers can occupy intermediate levels in the driver hierarchy.

Windows NT provides access to files on the LAN Manager network through a file system driver called the Windows NT redirector. The redirector accepts requests for remote files and directs them to a LAN Manager server on another machine.

2.3 Additional Windows NT Architectures

The tour thus far has not captured all the important elements of Windows NT. Indeed, coverage of many topics is deferred until later in this book, and other topics will be left for future writings. However, two topics in particular do not fit conveniently into any one component of the operating system (or any one chapter of this book) but are too important to omit. The first is Windows NT's internationalization support, which allows users located in many different countries to interact with the system in their native languages. It also gives application developers the tools they need to write international applications. The second topic is structured exception handling, a feature that is supplied in Microsoft C and bolstered by the NT kernel. It allows users to write robust applications. Windows NT, written mostly in Microsoft C, also uses the features of structured exception handling to make the operating system reliable.

Neither of these topics can be adequately presented in a few short pages. However, the following two sections give a glimpse of the issues surrounding internationalization and structured exception handling and summarize how both are addressed in Windows NT. Refer to the bibliography for sources of additional information.

2.3.1 Internationalization

With the widespread availability of jet travel and sophisticated telecommunications, the world is becoming a smaller and smaller place. Consequently, international markets are becoming increasingly important to the computing industry. International sales constitute an ever-larger slice of the applications market. The goal for Windows NT is to be a truly multilingual operating system, one that provides a solid foundation for developing and using international applications.

The user-visible aspects of international support appear in the Win32 control panel, shown in Figure 2-15.

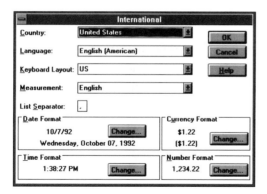

Figure 2-15. International Dialog Box

This dialog box has not changed from Windows 3.0. However, underneath the user interface, much has changed. International support is greatly streamlined in Windows NT, providing modular facilities for applications as well as for important system components such as the Win32 subsystem. The user interface to internationalization facilities will continue to evolve in future releases.

2.3.1.1 Locales

Different national or cultural markets, called *locales,* have different requirements for software. Chief among the requirements is to allow users to interact with the software in their native languages, using native conventions for representing data.

A locale consists of a language, a country, and a *code set,* the binary codes used to represent the characters of a particular language. (Windows ANSI is one such code set.) When installing Windows NT, the user selects a language to use and is assigned a default locale. The default locale gives the user culturally correct defaults for keyboard layout, sorting order, currency, and date and time formatting. The user can override any of these defaults.

Even more flexibility is desirable, however. In multilingual countries such as Canada, Switzerland, and Belgium, users require the ability to switch among two or more languages on a regular basis. Moreover, some companies, including Microsoft, have divisions in which several different languages are routinely spoken. Ideally, each user should be able to switch among locales at any time or to send data among locales without losing information. To accomplish this, applications (and in this case, Windows) must be separated into two pieces:

- Code, which can be used in all locales

- Data, which must be translated for different locales

In Windows, the data category consists of resources such as menus and messages. These resources are separated from the main body of the code and can be attached to or detached from Windows. When the user switches locales, the resource set changes to represent the new locale. Since the set of Windows resources is much smaller than Windows itself, many different resource sets can be loaded at installation time, allowing the user to switch between locales easily without loading new files from floppy disks. Moreover, a single Windows NT package can be shipped to all countries with localization support already built in. The only remaining task is to translate the resource files and the documentation.

To facilitate localization, Windows NT's Win32 subsystem provides a *national language support* (NLS) API that gives applications (and Windows NT) access to culturally correct string comparisons; collation tables for sorting the characters of different languages; date, time, and currency formatting routines; and routines for determining the locale that is in effect and the other locales present on the system. In addition, the NLS API provides routines to convert between the international code set used by Windows NT and other commonly used code sets. (More on this topic in the next section.) Both the Win32 subsystem and the C runtime library provide their own API routines based on NLS. Using these facilities allows applications to support localization without having to duplicate the substantial database (tables, code sets, and so on) required to do so.

2.3.1.2 Unicode

The lowest layer of localization support is in the representation of individual characters, the code sets. The United States has traditionally employed the ASCII (American Standard Code for Information Interchange) standard for representing data. For European and other countries, however, ASCII is not adequate because it lacks common symbols and punctuation. For example, the British pound sign is omitted, as are the diacritical marks used in French, German, Dutch, and Spanish.

The International Standards Organization (ISO) established a standard code set called Latin1 (ISO standard 8859-1), which defines codes for all the European characters omitted by ASCII. Microsoft Windows uses a slight modification of Latin1 called the Windows ANSI code set. Windows ANSI is a *single-byte coding scheme* because it uses 8 bits to represent each character. The maximum number of characters that can be expressed using 8 bits is 256 (2^8).

A *script* is the set of letters required to write in a particular language. The same script is often used for several languages. (For example, the Cyrillic script is used for both the Russian and Ukrainian languages.) Windows ANSI and other single-byte coding schemes can encode enough characters to express the letters of Western scripts. However, Eastern scripts such as Japanese and Chinese, which employ thousands of separate characters, cannot be encoded using a single-byte coding scheme. These scripts are typically stored using a double-byte coding scheme, which uses 16 bits for each character, or a multibyte coding scheme, in which some characters are represented by an 8-bit sequence and others are represented by a 16-bit, 24-bit, or 32-bit sequence. The latter scheme requires complicated parsing algorithms to determine the storage width of a particular character. Furthermore, a proliferation of different code sets means that a particular code might yield entirely different characters on two different computers, depending on the code set each computer uses.

To address the problem of multiple coding schemes and to accommodate a more comprehensive set of scripts, Windows NT employs the new *Unicode* standard for data representation. Unicode, a 16-bit character-coding scheme, can represent 65,536 (2^{16}) characters. This is enough to include all languages in computer commerce today, as well as several archaic or arcane languages with limited applications (such as Sanskrit and, eventually, Egyptian hieroglyphics). Unicode also includes representations for punctuation marks, mathematical symbols, and a set of graphical characters called dingbats,[5] with plenty of room remaining for future expansion.

Unicode separates the "essence" of a character from the font and formatting information used to display it. Each code corresponds to one (and only one) character; font information is applied to Unicode characters to display them in various styles and shapes. Figure 2-16 illustrates the layout of scripts and symbols in Unicode.[6]

Although the Win32 subsystem provides both ANSI and Unicode string API routines, Unicode is Windows NT's native code set. All character strings in the system, including object names, pathnames, filenames, and directory names, are represented with 16-bit Unicode characters. Even the Win32 subsystem converts any ANSI characters it receives to Unicode strings before manipulating them; it converts them back to ANSI, if necessary, upon exit from the system.

---

5. I have attempted, unsuccessfully, to determine why these characters are called dingbats. If anyone knows the answer, please satisfy my curiosity by sending the information to me in care of Microsoft Press.

6. Figure 2-16 was adapted from an illustration by Asmus Freytag, vice president of marketing for the Unicode Consortium.

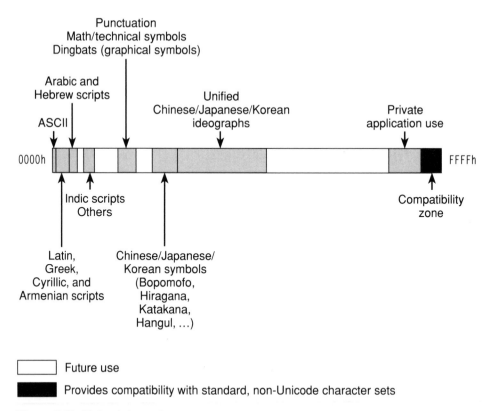

Figure 2-16. Unicode Layout

Using Unicode removes all limitations on the set of characters that Windows NT can represent. Because Unicode establishes a unique code for every character of every script, Windows NT can ensure that the round-trip character translation, into and out of the system, is always accurate.

2.3.2 Structured Exception Handling

The second special architecture supported and used by Windows NT is called structured exception handling. *Exceptions* are synchronous errors or atypical events that cause the execution of code outside the normal flow of control. Unlike interrupts, which are generated from an external source, exceptions occur when a program executes a particular code sequence, and exceptions can be reproduced.

For example, when a program calls the C function malloc(), the typical result is that malloc() allocates memory and returns a pointer to it. The exceptional condition occurs when some problem, such as a lack of available memory, causes the allocation to fail. In this case, the function returns a NULL pointer.

Returning a special value to indicate an exception is a common but primitive form of exception handling and has some drawbacks. First, a programmer must religiously check the return value and either act on any errors or propagate them to a higher layer of software. If one layer omits the check, bugs can surface in unrelated parts of the program. Second, the code becomes cluttered with If...Then...Else clauses that handle the atypical, rather than the typical, case. Third, information about why the operation went wrong might not be easily available to the code that must address the problem.

Exceptions can be detected by either hardware or software. For example, hardware generally detects divide-by-zero exceptions, whereas software detects memory access violations. Structured exception handling is the method used in Windows NT for processing both hardware and software exceptions, using the control structure (hence the name) of a programming language. Structured exception handling allows any block of code to determine what type or types of exceptions it wants to guard against and to register a special code sequence (the *exception handler*) that is executed if such exceptions occur within the guarded block of code.

The following code is a simple routine written in Microsoft C that includes an exception handler. It is a modified version of the standard C library function strlen(), which returns the length of a null-terminated string.

```
/* safelen: return valid length of string s,
   even if the string pointer was bad */

int safelen(char *s)
{
    int count = 0;

    try {
        while (*s++ != '\0')
        /* possible access violation */
            count++;
        return (count);
        }
    except (GetExceptionCode() == ACCESS_VIOLATION ?
                     EXCEPTION_EXECUTE_HANDLER :
                     EXCEPTION_CONTINUE_SEARCH)
        {
    /*  pointer was bad or string was not terminated */
        return (count);
        }
}
```

The normal strlen() function merrily plods through memory one character at a time until it finds a NULL character. But if the string is not null-terminated or if the string pointer is invalid, strlen() can terminate unexpectedly with an access violation exception.

This modified version of the code captures the exception and returns a valid value (not necessarily correct, merely valid), rather than terminating the program. The new C keyword, *try*, is used to mark the beginning of the block of code that might cause an access violation. If an exception occurs within this block, control is transferred to the *except* keyword, which is followed (in parentheses) by an exception filter. The exception filter allows the programmer to specify execution of the exception handler only for selected types of exceptions. If the exception filter resolves to TRUE, the exception handler—the *return (count)* statement, in this case—executes. Exception filters are powerful because they can access local data and can be of arbitrary complexity. They allow the exception handler to be executed under precise conditions. The transfer of control to an exception handler is called *raising an exception*. Notice how the error handling code is removed from the main line of the program.

Each block of code can have a separate exception handler, and exception handlers can even be nested within one another. When an exception occurs, the exception filter can test the type of exception and conditionally tell the operating system to execute the exception handler, continue the program, terminate the program, or look for an exception handler in an enclosing block of code.

Operating system exceptions aren't the only exceptions to which applications might want to respond. Applications can generate an exception using the Win32 API routine RaiseException(), causing control to transfer to a registered exception handler. The operating system supports this operation by registering exception handlers and searching for them in the proper order when exceptions are raised. If no exception handler takes care of the problem, the operating system terminates the program that caused the error. Windows NT's exception-handling facility is not language specific; a single mechanism is used across all languages. Each language defines how the underlying exception-handling mechanism is exposed.

Another type of exception handler, known as a *termination handler*, lets an application ensure that a particular block of code always executes, even if a guarded block of code terminates in an unexpected way. Termination handlers often contain code that frees allocated resources so that if a procedure terminates unexpectedly, the resources it allocated are released back to the system. The following is a Win32 code fragment illustrating the purpose of a termination handler:

```
/* allocate and initialize a
   global critical section object */
           .

           .

           .

LPSTR Buffer;
Buffer = NULL;

/* enter the critical section and
   allocate a buffer */
try {
        EnterCriticalSection(&CriticalSection)
        Buffer = LocalAlloc(LMEM_FIXED, 10);
        if(!Buffer) {
             return;
        }
        strcpy(Buffer, "Hello");
}
finally {
/* always leave the critical section and
   free the allocated buffer */
        if(Buffer != NULL)
             LocalFree(Buffer);
        LeaveCriticalSection(&CriticalSection);

}
           .

           .

           .
```

A critical section is a Win32 synchronization object that ensures that one and only one thread can execute a particular block of code at a time. In this example, a thread gains access to the critical section, allocates a buffer, and then modifies the buffer. If something goes awry (an unhandled exception, perhaps) and causes the routine to terminate while the thread is in the critical section, any other thread waiting to acquire the resource will be perpetually blocked. Furthermore, the buffer that the thread allocated will be lost, with the operating system unable to recover it. (Developers often refer to these types of errors as memory leaks. If too many occur, available memory gradually "drains away.") The termination handler ensures that the thread releases the critical section object and frees the buffer. Termination handlers always execute when the flow of control leaves the body of the try...finally block no matter how the exit occurs.

Exception handlers and termination handlers can be used separately or in combination to achieve robust behavior in any application. Windows NT uses both to ensure robust behavior at all levels of the system.

2.4   In Conclusion

There you have it—some of the highlights of Windows NT. It is a symmetric multiprocessing operating system base that supports multiple operating system environments. Windows NT has a Windows graphical user interface and runs Win32, 16-bit Windows, MS-DOS, POSIX, and OS/2 programs. It employs advanced operating system principles such as virtual memory, preemptive multitasking, structured exception handling, and operating system objects. It is secure, powerful, reliable, and flexible. It has the kind of capabilities that once were found only in mainframe and minicomputer operating systems. In other words, Windows NT is an express locomotive squeezed into a skateboard-sized package—it could very well represent the future of desktop computing. But you can judge for yourself. The following chapters of this book flesh out the details of Windows NT, beginning with objects—its means for representing, managing, and securing its resources.

CHAPTER THREE

THE OBJECT MANAGER
AND OBJECT SECURITY

Object-oriented languages, user interfaces, and operating systems became hot topics among computing enthusiasts in the latter half of the 1980s. Objects were suddenly touted as a cure-all for every programming affliction. However, objects are not new. They made their first appearance in the late 1960s in programming languages such as Simula that were developed primarily to create simulation programs. Computer simulations model the behavior of real-world objects. Therefore, object-oriented programming, which provides a way to represent and manipulate both physical and abstract objects, is a natural approach in that field.

Operating systems also manipulate objects. Their objects take the form of hardware resources, such as I/O devices and memory, or software resources, such as files, processes, and semaphores. Most operating systems focus on the differences between these shared resources and manipulate each type of resource differently. Implementing them as objects, however, exploits their similarities. It concentrates all resource management in one location and provides a cohesive model for using resources.

The tour inside Windows NT begins with the NT executive and specifically with NT executive objects. It's difficult to start anywhere else because processes, threads, files, and even the Win32 subsystem (a process) are objects. Hence, understanding the NT object system provides useful insights into wide-ranging parts of the operating system.

The first section of this chapter examines the types of objects that exist in Windows NT and describes how they are used. A discussion of object structure and of how the object manager administers objects is the subject of the second section. The third section focuses on a fundamental task of the Windows NT security system: protecting objects.

3.1 NT Executive Objects

What is an object? In the NT executive, an *object* is a single, runtime instance of a statically defined object type. An *object type* (sometimes called an *object class*) comprises a system-defined data type, services that operate on instances of the data type, and a set of object attributes. If you write Win32 applications, you encounter process, thread, file, and event objects, to name a few examples. These objects are based on lower-level objects that are created and managed by the NT executive. In NT, a process is an instance of the process object type, a file is an instance of the file object type, and so on.

An *object attribute* is a field of data in an object that partially defines the object's state.[1] An object of type stack, for example, would have a stack pointer as one of its most important attributes. *Object services,* the means for manipulating objects, usually read or change the object attributes. For example, the push service for a stack object would change the value of the stack pointer.

The most fundamental difference between an object and an ordinary data structure is that the internal structure of an object is hidden from view. You must call an object service to get data out of an object or to put data into it. You cannot directly read or change data inside an object. This separates the underlying implementation of the object from code that merely uses it, a technique that allows object implementations to be changed easily over time.

The NT executive design team decided to use objects to represent system resources because objects provide a centralized means for accomplishing three important (and often irksome) operating system tasks:

- Providing human-readable names for system resources

- Sharing resources and data among processes

- Protecting resources from unauthorized access

Not all data structures in the NT executive are objects. Only data that needs to be shared, protected, named, or made visible to user-mode programs (via system services) is placed in objects. Structures used by only one component of the executive to implement internal functions, for example, are not objects.

Despite its pervasive use of objects to represent shared system resources, Windows NT is not an object-oriented system in the strict sense. Most of the operating system code is written in C for portability and because develop-

---

1. Although there is a parameter called *ObjectAttributes* that a caller supplies when creating an object using either the Win32 API or native object services, that parameter should not be confused with the more general meaning of the term as used in this book.

ment tools are widely available. C does not directly support object-oriented constructs, such as dynamic binding of data types, polymorphic functions, or class inheritance. Therefore, Windows NT's C-based implementation of objects borrows from, but does not depend on, esoteric features of particular object-oriented languages.

The *object manager* is the component of the NT executive responsible for creating, deleting, protecting, and tracking NT objects. The object manager centralizes resource control operations that otherwise would be scattered throughout the operating system. Lou Perazzoli, engineering manager and project leader for Windows NT development, and Steve Wood, a nine-year veteran programmer of Microsoft operating systems, designed the object manager and set the following implementation goals:

- Provide a common, uniform mechanism for using system resources.

- Isolate object protection to one location in the operating system so that U.S. government Class C2 security compliance can be achieved.

- Establish an object-naming scheme that can readily incorporate existing objects, such as the devices, files, and directories of a file system, or other independent collections of objects.

- Create a way to charge processes for their use of objects so that a system administrator can set limits on the usage of system resources.

- Establish uniform rules for object retention (that is, keeping an object available until all processes have finished using it).

- Support the requirements of various operating system environments, such as the ability of a process to inherit resources from a parent process (needed by Windows and POSIX) and the ability to create case-sensitive filenames (needed by POSIX).

The following subsections present the basics of NT executive objects, including how these objects are structured and how they are used in the operating system.

3.1.1 Using Objects

The NT executive implements two kinds of objects: *executive objects* and *kernel objects*. Executive objects are objects implemented by various components of the NT executive. They are available to user-mode code (protected subsystems) through native NT services and can be created and manipulated either by subsystems or by the NT executive.

Kernel objects are a more primitive set of objects implemented by the NT kernel. These objects are not visible to user-mode code but are created and used only within the NT executive. Kernel objects provide fundamental capabilities, such as the ability to alter system scheduling, that can be accomplished only by the lowest layer of the operating system—the kernel. Many executive objects contain (encapsulate) one or more kernel objects. For now, we'll concern ourselves with only the user-visible object types, which are listed in Table 3-1 along with the executive components that define them.

Each Windows NT environment subsystem projects to its applications a different image of the operating system. The executive objects and object services are primitives that the environment subsystems use to construct their own versions of objects and other resources. The set of objects an environment subsystem supplies to its applications might be larger or smaller than that provided by the NT executive. Some subsystems, such as POSIX, do not support objects as objects at all. The POSIX subsystem uses executive objects and services as the basis for presenting POSIX-style processes, pipes, and other resources to its applications. Other subsystems, such as the Win32 subsystem, use NT executive objects to create their own versions of objects. The Win32 subsystem supplies to Win32 applications mutexes and semaphores, both of which are directly based on NT executive objects. In addition, the Win32 subsystem supplies named pipes and mailslots, resources that are based on NT executive file objects.

Executive Object Type	Defined By	Represents
Process	Process manager	A program invocation, including the address space and resources required to run the program
Thread	Process manager	An executable entity within a process
Section	Memory manager	A region of shared memory
File	I/O manager	An instance of an opened file or I/O device
Port	LPC facility	A destination for messages passed between processes
Access token	Security system	A tamperproof ID containing security information about a logged-on user
Event	Executive support services	An announcement that a system event has occurred

Table 3-1. Executive Objects

(continued)

Table 3-1. *continued*

Executive Object Type	Defined By	Represents
Event pair	Executive support services	A notification that a dedicated client thread has copied a message to the Win32 server or vice versa (used only by the Win32 subsystem)
Semaphore	Executive support services	A counter that regulates the number of threads that can use a resource
Mutant[2]	Executive support services	A mechanism that provides mutual exclusion capabilities for the Win32 and OS/2 environments
Timer	Executive support services	A counter that records the passage of time
Object directory	Object manager	A memory-based repository for object names
Symbolic link	Object manager	A mechanism for indirectly referring to an object name
Profile	Kernel	A mechanism for measuring the distribution of execution time within a block of code (for performance tuning)
Key	Configuration manager	An index key for referring to records in the Windows NT configuration database

This chapter focuses on executive objects, those that are provided by the NT executive. Executive objects should not be confused with the objects made available to application programs through the Win32 API, the POSIX API, or the OS/2 API.

3.1.1.1 File-Based Model

From a programming perspective, Windows NT looks like Windows or MS-DOS or POSIX or OS/2. Only system programmers who write an environment

---

2. The name *mutant* has a colorful history. Early in Windows NT's development, Dave Cutler created a kernel mutex object that implemented low-level mutual exclusion. Later he discovered that OS/2 required a version of the mutual exclusion semaphore with additional semantics, which Dave considered "brain-damaged" and which was incompatible with the original object. (Specifically, a thread could abandon the object and leave it inaccessible.) So he created an OS/2 version of the mutex and gave it the name *mutant*. Later Dave modified the mutant object to remove the OS/2 semantics, allowing the Win32 subsystem to use the object. The Win32 API calls the modified object *mutex*, but the native services retain the name *mutant*.

subsystem, a file system, a native device driver, or another specialized application are compelled to learn about executive objects and use them directly.

Executive objects are typically created either by a protected subsystem in direct response to some user activity or by various components of the operating system as part of their normal operation. For example, to create a file, a Win32 application calls the Win32 API routine CreateFile(). The Win32 subsystem, in turn, calls a native NT service that creates an executive file object. When the application later reads or writes to the file, the Win32 subsystem and the NT executive use the file object to access the file.

File operations represent an atypical case in the NT object system because files are a persistent resource and are not based in memory. However, files are important because the model used in most programming languages to manipulate files is a convenient one for creating and using NT objects. The relevant characteristics of the file model are these:

- In most programming languages, before you can read or write to a file, you must open it. The open operation can either open an existing file or create a new file with the name you specify. The filename can include a directory (or hierarchy of directories) in which the file is stored.

- When you open a file, you specify which operations you want to perform—for example, read, write, or append to the file.

- The file system opens the file and returns a file handle, which you use in subsequent operations to refer to the opened file. When you finish with the file, you close the file handle.

- Two programs share a file when they both open handles to it at the same time. Some file systems also allow applications to create temporary files, which the file system automatically deletes when all handles to them are closed.

With a few twists here and there, the Windows NT object model imitates the file model. The main differences are that the handles are called *object handles* and that the objects are stored in memory rather than on a physical device. The following section provides more details about the NT object model.

3.1.1.2 NT Object Model

Like most operating systems, Windows NT uses processes as a division of labor. Each process is allocated a set of resources that allows it to do its particular job: a thread so that it can execute programs and an address space in which to store code and data. When a thread runs, it can acquire additional resources for its process by creating objects or by opening handles to existing objects. Object handles are unique to a process and represent the process's access to system resources. They can be used to call native object services that manipulate the resources.

The Win32 subsystem is an NT process, one that acts as a server to Win32 applications. When an application calls a Win32 API routine that either directly or indirectly creates an object, the Win32 subsystem calls an NT object service. The NT object manager takes over from there, performing the following functions:

- Allocating memory for the object

- Attaching a *security descriptor* to the object, which specifies who is allowed to use the object and what they are allowed to do with it

- Creating and maintaining an object directory structure in which object names are stored

- Creating an object handle and returning it to the caller

All user-mode processes, including the environment subsystems, must own a handle to an object before their threads can use the object. Using handles to manipulate system resources is not a new idea. C and Pascal (and other language) runtime libraries, for example, return handles to opened files. Similarly, Win32 applications use different types of handles to control windows, the mouse cursor, and icons. In both cases, handles serve as indirect pointers to system resources; this indirection keeps application programs from fiddling directly with system data structures.

In the NT executive, object handles provide additional benefits. First, except for what they refer to, there is no difference between a file handle, an event handle, and a process handle. There is no need to remember ten different mechanisms for using ten different types of objects. Second, the object manager has the exclusive right to create handles and to locate an object that a handle refers to. This means that every user-mode action that affects an object can be scrutinized by the object manager. This gating effect lets the object manager satisfy three important Windows NT design goals:

- It protects objects. Each time a thread uses a handle, the object manager performs a security check to validate the thread's right to use the object in the way it is attempting.

■ It monitors who is using an object so that it can delete temporary objects when they are no longer needed. The object manager will not delete an object while any process has a handle to it (or while the system has a pointer to it).

■ It monitors resource usage. Each time a thread opens an object handle, the object manager charges the thread's process for the physical memory the object uses. The resource usage of a process's threads cannot exceed the memory limits (*quotas*) a system administrator has assigned to the user represented by the process.

The first task, protecting objects, is the essence of the Windows NT security system. Its implementation borrows heavily from the file model and is also somewhat visible to application programs that use the Win32 API. The following offers a brief introduction to object protection within the NT executive, a topic revisited later in this chapter.

To return to the file analogy: When you open a file, you must specify whether you intend to read or to write. If you try to write to a file that is opened for read access, you get an error. Likewise, in the NT executive, when a process creates an object or opens a handle to an existing object, the process must specify a set of *desired access rights*—that is, what it wants to do with the object. It can request either a set of standard access rights (such as read, write, and execute) that apply to all object types or specific access rights that vary depending on the object type. For example, the process can request delete access or append access to a file object. Similarly, it might require the ability to suspend or terminate a thread object.

When a process opens a handle to an object, the object manager calls the *security reference monitor*, the kernel-mode portion of the security system, sending it the process's set of desired access rights. The security reference monitor checks whether the object's *security descriptor* permits the type of access the process is requesting.[3] If so, the reference monitor returns a set of *granted access rights* that the process is allowed, and the object manager stores them in the object handle it creates.[4]

---

3. The Win32 subsystem allows an application process to assign a security descriptor to objects but does not require it. If the application does not assign a security descriptor, the Win32 subsystem does so on behalf of the application.

4. This is a simplification of the actual storage mechanism, which is described in greater detail later in this chapter.

Thereafter, whenever the process's threads use the handle, the object manager quickly checks whether the set of granted access rights stored in the handle corresponds to the usage implied by the object service the threads have called. For example, if the caller asked for read access to a section object but then calls a service to write to it, the service fails. How the security system determines who gets access to which objects is a topic explored in Section 3.3.

The second and third tasks that object handles facilitate—object retention and resource accounting—are described in Sections 3.2.2.1 and 3.2.2.2.

3.1.2 Object Structure

Every NT object is of a particular object type. The type determines the data the object contains and the native system services that can be applied to the object. To manage different objects uniformly, the object manager requires every object to contain several fields of standard information in a known location. As long as this data is present, the object manager neither knows nor cares what else is stored in the object. Each object has two parts—an object header and an object body—that separate the object's standard data from its variable data. The object manager controls the object header, and other executive components control the object bodies of the object types they create.

The object manager uses the data stored in an object's header to manage objects without regard to their type. Figure 3-1 shows the data, or attributes, that all object headers contain. Table 3-2 briefly describes the object header attributes.

p50

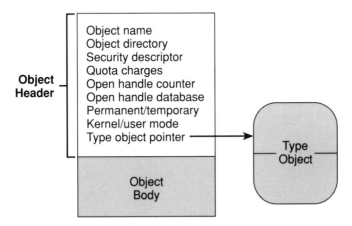

Figure 3-1. Contents of an Object Header

Attribute	Purpose
Object name	Makes an object visible to other processes for sharing
Object directory	Provides a hierarchical structure in which to store object names
Security descriptor	Determines who can use the object and what they can do with it
Quota charges	Lists the resource charges levied against a process when it opens a handle to the object
Open handle counter	Counts the number of times a handle has been opened to the object
Open handle database	Lists the processes that have opened handles to the object
Permanent/ temporary status	Indicates whether the object's name and storage can be deleted when the object is no longer in use
Kernel/user mode	Indicates whether the object is available in user mode
Type object pointer	Points to a type object that contains attributes common to a set of like objects

Table 3-2. Standard Object Header Attributes

The object manager provides a small set of generic services that operate on the attributes stored in an object's header and can be used on objects of any type (although some generic services don't make sense for certain objects). These generic services, some of which the Win32 subsystem makes available to Win32 applications, are listed in Table 3-3.

Service	Purpose
Close	Closes a handle to an object
Duplicate	Shares an object by duplicating a handle and giving it to another process
Query object	Gets information about an object's standard attributes
Query security	Gets an object's security descriptor
Set security	Changes the protection on an object
Wait for a single object	Synchronizes a thread's execution with one object
Wait for multiple objects	Synchronizes a thread's execution with multiple objects

Table 3-3. Generic Object Services

In addition to an object header, each object has an object body whose format and contents are unique to its object type; all objects of the same type share the same object body format. By creating an object type and supplying services for it, an executive component can control the manipulation of data in all object bodies of that type.

Every component of the NT executive can define object types, and most do. Defining an object type consists of determining what data will be stored in the body of each instance of the new type, telling the object manager the body's size so that it can allocate the proper amount of memory when objects are created, and supplying services for the new object type. For example, the process manager defines the body of process objects and provides native services that manipulate the data stored there. Similarly, the I/O manager defines the contents of a file object's body and exports services that get or set that data. The contents of various object bodies are described later in this book, along with the component of the NT executive that defines them.

3.1.3 Object Types

Object headers contain data that is common to all objects but that can take on different values for each instance of an object. For example, each object has a unique name and can have a unique security descriptor. However, objects also contain some data that remains constant for all objects of a particular type. For example, you can select from an object-type-specific set of access rights when you open a handle to objects of a particular type. The NT executive supplies terminate and suspend access (among others) for thread objects and read, write, append, and delete access (among others) for file objects. Another example of an object-type-specific attribute is synchronization, the ability of a thread to wait for objects of a particular type to be set to the signaled state, described shortly.

In order to save memory and reduce maintenance, the object manager sets these static, object-type-specific attributes once when creating a new object type. It uses an object of its own, called a *type object*, to record this data. As Figure 3-2 illustrates on the next page, a type object also links together all objects of the same type, allowing the object manager to find and enumerate them, if necessary.

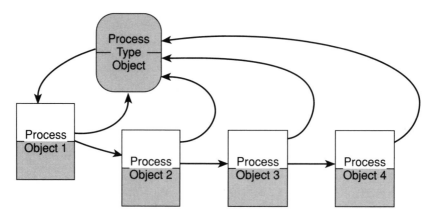

Figure 3-2. Process Objects and the Process Type Object

Type objects can't be manipulated from user mode because the object manager supplies no services for them. However, some of the attributes they define are visible through certain native services and through Win32 API routines. The attributes stored in the bodies of type objects are described in Table 3-4.

Attribute	Purpose
Object type name	The name for objects of this type ("process," "event," "port," and so on)
Access types	The types of access a thread can request when opening a handle to an object of this type ("read," "write," "terminate," "suspend," and so on)
Synchronization capability	Whether a thread can wait on objects of this type
Pageable/ nonpageable	Whether objects of this type can be paged out of memory
Methods	One or more routines that the object manager calls automatically at certain points in an object's lifetime

Table 3-4. Type Object Attributes

Synchronization, one of the attributes visible to Win32 applications, refers to a thread's ability to synchronize its execution by waiting for an object to change from one state to another. A thread can synchronize with executive process, thread, file, event, event pair, semaphore, mutant, and timer objects. Section, port, access token, object directory, symbolic-link, profile, and key objects do not support synchronization.

The last attribute in the list—methods—comprises a set of internal routines that are similar to C++ constructors and destructors, that is, routines that are automatically called when an object is created or destroyed. The NT object manager extends this idea by calling an object method in other situations as well, such as when someone opens or closes a handle to an object or when someone attempts to change the protection on an object. Some object types specify methods, while others don't, depending on how the object type is to be used. The methods (sometimes called *virtual methods*) are described in Section 3.2.3.

In summary, NT executive objects consist of two parts: an object header, which is controlled by the object manager, and an object body, which is controlled by the component of the operating system that creates an object type. One of the attributes in the object header is a pointer to a type object, a structure that defines static attributes for objects of the new type. Any component of the NT executive can define new object types, and each component supplies services for the object types it defines.

3.2 Managing Objects

As previously mentioned, the object manager provides a set of generic services that work on all object types. In addition, other components of the NT executive supply object-type-specific services for the object types they create. These services call the object manager by using internal interfaces. Hence, all services that manipulate an object must pass through the object manager on one level or another. This allows the object manager to centralize control over objects and to perform all object management tasks (or to explicitly relinquish control to a secondary object manager, if appropriate).

This section focuses on the primary functions of the object manager. How it locates objects and how it dispenses handles to them are the subjects of the first two subsections. The third subsection takes a closer look at object methods. The objects and services described are visible to user-mode subsystems, unless stated otherwise.

3.2.1 Object Names

An important consideration in creating a multitude of objects is devising a successful system for keeping track of them. The object manager requires the following in order to do so:

- A way to distinguish one object from another
- A method for finding and retrieving a particular object

The first requirement is served by allowing names to be assigned to objects. This is an extension of what most operating systems provide—the ability to name selected resources, files, pipes, or a block of shared memory, for example. The NT executive, in contrast, allows any resource represented by an object to have a name.

The second requirement, finding an object, is also satisfied by object names. If the object manager stores objects by name, it can find an object by looking up its name.

Object names also satisfy a third requirement, allowing processes to share objects. The NT executive's object namespace is a global one, visible to all processes in the system. One process can create an object and place its name in the global namespace, and a second process can open a handle to the object by specifying the object's name. If an object is not meant to be shared in this way, its creator need not give it a name.

To increase efficiency, the object manager does not look up an object's name each time someone uses the object. Instead, it looks up a name under only two circumstances. The first is when a process creates a named object: The object manager looks up the name to verify that it doesn't already exist before storing the new name in the global namespace. The second is when a process opens a handle to a named object: The object manager looks up the name, finds the object, and then returns an object handle to the caller; thereafter, the caller uses the handle to refer to the object. When looking up a name, the object manager allows the caller to select either a case-sensitive or a case-insensitive search, a feature that supports POSIX and other environments that use case-sensitive filenames.

Object names are global to a single computer (or to all processors on a multiprocessor computer), but they are not visible across a network. The object manager does, however, supply a hook—called a parse method—for accessing named objects that exist on other computers. For example, the I/O manager, which supplies file object services, extends the functions of the object manager to remote files. When asked to open a remote file object, the object manager calls a parse method, which allows the I/O manager to intercept the request and deliver it to a network redirector, a driver that accesses files across the network. A server process on the remote Windows NT system calls the object manager and the I/O manager on that system to find the file object and return the information back across the network. Future system extensions can exploit the same object manager hook to manage other remote objects. (The methods are described further in Section 3.2.3, and Windows NT networking is described in Chapter 9.)

3.2.1.1 Object Directories

In deciding how to form object names, the developers had as their primary constraint the MS-DOS and POSIX file systems, which have hierarchical naming schemes for files and file directories. In the NT executive, files and directories are represented as objects; therefore, the object manager had to understand the format of filenames in order to find file objects. It made sense, then, that object names should mimic filenames.

NT object names have some characteristics of both MS-DOS and POSIX filenames. Figure 3-3 depicts the NT object name hierarchy in tree form.

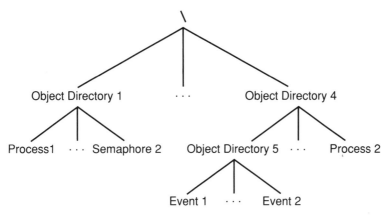

Figure 3-3. Object Name Hierarchy

Notice that the root of the object name tree is an MS-DOS-style backslash (\). Leaf nodes on the tree represent individual objects, and intermediate nodes represent names of object directories. Object names are formed by starting at the root and traversing the path to an object. As in MS-DOS and OS/2, backslashes are used to separate names in the path.

The *object directory object* is the object manager's means for supporting this hierarchical naming structure. It is analogous to a file system directory and contains the names of other objects, possibly even other object directories. The Win32 subsystem and other subsystems, as well as components of the NT executive, can create arbitrary hierarchies of object directories in which to store the named objects they create.

Figure 3-4 on the next page shows a conceptual summary of the important, unique characteristics of the object directory object. In this diagram and in others throughout the book, *object type* refers to the class of objects being described. *Object body attributes* refers to the fields of data stored in the bodies of objects of that type. *Services* are the native system services that a component of the NT executive provides for manipulating the object attributes. (The attributes stored in the object headers are not shown because they are the same for objects of all types. Likewise, the generic object services, described previously, manipulate objects of all types.)

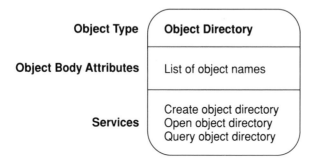

Object Type	**Object Directory**
Object Body Attributes	List of object names
Services	Create object directory Open object directory Query object directory

Figure 3-4. Object Directory Object[5]

The create and open services are used to create object directories and to open handles to them. Once a thread has opened a handle (with write access) to an object directory, it can create other objects and place them in the object directory.

The query service allows a caller to scan the list of object names stored in the object directory. The object directory object maintains enough information to translate these object names into pointers to the objects themselves. The object manager uses the pointers to construct the object handles that it returns to user-mode callers.

Both kernel-mode code and user-mode code (such as subsystems) can create object directories in which to store objects. For example, the I/O manager creates an object directory named \Device, which contains the names of objects representing I/O devices.

The create, open, and query trio of object services is repeated frequently throughout the NT executive. The I/O system implements a create file service for its file objects, and the process manager implements a create process service for its process objects. Although the NT developers considered establishing a single, virtual, create object service, such a routine would have been quite complicated in C because the set of parameters required to initialize a file object, for example, differs markedly from that required to initialize a process object. A single C routine would have become more complicated as

5. This depiction of an object is a simplified version of a format developed by Peter Coad and Edward Yourdon in *Object-Oriented Analysis* (Englewood Cliffs, N.J.: Prentice-Hall, 1990).

new object types were added to the system. Also, the object manager would have incurred additional processing overhead each time a thread called an object service to determine the type of object the handle referred to and to call the appropriate version of the service. For these reasons and others, the create, open, and query services are implemented separately for each object type.

3.2.1.2 Object Domains

The object namespace provides an umbrella under which self-contained sets of objects, called *object domains,* can be easily incorporated, thus allowing the object namespace to be extended. The I/O manager, for example, is a secondary object manager governing an object domain that consists of disk files, directories, and devices. The object manager allows the I/O system to tuck file system objects under a leaf node of the object manager namespace. For example, suppose you have the following directory structure on a floppy disk:

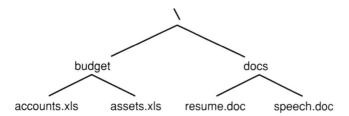

Within the object manager namespace, the directory structure takes the following form:

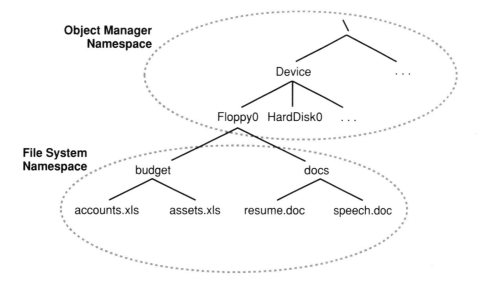

In this tree, each name represents an NT executive object. The file system namespace has been incorporated into the object namespace under the name \Device\Floppy0.

When a Microsoft Excel for Windows user attempts to open the file A:\budget\ accounts.xls, the object manager opens a handle to the file object named \Device\Floppy0\budget\accounts.xls.[6] To do so, the object manager searches its namespace until it reaches the object named Floppy0, which is a special device object that has a parse method associated with it. The object manager suspends its name search and calls the parse method, passing to it the name \budget\accounts.xls. The parse method is supplied by the I/O system, which asks the correct file system to locate and open this file stored on the floppy disk. Methods are described further in Section 3.2.3.

3.2.1.3 Symbolic Links

In certain file systems (on some UNIX systems, for example), a symbolic link lets a user create a filename or a directory name that, when used, is translated by the operating system into a different file or directory name. It is a simple method for allowing users to indirectly share a file or the contents of a directory, creating a cross-link between different directories in the ordinarily hierarchical directory structure.

The NT object manager implements an object called a *symbolic link object,* which performs a similar function for object names in its object namespace. When a caller refers to a symbolic link object's name, the object manager traverses its object namespace until it reaches the symbolic link object. It looks inside the symbolic link and finds a string that it substitutes for the symbolic link name. It then restarts its name lookup. A symbolic link can occur anywhere within an object name string. Figure 3-5 summarizes the attributes and services for the symbolic link object type.

One place in which the NT executive uses symbolic link objects is in translating MS-DOS device names into Windows NT object names. In MS-DOS, a user refers to floppy and hard disk drives using the names A:, B:, C:, and so on. Moreover, the user can add new drive or pseudo-drive names by creating extra partitions on a hard disk, for example, or by defining a drive name to refer to a disk directory on another computer. Once they are created, these drive names must be visible to all processes on the system.

---

6. This is a simplification of a mechanism described in the next section.

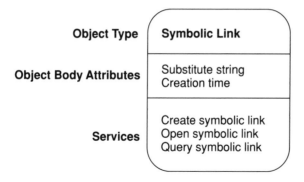

Object Type	Symbolic Link
Object Body Attributes	Substitute string Creation time
Services	Create symbolic link Open symbolic link Query symbolic link

Figure 3-5. Symbolic Link Object

The Win32 subsystem makes drive letters protected, global data by placing them in the object manager namespace. A special object directory is created specifically for this purpose, as shown here:

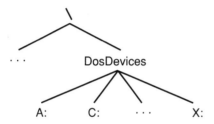

When the user or an application creates a new drive letter, the Win32 subsystem adds another object under the \DosDevices object directory. However, the objects that represent the actual physical devices exist elsewhere in the tree, as depicted here:

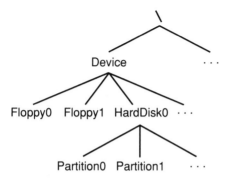

The objects named A:, B:, C:, and so on are symbolic link objects. Each of these symbolic links contains the object name of the physical device to which

67

the drive letter refers. So, for example, if an Excel for Windows user opens the spreadsheet stored in A:\budget\accounts.xls, the Win32 subsystem translates that name and opens a handle to the file object named \DosDevices \A:\budget\accounts.xls. To find this file object, the object manager traverses the object name tree until it reaches the object known as A: and discovers that this object is a symbolic link. It checks the contents of the symbolic link object, finding the string \Device\ Floppy0 stored inside, as shown here:

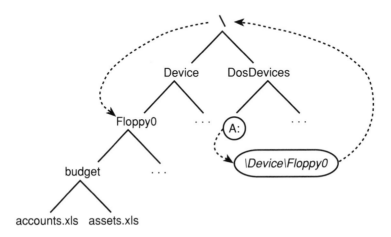

The object manager takes the string stored in the symbolic link object and appends the remainder of the original string to it (\Device\Floppy0 plus \budget\accounts.xls). Then it restarts the search for the file object from the top of the tree.

Symbolic links allow a subsystem (or other code) to create aliases for executive objects, which the subsystem can change as its needs change. Furthermore, a subsystem can realize performance gains by storing global data, such as drive names, directly in the NT executive rather than in the subsystem's address space. The topic of subsystem performance is discussed further in Chapter 5, "Windows and the Protected Subsystems."

3.2.2 Object Handles

Although object names are important for storing objects and for object sharing, they aren't used often. A process specifies an object's name when it first creates the object or when it opens a handle to it. Thereafter, the process uses the object handle. Referring to an object by its handle is faster than using its name because the object manager can skip the name lookup and find the object directly.

An NT object handle is an index into a process-specific *object table*. A process's object table contains pointers to all the objects that the process has opened a handle to. Processes acquire handles to objects by creating an object, by opening a handle to an existing object, by inheriting a handle from another process, or by receiving a duplicated handle from another process. Figure 3-6 illustrates the relationship between a process and its object table.

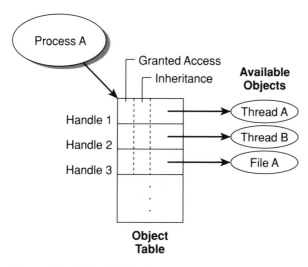

Figure 3-6. Object Table Structure

Each entry in the object table contains the corresponding handle's granted access rights and its *inheritance designation*—that is, whether processes created by this process will get a copy of the handle in their object tables. Although the term *handle*, strictly speaking, refers only to the index into the table, the developers use *handle* to refer also to the data stored in the corresponding table entry.

Two processes share an object when they both open handles to it. The two handles are unique, as illustrated in Figure 3-7 on the next page.

The creator of an object decides whether handles to the object can be inherited from one process by the processes it creates. This feature supports those environments, including Win32 and POSIX, that allow resource inheritance.

When a process terminates, the process object becomes a candidate for deletion from the system (dependent on whether any other process is still using it, as will be described shortly). Before deleting a process object, the object manager calls the delete method for process objects, which closes all the handles in the process's object table. (See Section 3.2.3 for more information.)

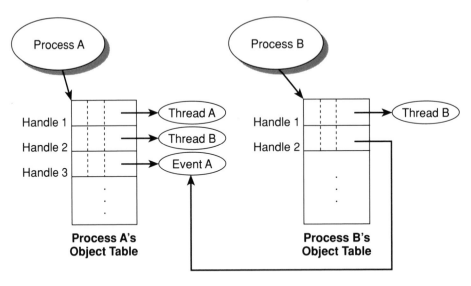

Figure 3-7. Sharing an Object

3.2.2.1 Object Retention

Because all user-mode processes that access an object must first open a handle to it, the object manager can easily track how many of these processes, and even which ones, are using an object. Tracking these handles represents the first step in implementing *object retention*—that is, retaining temporary objects only as long as they are in use and then deleting them.

The object manager implements object retention in two phases. The first phase is called *name retention,* and it is controlled by the number of open handles that exist to an object. Every time a process opens a handle to an object, the object manager increments the open handle counter in the object's header. (Refer to Figure 3-1 on page 57.) As processes finish using the object and close their handles to it, the object manager decrements the counter. When the counter drops to zero, the object manager deletes the object's name from its global namespace. This prevents new processes from opening a handle to the object. (Permanent object names are not deleted because these objects represent entities, such as physical devices, that remain in place even when no process is using them. The operating system must change permanent objects into temporary objects before it can delete them.)

The second phase of object retention is to stop retaining objects (that is, to delete them) when they are no longer in use. Because the operating system usually accesses objects by using pointers instead of handles, the object manager must also record how many object pointers it has dispensed to operating system processes. It increments a *reference count* for an object each time it gives out a pointer to the object; when operating system threads finish using the pointer, they call the object manager to decrement the object's reference count. So even after an object's open handle counter reaches zero, the object's reference count might remain positive, indicating that the operating system is still using the object. Ultimately, the reference count also drops to zero. When this happens, the object manager deletes the object from memory.

Because of the way object retention works, an application can ensure that an object and its name remain in memory simply by keeping a handle open to the object. Programmers who write applications that contain two or more cooperating processes need not be concerned that one process might delete an object before the other process has finished using it. In addition, closing an application's object handles will not cause an object to be deleted if the operating system is still using it. For example, one process might create a second process to execute a program in the background; it then immediately closes its handle to the process. Because the operating system needs the second process to run the program, it maintains a reference to its process object. Only when the background program finishes executing does the object manager decrement the second process's reference count and then delete it.

3.2.2.2 Resource Accounting

Resource accounting, like object retention, is closely related to the use of object handles. If an object has a positive open handle count, it indicates that some process is using that resource. It also indicates that some process is being charged for the memory the object occupies. When an object's handle count drops to zero, the process that was using the object should no longer be charged for it.

Many operating systems use a quota system to limit processes' access to system resources. However, the types of quotas imposed on processes are sometimes diverse and complicated, and the code to track the quotas is spread throughout the operating system. For example, in some operating systems, an I/O component might record and limit the number of files a process can open, whereas a memory component might impose a limit on the amount of memory a process's threads can allocate. A process component might limit a user to some maximum number of new processes she can create or a maximum number of threads within a process. Each of these limits is tracked and enforced in different parts of the operating system.

In contrast, the NT object manager provides a central facility for resource accounting. Every user is assigned quota limits that restrict the amount of system memory her processes can collectively use. Likewise, each object header contains an attribute called quota charges that records how much the object manager subtracts from a process's allotted quota when a thread in the process opens a handle to the object. A process's threads can open many handles during their lifetimes, and the object manager subtracts the specified amount from their process's quota every time. If a user's processes open too many handles and exhaust the user's quota, their threads must close some object handles before they can open any more. The object manager, therefore, limits a process's (and ultimately, a user's) use of resources by monitoring the amount of memory occupied by objects that the process has opened handles to. (In addition to the object-based quotas, the NT process manager imposes a quota on the amount of processor time each user's processes can use.)

3.2.3 Object Methods

The object manager exploits the similarities of objects so that it can manage them uniformly. However, objects also have their differences, some of them significant. The object manager would have to be much bigger and more complicated if it were to accommodate the idiosyncrasies of all the different object types. It would also have to change if a new object type were added to the system in the future. To prevent this, the object manager supplies hooks that other NT executive components can use to perform tasks unique to their object types. These hooks are called *object methods*.

When an executive component creates a new object type, it can register one or more methods with the object manager. Thereafter, the object manager calls the methods at well-defined points in the lifetime of objects of that type, usually when an object is created, deleted, or modified in some way. The methods that the object manager supports are listed in Table 3-5.

An example of the use of a close method occurs in the I/O system. The I/O manager registers a close method for the file object type, and the object manager calls the close method each time it closes a file object handle. This close method checks whether the process that is closing the file handle owns any outstanding locks on the file and, if so, removes them. Checking for file locks is not something that the object manager itself could or should do.

The object manager calls a delete method, if one is registered, before it deletes a temporary object from memory. The virtual memory (VM) manager, for example, registers a delete method for the section object type that frees the physical pages being used by the section. It also verifies that any

Method	When Method Is Called
Open	When an object handle is opened
Close	When an object handle is closed
Delete	Before the object manager deletes an object
Query name	When a thread requests the name of an object, such as a file, that exists in a secondary object domain
Parse	When the object manager is searching for an object name that exists in a secondary object domain
Security	When a process reads or changes the protection of an object, such as a file, that exists in a secondary object domain

Table 3-5. Object Methods

internal data structures the VM manager has allocated for a section are deleted before the section object is deleted. Once again, this is work the object manager cannot do because it knows nothing about the internal workings of the VM manager. Delete methods for other types of objects perform similar functions.

The parse method (and similarly, the query name method) allows the object manager to relinquish control of finding an object to a secondary object manager. The secondary object manager finds an object that exists outside the object manager namespace in a different object domain. The I/O system provides the simplest example. Take another look at a figure that appeared earlier.

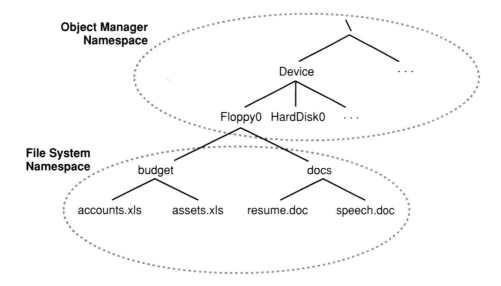

The object named Floppy0 is a device object, a special object type defined and used by the I/O system. In the object manager namespace, the device object represents a launching point into a file system's object domain, one that the object manager knows nothing about.

When the I/O system created the device object type, it registered a parse method for it. When the object manager looks up an object name, it suspends its search when it encounters an object in the path that has an associated parse method. The object manager calls the parse method, passing to it the remainder of the object name it is looking for.

For example, when a process opens a handle to the object named \Device\Floppy0\docs\resume.doc, the object manager traverses its name tree until it reaches the device object named Floppy0. It sees that a parse method is associated with this object, and it calls the method, passing to it the rest of the object name it was searching for—in this case, the string \docs\resume.doc. The parse method for device objects is an I/O routine. The routine takes the name string and passes it to the appropriate file system, which finds the file on the disk and opens it.

The symbolic link objects described in Section 3.2.1.3 are also translated by a parse method. The symbolic link object type has a parse method associated with it. The method takes one name, substitutes another name for it, and then calls the object manager to restart its search for the object. (If the new name also contains a symbolic link object name, the parse method is called again.)

The security method, which is used by the I/O system, is similar to the parse method. It is called whenever a thread tries to change the security information protecting a file. This information is different for files than for other objects because security information is stored in the file itself rather than in memory. The I/O system, therefore, must be called in order to find the security information and change it.

3.3   Protecting Objects

Although naming, sharing, and accounting for system resources in a uniform way are all good reasons for the NT executive to use an object model, probably the most important reason is to ensure that Windows NT is a secure operating system.

Operating system security is a battle fought on many fronts. A secure multiuser system must protect one user's files, memory, and other resources from other users. It must protect the operating system's data, files, and memory from user programs. It should monitor attempts to bypass its security features, and so on. The U.S. Department of Defense has identified features of an operating system that make it secure. These features are categorized into seven levels of security, each one more stringent than the last.[7]

At the Class C2 level, the initial target for Windows NT, the following features must be present:

- A *secure logon facility* requires users to identify themselves by entering a unique logon identifier and a password before they are allowed access to the system.

- *Discretionary access control* allows an owner of a resource to determine who can access the resource and what they can do to it. The owner does this by granting access rights to a user or a group of users.

- *Auditing* provides the ability to detect and record important security-related events or any attempt to create, access, or delete system resources. It uses logon identifiers to record the identity of the user who performed the action.

- *Memory protection* prevents anyone from reading information written by someone else after a data structure has been released back to the operating system. Memory is reinitialized before it is reused.

Not all Windows NT installations will require all the security mechanisms that the system provides. The security system, therefore, allows a system administrator to streamline the logon sequence, for example, or to adjust whether information is collected in an audit log and, if so, how much.

Facilities that are extremely security conscious, such as military installations, require an even higher level of security than Windows NT initially provides. Therefore, Windows NT is designed to evolve toward Class B2 security, a level known as Mandatory Access Control, in which each user is assigned a security clearance level and is prevented from giving lower-level users access to protected resources. For example, in secure U.S. government facilities, one user might have a "Secret" security clearance and another a "Top Secret" security clearance. Mandatory access control ensures that the user with the "Top Secret" clearance can never allow the former user access to any "Top Secret" information, even by using discretionary access control. Similarly, B2 security requires the recognition of "compartments," the separating of groups of users from one another. This type of protection is useful in industries such as financial security exchanges, in which inappropriate access to stock offerings or mergers might create conflicts of interest.

---

7. Department of Defense Trusted Computer System Evaluation Criteria, DOD 5200.28-STD (December 1985).

The Windows NT security system is multifaceted, but protecting objects is the essence of discretionary access control and auditing (and later, of mandatory access control). The idea behind Windows NT security is to create a gate through which every user of system resources must pass. Because all system resources that can be compromised are implemented as objects, the NT object manager becomes the gate. One need not poke around in numerous dark corners of the operating system to validate the integrity of Windows NT's security system; the critical security-related operations can be found in a central location.

The following subsections examine object protection from two perspectives: first, verifying the identity of users and, second, controlling which users can access which objects.

3.3.1 Access Tokens

In order to control who can manipulate an object, the security system must first be sure of each user's identity. Therefore, the first line of protection in Windows NT is the requirement that every user log onto the system.

As Chapter 2, "System Overview," described, an integral protected subsystem, the *security subsystem*, is responsible for *authenticating* users—that is, for verifying that the logon information a user supplies matches the information stored in a security database. After the security subsystem determines that a logon is authentic, it constructs an object that it permanently attaches to the user's process. This object is called an *access token*, and it serves as the process's official identity card whenever it tries to use a system resource. A sample access token is depicted in Figure 3-8.

The first attribute shown in this example is the user's personal *security ID*, an identifier that usually corresponds to the user's logon name. In large installations, a security ID might also incorporate the name of the user's divi-

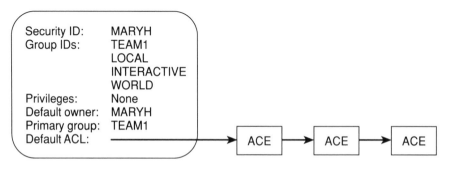

Figure 3-8. Sample Access Token

sion or department (for example, ENGINEERING_MARYH). Group security IDs are formed from lists of user IDs. The second attribute shown in Figure 3-8 is the list of groups to which MARYH belongs. Windows NT defines several standard group identifiers that are included in MARYH's token.

When a process tries to open a handle to an object, the object manager calls the security reference monitor. The security reference monitor gets the token associated with the process and uses its security ID and list of groups to determine whether the process can access the object.

A small number of security-sensitive system services (such as create token) are also protected from use. The privileges attribute lists any of these special services that a user can call. Most users have no privileges.

The user who creates an object generally becomes its owner and can decide who else can use it. The access token's default *access control list* (ACL) attribute is an initial list of protections applied to the objects the user creates. The primary group attribute provides the capability to collect security IDs into groups for organizational purposes, a feature of several operating system environments, including POSIX.

Details about security IDs and ACLs are explained in the next section. For now, look at Figure 3-9, which summarizes the attributes and services applicable to access token objects.

In addition to the create, open, and query services, the set token service also appears. Setting attributes in an object is a common service that is provided for many NT executive objects. The remaining three services are intended for use primarily by security administration software.

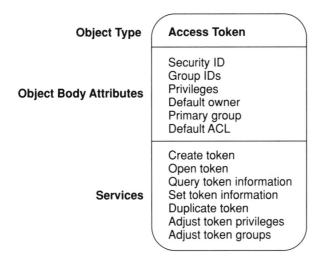

Figure 3-9. Access Token Object

3.3.2 Access Control Lists

All objects, including files, threads, events, and even access tokens, are assigned security descriptors when they are created.[8] The main feature of a security descriptor is a list of protections that apply to the object, called an access control list (ACL). The owner of an object, usually the user who creates it, has discretionary access control over the object and can change the object's ACL to allow others to access the object or to disallow them from accessing it. Figure 3-10 is a simplified picture of a file object and its ACL.

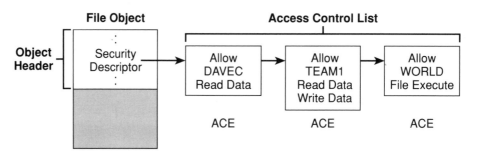

Figure 3-10. Access Control List (ACL)

Each entry in an ACL is known as an *access control entry* (ACE). An ACE contains a security ID and a set of access rights. A user with a matching security ID might be allowed the listed access rights, denied them, or allowed them with auditing. The accumulation of access rights granted by individual ACEs forms the set of access rights granted by an ACL.

Suppose you attempt to list a file, for example. If the file object's ACL contains an ACE with your security ID or one of your group IDs in it, and if that ACE contains the access right called read data, you are allowed to list the file. In addition, if the operation you are attempting is a privileged operation, such as create token, you must have the privilege to create an access token. Otherwise, accessed is denied.

As shown in Figure 3-10, an ACE can also be created for a group security ID. DAVEC has read access to the file object, the members of group TEAM1 have read and write access, and all other users have execute access.

---

8. There are exceptions. Only objects that can be shared by more than one process are required to have a security descriptor. This group includes all named objects plus all named and unnamed process, thread, and token objects.

To determine which ACL to assign to a new object, the security system applies one of three mutually exclusive rules, in the following order:

1. If a caller explicitly provides an ACL when creating the object, the security system applies that ACL to the object.

2. If a caller does not supply an ACL and the object has a name, the security system looks at the ACL on the object directory in which the new object name is stored. Some of the object directory's ACEs might be marked "inherit," meaning that they should be applied to new objects created in the object directory. If any of these inheritable ACEs are present, the security system forms them into an ACL, which it attaches to the new object.

3. If neither of the first two cases occurs, the security system retrieves the default ACL from the caller's access token and applies it to the new object.

In addition to an ACL, an object's security descriptor contains a field that regulates auditing of the object. *Auditing* refers to the security system's ability to "spy" on selected objects and their users and to generate messages or alarms when someone attempts a restricted operation on an object. For example, the security system can audit attempts to read or modify a system-owned file. If someone tries to change the file, the security system writes a message to the audit log, identifying the user by security ID. The system manager can generate security reports that retrieve information from the log. For highly secure systems, the security system is even designed to generate an audible or a visible alarm on a security administrator's machine when the action occurs. Auditing can help reduce the risk of computer tampering.

3.3.3 Putting It All Together

An access token identifies a process (and its threads) to the operating system, whereas a security descriptor enumerates which of these processes (or groups of processes) can access an object. When a thread opens a handle to an object, the object manager and the security system put this information together to determine whether the caller should be given the handle it is requesting.

Figure 3-11 on the next page illustrates what happens when user LEES opens a handle, requesting synchronize access to an event object.

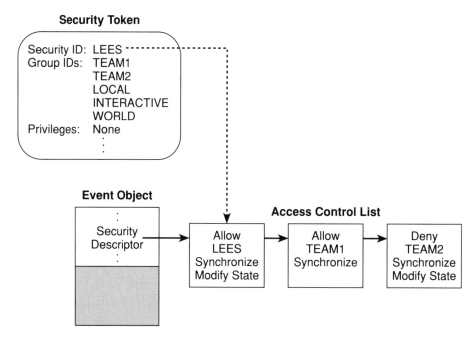

Figure 3-11. Checking an Object's Protection

When checking an ACL, the security system proceeds through the list from first ACE to last. When it finds the security or group ID of the caller, it stops its search and checks whether the ACE allows the type of access the user is attempting. If it finds an ACE that allows the access, it stops searching and returns a handle to the caller. If it reaches the end of the list without finding the security or group ID of the caller, the caller's request is denied.

In Figure 3-11, the event object's ACL allows LEES synchronize access in its first entry. Because LEES requested synchronize access, the security system immediately stops its search, and the object manager returns to LEES a handle that contains synchronize access to the event. Notice that the third ACE explicitly denies LEES synchronize access, based on her membership in TEAM2. However, because of the order of the ACEs in this access control list, the third ACE is ignored in this case. (This is a somewhat artificial example because the system generally places ACEs that deny access at the beginning of the list.)

It would not be efficient for the security system to make this check every time a process uses a handle. An ACL can have many entries, a process can access many objects during its lifetime, and numerous processes can be active at any time. Therefore, the check takes place only when a handle is opened, not each time the handle is used. (Note that since kernel-mode code uses pointers rather than handles to access objects, the access check is not performed when the operating system uses objects. In other words, the NT executive "trusts" itself in a security sense.)

The next time LEES uses the event handle, the object manager simply compares the granted access (synchronize) stored in the handle with the type of access implied by the service she has called. If she calls a wait service, the call will succeed. If she calls set event, however, the service will fail. In order to call set event, either she must have opened the first handle requesting both synchronize and modify-state access or she must now open a new handle and request modify-state access.

Note that once a process successfully opens a handle, the access rights that have been granted cannot be revoked by the security system, even if the object's ACL changes. The old handle is essentially grandfathered in because the developers decided efficient security checks were more important than the ability to revoke granted access rights. The latter capability would have required a complete security check each time a handle is used, rather than only when the handle is originally created as the current design specifies. The performance improvement achieved by storing granted access rights directly in handles is significant, especially for objects with long ACLs attached.

3.4 In Conclusion

NT executive objects represent a unifying theme in Windows NT. They provide a basis for managing system resources uniformly. They also serve as a focal point for important tasks such as naming, sharing, and protecting resources. In addition, they supply a set of primitives that environment subsystems use to implement their versions of objects and object-like resources. Each environment subsystem uses executive objects to provide the facilities and resources that its client applications expect.

The user-mode objects presented in this chapter are based on a set of more primitive objects implemented by the NT kernel. The discussion of kernel objects and their capabilities is deferred until Chapter 7, "The Kernel." In the next chapter, we'll examine two special objects that are integral to Windows NT's functioning: processes and threads.

PROCESSES AND THREADS

Under early versions of MS-DOS, users could run only one program at a time. They ran a program, waited for it to finish, and then ran another one. Under Windows, however, users can execute more than one program at a time or even multiple copies of the same program at the same time. This change highlights a subtle distinction that is important to this chapter: the difference between a program and a process. A *program* is a static sequence of instructions, whereas a *process* is the dynamic invocation of a program along with the system resources required for the program to run.

A process represents a unit of resource ownership and work to be done. It's an operating system's means of organizing the many tasks it must perform. The operating system allocates a portion of the computer's resources to each process and ensures that each process's program is dispatched for execution in an orderly and timely way.

Operating systems generally have a body of code that manages the creation and deletion of processes and the relationships between processes. This code is referred to as the *process structure* and in Windows NT is implemented by the *process manager*. Mark Lucovsky, a Windows NT developer who has written process structure components for both a UNIX system and an object-based operating system, designed and wrote the NT executive's process manager. He identifies its fundamental goal in a single sentence: to provide a set of native process services that environment subsystems can use to emulate their unique process structures. This goal evolved with the Windows NT objective of providing multiple operating system environments that run in user mode.

Different operating systems implement processes in different ways. Processes vary in how they are represented (their data structures), how they are named, how they are protected, and the relationships that exist among them.

Native NT processes have several characteristics that differ from processes in other operating systems:

- NT processes are implemented as objects and are accessed using object services.

- An NT process can have multiple threads executing within its address space.

- Both process objects and thread objects have built-in synchronization capabilities.

- The NT process manager maintains no parent/child or other relationships among the processes it creates.

This chapter examines the nature of processes in general and the structure of NT executive processes in particular. It begins by defining a process and then examines how NT's process manager implements its version of a process. An introduction to threads follows, including discussion about why threads are needed, the terminology relating to threads, and how the NT process manager implements threads. The chapter closes with a description of the relationship between the NT executive's version of processes and the version of processes that NT environment subsystems make available to application programs.

4.1   What Is a Process?

At the highest level of abstraction, a process comprises the following:

- An executable program, which defines initial code and data

- A private *address space*, which is a set of virtual memory addresses that the process can use

- System resources, such as semaphores, communication ports, and files, that the operating system allocates to the process as the program executes

In Windows NT, a process must include a fourth element before it can do any work:

- At least one *thread of execution*

A thread is the entity within a process that the NT kernel schedules for execution. Without it, the process's program cannot run.

The following subsections look at processes in more detail, examining first a process's address space and then its resources. A subsequent section explores the topic of threads.

4.1.1 Address Space

Common sense dictates that one process should be prevented from wielding unlimited control over other processes. Using a *virtual memory* system is one way in which Windows NT accomplishes this. With virtual memory, programmers (and the processes they create) have a logical view of memory that does not correspond to its physical layout. See Figure 4-1.

Each time a process uses a memory address, the virtual memory system translates the address into a physical address. It also prevents processes from directly accessing virtual memory occupied by other processes or by the operating system. To execute operating system code or to access operating system memory, a thread must be running in the unrestricted processor

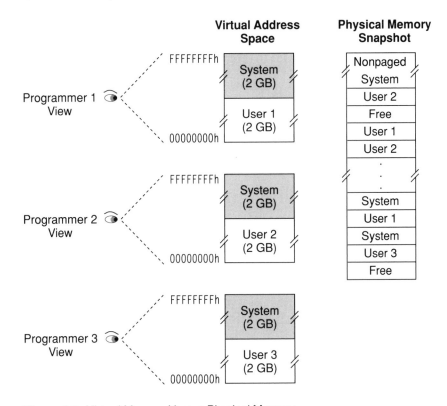

Figure 4-1. Virtual Memory Versus Physical Memory

mode called *kernel mode*. However, most processes are user-mode processes—that is, processes whose threads run primarily in the restricted processor mode called *user mode*.

A user-mode thread gains access to the operating system by calling a system service. When the thread calls the service, the processor traps it and switches its execution from user mode to kernel mode. The operating system takes control of the thread, validating the arguments the thread passed to the system service and then executing the service. The operating system switches the thread back to user mode before returning control to the user's program. In this way, the operating system protects itself and its data from perusal and modification by user processes.

This chapter focuses on user-mode processes, which represent the majority of processes in the Windows NT system at any given time. Application programs run in user mode, but so do Windows NT's protected subsystems. The latter are user-mode server processes that provide important operating system capabilities. They are implemented as servers to simplify the base operating system and to make it extensible. The subsystems run in user mode so that each one's address space is protected from application processes and from other subsystems. (See Chapter 5 for more information.)

4.1.2 Collection of Resources

In addition to a private address space, each process has a diverse set of system resources attached to it. Figure 4-2 shows a typical process and its resources.

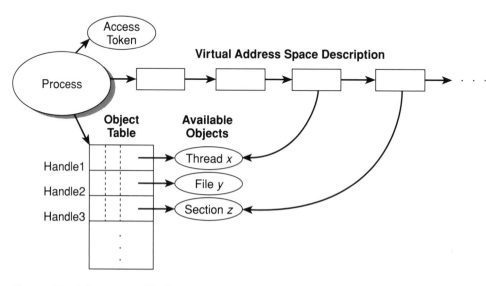

Figure 4-2. A Process and Its Resources

At the top of the diagram is the process's access token, which was described in Chapter 3, "The Object Manager and Object Security." Notice that the token object is directly attached to the process by the operating system. If the process needs to get information about its access token or perhaps change some of its attributes, the process must open a handle to its token object. The security system determines whether it can do so. This particular process has not opened a handle to its access token; hence, there is no arrow extending from the object table to the access token.

Below the access token is a series of data structures the virtual memory (VM) manager has created to keep track of the virtual addresses the process is using. The process cannot read or alter these structures directly; the VM manager creates and modifies them indirectly as the program allocates memory. (These data structures are described in more detail in Chapter 6, "The Virtual Memory Manager.")

The process's object table is shown at the bottom of the figure. The process has opened handles to its one thread, to a file, and to a section of shared memory. (The virtual address description records the virtual addresses occupied by the thread's stack and the section object, as indicated by the arrows from the virtual address description to those objects.)

In addition to the tangible resources shown in the figure, each process has a set of resource quota limits that restrict how much memory its threads can use for opening handles to objects. Each process also has a base execution priority and a default processor affinity, topics described later in this chapter.

4.1.3 Process Object

In the NT executive, processes are simply objects created and deleted by the object manager. The process object, like other objects, contains a header that the object manager creates and initializes. The header stores standard object attributes, such as the process object's security descriptor, the process's name (if it has one for sharing purposes), and the object directory in which its name is stored, if applicable.

The process manager defines the attributes stored in the body of process objects and also supplies system services that retrieve and change these attributes. The attributes and services for process objects are illustrated in Figure 4-3 on the next page.

Notice that the object table and the address space description are not listed as part of the process object. This is because although they are attached to the process object, they cannot be modified directly by user-mode processes. The figure depicts only data that user-mode code can read or set by calling process object services. Table 4-1 on the next page summarizes the attributes of the process object.

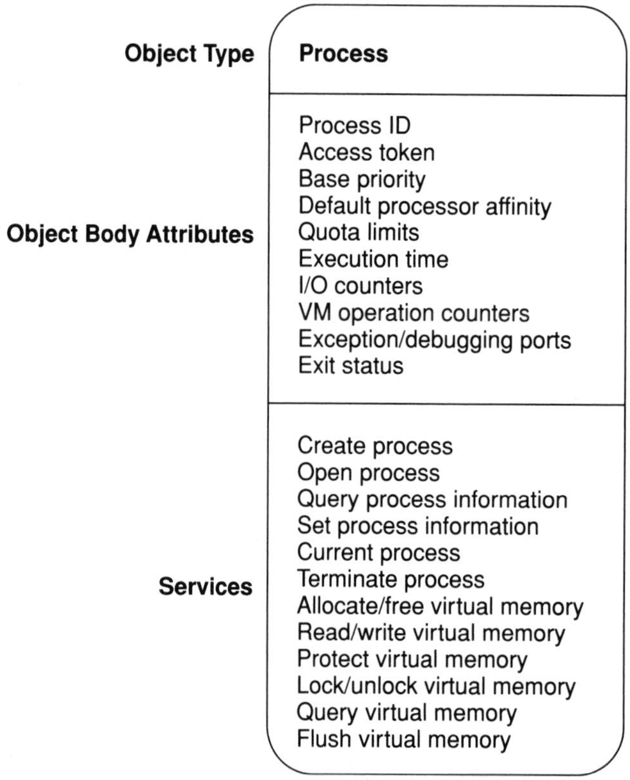

Object Type | Process

Object Body Attributes

Process ID
Access token
Base priority
Default processor affinity
Quota limits
Execution time
I/O counters
VM operation counters
Exception/debugging ports
Exit status

Services

Create process
Open process
Query process information
Set process information
Current process
Terminate process
Allocate/free virtual memory
Read/write virtual memory
Protect virtual memory
Lock/unlock virtual memory
Query virtual memory
Flush virtual memory

Figure 4-3. Process Object

Attribute	Purpose
Process ID	A unique value that identifies the process to the operating system
Access token	An executive object containing security information about the logged-on user represented by this process
Base priority	A baseline execution priority for the process's threads
Default processor affinity	The default set of processors on which the process's threads can run
Quota limits	The maximum amount of paged and nonpaged system memory, paging file space, and processor time a user's processes can use

Table 4-1. Process Object Attributes

(continued)

Table 4-1. *continued*

Attribute	Purpose
Execution time	The total amount of time all threads in the process have executed
I/O counters	Variables that record the number and type of I/O operations the process's threads have performed
VM operation counters	Variables that record the number and type of virtual memory operations the process's threads have performed
Exception/debugging ports	Interprocess communication channels to which the process manager sends a message when one of the process's threads causes an exception
Exit status	The reason for a process's termination

Several of the process object attributes impose constraints on the threads that execute within the process. For example, on a multiprocessor computer, the processor affinity might restrict the process's threads to running on a subset of the available processors. Similarly, the quota limits regulate how much memory, paging file space, and execution time the process's threads can collectively use.

The process's base priority helps the NT kernel regulate the execution priority of threads in the system. The priority of individual threads varies but always stays within range of their process's base priority. Environment subsystems can use the process object's base priority to influence which process's threads are selected first by the NT kernel. For example, the Win32 subsystem calls NT services to raise the base priority of the foreground application process and lower the base priority of the background application processes, giving interactive applications an edge over the others. (See Section 4.2.3.) Quota limits, processor affinity, and base priority are among the process attributes and data structures that can be inherited from one process to another. Process inheritance is described in Section 4.3.2.1.

A process's exception and debugging ports are interprocess communication channels to which the operating system sends messages when one of the process's threads generates an exception or when the process is being debugged. A thread in another process waits at the port to receive the message and take suitable action. For example, an environment subsystem thread can "listen" at the exception port to capture errors generated by its client processes, and a debugger can capture exceptions such as debugger breakpoints. (See Chapter 5, "Windows and the Protected Subsystems," for more information about port objects and environment subsystems.)

Of the process object services, most are self-explanatory. The create process service is flexible, allowing different subsystems to create processes with different initial attributes. The current process service lets a process quickly acquire a handle to itself without passing through the object manager. The terminate process service stops a process's threads, closes any open object handles, and deletes the process's virtual address space.

The virtual memory services shown in Figure 4-2 are actually implemented by the VM manager, but each of them requires a process handle as a parameter, designating a process whose virtual memory will be accessed. The virtual memory operations are described in Chapter 6, "The Virtual Memory Manager."

4.2 What Are Threads?

If you are familiar with the subject of threads, you have likely encountered various definitions for a thread, including "a unit of execution," "an independent program counter," or "a schedulable entity within a process." Although each of these definitions is essentially correct, none of them is satisfying. What exactly does it mean to be "a unit of execution"? Just what is the thing that executes on a processor?

While a process logically represents a job the operating system must do, a thread represents one of possibly many subtasks needed to accomplish the job. For example, suppose a user starts a database application in a window. The operating system represents this invocation of the database as a single process. Now suppose the user requests that a payroll report be generated from the database and sent to a file—conceivably a lengthy operation. While this operation is in progress, the user can enter another database query. The operating system represents each request—the payroll report and the new database query—as separate threads within the database process. The threads can be scheduled for execution independently on the processor, which allows both operations to proceed at the same time (concurrently). Operating systems provide threads in order to achieve this concurrency in a convenient and efficient way. More on that topic later.

The following are the essential components of a thread in the NT executive:

- A unique identifier, called a client ID

- The contents of a set of volatile registers representing the state of the processor

- Two stacks, one for the thread to use while executing in user mode and the other for it to use while executing in kernel mode

■ A private storage area for use by subsystems, runtime libraries, and dynamic-link libraries (DLLs)

The volatile registers, the stacks, and the private storage area are called the thread's *context*. The actual data composing a thread's context varies from one processor to another.

A thread resides within a process's virtual address space, using the address space for storage during the thread's execution. If more than one thread exists in the same process, they share the address space and all the process's resources, including its access token, its base priority, and the object handles in its object table. The NT kernel schedules threads for execution on a processor. Therefore, every NT process must have at least one thread before it can execute.

4.2.1 Multitasking and Multiprocessing

A processor is capable of executing only one thread at a time. However, a *multitasking* operating system allows users to run multiple programs, and it appears to execute all of them at the same time. It achieves this in the following way:

1. It runs a thread until the thread's execution is interrupted or until the thread must wait for a resource to become available.

2. It saves the thread's context.

3. It loads another thread's context.

4. It repeats this sequence as long as there are threads waiting to execute.

Switching the processor's execution from one thread to another in this manner is called *context switching*. In Windows NT, context switching is performed by the kernel component of the executive.

As illustrated with two threads in Figure 4-4 on the next page, a multitasking operating system continually alternates its execution from one thread to another. Each thread eventually finishes its subtask and then is either terminated or given another task. The extraordinary speed of the processor provides the illusion that all the threads execute at the same time.

Multitasking increases the amount of work the system accomplishes because most threads cannot execute continuously. Periodically, a thread stops executing and waits while a slow I/O device completes a data transfer or while another thread is using a resource it needs, for example. When one thread

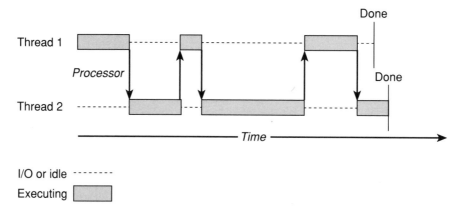

Figure 4-4. Multitasking

must wait, multitasking allows another thread to execute, taking advantage of processor cycles that otherwise would be wasted.

Preemptive multitasking is a form of multitasking in which the operating system does not wait for a thread to voluntarily yield the processor to other threads. Instead, the operating system interrupts a thread after the thread has run for a preset amount of time, called a *time quantum,* or when a higher-priority thread (such as one responding to user input) becomes ready to run. Preemption prevents one thread from monopolizing the processor and allows other threads their fair share of execution time. The NT executive is a preemptive multitasking system, as is its primary Windows environment, the Win32 subsystem. In the MS-DOS-based, nonpreemptive versions of Windows, a thread had to voluntarily relinquish control of the processor in order for multitasking to occur. Ill-mannered or primitive applications could hoard the processor to the detriment of other applications or of the system as a whole.

Sometimes two threads require the ability to communicate with one another to coordinate their activities toward achieving a common goal. For example, a C compiler might have one thread that preprocesses a C program and another thread that takes the first thread's output and compiles it into object code. The two threads must have a way to pass data between them.

Until the latter half of the 1980s, most operating systems allowed a process to have only one thread of execution.[1] (In fact, most operating systems used the term *process* to refer to an executable entity. *Thread* is a relatively new

---

1. Dave Cutler, chief architect of Windows NT, notes that VAX ELN, a real-time operating system he and others on the Windows NT team designed for Digital Equipment Corporation, had threads as early as 1983.

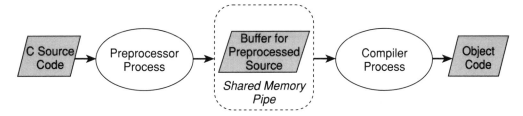

Figure 4-5. Two-Process Compiler

term.) Because every process had a separate address space, two processes had to establish either a region of shared memory or a shared file if they wanted to communicate with one another. Pipes were (and are) commonly used to accomplish this sort of interprocess communication. See Figure 4-5.

Using two processes (each with one thread) to preprocess and compile a program would likely be faster than using a single process because a multitasking operating system can interleave the execution of the preprocessor thread and the compiler thread. As soon as the preprocessor places something in the shared buffer, the compiler can begin its work. Applications such as this that execute in two or more locations are called *concurrent applications.*

Concurrency in an application is useful on a single-processor computer but becomes even more useful on a multiprocessor computer. With multiple processors, the preprocessor and the compiler, using this example, can execute concurrently. If a concurrent application is well designed and minimizes its threads' contention for resources, it can execute faster on a multiprocessor computer than on a single-processor computer. Figure 4-6, when compared to Figure 4-4, illustrates this point.

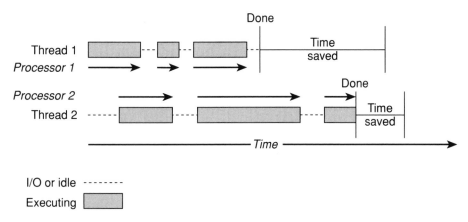

Figure 4-6. Multiprocessing

A *multiprocessing* operating system is one that is specially designed to run on computers with more than one processor. A *symmetric multiprocessing* (SMP) operating system, such as Windows NT, can run both operating system code and user code on any available processor. When there are more threads to run than processors to run them on, an SMP operating system also performs multitasking, dividing each processor's time among all waiting threads. (See Chapter 7, "The Kernel," for more information about thread scheduling on Windows NT.)

4.2.2 Multithreading

Using two processes to achieve concurrency is not always efficient. On some UNIX systems, for example, when one process creates (or forks) another, the system must copy everything in the first process's address space to the address space of the new process. For a large address space, this operation is time-consuming. Furthermore, the two processes must establish a way to share data, a job that is fast and easy on some operating systems but not on others. Windows NT addresses these problems by providing convenient mechanisms for sharing memory: by using copy-on-modify memory to avoid copying an entire address space from one process to another and by implementing a locally optimized message-passing facility. (The first two capabilities are described in Chapter 6, "The Virtual Memory Manager," and the third—the local procedure call (LPC) facility—is described in Chapter 5, "Windows and the Protected Subsystems.")

Even with such enhancements, there are times when a different approach to concurrency is beneficial—namely, *multithreaded processes*. As stated previously, the term *thread* refers to the movement of a processor through a program's instructions; each thread represents a separate program counter. A multithreaded process has two or more threads (and program counters) within a single process, sharing the same address space, object handles, and other resources.

Every NT process is created with a single thread. A program can create additional threads in the process as it needs to. These additional threads are often used for *asynchronous operations* in a program—that is, operations that can happen at any time without regard to the main flow of the program. I/O operations often fit into this category. For example, one might use a thread to periodically save a document being edited or to monitor a device, such as a keyboard or a mouse, for user input. By using one thread to run the main program and creating another thread to monitor a device, the system can schedule both operations separately on a processor, and multitasking occurs. When running on a multiprocessor computer, the two threads can execute simultaneously without the overhead of creating a second process and initializing its address space.

To achieve concurrency using threads, a program creates two or more threads to execute different parts of its program within the same process. A multithreaded compiler is depicted in Figure 4-7.

Compiler Process

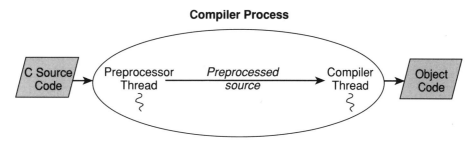

Figure 4-7. Multithreaded Compiler

Multithreaded processes achieve concurrency without the disadvantages of using two processes. Threads require less overhead and are faster to create than are processes. (They are sometimes called "lightweight processes" for this reason.) Also, because all threads in a process share the same memory except for their stacks and register contents, no special data-passing mechanisms are required. One thread simply writes its output to memory, and another thread reads it as input. Similarly, all the process's resources (objects) are equally available to all the threads in the process.

The NT kernel uses a priority-based scheme to select the order in which threads execute. Higher-priority threads execute before lower-priority threads, and the kernel changes a thread's priority periodically to ensure that all threads will execute. An application can allow its threads to execute on any processor in a multiprocessor computer, or it can limit their execution to a subset of the processors.

Creating a multithreaded process is an ideal solution for server applications (such as Windows NT's protected subsystems) that accept requests from clients and execute the same code for each request. For example, a file server performs operations on files; it opens files, reads from them, writes to them, and closes them. Although each request might require the server to operate on a different file, the server's program is loaded into memory only once. Each incoming request is received and handled by a separate server thread, which executes the appropriate server function. All the clients' requests are serviced concurrently. Figure 4-8 on the next page illustrates this point.

In this figure, two client processes (each with a single thread, represented as a squiggly line) use the message-passing facility to send a message

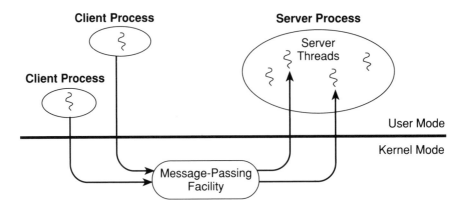

Figure 4-8. Multithreaded Server

to the server process. Multiple server threads are available to execute server code and reply to the clients.

Note that writing multithreaded applications requires great care because all the threads within a process have complete access to the process's address space. Threads can accidentally get in each other's way, reading or writing memory out of turn.

Such is not the case for applications that use two processes to achieve concurrency and that communicate explicitly through messages or pipes. One process cannot accidentally or deliberately destroy or corrupt another process's address space. This is the reason why Windows NT protected subsystems are implemented as separate server processes (and why they are called "protected" subsystems). Each subsystem maintains control over its private address space, without interference from other subsystems or from user processes. Within a server, however, it is advantageous for multiple threads to run, sharing the same address space and resources.

Achieving concurrency by using multiple processes and by using multiple threads within a process are both useful techniques. The goals of the application determine which structure is more beneficial in any particular program.

In review, the following terms refer to an operating system's implementation of processes:

- Multitasking. Dividing the processor's time among threads waiting for execution and creating the illusion that all threads are executing simultaneously.

- Multiprocessing. Running the same operating system code on both single-processor and multiprocessor computers. A symmetric multiprocessing operating system runs system code and user code on all available processors.

■ Multithreading. Supporting more than one thread within a single process.

An advanced operating system should supply all of these capabilities. And Windows NT does.

4.2.3 Thread Object

An NT process remains inanimate until it has a thread that can be scheduled for execution. Once a process has a thread, that thread can create additional threads.

Like processes, NT executive threads are implemented as objects, created and deleted by the object manager. The process manager defines the body of thread objects and the system services used to manipulate threads once they are created. The thread object is depicted in Figure 4-9.

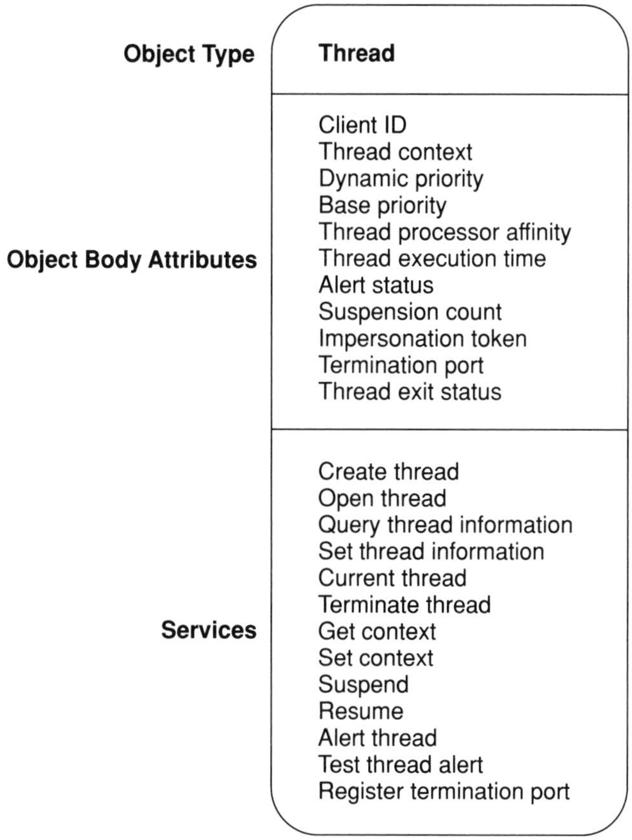

Object Type	Thread
Object Body Attributes	Client ID Thread context Dynamic priority Base priority Thread processor affinity Thread execution time Alert status Suspension count Impersonation token Termination port Thread exit status
Services	Create thread Open thread Query thread information Set thread information Current thread Terminate thread Get context Set context Suspend Resume Alert thread Test thread alert Register termination port

Figure 4-9. Thread Object

97

Table 4-2 describes the thread object's attributes.

Attribute	Purpose
Client ID	A unique value that identifies a thread when it calls a server
Thread context	The set of register values and other volatile data that defines the execution state of a thread
Dynamic priority	The thread's execution priority at any given moment
Base priority	The lower limit of the thread's dynamic priority
Thread processor affinity	The set of processors on which the thread can run, a (nonproper) subset of the processor affinity of the thread's process
Thread execution time	The cumulative amount of time a thread has executed in user mode and in kernel mode
Alert status	A flag that indicates whether the thread should execute an asynchronous procedure call (APC)
Suspension count	The number of times the thread's execution has been suspended without being resumed
Impersonation token	A temporary access token allowing a thread to perform operations on behalf of another process (used by subsystems)
Termination port	An interprocess communication channel to which the process manager sends a message when the thread terminates (used by subsystems)
Thread exit status	The reason for a thread's termination

Table 4-2. Thread Object Attributes

As you can see, some of the attributes in the thread object resemble those in the process object. Certain attributes, such as the thread's processor affinity and dynamic priority, actually restrict or qualify the values applied to the process as a whole. For example, each thread has a processor affinity that is a nonproper subset of (equal to or less than) the processor affinity assigned to its process. Therefore, different threads within a process can be forced to run on different subsets of processors.

Similarly, each thread has a base execution priority that ranges from two levels below the process's base priority to two levels above it, as shown in Figure 4-10.

As shown in the figure, each thread also has a dynamic priority that begins at the thread's base priority and varies upward depending on the type

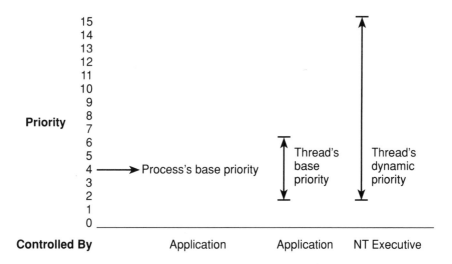

Figure 4-10. Priority Relationships[2]

of work the thread is doing. For example, if a thread is responding to user input, the NT kernel raises its dynamic priority; if it is compute bound, the kernel gradually lowers its dynamic priority to its base priority. By lowering one thread's base priority and raising another thread's base priority, subsystems can control the relative priorities of threads within a process. The process's base priority controls how far apart the priorities of threads within the process can range and how the threads' priorities relate to those of other processes.

Like thread priorities, other attributes in the thread object exist to allow the operating system (and particularly the environment subsystems) to control the threads it creates. For example, the thread context attribute contains everything the operating system needs to know to continue a thread's execution after it has been interrupted—namely, the values stored in the processor's registers and on the thread's user-mode and kernel-mode stacks. By suspending a thread, altering its user-mode context, and then restarting the thread, an environment subsystem can modify the thread's behavior or start it executing at a location different from where it was suspended. (User-mode debuggers can also use this capability to control the execution of threads.)

Alerting a thread, another service provided for thread objects, is a capability that allows an environment subsystem or other parts of the operating

2. This figure illustrates only the variable-priority threads, which run at priorities 0 through 15. Real-time threads run at priorities 16 through 31. See Chapter 7, "The Kernel," for more information.

system to asynchronously notify some thread that it must execute a special procedure. A thread that expects to be alerted can call a service to test whether an alert is pending. (See Section 4.2.5.)

A thread's termination port is similar to a process's exception and debugging ports. The termination port allows an environment subsystem to be notified when a thread in one of its client processes terminates. It can then update any information it maintains about the thread or the process in which the thread resides.

The current thread service allows a thread to quickly acquire a handle to itself without explicitly opening one. It can use the handle, for instance, to retrieve information about itself, such as its total execution time, its current execution priority, and its processor affinity.

Subsequent sections provide more information about both process and thread services. The next chapter describes the Windows NT protected subsystems.

4.2.4 Synchronization

When a concurrent application runs, its threads often require a way to communicate with one another to coordinate their activities. Passing data through pipes is one example of communication. However, the simplest form of communication is called *synchronization*. Synchronization refers to the ability of one thread to voluntarily stop executing and wait until another thread performs some operation.

In the compiler examples presented earlier, the preprocessor reads C source code and writes its output into a memory buffer that it shares with the compiler. The compiler reads this output as its input, compiles it, and generates object code. When the program starts, the compiler thread must wait until the preprocessor thread has put something into the buffer before it tries to read from the buffer. Likewise, if the buffer becomes full, the preprocessor must wait until the compiler removes data from the buffer before placing more data into it.

All multitasking or multiprocessing operating systems must provide a way for threads to wait for another thread to do something—for example, to release a tape drive or to finish writing to a shared memory buffer. The operating system must also allow a thread to signal other threads that it has finished such an operation. Once notified, a waiting thread can continue its execution.

In the NT executive, these wait and signal capabilities are implemented as part of the object architecture. *Synchronization objects* are executive objects with which a thread can synchronize its execution. The synchronization objects include the following:

- Process objects

- Thread objects

- File objects

- Event objects

- Event pair objects

- Semaphore objects

- Timer objects

- Mutant objects

The first three objects listed serve other purposes in addition to synchronization, but the last five objects exist solely to support synchronization. Together, these executive objects allow threads to coordinate their activities with a variety of system occurrences, applying different rules for different situations.

At any given moment, a synchronization object is in one of two states, either the *signaled state* or the *nonsignaled state*. The signaled state is defined differently for different objects. A thread object is in the nonsignaled state during its lifetime and is set to the signaled state by the NT kernel when the thread terminates. Similarly, the kernel sets a process object to the signaled state when the process's last thread terminates. In contrast, the timer object, like a stopwatch, is set to "go off" at a certain time. When its time expires, the kernel sets the timer object to the signaled state.

To synchronize with an object, a thread calls one of the wait system services supplied by the object manager, passing a handle to the object it wants to synchronize with. The thread can wait on one or several objects and can also specify that its wait should be canceled if it is not ended within a certain amount of time. Whenever the kernel sets an object to the signaled state, it checks to see whether any threads are waiting on the object. If so, the kernel releases one or more of the threads from their waiting state so that they can continue executing.

When choosing a synchronization mechanism, a program must take into account the rules governing the behavior of different synchronization objects. Whether a thread's wait ends when an object is set to the signaled state varies with the type of object the thread is waiting on, as Table 4-3 on the next page illustrates.

Object Type	Set to Signaled State When	Effect on Waiting Threads
Process	Last thread terminates	All released
Thread	Thread terminates	All released
File	I/O operation completes	All released
Event	Thread sets the event	All released
Event pair	Dedicated client or server thread sets the event	Other dedicated thread released
Semaphore	Semaphore count drops to zero	All released
Timer	Set time arrives or time interval expires	All released
Mutant	Thread releases the mutant	One thread released

Table 4-3. Definitions of the Signaled State

When an object is set to the signaled state, waiting threads are generally released from their wait states immediately. For example, an event object is used to announce the occurrence of some event. When the event object is set to the signaled state, all threads waiting on the event are released. The exception is any thread that is waiting on more than one object at a time; such a thread might be required to continue waiting until additional objects reach the signaled state.

In contrast to an event object, a mutant object (made visible as a mutex object to Win32 programmers) has ownership associated with it. It is used to gain mutually exclusive access to a resource, and only one thread at a time can hold the mutant. When the mutant object becomes free, the kernel sets it to the signaled state and then selects one waiting thread to execute. The thread selected by the kernel acquires the mutant object, and all other threads continue waiting. (Chapter 7, "The Kernel," describes synchronization in greater detail.)

The NT executive's synchronization semantics are visible to Win32 programmers through the WaitForSingleObject() and WaitForMultiple-Objects() API routines, which the Win32 subsystem implements by calling analogous system services supplied by the NT object manager. A thread in a Win32 application can synchronize with a Win32 process, thread, event, semaphore, mutex, or file object. For example, a thread might synchronize with another thread in a spreadsheet program. Assume that the application has a main thread that performs ordinary spreadsheet functions and a secondary thread that spools spreadsheet files to the printer. Now suppose the user prints a spreadsheet and, before spooling is complete, enters a command to exit the program. The main thread, which accepts the exit request, doesn't terminate the process immediately (although it might clear the screen). Instead, it calls the WaitForSingleObject() routine to wait for the spooler thread to finish spooling and terminate. After the spooler thread terminates, the main thread is released from its wait operation and terminates itself, which ends the spreadsheet program and terminates the spreadsheet process.

4.2.5 Alerts and Asynchronous Procedure Calls

In some situations, it is useful to allow one thread to asynchronously notify another thread to stop what it is doing. This operation, called an *alert* in the NT executive, is closely related to synchronization. Suppose a database application is responding to a query operation. It might not know whether the data it needs is available on a local computer or on a remote computer. To hedge its bets, it starts two threads; one searches for the data locally, and the other looks for the data on the network. As soon as one thread finds the data, it alerts the other thread. In response, the alerted thread stops what it was doing and returns, ready to work on a new task.

The alert capability is not used extensively in Windows NT except in combination with another asynchronous notification mechanism, called an *asynchronous procedure call* (APC). From time to time, the operating system needs to notify a thread that the thread must perform some action. Sometimes the thread must do the work after an event occurs. For example, a user can tell Windows to send a message reminding him of a scheduled meeting time. In Windows NT, this type of asynchronous notification is accomplished by employing a user-mode APC—that is, the Win32 subsystem calls the NT executive to set a timer and provides a pointer to a procedure (an APC) that will send a message to the user. When the timer goes off, the NT executive prompts a Win32 subsystem thread to execute the APC procedure. Afterward, the Win32 thread proceeds with what it was doing.

Although some asynchronous operations are generated by user-mode programs, most are generated by the operating system, and particularly by the NT I/O system. The NT I/O system is asynchronous, which means that a caller can start an I/O operation and then do other work while a device completes the operation. When the device finishes transferring data, the I/O system must interrupt whatever the calling thread is doing and copy the results of the I/O operation to the thread's address space. The I/O system uses a kernel-mode APC to perform this action.

User-mode and kernel-mode APCs vary in several respects, but one difference is especially notable. A kernel-mode APC can interrupt a user-mode thread's execution at any time and force it to execute the procedure. Ordinarily this happens unbeknownst to an application. A software interrupt occurs and, as with a hardware interrupt, the system simply "steals" the application's thread for a short time and causes it to execute the APC procedure. A user-mode APC, in contrast, can be delivered only at control points when the thread that requested it is prepared to execute it.

NT provides two ways in which a thread can control when it receives a user-mode asynchronous notification (an alert or a user-mode APC). The thread can either call a native service to test whether it has been alerted, or it can wait on an object handle, specifying that its wait can be interrupted by an alert. In either case, if a user-mode APC is pending for the thread, the NT kernel delivers it, and the thread executes the procedure. The kernel then resumes the thread's execution from the point at which it was interrupted.

The Win32 API makes alerts and APCs visible through its extended (NT-only) I/O routines. The ReadFileEx() and WriteFileEx() API routines allow a thread to read from or write to a file asynchronously, supplying an APC routine that the thread will execute after the I/O operation is complete. The WaitForSingleObjectEx() and WaitForMultipleObjectsEx() routines let the thread wait in an alertable state at some point after issuing the I/O call. The POSIX subsystem doesn't provide APC capabilities to POSIX applications, but it uses kernel-mode APCs to emulate the delivery of POSIX signals to POSIX processes. Similarly, future environment subsystems can use APCs to implement other asynchronous notification facilities. The topic of APCs reappears in later discussions of the NT kernel, which controls APC processing, and the NT I/O system, which uses APCs extensively.

4.3   Process Structure

Processes are dynamic entities, created and destroyed as the operating system runs. One process creates another, which in turn can create others. The term *process structure* refers to how an operating system creates, manages, and discards processes and threads and how one process relates to others while it exists.

Programmers who write Win32, MS-DOS, OS/2, or POSIX applications never see NT's native processes and threads. The Win32 subsystem and other subsystems shield programmers from them, creating customized environments in which a Win32 programmer sees only Win32-like processes, a POSIX programmer sees only POSIX-like processes, and so on. However, it is largely the underlying capabilities of the NT executive's process structure that allow these disparate environments to coexist in the same operating system.

The next section discusses some of the requirements of various environment subsystems, and the subsequent section describes the mechanisms that the NT process manager provides for the subsystems.

4.3.1 Environment Subsystem Requirements

One of the main tasks of a Windows NT environment subsystem is to emulate the API that the subsystem's client applications expect (the Win32 or POSIX APIs, for example). Another major function is to implement the process structures required by those clients. Mark Lucovsky and Steve Wood, who designed Windows NT's original POSIX and OS/2 environment subsystems, carefully considered the capabilities these and future subsystems would require in order to emulate their respective APIs. They identified the following process-related capabilities required of a typical environment:

- Creating and terminating processes and threads

- Recording and maintaining relationships between processes

- Performing operations (both local and network) on behalf of a client process

- Reading to, writing from, and otherwise manipulating a client process's address space

- Stopping a client's thread, possibly altering its user-mode context, and restarting it

- Capturing and handling exceptions generated by client processes

Process creation, the first item in the list, is a common operation for a subsystem and one that illustrates how environment subsystems accomplish their work using native process services. Figure 4-11, shown on the following page, depicts the relationship between creating a process from an application program and creating an NT executive process.

A client application—Win32, POSIX, or OS/2 in this example—creates a process using the API appropriate for its environment. The process creation call is transmitted via the NT executive's message-passing facility (described in Chapter 5, "Windows and the Protected Subsystems") to the appropriate server, which calls the NT process manager to create a native process.

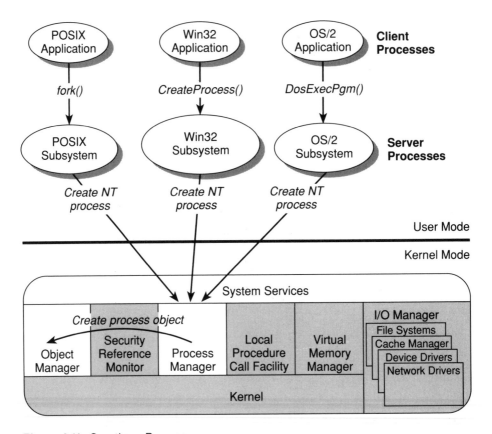

Figure 4-11. Creating a Process

After creating a native process, the NT process manager returns a handle to a process object. The environment subsystem takes the handle and constructs the appropriate return value expected by the original client application. What each subsystem returns is shown in Figure 4-12.

Note that an environment subsystem must do some additional work after it receives a process handle from the process manager and before it returns a result to the client application. For example, the subsystem calls the process manager again to create a thread for the new process.

As you can see in Figure 4-12, different operating system environments return different results when a process is created. Similarly, operating systems vary in the rules and conventions they adopt for managing processes. One of the fundamental differences among the operating system environments available on Windows NT is their ability to support multithreaded processes. Win32 and OS/2, for example, allow multiple threads per process, whereas POSIX, MS-DOS, and the Windows 16-bit environment do not.

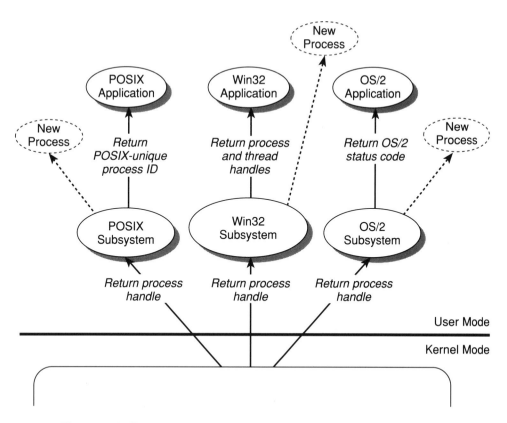

Figure 4-12. Returning from Process Creation

Another example of the differences among operating system environments is the way in which each subsystem's processes relate to one another. POSIX and OS/2, for example, organize their client processes into hierarchies, or *process trees*. They each create an initial process that creates the so-called *child processes*. The child processes, in turn, create their own child processes. Except for the initial process, every process has a parent from which it inherits certain resources and characteristics. Figure 4-13, shown on the next page, illustrates these relationships.

Both POSIX and OS/2 use the relationships between their client processes to manage them. For example, when a POSIX process or an OS/2 process terminates, the operating system tracks down and terminates all of its descendant processes. Moreover, a POSIX-compliant operating system maintains other types of relationships between processes, including *process groups* (collections of related processes) and *sessions* (collections of process groups). POSIX systems implement detailed process-control semantics related to

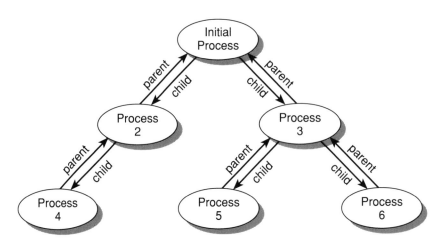

Figure 4-13. POSIX or OS/2 Process Hierarchy

process groups and sessions that have no precise counterparts in other operating systems. The NT executive must allow each of its environment subsystems to support whatever process relationships it requires.

In addition to differences in process groupings and in the use of single-threaded processes or multithreaded processes, environment subsystems differ in the rules they use for creating new processes. Table 4-4 details some of the differences among the process structures of three operating system environments Windows NT supports.

	Windows (32-bit)	POSIX	OS/2
API routine	CreateProcess()	fork()	DosExecPgm()
Process hierarchy	Maintains no formal parent/child relationships	Creates new process as child of caller	Creates new process as child of caller
Inheritance	Copies to child process all object handles that were opened with the inheritance attribute	Copies parent's file descriptors to child process	Copies to child process all of parent's file, pipe, and semaphore handles that were opened with inheritance rights

Table 4-4. Process Creation Semantics

(continued)

Table 4-4. *continued*

	Windows (32-bit)	POSIX	OS/2
Address space initialization	Initializes process's address space with an executable program	Initializes child's address space by copying parent's address space	Initializes child's address space with an executable program
Process identification	Returns a handle to the new process	Returns process ID for new child	Returns process ID for new child (if child runs asynchronously)
Threads	Creates one thread and supports multithreading	Creates one thread but does not support multithreading	Creates one thread and supports multithreading

As you can see, process hierarchies, address space initialization, and process identification vary in different environments. Although some of the differences seem minor, the process manager must support all environments equally well and must allow their different process structures to coexist without conflicting. The following section explains how this is done.

4.3.2 Native Process Structure

While designing the native NT process structure, the developers quickly realized that even if it were possible, providing multiple types of process structures in the base operating system would result in a highly complex and chaotic system. Fortunately, most details pertaining to process structure are not fundamental to the operation of the underlying operating system. Process structures could be implemented in the user-mode environment subsystems outside the NT executive. To accomplish this, the NT executive's process structure does not enforce any set of rules that might preclude another. Instead, it supplies a basic set of mechanisms that the subsystems can use as a foundation for implementing their own process structures. As an example of this approach, Table 4-5, shown on the next page, details the NT executive's flexible process creation rules.

The NT executive views process creation as the creation of an object—nothing more. When the process manager finishes creating a new process, it returns the new process's handle to the environment subsystem. The subsystem is responsible for calling the process manager to create a thread in the process.

NT	
API routine	NtCreateProcess()
Process hierarchy	Creates new process as independent peer of caller and returns an object handle
Inheritance	Caller specifies a parent from which the new process inherits object handles that were opened with the inheritance attribute
Address space initialization	Initializes new process's address space with an executable program or as a copy of the parent's address space
Process identification	Returns NT object handle for new process
Threads	Does not create a thread in the new process automatically, but supports multithreading

Table 4-5. Native NT Process Creation Semantics

The NT process manager does not record which process created which. Therefore, in order to emulate the unique process relationships required by their applications, each environment subsystem maintains records of client processes it has created and the relationships that exist among them. The following sections describe some of the facilities the NT executive provides the subsystems for managing their clients.

4.3.2.1 Managing Client Processes

A native NT process must be given a minimal set of resources, in addition to a thread, before it can do any work. If you refer back to Figure 4-2 on page 86, you'll see that a process has an access token, address space contents, and handles to objects. These resources, plus process-specific quotas and other settings, are in whole or in part inherited from another process, a "parent process."

The term "parent process" is enclosed in quotation marks because of the NT executive's unique notion of an assignable parent. Consider the illustration shown in Figure 4-14.

In this figure, a POSIX application calls the POSIX subsystem to create a new POSIX process. The subsystem, also a process, calls the NT executive to create a native process. Because the POSIX subsystem is acting on behalf of the client application, the new process should inherit its resources from the client, not from the subsystem. The same holds true for Win32 and OS/2 applications that create new processes. To allow the environment subsystems to emulate the process inheritance semantics their applications require, the NT executive's create process service lets a caller (the subsystem in this case) optionally specify the new process's parent.

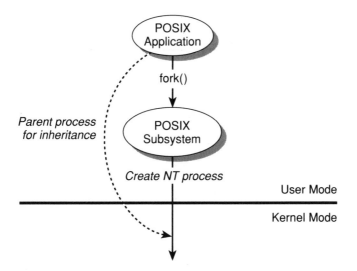

Figure 4-14. Assigning a Parent Process

The new native NT process inherits the parent's access token, quota limits, base priority, and default processor affinity. It also inherits any handles in the parent's object table that were opened with an inheritance designation. The parent's address space can also be inherited if the subsystem requests it. The POSIX subsystem uses this feature to emulate the POSIX fork() API routine, whereas the Win32 and OS/2 subsystems specify an executable image to load into the new process's address space.

Before it can execute, a new process must be given a thread. To a Win32 or an OS/2 application, creating a thread is not considered a separate operation from creating a new process. Win32 and OS/2 applications expect the thread to be there already when the process creation routine returns. The thread is not automatically created in NT, however, so the subsystems must call the process manager again to create a thread in the new process. When creating a thread, the process manager allows subsystems to specify a process to which the new thread belongs. This lets the Win32 subsystem, for example, create a process for one of its clients and then place a thread in that client's address space. The new thread begins executing at the client process's base priority, on the set of processors listed in the client's processor affinity, and under the constraints of the client's access token.

In addition to creating processes and threads on behalf of other processes, the NT process manager provides facilities that allow a subsystem to attach to a client's address space and read and write to it, to allocate and free a client's virtual memory, and to suspend a client's threads, alter the threads'

111

execution states, and restart them. The subsystem can also duplicate object handles from its own object table into the client's object table. Furthermore, it can terminate a client's threads or a client process.

These powerful capabilities give user-mode subsystems control that in most operating systems is limited to kernel-mode operating system code. They allow the environment subsystems freedom to control their client applications and to establish an operating system environment for them that differs from the NT executive's native environment.

4.3.2.2 Preventing Misuse

Creating processes and threads on behalf of another process, reading and writing another process's virtual memory, and controlling another process's threads are operations that should not be used indiscriminately. To prevent misuse, the Windows NT security system (specifically its object protection mechanisms) ensures that such operations are carefully controlled.

At their most basic level, the Windows NT environment subsystems are simply ordinary processes. Like other processes, they determine what access rights are granted to the processes they create. Because virtually all user-mode processes are created by environment subsystems, the subsystems control the actions of all user processes in the system.

For example, when creating a client process, a subsystem denies the client the ability to bypass the subsystem and terminate itself by calling a native NT service. Were this not the case, the process could leave the subsystem's global data structures in an inconsistent state, possibly disrupting other processes that are under the control of that environment. The subsystem prevents this by not giving the new process delete access to its own process object in the object's access control list (ACL). (See Chapter 3, "The Object Manager and Object Security.") Without delete access, the process can never open an object handle that lets it terminate itself, and the security system will not allow the terminate service to succeed unless it is given a valid handle.

Because of the way object security works, unless a subsystem explicitly gives a client process a capability, the client cannot acquire it. Thus, a subsystem designer doesn't need to think of all the devious things a user process could do and prevent them. Instead, it is enough to decide only what the process should be able to do and to grant the client those capabilities. For the most part, this means that no ordinary user-mode process can successfully call native NT services. A user-mode process can call only the API routines provided by the subsystem that created it.

These same mechanisms also prevent user-mode processes from terminating or manipulating other processes. A process can call only those API routines available in its environment (Win32 or POSIX, for example) to manipulate another process. Furthermore, a process's ability to call even those services is constrained by its access rights to the native objects it would be affecting. Once again, by not giving a client process access rights to native objects, an environment subsystem can prevent the client from misbehaving. The Windows NT security architecture, working tirelessly in the background, guarantees it.

4.4   In Conclusion

Processes are a fundamental division of labor and resources within Windows NT. They allow the operating system to divide its work into functional units to achieve efficient use of the processor. Windows NT divides processes into executable units called *threads*. Threads allows a single process to concurrently execute different parts of its program and achieve better processor utilization, especially on multiprocessor computers. A process consists of an address space and a set of resources that all of its threads share as they execute.

The NT executive's process structure is primitive and flexible, allowing environment subsystems to construct whatever semantics they require in order to support their clients. They are free to establish process hierarchies, to implement process inheritance, and to initialize the address spaces of their clients as they see fit. They can also control client processes in other ways, by performing actions on behalf of their clients and by reading and writing their clients' virtual memory. All of these capabilities are monitored by the security system, which checks the access rights a process has on the objects it is trying to manipulate before allowing such operations.

The next chapter focuses in more detail on the structure of the Windows NT subsystems and on the LPC message-passing facility, which allows client and subsystem processes to communicate with one another.

WINDOWS AND THE PROTECTED SUBSYSTEMS

During Windows NT's development, the trade press variously referred to it as a chameleon operating system, as the mother of all operating systems, and once as a many-headed Hydra. Its protected subsystems, and specifically its environment subsystems, were the reason for these whimsical nicknames.

As evidenced by the name Windows NT, a 32-bit version of Windows supplies the NT executive's user interface. To a user, Windows NT looks like Windows on MS-DOS. To a programmer, however, Windows NT adopts several personas.

The idea that one operating system can run different types of programs is not new. Windows NT borrowed the idea from the Mach operating system, which was designed to support different, incompatible versions of UNIX application programming interfaces (APIs) within the same operating system. Mach accomplished this by implementing the different API environments as user-mode server processes. Windows NT uses the same approach to achieve different goals.

From the beginning of Windows NT's development, its designers focused on extending existing Microsoft APIs, not replacing them, so that existing applications could continue to run as new applications were developed. The most important result of this effort is a new 32-bit Windows interface called the *Win32 API*. The Win32 API allows applications to take advantage of sophisticated operating system capabilities that were not available in the 16-bit Windows API. In addition to running Win32 applications, however, Windows NT runs existing MS-DOS and 16-bit Windows applications as well as many OS/2 and all POSIX-conformant (IEEE 1003.1) applications.

To achieve this flexibility, the NT executive is necessarily rather generic. It handles low-level process and thread creation, thread scheduling, memory management, interrupt handling, and I/O while relying on user-mode servers to provide the niceties of a graphical user interface and the other features that applications and users expect. Using NT system services as a base, separate user-mode servers implement Win32, 16-bit Windows, MS-DOS, POSIX, and OS/2 APIs. Any number of these APIs and application execution environments can coexist in Windows NT.

The servers that provide API environments are called *protected subsystems* and, specifically, *environment subsystems*. Although each subsystem had different, and sometimes many, designers, the overall client/server approach and the first two environment subsystems (rudimentary versions of OS/2 and POSIX) were designed by Steve Wood and Mark Lucovsky. The general goals they established for the Windows NT environment subsystems are these:

- Make each subsystem *robust* so that client applications cannot negatively affect one another or the subsystem as a whole. Also ensure that one subsystem cannot arbitrarily influence another subsystem or its client applications.

- Ensure that the *performance* of each environment compares favorably with the performance of the operating system it emulates. For example, 16-bit Windows applications must run as fast on Windows NT as they do on 16-bit Windows. Similarly, the execution of MS-DOS applications on Windows NT must compare favorably with their execution on a native MS-DOS system.

- Ensure that each subsystem meets U.S. government requirements for a *secure operating system environment*. This includes fully shielding each process's memory from other processes and controlling each client process's access to subsystem resources and to the resources of other clients.

- Allow the subsystems to *interoperate* when users would expect them to. For example, 16-bit and 32-bit Windows applications should be able to pass data to one another via the Clipboard or to communicate by using dynamic data exchange (DDE) or object linking and embedding (OLE). A single character-mode command interpreter should execute MS-DOS, OS/2, or POSIX programs and allow I/O redirection between them, when appropriate. Character-mode applications of all types should be able to send their output to standard I/O and have the system automatically display it in a window.

This chapter does not describe each subsystem in detail. Instead, it focuses on the Win32 environment, the 16-bit Windows environment, and the MS-DOS environment. The Win32 environment subsystem is a crucial component of Windows NT and provides the system's user and programming interface. The 16-bit Windows and MS-DOS environments are important for compatibility with existing applications.

The first section of this chapter describes Windows NT's client/server model and how it was selected. The second section examines the ways in which the subsystems interact, and the third section focuses on the Win32 subsystem. A section on the MS-DOS and 16-bit Windows environments follows, and a discussion of the system's message-passing facility closes the chapter.

5.1   Protected Subsystems Overview

Windows NT's protected subsystems are user-mode server processes created by Windows NT when the operating system is booted. Once created, they run continually, responding to messages sent to them from application processes and from other subsystems. Whereas the environment subsystems implement operating system APIs, another type of subsystem, called an *integral subsystem,* performs necessary operating system tasks. Much of Windows NT's security system is implemented as an integral subsystem, and network servers can also be implemented as integral subsystems.[1]

Each protected subsystem does its work in user mode, calling NT executive system services for kernel-mode operating system support. Network servers can run either in user mode or in kernel mode, depending on how they are designed. The Windows NT subsystems are shown in Figure 5-1 on the next page.

Subsystems communicate by passing messages to one another. When a user application calls an API routine, for example, the environment subsystem providing the routine receives a message and implements it by calling NT system services or by passing messages to other subsystems. When finished, the environment subsystem sends a message containing the return values back to the application. The message passing and other activities of the protected subsystems are invisible to the user.

The glue that holds the Windows NT client/server model together is known as the *local procedure call* (LPC) facility. It is a message-passing facility

---

1. Network servers can be implemented either as integral subsystems or as drivers. The built-in Windows NT server is implemented as a loadable driver, but future network servers can be created as subsystems.

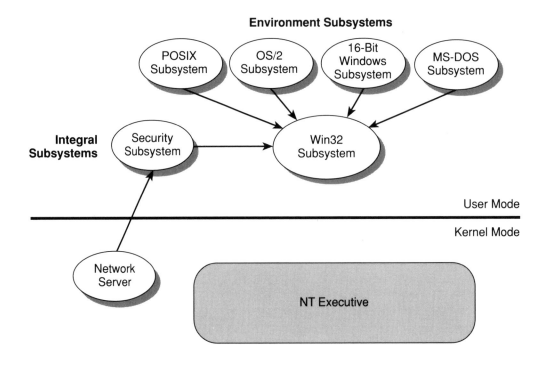

Figure 5-1. Windows NT's Protected Subsystems

through which clients make requests of servers and servers reply. LPC is a locally optimized version of a more general message-passing facility called *remote procedure call* (RPC), which is used for communication among client and server processes residing on different computers in a network.

The LPC facility supplies several ways to pass data between clients and servers: one used to send short messages, another used to send long messages, and a third that is optimized for use by the Win32 subsystem. Each subsystem establishes a *port*—a communication channel through which other processes can communicate with the subsystem. Ports are implemented as NT executive objects.

This section examines Windows NT's client/server model from a primarily historical perspective—that is, how the model evolved during the early phases of designing Windows NT. The first subsection focuses on how the client/server model helps Windows NT achieve its design goals. The second subsection addresses a major consideration when using a client/server model: system performance.

5.1.1 Why Use a Client/Server Model?

Implementing portions of the operating system in user-mode servers is a significant part of Windows NT's design and thus has far-reaching implications for how the system works. Although the client/server approach is not unique to operating system design, it does break with long-standing tradition. Until relatively recently, most operating systems were structured around either a monolithic or a layered model. In both of these models, the operating system runs in a privileged processor mode (or perhaps more than one privileged mode) that distinguishes the operating system from nonprivileged application code. Furthermore, in a monolithic or layered model no part of the operating system runs in a process of its own. Instead, the operating system creates user-mode processes to run applications, and the operating system code executes on behalf of these applications when they call system services or when external interrupts occur.

In contrast, Windows NT is composed of two parts: a traditional operating system portion and a set of user-mode "applications" that perform operating system tasks. The "applications" are Windows NT's protected subsystems. Like ordinary applications, they execute within a process with a private address space. The NT executive's kernel component schedules their threads on processors exactly as it does for other applications.

Windows NT uses protected subsystems to meet the following goals:

- To provide multiple application programming interfaces (APIs) while keeping the base operating system code (the NT executive) simple and maintainable

- To shield the base operating system from changes in or extensions to the provided APIs

- To consolidate the global data required by each API and, at the same time, separate the global data required by one API from that required by other APIs

- To protect each API environment from applications and from each other and to protect the base operating system from the different environments

- To allow the operating system to be extended with new APIs in the future

The first item in this list, providing multiple APIs, was an important goal for Windows NT, and it posed a dilemma for which a solution was not immediately obvious. This subsection chronicles the debate that ensued over how this goal could be achieved and documents why the client/server model was selected.

5.1.1.1 Providing Multiple Environments

As discussed in Chapter 1, "The Mission," the original market requirements for NT called for it to supply primarily OS/2 and POSIX programming interfaces and to allow other APIs to be added in the future. This was the assumption the team members made when they set out to design a structure for NT (as the system was called in 1988).

When first examining this issue in 1988, the team soon realized that it wasn't enough merely to implement multiple APIs because APIs do not exist in a vacuum. For example, an OS/2 application that calls DosExecPgm() to create a process and run a program rightfully expects the routine to do its work and return the correct values. In addition, and this is the crux of the issue, the application also expects the routine to create a process that behaves exactly as it would on an OS/2 system. The same is true for Windows, MS-DOS, and POSIX applications; that is, the API routine *and its underlying execution environment* must be wholly compatible with the application's native environment. Each native operating system has a different process structure, different memory management, different exception and error handling, different resource protection mechanisms, and different semantics for file access and I/O. How do you supply an execution environment that is compatible with several different operating systems? This was the great challenge in designing Windows NT.

The team started by examining the OS/2 and POSIX APIs and trying to select a structure for NT that could accommodate both. An additional goal was to ensure that the system could also provide other, as yet unknown, APIs for future extensibility. (Windows and MS-DOS APIs, of course, were obvious choices.)

The first idea centered around making NT a standard layered operating system that presented one selected API as native system services. The OS/2 API was the first choice at that time. POSIX and other future environments would exist as runtime interfaces that called the OS/2–like services to do their work. (See Figure 5-2.)

As this option came under increasing scrutiny, it became clear that the behavior of nearly all the OS/2 API routines was sufficiently different from the behavior of the POSIX routines that the OS/2 API routines would need to change. For example, OS/2's process creation routine DosExecPgm() would need to support the option of copying an address space from a parent to a child process. (The routine's normal behavior initializes the child process's memory with an executable image.) More inconvenient, however, was the fact

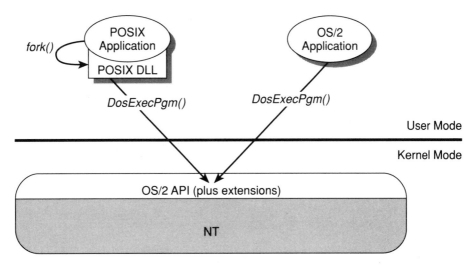

Figure 5-2. Implementing Multiple APIs (Option 1)

that the OS/2 and POSIX semantics could not be separated cleanly from one another or from NT. For example, if a multithreaded OS/2 application accidentally called the routine DosExecPgm() and specified a POSIX option, the operating system could fail because NT would not expect a POSIX process to have more than one thread. This first design option was subsequently rejected because it could not guarantee a robust, maintainable, or extensible operating system.

The second design option was to make NT a dual-API system, placing both OS/2 and POSIX APIs directly in NT, running in kernel mode, as illustrated in Figure 5-3.

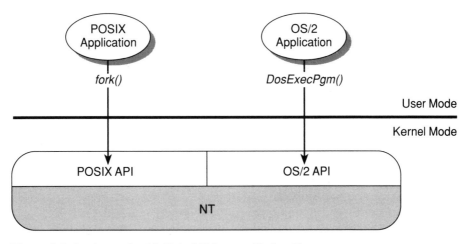

Figure 5-3. Implementing Multiple API Layers (Option 2)

With this option, the API layers would not manage global data or track the state of processes, memory, and so on but would simply call the NT layer, which would implement a generic operating system environment that supported both OS/2 and POSIX semantics.

As this idea was examined in detail, it became apparent that it was only a tiny improvement over the previous option. Although it would be impossible for a user-mode program to call NT with dangerous parameters, NT would still need to support two incompatible application execution environments. For example, the process creation routine would need to implement both OS/2 and POSIX semantics, using a flag that indicated which type of process the caller wanted to create. Similarly, when a process terminated, NT would need to determine whether it was an OS/2 process created by using the EXEC_SYNC option. If so, its process identifier could be reused by another process. If it were a POSIX process and if its parent were not the initial process, NT would send it a POSIX-style signal; if the process were a session group leader, the executive would generate a hangup signal to all members of the session group using the same controlling terminal and would possibly free the controlling terminal, and so on, and so on, and so on. A complicated mess.

Process structure wasn't the only area of difficulty, however. Problems arose as a result of subtle differences between OS/2 and POSIX in many areas, including timers, time-of-day format, file locks, pipes, exception handling, and others. To support these differences, each process and thread in the system would need to carry around baggage identifying its characteristics and pointing to special tables to keep track of possible combinations and actions. Simple functions, such as waiting for a child process (common to both OS/2 and POSIX), would be difficult to implement because NT would need to manage two slightly different cases (not to mention future ones). As Mark Lucovsky aptly stated, "The list of 'chicken wire' and 'voodoo' interfaces required by this design threatened the goals of extensibility and maintainability." Indeed, supporting Windows and MS-DOS applications as well as OS/2 and POSIX applications using this structure would have been well-nigh impossible.

The system designers had to explore some new alternatives. What they needed was a way to separate the basic mechanisms of process and memory management, exception handling, and so forth from the policies governing how these mechanisms were presented to application programs. In addition, the designers needed a way to separate the global data and policies required by the different API layers from NT in order to keep NT small and uncluttered.

The Mach operating system successfully solved some of these problems in the 1980s. It is a client/server implementation of UNIX that separates operating system mechanisms, such as memory management and thread scheduling, from the various UNIX (and non-UNIX) APIs its servers provide. The Windows NT designers borrowed from Mach and adapted its approach to their needs. The resulting design, with the critical addition of the 32-bit Windows subsystem, is shown in Figure 5-4.

The NT executive is a generic, all-purpose operating system. It supplies basic operating system mechanisms and allows the environment subsystems to establish policies and semantics for the applications they support. Each environment subsystem is a peer of the others and can call the native NT services it needs to create appropriate execution environments for its client applications.

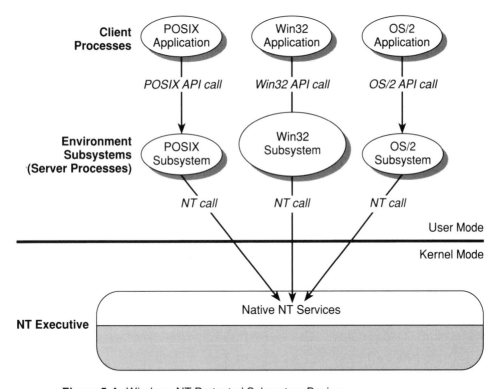

Figure 5-4. Windows NT Protected Subsystem Design

5.1.1.2 Memory Protection

Moving the APIs out of the NT executive resulted in a clean separation between the operating system "proper" and the semantics and policies required by the different APIs. An additional benefit of this structure is that it facilitates another of Windows NT's important goals: to protect each API environment from user applications and to protect the NT executive from the environments.

The OS/2 and 16-bit Windows systems use a DLL model to implement their APIs. In that model, the API is provided in one or more shared DLLs that application programs link to and call as regular procedure calls. The system modifies the caller's executable image to point to the shared DLL segments at runtime. (See Figure 5-5.)

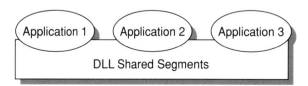

Figure 5-5. DLL Model for APIs

Although the OS/2 and Windows systems implement DLLs differently,[2] the result is the same: Every application that links to the DLL can modify data that is in use by all applications. In Windows NT, such a scenario is unacceptable because two important requirements are robustness and security. An application program must not be able to negatively affect the operating system or other applications. For example, Windows code keeps track of how many windows are on the screen. If a user program were to overwrite that data, Windows could hang or become erratic, which could stop or even corrupt executing applications. Windows NT does not shun DLLs, but the way in which OS/2 and Windows use them illustrates the problem of code and data protection in an operating system. For an operating system to be fully secure, operating system code and data should not be accessible to user-mode applications.

Windows NT's client/server model goes a long way toward solving the problem of memory protection. Each protected subsystem runs in a process with a private address space. For an application to gain access to a subsystem, it must send a message. The server receives the message, validates all parameters, executes the required function, and returns the results to the caller. Using this procedure, the caller never gets direct access to the subsystem's address space. Any global data the subsystem maintains is accessible only to the subsystem.

---

2. The Windows system maps a DLL once into a single address space that is accessible to all applications. OS/2 maps shared DLLs into each process's address space, but all processes share the same DLL data.

At first glance, it might seem that an application running on Windows NT would need to be rewritten to pass messages to servers instead of calling API routines, but this is not the case. Applications still link to DLLs as before. Each DLL contains API entry points, called *stubs*, that package the caller's parameters into a message and send the message to the correct server. The server implements the API routine and then returns the results to the DLL code via the LPC facility. The DLL returns in the normal way to the application so that the message passing is invisible to the application programmer. Figure 5-6 illustrates this round-trip behavior with the Win32 subsystem. The mechanism works in the same way for the other protected subsystems.

Using this model, it is impossible for a Win32 application, for example, to corrupt the Win32 subsystem's global data and negatively affect other applications. Moreover, each subsystem is separate and thus protected from the other subsystems. Each subsystem can independently create and maintain data structures and establish any special semantics it requires for process structure, exception and error handling, I/O, and so on.

Furthermore, because the subsystems are user-mode applications, they cannot modify the NT executive's data structures or call internal operating system routines. The only way they can gain access to the NT executive is by

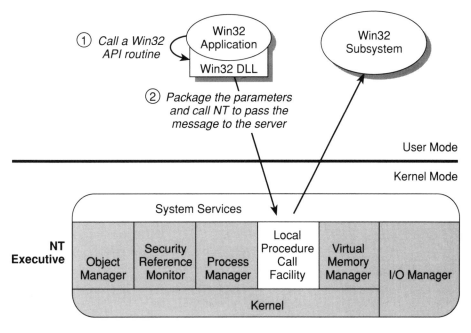

Figure 5-6. Windows NT's DLL Model for APIs

calling system services. No complicated ring structure or other cumbersome protection mechanism is required. The client/server model enforces the separation between the subsystems and the kernel-mode portion of the system.

A final benefit of using the client/server model is that any number of subsystems can run simultaneously, providing multiple API environments. Each subsystem is simply a user-mode process whose threads can be scheduled independently on a processor, improving parallelism in the system. With all these benefits, the client/server model appeared to be the right design for Windows NT.

5.1.2 Performance Considerations

The biggest worry the developers had in selecting the client/server model for Windows NT was performance. Calling an API routine or a system service on a traditional operating system generally requires less overhead than does calling an API routine in a client/server configuration.

Monolithic and layered operating systems implement their system services in the kernel-mode portion of the system. On such systems, when a user-mode thread calls a service, the hardware traps the thread and changes the processor mode to kernel-mode execution. The operating system then executes the service. When the service ends, the operating system switches the processor mode back to user mode and the thread resumes executing in application code. On most processors, this sequence is quite fast.

In Windows NT, however, when a Win32 application calls the Win32 API, the API routine is not implemented in the kernel-mode portion of the operating system. If you refer back to Figure 5-6, you'll see that the Win32 DLL calls an NT system service to send a message. The service sends a message to the server and then waits for the server to receive it, execute the service, and reply. For the server to get the message and execute it, a *context switch* must occur—that is, the NT executive must perform the following sequence:

1. Save the client thread's context (volatile machine state)

2. Select a server thread for execution and load the server thread's context

3. Execute the Win32 API routine using the server's thread

4. Save the server thread's context

5. Reload the client thread's context and process the results of the API routine

Depending on the hardware on which the operating system is based, a context switch adds processing overhead to a system trap. Given that, a thread that calls an API routine implemented in a server would theoretically take a performance hit each time it called the routine, as compared to calling an API routine implemented as a system trap. Because performance was considered crucial to Windows NT's success, the designers examined this issue carefully before proceeding.

Context switching, the process of saving one thread's machine state and loading another, is a relatively fixed-cost operation. Depending on the processor, certain optimizations can be performed, such as ordering the load and store operations intelligently and only loading and storing those portions of a thread's context that are required. Dave Cutler, who wrote the context-switching code for the MIPS processors, and Bryan Willman and Shie-Lin Tzong, who rewrote it for the Intel CISC processors, are all highly experienced in this task, so any optimizations that could be achieved in the software were achieved.

The system's message-passing facility is the other performance variable in a call from a client to a server and back. Steve Wood, who designed and implemented the LPC facility, created it with flexible options for the transmission of data. For example, the LPC facility provides a way to send short messages easily and a way to send longer messages efficiently. A third method of message passing was created specifically to optimize performance in the Win32 subsystem, an important goal because this subsystem processes all user input and generates all graphical output on Windows NT.

In addition to a flexible, optimized message-passing facility, the Windows NT developers established some "tricks" that reduce the number of interactions a client must make with a server:

- Using client-side DLLs to implement the API routines that don't use or modify global data

- Storing certain subsystem data in the executive, or caching subsystem data in the client-side DLL

- Batching client API calls and sending them to the server in a single message

The first strategy provides the biggest benefit of the three. As detailed previously, one major purpose for using the client/server model is to ensure that processes cannot modify the global data maintained by a particular environment. This data includes information such as the number of windows on the screen for the Win32 subsystem, handle translation tables for the POSIX or OS/2 subsystems, and environment-specific process or session IDs that all the subsystems maintain. Because this data resides in the subsystem's address space, a client must pass a message to gain access to this data.

When you examine the various APIs, however, you realize that API routines can be divided into two categories: those that use or change global data and those that don't. The API routines in the latter group need not call the subsystem. That is, they can be implemented directly in a private DLL, as shown in Figure 5-7. The DLL calls native NT services to do its work, avoiding context switching and message passing altogether.[3]

Developers of the various Windows NT subsystems took pains to implement their most frequently used API routines in DLLs. Win32 API routines that get information about the executing thread or its process, for example, or even Win32 API routines that set process or thread characteristics are implemented in a Win32 DLL because they can call NT services to get the infor-

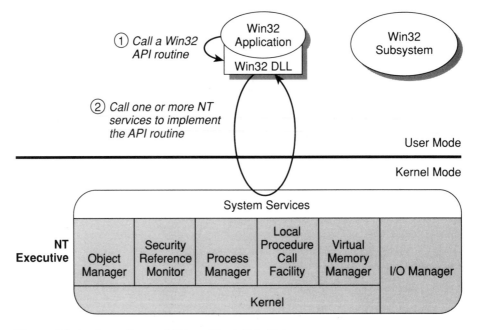

Figure 5-7. Implementing an API in a Client-Side DLL

---

3. The DLL code is actually shared among applications by the operating system, but it is protected with copy-on-write page protection. See Chapter 6, "The Virtual Memory Manager," for more information.

mation they need without going to the Win32 server. A similar approach was adopted for the other environment subsystems, a strategy that places the performance of frequently used API routines within the same ballpark as API calls on layered or monolithic operating systems.

Close examination revealed that most API routines do not require the use of global data and therefore do not require a call to the server. Those API routines that do require it tend to be operations that are infrequently used or are already "high-cost" services, such as creating a process or opening a file. The cost of context switching and message passing in these cases is not noticeable to a user.

The second and third client/server optimizations are slightly smaller in scope but are no less important. The second optimization stores subsystem data in the NT executive or caches it in the DLL. Drive letters, as mentioned in Chapter 3, "The Object Manager and Object Security," are an example of subsystem data that is stored in the NT executive. Both MS-DOS and OS/2 require global symbols for the drive letters A, B, and C, as well as any others the user might create. To avoid calling the server each time an application refers to a drive, drive letters are created as NT named objects whose names are translated by the object manager into device destinations at runtime. Similarly, the Win32 subsystem caches global data in the application's address space. For example, when an application draws an object, the Win32 subsystem keeps a copy of the object in the client-side DLL so that the DLL has the data it needs to execute more API routines without requesting information from the Win32 server.

The third optimization, devised by Chuck Whitmer, architect of the graphics portion of the Win32 subsystem, batches information in the client and sends it as a single message to the server. For example, the application might call several consecutive line-drawing routines; the DLL collects them into a batch, sending the calls to the server in a single message. Or the application might set the pen color; the DLL remembers that the pen color has changed and only transmits that information to the server the next time it draws something on the screen. Batching API calls or information in this way results in fewer large data transmissions between client and server and, thus, better performance for drawing operations.

The improved protection and robustness guaranteed by the use of the client/server model in Windows NT was important enough to the developers that they were willing to accept a 10-percent reduction in application execution speed compared to the speed of applications running on Windows 3.1. However, the performance enhancements listed here greatly reduce the number of API routines that actually call the server. Those that do are optimized using batching and caching techniques and a streamlined form of LPC (described in Section 5.5). With these techniques (and a few others) in use, only a handful of API calls carry significant overhead, and that overhead appears to fall well below the 10-percent mark.

5.2 Interacting with Windows NT Subsystems

Windows NT's environment subsystems not only interact with client applications when applications call API routines, the subsystems also interact with one another in predictable ways. Figure 5-8 illustrates some of the Windows NT protected subsystems and the typical interactions that occur among them.

In addition to other responsibilities, the Win32 subsystem controls the user interface. It manages the windows on the screen, displays output for other environment subsystems, and captures input from users and directs it to the correct subsystem or application. The Win32 subsystem starts applications in response to requests from the Windows Program Manager or the command shell application (console).

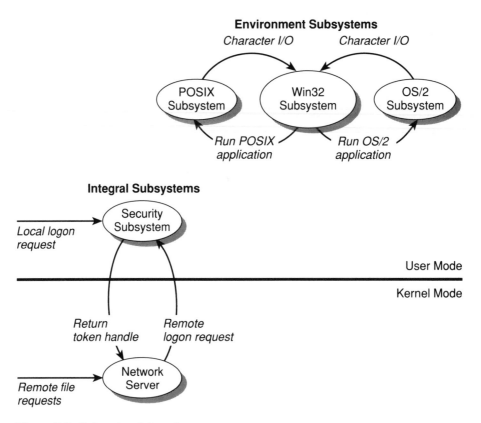

Figure 5-8. Subsystem Interactions

In addition to the environment subsystems shown in a row at the top of the figure, two integral subsystems are depicted. These are system components that benefit from the protection offered by a client/server structure and their ability to be scheduled independently for execution. The security subsystem processes user logons, creates security tokens to represent user processes, and maintains a database of security information about user accounts. Network subsystems respond to requests that arrive from the network. More than one network subsystem (commonly called a network server) can be loaded into Windows NT to handle requests originating from different networks.

The following subsections discuss in more detail two types of interactions that occur among subsystems when users enter certain kinds of input. The first type of subsystem interaction occurs when a user attempts to log on to Windows NT, and the second type of interaction occurs when a user executes applications other than Win32 applications.

5.2.1 Logon

User logon is a new feature in Windows NT, designed to help make the operating system truly secure (as defined by the U.S. government). Logon prevents unauthorized users from accidentally or maliciously doing things they aren't supposed to do with other people's data.

There are two ways to gain access to Windows NT: through an interactive logon or by logging on over a network connection. The security subsystem ensures that any user who tries to access Windows NT has been given the authority to do so by a system administrator. In most cases, "authority" means that an entry exists for the user in Windows NT's security account manager (SAM), a database containing user names, passwords, and other security information.

Jim Kelly and Cliff Van Dyke, developers with many years of security and networking experience, designed the security subsystem. One of many goals in their design was to ensure that Windows NT be flexible in the number and types of external logon devices it can support. To accomplish this, the logon architecture takes the form shown in Figure 5-9 on the next page.

Requests from users can be made either from a keyboard attached to a Windows NT system or over a network. Network requests generally manifest themselves as requests to connect to a network resource and/or to perform I/O operations. For both interactive and network requests, a local process must intercede and verify that the access is legitimate. The built-in Windows NT server or other network server performs this task for network requests. For

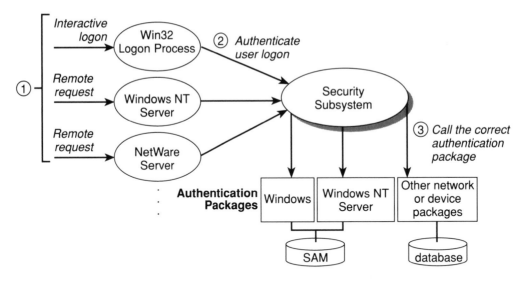

Figure 5-9. Logon and the Security Subsystem

interactive requests, a Win32 process waits for the user to press the Ctrl-Alt-Del key combination. When it detects this input, the logon process prompts the user for logon information.

Two types of information are needed to verify a user's identity: identification information and authentication information. The first is a user's account name and the second is a password. However, Windows NT's security system is flexible enough that the ID information could take the form of an ATM card, for example, and the authentication information could be a personal information number. Similarly, if a retinal or fingerprint scanner were used to identify users, the ID information could be a user's name, and the authentication information could be a picture of the user's eyeball or a thumbprint.

After the security subsystem receives the logon information, it uses an *authentication package* to verify the information. Different authentication packages can be plugged into Windows NT's security system so that future input devices are easily supported. However, in a normal logon, the Windows or network authentication package checks the SAM database, and if the entered password matches one currently in the database, the authentication package returns the user's ID and a list of the group IDs to which the user belongs.

The security subsystem then obtains additional information about the user from its local policy database, including any privileges owned and quota limits. Finally, the security subsystem constructs an access token to represent the user and passes the token handle to the logon process, as shown in Figure 5-10. With that, the user has established a logon session with Windows NT.

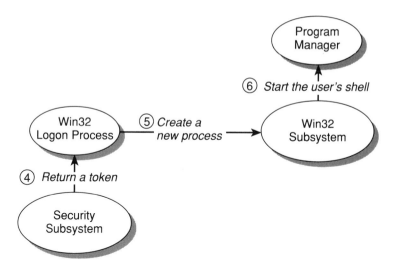

Figure 5-10. Starting an Interactive User Session

For interactive logons, the Win32 logon process calls the Win32 subsystem to create a new process and attach the user's token to it. The subsystem starts a user shell in the process. Typically the shell is the Program Manager, as Figure 5-10 shows, although it could be a POSIX or other type of command shell.

For network logons, the network server uses the access token to impersonate the user and gain access to system resources. It can then copy a file or perform whatever action the remote user requested.

5.2.2 Running Applications

After an interactive user is logged on, the Win32 subsystem creates processes to run the various applications the user starts. When the user clicks on an icon, for example, the Win32 subsystem directs that mouse input to the Program Manager application. As Figure 5-11 on the next page illustrates, the Program Manager in turn calls the Win32 subsystem to create a new process and start the application in it. The application then calls the Win32 subsystem to create windows, send messages, and so forth. When the user enters input, the Win32 subsystem directs the input to the correct application.

The Win32 subsystem is the link between the user and the rest of the operating system. Applications that call the Win32 API are clients of the Win32 subsystem and are "served" directly by it. However, the Win32 subsystem cannot run other applications directly because it does not implement 16-bit Windows, MS-DOS, OS/2, or POSIX APIs. Therefore, whenever a user

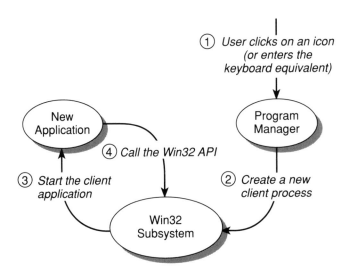

Figure 5-11. Starting a Win32 Application

starts an application whose image-file format the Win32 subsystem doesn't recognize,[4] the subsystem creates a process in which to run the application, but instead of starting it, the subsystem passes control of the process to another subsystem, as shown in Figure 5-12. Thereafter, that application's API calls go directly to the subsystem that implements the API that the application requires.

Windows NT does not allow applications to call API routines from different operating system environments (Win32 and POSIX, for example) because doing so doesn't make sense from the standpoint of application portability and because it probably wouldn't work correctly. Each subsystem maintains its own notion of what constitutes a process or a file handle, for example, and the data structures used in one environment are unlikely to match those in other environments. Therefore, once the Win32 subsystem has assigned an application process to another subsystem, the application remains a client of that subsystem until the process exits. The Win32 subsystem continues to direct user input to the application.

In addition to managing user input, the Win32 subsystem displays application output on the screen. For output purposes, the Win32 subsystem views applications as one of two types: graphical or character based. Ordinary

---

4. The Win32 subsystem actually calls the NT executive's virtual memory (VM) manager to load the application. The VM manager determines the application's image-file format, returning a status message to the Win32 subsystem.

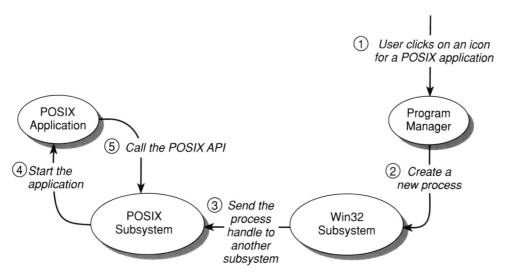

Figure 5-12. Starting a Non-Windows Application

Win32 and 16-bit Windows applications are graphical in nature. They use menus and dialog boxes, they draw text and lines in a window, and so on. Character-based applications, in contrast, simply write line-oriented, textual output to the screen at the current position of the cursor. They are generally started from a command interpreter and exit to a command interpreter prompt upon completion. MS-DOS applications, such as CHKDSK and FOR-MAT, are character based, as are character-mode OS/2 applications[5] and all POSIX (IEEE 1003.1-conformant) applications.

In Windows NT, character-based applications are transformed, in a sense, into graphical applications because their simple, line-oriented output is displayed inside a window. To achieve this effect without requiring programmers to rewrite character-based applications, Therese Stowell, formerly a programmer in the OS/2 file systems group, developed a set of Win32 API routines that direct the output of character-based applications to text windows managed by the Win32 subsystem. These windows are called *consoles.* The C runtime library, for example, calls the console routines to direct standard output for POSIX applications to a console window. Likewise, when an OS/2 application calls VIO functions or an MS-DOS application calls INT(10) functions, the OS/2 or MS-DOS environment subsystem, respectively, calls Win32 console routines to display the textual output.

---

5. Presentation Manager applications are not supported in Windows NT's first release.

Console windows sit alongside graphical windows in Windows NT, and users can pass text between the two via the Win32 Clipboard. Furthermore, with the availability of the new Win32 console routines, developers can write 32-bit, character-based applications for Windows NT. Most of the command-line utilities shipped with Windows NT are Win32 applications.

5.3 Win32 Subsystem

Although it runs different types of applications, Windows NT is first and foremost a Windows operating system. To be precise, it is the high-end Windows operating system in a family of Windows systems. With the release of Windows NT, computers from the smallest notebooks to large, multi-processor workstation computers can all run Windows applications. For application developers, this means that one development effort allows their applications to run on a broad range of computer hardware.

As mentioned earlier in this book, the Windows NT team started writing the system with the assumption that it would be a high-end OS/2 operating system that also supported the POSIX API. The switch from OS/2 to Windows came halfway through Windows NT's development, and although it was painful from a personnel and project-management point of view (that is, the OS/2 team had to scrap its code and begin anew), the change was somewhat inconsequential from an operating system design point of view. A Windows environment subsystem would plug into the NT executive and replace the OS/2 subsystem. Because the Windows subsystem would be the primary application programming and graphical user interface for Windows NT, it needed to provide a "super-Windows" environment, extending the capabilities available in the 16-bit Windows system with a 32-bit API and other advanced features.

Therefore, when creating the new Windows environment, Scott Ludwig, Chuck Whitmer, and others in Leif Pederson's 32-bit Windows team began to examine existing Windows software through the lens of Windows NT. The Windows environment on NT would have to provide a programming environment suitable for high-end workstations. It would also have to achieve many of the NT executive's goals, such as the following:

- Establish a 32-bit, linear (flat) memory model

- Implement preemptive multitasking

- Ensure robustness and security

Although these goals represent some far-reaching changes to the 16-bit Windows system, to an application developer or a user, Windows NT is a familiar environment. Windows NT provides additional capabilities, but wherever possible it retains existing Windows functionality. To the NT executive, the Win32 subsystem is a native NT application, albeit a sophisticated one. It is completely rewritten for Windows NT and uses native NT services as its base. Although the subsystem resides in an application process, Windows NT is dependent on it to interact with the user and to provide a programming environment and an API for other applications.

The Win32 subsystem takes its name from Microsoft's new 32-bit Windows API. This API, available on Windows NT and MS-DOS, extends the 16-bit Windows API not only to use a 32-bit flat memory model but also to augment its operating system capabilities. The Win32 API adds features such as I/O, sophisticated memory management, object management, multithreaded processes, and security, as well as enhanced graphics and window management.

The Win32 subsystem is not entirely new. A team of developers took the window management code and the user interface code from Windows 3.0 and used as much of it as they could, discarding and rewriting those portions that could not be made robust, secure, preemptive, and so on. This team also incorporated Windows 3.1 features so that the user interface of Windows NT would be compatible with Windows 3.1. In contrast, the graphics portion of the Win32 subsystem is almost all new; a separate team redesigned the graphics engine from the ground up, writing it largely in C++.

The following subsections offer some general information about the Win32 API, outline the basic structure of the Win32 subsystem, and detail some of the ways in which the design of the Win32 subsystem differs from the design of the 16-bit Windows system.

5.3.1 32-Bit API

Microsoft put a lot of energy and resources into establishing Windows as its preeminent application development environment. In 1990, Steve Ballmer, then Senior Vice President of Microsoft's Systems division, began shouting his favorite new slogans to whomever would listen: "Windows, Windows, Windows!" and "Windows Everywhere!"[6] Although his exuberant humor always yielded a laugh at company meetings, his latter slogan has some notable implications. As Chapter 1, "The Mission," noted, Microsoft saw a need to create a high-end operating system that could exploit advances in hardware

---

6. Given his penchant for slogans, Ballmer was appropriately promoted to Executive Vice President in charge of Worldwide Sales and Support. After the promotion, he updated his slogan to "Windows, Windows, Windows for customers, customers, customers!"

technology. The Windows 3.0 API, which was designed for use on top of MS-DOS, was restricted in this regard. In order to become an advanced operating system environment, the Windows 3.0 API needed to evolve.

The Windows API needed to provide a complete and sophisticated application development environment, one not limited by old software technology or reliant on any particular hardware architecture. The API needed to support larger amounts of memory, a variety of processors, and multiprocessor computers, and create a secure environment for "you bet your business" applications.

Despite these ambitious goals, Microsoft's number-one priority in the evolution of the Windows API was the following: Make the new API compatible with the 16-bit Windows API in function names, semantics, and use of data types whenever possible. All Win32 API routines must provide an upwardly mobile path for the migration of existing 16-bit Windows applications to Windows NT.

With that goal firmly in mind, the Windows and Windows NT developers set about establishing the following additional goals for the new Windows API:

■ Change the API to use a 32-bit, linear memory architecture. The API should break its reliance on the segmented memory model established by the Intel *x*86 family of processors to free applications from the constraints of its 64-KB code and data limits and allow them to maximize their portability to RISC and other nonsegmented hardware platforms.

■ Make the 32-bit API the same on MS-DOS and on Windows NT so that developers can run their applications without modification on a broad range of computers, from the low end to the high end.

■ Make the application environment a secure one by instituting a virtual memory system in which each application runs in its own address space and by providing object protection mechanisms in the API.

■ Add advanced operating system capabilities to the API, such as multithreaded processes, API-based I/O capabilities, process synchronization, memory management, and national language (internationalization) support.

To create the new Win32 API, Microsoft developers and program managers took the Windows 3.0 API and modified it to meet the goals listed above.

Microsoft then recruited "guinea pigs" from both inside and outside the company to help hone the result for ease of use and ease of porting.

The Win32 subsystem makes the Win32 API available to applications on Windows NT. Because the NT executive's virtual memory system is based on a 32-bit, per-process, linear address space, applications that call the Win32 API incur less overhead than those using the 16-bit Windows API or the MS-DOS API. Therefore, Microsoft encourages programmers writing new applications to use the Win32 API, which is available on both Windows NT and on MS-DOS.

The Win32 API functions differ in several uniform ways from the same API functions provided in Windows 3.0. The biggest difference is that certain data structures, such as handles, pointers, and drawing coordinates, have been widened from 16 bits to 32 bits and are no longer based on a segmented view of memory. In cases in which the wider parameters would affect existing applications, the Win32 API adds a new function that parallels the capabilities of the existing function so that existing applications do not break and can migrate to the Win32 API over time. For example, integer parameters and pointers have been changed from a segment:offset format to a flat, 32-bit format, and coordinates used in drawing functions are 32 bits wide rather than 16 bits wide.

A whole new set of Win32 API routines provides advanced operating system capabilities, such as I/O, synchronization, memory management, security, and threads. Although designed to retain the feel of the old Windows API, the new services more or less directly export native NT services, making the power of NT available to Win32 programmers. And although many of these Win32 features were directly borrowed from the NT executive, they are also being re-created for MS-DOS. Certain advanced features, such as asynchronous I/O capabilities, are available only on Windows NT, however.

One new feature the Win32 API provides—security—pervades the interface. Win32 security was implemented by Jim Anderson, a developer whose varied software background includes, among other things, building quality-control computers for Ford Motor Company engine plants. The security features he developed for the Win32 subsystem are user-mode extensions to the security capabilities that Jim Kelly, Robert Reichel, and others designed into the NT executive's object architecture.

The Win32 subsystem implements object-based security in the same way the NT executive does; the Win32 subsystem protects shared Windows objects from unauthorized access by placing NT security descriptors on them. As in the NT executive, the first time an application tries to access a shared object, the Win32 subsystem verifies the application's right to do so. If the security check succeeds, the Win32 subsystem allows the application to proceed.

139

The Win32 subsystem implements object security on a number of shared objects, some of which were built on top of native NT objects. The Win32 objects include desktop objects, window objects, menu objects, and—as in the NT executive—files, processes, threads, and several synchronization objects.

Redesigning certain parts of the Windows graphical user interface for the Win32 subsystem (a topic described shortly) and adding security features to the Win32 API make the Win32 subsystems, as well as the NT executive, secure and robust.

5.3.2 Structure

The Win32 subsystem retains the basic structure of the 16-bit Windows system. It consists of the components shown in Figure 5-13.

The subsystem is divided into five modular pieces: the window manager, which handles input and manages the screen; the graphics device interface (GDI), which is a drawing library for graphics output devices; operating system functions; the console, which provides text window support; and the Win32 graphics device drivers.[7] Each component implements API routines that application programmers can use to create graphical applications. Together, these programming interfaces make up the Win32 API.

The window manager does the work that makes Windows NT look like Windows. The window manager controls windows on the screen, directs user

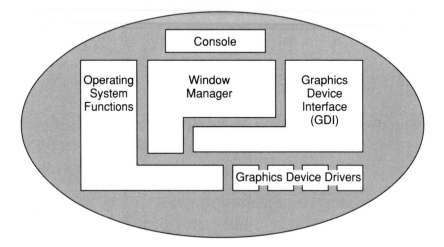

Figure 5-13. Win32 Subsystem

---

7. Each of these components resides in a separate DLL. The DLL for the window manager is called User32, and the DLL containing operating system functions is called Kernel32 (not to be confused with the NT kernel).

input to applications, establishes standard Windows objects, transfers data to and from the clipboard, and handles other visible and invisible tasks. It also provides API routines that let applications create graphical user interfaces. For example, it shields applications from dealing directly with devices by providing standard routines they can call to get information from input devices. The window manager also keeps track of the windows on the screen, their sizes, and their layering. When a user makes a window larger or smaller, for example, the window manager notifies the affected application. Similarly, it tells applications when they should repaint their windows, and when they do so, it repaints only the portions of the window that should be visible. The window manager also allows applications to cut information to the Clipboard and then places the information in the input stream of the application to which the user pastes it.

The GDI component of the Win32 subsystem provides a rich set of API routines for drawing lines, figures, symbols, and text on graphics output devices (such as the video display or a plotter) and for performing sophisticated graphics manipulations. The window manager calls these routines to draw windows and other symbols, and the console component calls them to draw text in a window, but applications can also call the GDI API routines directly. GDI, in turn, calls the graphics device drivers to display figures and text, and the graphics device drivers call NT device drivers to manipulate device hardware.

Like the console component, the operating system component of Win32 is largely new. It allows Win32 applications to perform full-featured I/O, manipulate operating system objects (in addition to graphical objects), synchronize their threads' execution with system events and with other applications, manage memory in a sophisticated way, share resources securely, and create multithreaded applications. These Win32 functions are based on features of the NT executive, and they call NT system services directly.

5.3.3 Design Changes

MS-DOS/Windows is a small, streamlined operating system environment. It was designed to run on personal computers that did not have large amounts of memory and certainly didn't have the fast processors Intel and RISC manufacturers are producing today. On the smaller computers in which every byte and every CPU cycle counts, it was not practical to make Windows a completely robust environment because doing so carries with it a certain cost in terms of code size and speed.

Windows NT, on the other hand, is designed as an operating system that can serve any number of networked users and that can run sophisticated banking or sensitive government applications. In such environments, it is not acceptable to allow one application to adversely affect others or to hang the operating system. Therefore, making the Win32 subsystem robust was an important goal.

To protect the operating system from applications, the Win32 window manager needed to operate a bit differently than did the original window manager. Led by Scott Ludwig, an 8-year veteran of Windows and Presentation Manager programming, the Window Manager team set about making the 32-bit version a more robust and reliable environment than was the 16-bit window manager. Some key changes include the following:

- Desynchronize the Windows input model
- Institute preemptive thread scheduling
- Add object-handle validation and object locking

The first change refers to how the Win32 subsystem handles user input, such as keystrokes and mouse clicks. The 16-bit window manager had a synchronous input model, which means that it placed all user input into a single queue (first in, first out) and parceled it out to applications as they requested it. After entering input, the user had to wait until the application processed it before any subsequent input he entered would be processed. Because only one application at a time could retrieve its input, each application had to retrieve input from the queue in a timely way in order for all applications to execute unhindered. Figure 5-14 illustrates the synchronous input model.

Using this model, things sometimes went wrong. Perhaps an application got in a muddled state and stopped retrieving input or perhaps it was too busy doing something else to get its input quickly. When this happened, other applications might stop because they couldn't get the input they needed to continue. To the user, the operating system appeared to hang.

The input model for the 16-bit window manager required significant redesign, but as a result, the robustness of the Win32 subsystem is greatly improved. In the new input model, designed by David Pehrson and Scott Ludwig, each application gets a private input queue, as shown in Figure 5-15 on page 144.

When a user enters input, the Win32 subsystem immediately determines which application the input is intended for (by checking which window is currently active or on which window the mouse cursor is positioned). The 32-bit window manager places the input in the correct application queue, and the application retrieves the input when it is ready. If the application stops retrieving its input for some reason, other applications are not affected.

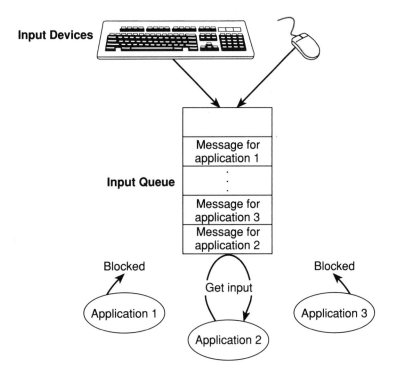

Input Devices

Input Queue

Message for application 1

:
:

Message for application 3

Message for application 2

Blocked

Blocked

Get input

Application 1

Application 2

Application 3

Figure 5-14. 16-Bit Windows Input Model

The Win32 subsystem's second major change from 16-bit Windows is full preemptive multitasking. In a robust operating system, it is unacceptable for one application to stop working with no way for the operating system to break into or terminate the application's execution. The 16-bit Windows system relies on applications to yield the processor occasionally so that other applications can run, something that doesn't always happen. In Windows NT, the Win32 subsystem (with crucial support from the NT kernel) forces applications to yield the processor. Each application thread is allowed to run only for the duration of its time quantum. The NT kernel then interrupts the thread and checks whether a higher priority thread should run.

With true preemption, the Win32 subsystem not only forces each application to yield the processor, but it can also force a Win32 application to terminate. For example, if an errant application hangs or if the user just doesn't want it around anymore, he can click on the End Task button in the Windows Task Manager. When running under the 16-bit Windows system, a poorly behaved application can prevent itself from being terminated or, in especially nasty cases, can even prevent the Task Manager from coming to the

Input Devices

Input Queues

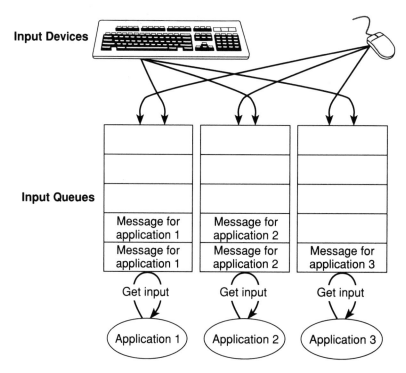

Message for application 1

Message for application 1

Message for application 2

Message for application 2

Message for application 3

Get input

Get input

Get input

Application 1

Application 2

Application 3

Figure 5-15. Win32 Input Model

foreground. In Windows NT, however, the Win32 subsystem calls the NT executive to force the application to terminate, and it always succeeds. Also, because the application thread is based on an NT thread object, the NT process manager sends a message to the termination port registered for the thread. The environment subsystem that is responsible for the application receives the message and cleans up any global information it was maintaining about the terminated application.

In addition to desynchronizing the input model and implementing preemption, the Win32 subsystem validates object handles. Object handles are sometimes a problem in the 16-bit Windows system because it assumes that applications always pass valid handles—that is, handles that actually point to the objects that Windows expects them to point to. If Windows expects a handle to a window and an application passes it something that doesn't point to a window, the Windows software can become disastrously confused.

The Win32 subsystem, in contrast, validates the handles that applications pass to it. It does so by examining the contents of the handles it receives. Like an NT object handle, a Win32 object handle is an index into a table. The handle and its corresponding table entry contain specific information about the object to which the handle refers. The Win32 subsystem can verify that the handle points to an object of the type the Win32 subsystem expects. It can even determine whether the handle points to the correct instance of the type. In addition to validating object handles, the Win32 subsystem implements a form of object retention similar to that in the NT executive. In the 16-bit Windows system, it's possible for an application to delete an object while the operating system is still using it, a situation that can lead to unpleasant system errors. The Win32 subsystem, however, maintains a reference count for the objects it needs. An application can still "delete" the object, but the subsystem won't remove the object from memory until the system has finished using it.

Win32's GDI component wasn't simply a revision of the 16-bit version—it was entirely rewritten. The new version was designed by Chuck Whitmer and written by a team of developers managed by Kent Diamond. The primary goals for the GDI component of the Win32 subsystem were to replace assembly language code with portable C code and to redesign the GDI's inner workings to support some advanced capabilities. The new GDI's features include Bézier curves, which give users of drawing packages fine-tuned control in drawing arcs; paths, which let users create arbitrarily shaped objects using sequences of drawing commands; object transformation, which lets applications map the contents of one coordinate space into another; and later, correlation, a way by which applications can easily determine whether one object or region overlaps another.

Another design change in Win32's GDI is the new device driver interface, which borrowed from the GDI team's collective experience with both the 16-bit Windows and the Presentation Manager graphics engines. This new interface improves upon both previous engines, giving Win32 graphics device drivers (which are responsible for creating device-specific images and sending them to output devices) a finer degree of control. For example, the GDI tailors the input it provides to a driver depending on what operations the driver understands. For example, if a particular driver understands Bézier curves, the GDI passes complete Bézier curves to it as input. If a driver doesn't understand Béziers, the GDI breaks the curve into simple line segments before sending it to the driver. In addition, the GDI incorporates powerful new functions for creating bitmap images, which video and printer drivers in particular can use in lieu of writing their own functions. With this support, it is easier for developers to get device drivers up and running quickly. Developers can rely on the GDI to do most of the work, adding only device-specific enhancements and optimizations to the device driver.

Despite all the improvements mentioned thus far, perhaps the biggest change in both the window manager and in the GDI was the implementation of Win32 as a protected subsystem, that is, as a server process. As described earlier in this chapter, the designers of each Windows NT environment subsystem divided their API routines into two groups: those routines that use only private data and those that use global data. The former subset can be implemented in the client-side DLL to optimize performance. The latter subset, however, must be implemented in the subsystem's address space so that global data is protected and yet is available to all clients of the subsystem. This change in design affects how one might choose to write a Win32 application, particularly when calling GDI functions.

Although the GDI regards virtually all data as private to a client process, when drawing objects, all the processes share their output device—the screen. The screen, then, is effectively "global data," and GDI functions that change the state of the screen must be implemented in the Win32 server instead of in the client-side DLL. To achieve maximum performance for these functions, the GDI component implements several optimizations. For example, to change the colors on the screen, a Win32 application might call a GDI function to set the foreground color, call again to set the background color, and then perform several other operations before drawing anything on the screen. Instead of calling the subsystem once for each of these GDI functions, the client-side DLL stores the changed information in a buffer. When the application draws something on the screen, the DLL sends all the changed data to the subsystem in a single message. In the present example, the subsystem would update the screen colors in the DLL, waiting to send the color changes to the server until it draws its first line. *Attribute caching*, as this buffering technique is called, minimizes the number of context switches and the time spent passing messages between the client and the subsystem.

The GDI uses a similar optimization, called *batching*, to minimize context switching between the client and the server. Batching is a technique in which, for example, the GDI DLL stores multiple function calls in a queue, sending them to the server in a single message when the queue gets full or when the user enters input. When the Win32 server receives the message, it executes the functions in sequence before returning control to the client. Before implementing this technique, the GDI developers tested it to be sure that screen output would not appear jumpy or intermittent. Their testing indicated that function calls are sent to the server frequently enough that output appears smooth and measured.

Application writers must keep these performance optimizations in mind when writing new multithreaded Win32 applications. If two threads are working together, they must synchronize their execution to be sure that their operations execute in the proper order. For example, they must be aware that simply because a thread has called an API function doesn't mean that the result is visible on the screen immediately. The function call might be stored in the thread's buffer, waiting to be flushed to the screen. GDI provides the GdiFlush() function to let threads force cached function calls to be sent to the Win32 server.

Another effect of the client/server model is that applications that repeatedly manipulate and redraw large bitmaps can perform poorly compared to device-independent figures drawn using GDI calls. Because each object or bitmap is private to the client application, it must be sent in a message to the server each time the screen is updated. To maintain optimum performance, applications should either redraw only the modified portions of a bitmap image, if possible, or rely on GDI functions to draw all images, taking advantage of the GDI's caching and batching techniques to optimize performance. The new Win32 GDI API is better equipped than the 16-bit Windows GDI API to provide all the drawing capabilities sophisticated applications require.

5.4 MS-DOS and the 16-Bit Windows API

One of the first thoughts a potential Windows NT user is likely to have is, "Well, the high-end features are nice, but will Windows NT run my favorite MS-DOS and Windows applications?" It's an important question, given the investment that most users have in existing applications. Clearly, the bulk of potential Windows NT users depend heavily on MS-DOS and 16-bit Windows applications and will continue to do so for a long time. Supporting these users was an important consideration in Windows NT's development.

Fortunately, Windows NT's client/server model can easily accommodate multiple application execution environments. Including an MS-DOS environment and a 16-bit Windows environment involved complicated and detailed work, but it didn't change the design of the operating system.

Matthew Felton, who has an extensive MS-DOS background and who worked previously on OS/2's MS-DOS compatibility environment, led the team that created the MS-DOS and 16-bit Windows subsystems on Windows NT. The two projects are closely related and shared a set of broad goals:

- Allow users to easily migrate from MS-DOS or 16-bit Windows to Windows NT

- Run all major MS-DOS and 16-bit Windows applications while protecting the rest of the operating system from them

147

- Maintain binary compatibility for applications between CISC and RISC hardware platforms

- Allow 16-bit Windows applications to run as peers of 32-bit Windows applications

On MS-DOS, Windows is a sophisticated graphical application that extends the capabilities of the underlying operating system. On Windows NT, both MS-DOS and 16-bit Windows are applications: They are environment subsystems that call the Win32 API and occasionally native NT services. Figure 5-16 illustrates how MS-DOS and 16-bit Windows fit into Windows NT's system structure.

The MS-DOS and the 16-bit Windows subsystems run in user mode in the same way that other environment subsystems do. However, unlike the Win32, OS/2, and POSIX subsystems, they are not server processes, per se. MS-DOS applications run within the context of a process called a *virtual DOS machine* (VDM). A VDM is a Win32 application that establishes a complete virtual computer running MS-DOS. For example, it allows MS-DOS applications to issue machine instructions, to call the BIOS, to directly access certain devices, and to receive interrupts. Any number of VDM processes can run at the same time, each within a separate console window.

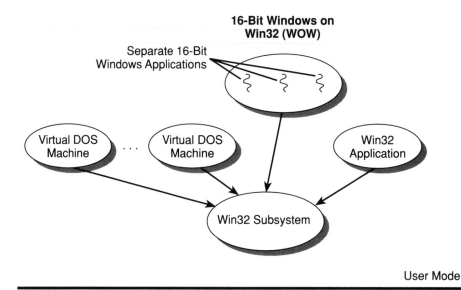

Figure 5-16. MS-DOS and 16-Bit Windows Subsystems

The 16-bit Windows environment is a hybrid application, one that runs within the address space of a VDM process. It calls the Win32 API to do most of its work but occasionally calls NT services as well. The developers of the 16-bit Windows environment refer to it as *WOW*, which is short for *Windows On Win32*.

Creating MS-DOS and the 16-bit Windows environments as user-mode subsystems gives them the same code and data protection that the other subsystems have. It protects the NT executive from problems that might occur in the environments because they can access the NT executive only by calling system services. This strategy also protects the MS-DOS applications from the 16-bit Windows applications and vice versa, and it partitions their address spaces from those of the 32-bit Windows applications.

5.4.1 Virtual DOS Machines (VDMs)

A VDM is an MS-DOS session created whenever a user starts an MS-DOS application on Windows NT. Windows NT allows any number of MS-DOS applications to run simultaneously, and they can pass textual data to each other and to Windows applications via the Clipboard.

It is a tricky endeavor to run MS-DOS applications on Windows NT because they are, naturally, written in assembly language, and they assume that they have free access to memory, devices, and so forth. In a full-fledged, multiuser operating system, MS-DOS applications can't have free rein, but they must be allowed to run as if they do. Sudeep Bharati and Dave Hastings, VDM's primary developers, accomplished this subterfuge by placing each MS-DOS application in its own process—the VDM—with a private virtual address space containing all the MS-DOS code and the MS-DOS drivers that the application needs to run.[8] Within its virtual address space, the application can do what it likes. The NT executive's virtual memory (VM) manager controls the physical memory usage of the application and ensures that it doesn't overrun other processes.

When a user clicks on the MS-DOS icon (or on an MS-DOS application icon), the Win32 subsystem starts Windows NT's command shell in a console window. The command shell departs from the OS/2 model of executing 32-bit commands in one shell and MS-DOS commands in another. Although it

---

8. Windows NT's initial MS-DOS environment uses MS-DOS 5.0 source code and is therefore compatible with MS-DOS 5.0. It is also compatible with LIM-EMS 4.0, DPMI .9, and XMS 3.0. VCPI is supported on the MIPS processors but not on the Intel x86 processors. Windows NT's MS-DOS environment also does not support applications that write directly to the hard disk or floppy disk, as doing so would compromise the integrity of the file system.

looks like the MS-DOS command shell, it is equally capable of executing 32-bit Windows NT commands and 16-bit MS-DOS commands within the same console window, even piping output between the command-line applications. When the user enters a command, the command shell simply calls the Win32 CreateProcess( ) routine to execute the image. If the command is an MS-DOS image, the Win32 subsystem starts a VDM process, which loads the MS-DOS application into the VDM's virtual address space and executes it. When the MS-DOS application generates output, the VDM calls Win32 console routines to display the output in its console window.

As it runs, an MS-DOS application must have access to the MS-DOS operating system, or at least to something that looks and works like MS-DOS. A VDM is, in essence, a virtual MS-DOS operating system running on a virtual, Intel x86-based computer. Figure 5-17 shows the layout of the VDM's virtual address space on Intel x86-based machines.[9]

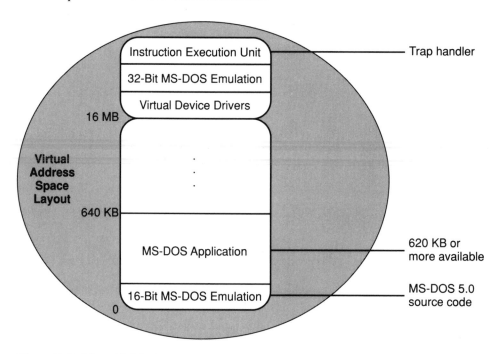

Figure 5-17. Virtual DOS Machine (VDM)

9. The memory layout and contents are roughly the same on the MIPS platforms with the instruction execution unit replaced. On the MIPS-based platform, the instruction execution unit emulates Intel instructions using MIPS processor instructions. Insignia Solutions, Ltd., created this code as well as the virtual device drivers shown in Figure 5-17. Insignia's virtual device drivers are used on both the Intel and MIPS platforms for compatibility.

The 16-bit MS-DOS emulation is derived from MS-DOS 5.0 source code minus file system support. It resides in the lowest portion of the VDM's virtual address space, with the MS-DOS application directly above it. The application has access to at least 620 KB of memory.

Although the code below the 16-MB boundary is based on 16-bit segmented addresses, the code above this boundary is written with 32-bit flat addresses, Windows NT's format. The 32-bit portion of the VDM's address space is sophisticated. It includes a collection of virtual device drivers and 32-bit MS-DOS emulation code that is the same across different processor architectures. The *instruction execution unit* is a processor-dependent block of code. The Intel *x*86 version, written by Microsoft's Dave Hastings, acts as a trap handler (see Chapter 7, "The Kernel"), capturing instructions that cause hardware traps and transferring control to the code that handles them, such as the virtual device drivers. On the MIPS processors, this code is an instruction emulator, converting *x*86 instructions to MIPS instructions.

The virtual device drivers act as a layer between MS-DOS applications and the hardware attached to the Windows NT machine. In its first release, the VDM environment provides virtual device drivers for standard PC devices, including the mouse, keyboard, printer and COM ports, and so on. The 32-bit VDM code handles MS-DOS I/O operations by trapping them and calling either Win32 API functions or the NT executive to carry out the I/O. For example, the VDM processes COM port requests by opening the COM device driver and sending it I/O control codes (IOCTLs). To update the video, a thread within the VDM periodically examines the video RAM in which the MS-DOS application is writing and calls the Win32 console APIs to update the screen pixels that have changed.

Although many MS-DOS sessions can run at once, their memory usage remains relatively low. The first 640 KB of virtual memory in each process, plus any memory the process uses up to the 16-MB boundary, is unique and not shared among VDMs. Above the boundary, however, the NT executive's VM manager shares one copy of the 32-bit code among all VDM processes. Furthermore, because VDMs are simply user-mode processes, they are entirely pageable. This means that NT's VM manager loads into physical memory only those portions of the MS-DOS 5.0 code and the MS-DOS application code that the application uses, as it uses them. It also temporarily transfers the applications' memory contents to disk if memory usage on the system is high. (See Chapter 6, "The Virtual Memory Manager," for more information about virtual memory management.)

MS-DOS applications are not multitasking because each application assumes it is the only one running on an MS-DOS machine. However, NT's kernel component treats an MS-DOS thread like any other thread. When the thread's time quantum expires, the kernel interrupts it and context switches to another thread, rescheduling the MS-DOS thread later. Because some MS-DOS applications simply sit in a tight loop checking for keyboard input (and hogging CPU cycles), the VDM environment detects this idle state and, when it occurs, gives other waiting threads higher scheduling priority.

5.4.2 Windows on Win32 (WOW)

One of the primary goals for the 16-bit Windows environment (WOW) was to make no user-visible distinctions between 16-bit and 32-bit Windows applications. Users start 16-bit applications in the same way they start Win32 applications. Both types of applications run simultaneously, indistinguishable from one another.

Although 16-bit and 32-bit applications look the same to a user, they actually run under the control of different parts of the operating system. The WOW environment, designed and implemented by Jeff Parsons, Matthew Felton, Chandan Chauhan, and Ramakrishna Nanduri is essentially a multithreaded VDM, each of whose threads executes a 16-bit Windows application. Running the applications within a single virtual address space mimics the normal behavior of 16-bit Windows, in which all applications are single-threaded and reside within the same address space. The WOW environment calls the Win32 API to create and manage on-screen windows for each of its 16-bit applications. With regard to user input, the WOW environment is treated as a single Win32 application, as shown in Figure 5-18.

Like an MS-DOS application, the first time the user starts a 16-bit Windows application, the Win32 subsystem detects that the executable image runs on MS-DOS, and it starts a VDM process. Once started, the VDM loads the WOW environment. The virtual address space for the WOW VDM is shown in Figure 5-19 on page 154.

The address space of the WOW subsystem is structured similarly to that of an MS-DOS application process. The same MS-DOS code resides in the lowest portion of WOW's address space, with the Windows 3.1 kernel code above it. The kernel code, with its multitasking support removed, handles Windows 3.1 memory management functions and loads executable images and dynamic-link libraries for the 16-bit Windows applications. Above that code lie the window manager and the GDI stub routines, and the 16-bit Windows applications reside above the stub routines. Any number of applications can run there, their code and data paged into memory by NT's VM manager as the applications access it.

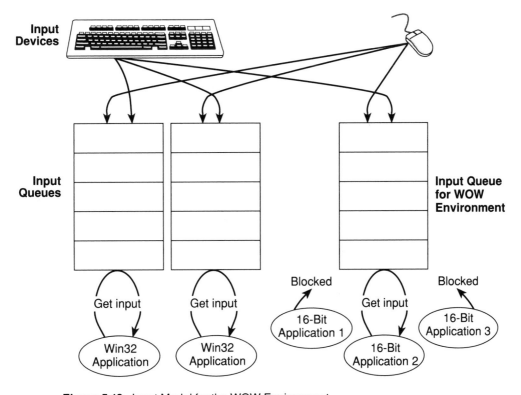

Figure 5-18. Input Model for the WOW Environment

In the WOW subsystem, 16-bit Windows multitasking code is replaced by WOW code, by calls to the Win32 API, and by the NT executive's multitasking code. Once the WOW environment is running, the Win32 subsystem sends it a message each time the user starts a 16-bit application. WOW responds by loading the application into memory and calling the Win32 CreateThread() API routine to create a thread to run the application. Although all other threads are scheduled preemptively in Windows NT, the Win32 subsystem schedules WOW threads nonpreemptively to make the WOW environment compatible with 16-bit Windows. This does not mean that WOW threads are allowed to run as long as they want. The NT kernel still interrupts a WOW thread's execution to let non-WOW threads in the system run. However, when it switches back to WOW, the kernel selects only the interrupted WOW thread to continue; all other WOW threads remain blocked until the current one yields the processor. This behavior parallels the nonpreemptive multitasking that Windows 3.*x* applications expect, without affecting Win32 or other applications running on Windows NT.

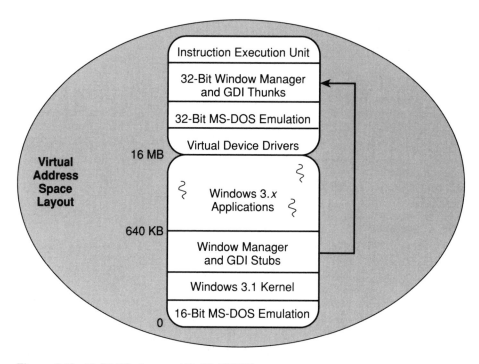

Figure 5-19. 16-Bit Windows on Win32 (WOW)

Above the 16 MB boundary in the WOW subsystem's address space is the same code found in the MS-DOS application processes: the virtual MS-DOS device drivers, 32-bit MS-DOS emulation, and the hardware-dependent instruction execution unit. In addition, there is a block of 32-bit window manager and GDI code, which mirrors the 16-bit code in the lower portion of the address space. This 32-bit code is responsible for translating 16-bit segmented addresses into 32-bit flat addresses. For example, when a 16-bit Windows application calls the window manager or the GDI functions, the 16-bit stubs shown in Figure 5-19 call equivalent 32-bit API functions in the high portion of the WOW subsystem's address space. The 32-bit window manager and GDI code takes the 16-bit addresses supplied by the application and modifies (or "thunks") them to conform to the 32-bit flat addressing model. It then calls the Win32 API to carry out the operation. When the Win32 subsystem returns its results, the 32-bit WOW code thunks the 32-bit addresses back to 16-bit segmented addresses and returns the results to the application. Because the 16-bit API is not really implemented in WOW, any 16-bit Windows applications that rely on the internal structure of the 16-bit window manager or GDI are not guaranteed to work on Windows NT.

5.5 Message Passing with the Local Procedure Call (LPC) Facility

In Windows NT's client/server model, much hinges on the success of the local procedure call (LPC) facility. Although, ironically, each subsystem does its best not to send LPC messages (see Section 5.1.2), the subsystems must do so upon occasion.

When two threads exist within the same process, they share an address space and can communicate and pass data easily. They use simple synchronization mechanisms to access data in the proper sequence. When two threads are in different processes, however, they must bridge the gap between their separate virtual address spaces by copying data from one address space into another or by creating a region of shared memory that is visible in both address spaces. LPC is a message-passing facility provided by the NT executive. It is used in the latter situation—that is, between two processes, a client and a protected subsystem (server), located on the same computer. The design of the LPC facility mimics the procedure-call model used by the industry-standard, remote procedure call (RPC) facility, which is used for passing messages between client and server processes on different computers. In the RPC facility, the application sending the message does not know it is passing a message; it simply calls an API routine that resembles any other API routine. A stub procedure repackages the parameters to the routine and calls the RPC facility to send them to a remote server. Results are returned through the same channel. (See Chapter 9, "Networking," for more information.)

Windows NT's LPC facility works like the RPC facility but is optimized for two processes running on the same Windows NT system. An application calls an API routine in a DLL to which it is linked, and the DLL does the work necessary to send the message to a Windows NT protected subsystem. Although the RPC facility is a general mechanism used on different types of operating systems, the LPC facility is specific to Windows NT and therefore takes advantage of Windows NT features to make it faster and more efficient than a generalized RPC facility.[10]

---

10. The LPC facility is not available directly to Win32 applications on Windows NT, but the RPC facility is available. Based on the machine's configuration, RPC will use LPC for passing messages locally and will use named pipes for passing messages between computers. Win32 applications can use named pipes or RPC.

The NT executive's LPC facility supplies three different ways to pass messages, each designed for a different situation:

- Sending a message to a port object, which is associated with a server process

- Sending a message pointer to a server's port and passing the message in shared memory

- Passing a message to a particular server thread through a dedicated shared memory region

In addition, the LPC facility supplies a sophisticated *callback* mechanism that allows a server to reply to a message by requesting more information from the client.[11]

The following subsection examines how a client process establishes a connection with a server process by using a port object. The subsequent subsection examines the different types of LPC message passing and LPC callbacks in more detail.

5.5.1 Port Object

In all forms of LPC message passing, a client process must establish a communication channel with a protected subsystem before it can send a message to the subsystem. The NT executive, like the Mach operating system, uses a port object as its means for establishing and, in most cases, maintaining a connection between two processes.

Any number of clients can call a protected subsystem, and ultimately, each needs a secure and private communication channel. To accommodate this need, the NT executive implements two types of ports. They are structurally equivalent but differ in their common names and in how NT uses them. One type of port is called a *connection port*, and it gives client applications a place to call to set up a communication channel with the server. Connection port objects have names, which makes them visible to all NT processes. Figure 5-20 illustrates, step by step, how a client process initiates contact with a protected subsystem and how subsequent messages are transmitted.

To initiate contact with a protected subsystem, a client process opens a handle to the protected subsystem's connection port object and then sends it

---

11. Callbacks in the NT executive's LPC facility should not be confused with callback procedures in Windows applications.

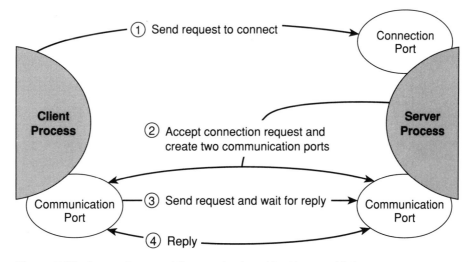

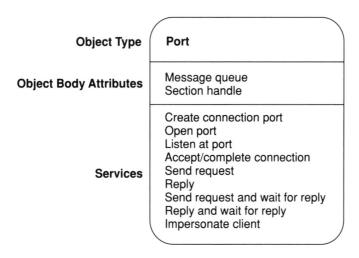

Figure 5-20. Connecting to and Communicating with a Protected Subsystem

a connection request. The server, which has one or more threads waiting to receive such requests, responds by creating two unnamed (and therefore private) communication port objects, keeping one handle and returning the other handle to the client. The client uses its communication port handle to send subsequent messages or callbacks to the protected subsystem and to listen for replies from the subsystem. The subsystem uses its handle in the same way to communicate with the client.

Figure 5-21 summarizes the attributes and native NT services for manipulating port objects.

Object Type	Port
Object Body Attributes	Message queue Section handle
Services	Create connection port Open port Listen at port Accept/complete connection Send request Reply Send request and wait for reply Reply and wait for reply Impersonate client

Figure 5-21. Port Object

Handles to port objects, unlike most other NT object handles, cannot be inherited by a newly created process. If inheritance were allowed, the server would need to figure out which process was calling it each time it received a message. By disallowing inheritance, the server always knows which process is calling it on a particular channel, the server's processing overhead is thus reduced, and clients get faster service.

5.5.2 Types of LPC Message Passing

When a client process establishes a communication channel with a protected subsystem, it specifies which of three types of LPC message-passing techniques it wants to use:

- Passing messages into the port object's message queue is a technique used for small messages.

- Passing messages through a shared memory object is a technique used for larger messages.

- Quick LPC is used exclusively by portions of the Win32 subsystem to achieve minimum overhead and maximum speed.

These three forms of message passing and the callback mechanism are the topics of the following subsections.

5.5.2.1 Copying a Message to a Port

The first and most common form of message passing bridges the address spaces of the client and the protected subsystem by copying a client's message to an intermediary location and then copying it into the subsystem's address space. The intermediary location it uses is a message queue in the communication port object.

As Figure 5-21 showed, each port object contains a queue of fixed-size message blocks. (Connection port objects contain a queue for connection requests, and communication port objects contain a queue for service requests.) When a client sends a message, the LPC facility copies it into one of the message blocks in the subsystem's port object. After the NT kernel context switches from the client to the subsystem process, a subsystem thread copies the message into the subsystem's address space and processes it. When the subsystem is ready to reply, it sends a message back to the client's communication port, as shown in Figure 5-22.

At any given time, the NT executive has access to either the client's address space or the subsystem's address space, but not both. However, like other

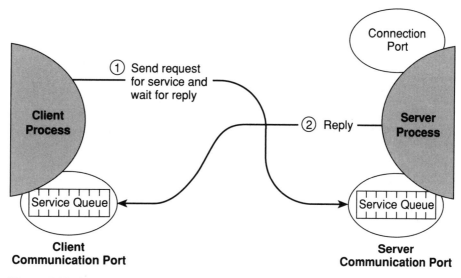

Figure 5-22. Message-Copying LPC

objects, port objects are stored in system memory, so access to the message is not lost when the NT kernel context switches from the client process to the subsystem process.

When creating a port object, the LPC facility allocates memory for it from nonpaged pool, that is, system memory that is always resident. Because nonpaged pool is a finite system resource, the message blocks in a port object are necessarily limited both in size and in number. The size of a message block is 256 bytes, enough room to send most ordinary messages.

5.5.2.2 Passing a Message in Shared Memory

When a client needs to pass messages that are greater than 256 bytes in size, it cannot copy them to the server port's message queue. Instead, it must pass them through shared memory objects, whose size is limited only by the client's resource quota limits.

To pass messages by using shared memory, the client creates a shared memory object, called a *section object.* A section object (described in more detail in Chapter 6, "The Virtual Memory Manager") is a block of shared memory that the LPC facility makes visible in the address spaces of both the client and the protected subsystem.[12] To send a large message, the client

---

12. The LPC facility calls the VM manager to double-map the section object into both address spaces. To accomplish this, the VM manager uses virtual address aliasing, a capability that the processor must provide.

places it in the section object and then sends to the server's port a small message containing a pointer and size information about the larger message. After the NT kernel context switches to the subsystem process, the subsystem retrieves the information from the message block and then uses it to find the message in the section object, as Figure 5-23 illustrates.

Note that a client must decide when it first establishes a communication channel whether its messages will be large or small. If it expects them to be small, it doesn't ask for a section object, but if it expects at least one of its messages to be large, it requests the section object. As the figure shows, the section object is associated with the client's communication port. If the subsystem also expects its reply messages to be large, it can create a section object associated with its own communication port in which it stores the large replies when transmitting them back to the client.

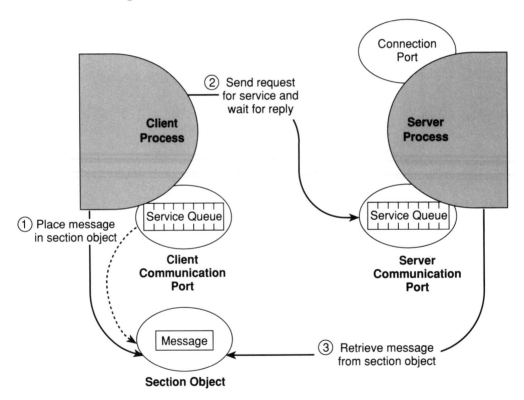

Figure 5-23. Shared Memory LPC

Using a section object means that the client must do a bit of extra work. The LPC facility does not assume any particular format for the section object, for example, so the client must manage the section object's memory itself, telling the subsystem the size of the last message and where it is stored within the section object. This bit of memory management makes passing messages via shared memory a little more complicated for the client than using the port object directly. However, it allows large messages to be accommodated without having to copy them multiple times. Copying a large amount of data from one address space to another can be a slow operation, and using shared memory avoids this processing overhead.

5.5.2.3 Callbacks

Under normal circumstances, a subsystem has several, possibly many, communication ports. Each one serves as a communication channel for one client process. To service the requests it receives on its various communication ports, the subsystem generally creates a pool of threads that wait to receive requests and process them; any of the subsystem threads can reply to any request. This gives the subsystem great flexibility but requires the LPC facility to maintain a careful scheme for identifying client callers and their messages so that it can reply to the correct client at the correct communication port.

To keep track of which client sent which message, each message contains the calling thread's client ID (an attribute of every thread object) and a serial number that the LPC facility assigns to each message. When the subsystem replies to a message, it records in its reply the client ID of the thread the reply is intended for and the serial number of the message to which it is replying. The LPC facility then verifies that a client with that client ID is waiting for a reply to that message number. If not, the LPC facility returns an error.

Sometimes, the subsystem might not be able to send a reply immediately. It might need to request more information from the client. The LPC facility provides a callback mechanism to accommodate this situation. Figure 5-24 on the next page illustrates a typical exchange. (Step 2 is the callback message.)

Typically a client sends a request and then waits for a reply. If the client supports callbacks, however, it can handle getting a request from the subsystem when it is expecting a reply. Using native LPC routines, the client can respond to the request and then continue waiting for the original reply.

Message-passing facilities on many operating systems do not have the NT executive's flexibility in the implementation of callbacks. For example, NT's LPC callback mechanism is completely symmetrical. Both the client and the server can issue callbacks to the other. Moreover, the LPC facility allows an arbitrary number of outstanding callbacks to exist at one time. In step 3 in Figure 5-24, for example, instead of replying to the server's callback, the

161

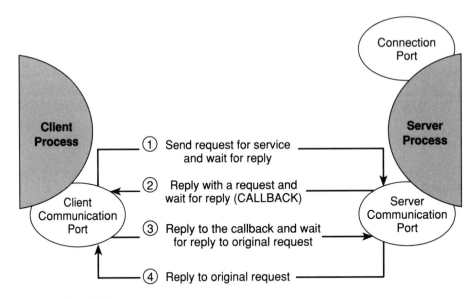

Figure 5-24. Callbacks

client could have requested more information from the server regarding the server's callback. If so, the client would send a callback to the server and then wait for both a reply to its callback and a reply to its original request. In other words, step 2 can be repeated any number of times by either the client or the server, and the unresolved callbacks would "stack up" on both sides. One by one, each callback would be resolved by a reply until all the callbacks are resolved on both sides. When this happens, the server finally sends a reply to the client's original request, and the message exchange ends.

5.5.2.4 Quick LPC

As you might imagine, Win32 is a high-use subsystem. Because it interacts with all applications running on Windows NT, it is likely to have many callers at any given time. Because of the subsystem's potential to be a performance bottleneck, its developers, along with Mark Lucovsky and Steve Wood, implemented *quick LPC*, an optimized form of LPC message passing for use by the Win32 subsystem. The Win32 subsystem's window manager and GDI component use quick LPC to minimize the time required for a round-trip LPC call from a client to the Win32 server.

Much of the overhead involved in using LPC message passing is in opening a handle to a port object and copying messages to and from the message queue. Even when a client uses shared-memory LPC, it sends a message to the message queue, which must be copied to the subsystem's address space.

In quick LPC, a client thread sends a message to the server's connection port to establish contact, indicating that it wishes to use quick LPC message passing to communicate. In response, the server creates three resources for the client:

- A dedicated server thread to handle this and subsequent requests
- 64 KB of shared memory (a section object) for passing messages
- An event pair object

Thereafter, the client and server threads using quick LPC bypass ports altogether and pass their messages via shared memory. The event pair object, which contains one event for the client thread and one event for the server thread, provides an implicit synchronization mechanism. The client, for example, places a message in the section object and then sets the server's event while simultaneously waiting on its own event. The NT kernel awakens the dedicated server thread, and because the thread's only job is to service this one client thread, it knows immediately where to look for the message. When the server thread finishes processing the message, it sets the client's event and simultaneously waits on its own event. The communication continues in this way until the quick LPC connection is closed.

By eliminating the overhead of using the port object and the overhead of copying messages between the two processes' address spaces, quick LPC gives the Win32 subsystem a boost in performance. In addition, because a dedicated server thread is created to service every client thread, the subsystem avoids figuring out which client thread is calling it each time it receives a message. Using quick LPC, context switching from the client to the subsystem (or vice versa) becomes the delimiting factor in the performance of the message passing. And the NT kernel minimizes even this by giving these threads preference in scheduling.

So why limit the use of quick LPC message passing to the Win32 subsystem? If it's so fast, why not use this method for all forms of message passing on Windows NT? The answer is that quick LPC trades one type of system overhead for another. What it gains in speed, it loses in resource usage. Instead of maintaining a pool of threads, each of which can respond to numerous clients, quick LPC requires the subsystem to create a server thread for each client thread that calls it. Not only does this consume system memory (some of it nonpaged resident memory), but these dedicated threads spend half of their time waiting to be awakened by the client. Another resource cost is the use of the section object. In ordinary LPC, each process can create a section

163

object for passing messages. If more than one thread in the process passes messages, the threads share a section object. In quick LPC, each thread has its own section object.

Some of these resource costs are mitigated by the fact that thread stacks and the section object memory are pageable and can be transferred to disk when memory usage is high. However, it would not be practical to use quick LPC for all message passing. Quick LPC is used only by the Window Manager and GDI components of the Win32 subsystem. The console and operating system components, as well as all other Windows NT subsystems, use normal LPC.

5.6   In Conclusion

The client/server model is a fundamental part of Windows NT's design, affecting not only how the system works, but also how applications run. It was originally selected for its flexibility in providing OS/2 and POSIX APIs within the same operating system but became the basis for the Win32 protected subsystem as well. Using the client/server model, MS-DOS and 16-bit Windows applications coexist peacefully with Win32, OS/2, and POSIX applications, and all applications can pass data to one another via the Clipboard. The client/server model also protects the different applications from one another and the protected subsystems from applications.

This chapter examined how Windows NT appears to users and to application programs. The next chapter takes a step downward, back into the fundamental workings of the NT executive and, specifically, its VM manager. Although different environment subsystems present whatever view of memory their applications expect, underneath the subsystems lies the NT executive's virtual memory system. The VM manager, the NT component that keeps all the applications and protected subsystems from bumping into each other, is the subject of the next chapter.

CHAPTER SIX

THE VIRTUAL
MEMORY MANAGER

At one time, computers were single-process, single-thread systems. Programmers, both experienced and aspiring, had to reserve time to work from the computer's one console. The programmer *was* the operating system, responsible for manually loading a program into memory using switches, paper tape, or keypunched cards. Once a program was loaded, the programmer entered a starting address and directed the processor to jump to it and begin executing. Loading and executing more than one program at a time was not possible. Needless to say, the processor sat idle much of the time.

In operating system technology, advancement has meant finding ways to keep the processor busy more of the time and, thus, get more work done. Multitasking systems load multiple programs into memory and keep the processor busy by switching among them. How the operating system distributes the available memory among processes while protecting the code and data of one process from the other processes is the subject of memory management, and in the case of Windows NT, *virtual memory management.*

In the early days of computing, it was not possible to execute a program that was bigger than the computer's physical memory. Later, programmers began writing overlays, programs that swap portions of their code to disk and load other parts of the program into memory. When the code on disk was needed, the program would load it back into memory, overlaying code that was not in use. Aside from being tedious to program and difficult to maintain and update, overlays required each application to recreate the code that swapped memory contents to disk.

Virtual memory (VM), first implemented in 1959,[1] took the onus of memory management off the programmer and placed it on the operating system. VM is a centralized system for swapping memory contents to disk when memory gets full. It allows programmers to create and run programs that require more memory than is present on their computers, and it has become the standard memory management technique for all but the simplest operating systems.

The NT executive's virtual memory component, the *VM manager,* is the native memory management system for Windows NT. Any memory management capabilities an environment subsystem provides are based on NT's VM manager. The VM manager was designed and implemented by Lou Perazzoli, who also served as the engineering manager and project leader for NT. Together with other team members, Lou established the following goals for the VM manager:

- Make it as portable as possible.

- Make it work reliably and efficiently on all sizes of applications without requiring system tuning by a user or an administrator.

- Provide modern memory management features, such as mapped files, copy-on-write memory, and support for applications using large, possibly sparse, address spaces.

- Allow processes to allocate and manage private memory.

- Provide mechanisms that support environment subsystems, such as allowing a subsystem (with the proper access rights) to manage the virtual memory of a client process.

- Balance the needs of multiprocessing with the speed of memory access. (For example, protecting data structures using multiple levels of locking can increase parallelism in the VM manager, but each lock creates additional overhead.)

The next section begins with an introduction to virtual memory systems. Following that is an examination of NT's version of virtual memory—the VM manager—and additional features and services the VM manager

---

1. The Atlas computer, developed at Manchester University around 1959, provided virtual memory. However, the concept did not become popular until at least a decade later with the creation of the Multics operating system.

provides to environment subsystems. A description of the VM manager's implementation follows, including coverage of key data structures and algorithms.

6.1 Virtual Memory

Memory has several characteristics: a physical structure, a logical structure, and the manner in which the operating system translates (or doesn't translate) from one structure to the other.

Physical memory is organized as a series of 1-byte storage units. Bytes are numbered starting with 0 and extending to the amount of memory available in the system configuration (minus 1), as shown in Figure 6-1. This set of numbers (shown here in hexadecimal form) comprises the physical address space of the machine.[2]

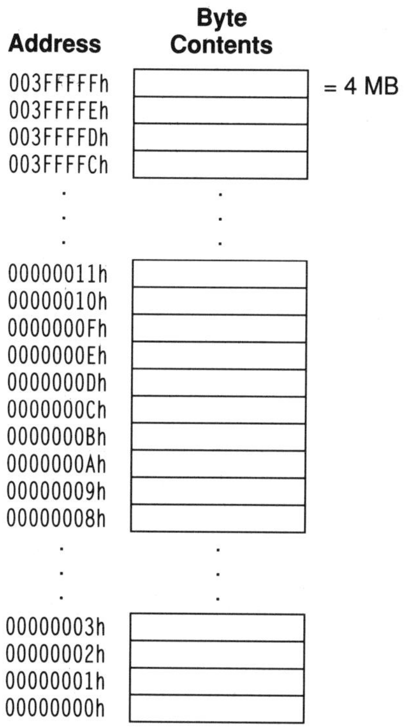

Address	Byte Contents	
003FFFFFh		= 4 MB
003FFFFEh		
003FFFFDh		
003FFFFCh		
.	.	
.	.	
.	.	
00000011h		
00000010h		
0000000Fh		
0000000Eh		
0000000Dh		
0000000Ch		
0000000Bh		
0000000Ah		
00000009h		
00000008h		
.	.	
.	.	
.	.	
00000003h		
00000002h		
00000001h		
00000000h		

Figure 6-1. Physical Address Space

---

2. Word-oriented machines also exist, but this chapter is concerned only with byte-oriented machines.

167

Logical memory, more commonly called *virtual memory,* is the way in which a program views memory, and in modern operating systems it rarely corresponds to the physical memory structure. Virtual memory systems usually adopt either a segmented view or a linear view of memory. All early personal computers based on Intel chips, from the Intel 8086 through the 80286, use a segmented model. A segmented addressing system divides physical memory into units of (usually) contiguous addresses, called segments. A typical address includes the segment number and an offset within the segment.

In contrast, most RISC processors, and even the recent CISC processors from Intel, support a linear addressing architecture. Linear addressing coincides more closely with the actual physical structure of memory than does segmented addressing. Addresses in a linear scheme begin at 0 and extend, byte by byte, to the uppermost boundary of the address space.

A *virtual address space* is the set of memory addresses available for a process's threads to use. Every process has a unique virtual address space that is generally much larger than physical memory. Although the number of physical addresses on a particular computer is limited by how much memory the computer has (with each byte claiming a unique address), the number of virtual addresses is limited only by the number of bits in a virtual address. Each bit can be either turned on or turned off; thus, for example, the MIPS R4000 processor, which has 32-bit addresses,[3] boasts a virtual address space of 2^{32}, or four billion bytes (4 gigabytes), as illustrated in Figure 6-2.

The discrepancy between a physical address space and a virtual address space necessitates the two tasks of a virtual memory system:

■ To translate, or *map,* a subset of each process's virtual addresses into physical memory locations. When a thread reads or writes its virtual address space, the virtual memory system (some of which can be implemented in hardware) uses the virtual address to find the correct physical address before transferring data.

■ To swap some of the contents of memory to disk when memory becomes overcommitted—that is, when threads in the system try to use more memory than is physically available.

---

3. The MIPS R4000 actually provides 64-bit addresses but allows an operating system to use either 32-bit or 64-bit addresses. The first version of Windows NT uses 32-bit addresses for compatibility with the Intel 386.

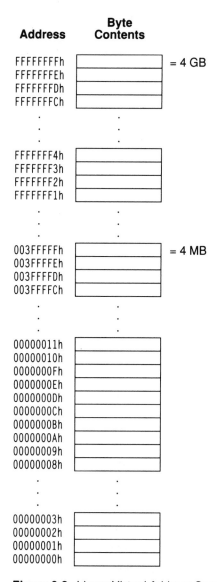

Figure 6-2. Linear Virtual Address Space

The first task, mapping virtual addresses to physical addresses, allows a program to be easily relocated in memory as it is executing. The virtual memory system moves portions of the program to disk and then back to memory, possibly locating them in a different place. It then updates the logical-to-physical memory mappings to point to the new location.

The second task, swapping memory contents to disk, results from the first task. It's clearly impossible for a process to address 4 GB of memory when only 4 MB of physical memory is present on a machine. Virtual memory systems accomplish this feat by using the disk drive as backup "memory" (called a *backing store*). When physical memory becomes overcommitted, the virtual memory system selects data stored in memory for removal and then transfers it temporarily to a file on disk. When the data is again required by an executing thread, the virtual memory system transfers it back into memory.

Moving data back and forth between memory and disk would be unacceptably slow if the virtual memory manager moved it a byte at a time. Therefore, the virtual address space is divided into blocks of equal size called *pages*. Likewise, physical memory is divided into blocks called *page frames*, which are used to hold pages. Each process has a set of pages from its virtual address space that are present in physical memory at any given time. Pages that are in physical memory and immediately available are called *valid pages*. Pages that are stored on disk (or that are in memory but are not immediately available) are called *invalid pages*, as illustrated in Figure 6-3.

When an executing thread accesses a virtual address in a page marked "invalid," the processor issues a system trap called a *page fault*. The virtual

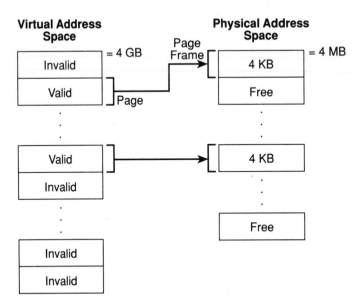

Figure 6-3. Mapping Virtual Pages to Physical Page Frames

memory system locates the required page on disk and loads it into a free page frame in physical memory. When the number of available page frames runs low, the virtual memory system selects page frames to free and copies their contents to disk. This activity, known as *paging*, is imperceptible to the programmer.

Page faults can be expensive operations, requiring many processor cycles to complete. Large page sizes offset this cost, however, because more data is loaded into memory for each page fault, and therefore, fewer page faults tend to occur. (Of course, too large a page size can result in more data than necessary being loaded, so a balance between large and small page sizes must be achieved.) The number of bytes in a page is generally a power of 2 and is often determined by hardware. Windows NT adopts the page size established by the Intel 386, which is 2^{12}, or 4 KB. (The MIPS R4000 allows software to determine the page size.)[4]

Although mapping virtual addresses to physical addresses and transferring data to and from the backing store are the primary tasks of a virtual memory system, it must perform several other duties as well:

- It must allow two processes to share memory easily and efficiently.

- It must protect both shared and private memory from unauthorized access.

- If it runs on multiprocessor computers, as does Windows NT, it must respond to page faults from more than one thread at a time.

The way in which the NT executive's virtual memory system, the VM manager, performs these tasks is the subject of the rest of this chapter.

6.2 User-Mode Features

The NT VM manager provides rich functionality to user-mode processes through its native services. The environment subsystems use the services to manage their client processes. The Win32 subsystem also exports some of the capabilities provided by the native memory services in the Win32 API.

The VM manager allows user-mode subsystems to share memory efficiently using objects that are protected, named, and manipulated like other executive objects. The subsystems can set page-level protection on private

---

4. Unless otherwise indicated, when this chapter refers to the Intel 386, you can assume that the information is also true for 386-compatible processors (such as the AMD386 by Advanced Micro Devices) and upwardly compatible Intel processors (such as the Intel 486).

memory, and they can lock selected pages in memory. They can also take advantage of mapped files and manage the virtual address spaces of their clients.

The following subsections focus on the capabilities the VM manager makes available to user mode: managing a process's virtual address space, sharing memory between processes, and protecting one process's virtual memory from other processes.

6.2.1 Managing Memory

As Chapter 4, "Processes and Threads," showed in the diagram of attributes and services for process objects (Figure 4-3), the VM manager furnishes a set of native services a process can use to directly manage its virtual memory. These services allow a process to do the following:

- Allocate memory in a two-stage process
- Read and write virtual memory
- Lock virtual pages in physical memory
- Get information about virtual pages
- Protect virtual pages
- Flush virtual pages to disk

The VM manager establishes a two-phased approach to memory allocation—reserving it and then committing it. *Reserved memory* is a set of virtual addresses that the VM manager has reserved for a process's future use. Reserving memory (that is, virtual addresses) is a fast and cheap operation in Windows NT. *Committed memory* is memory for which the VM manager has set aside space in its *paging file*, the disk file to which it writes virtual pages when removing them from memory. When a thread allocates virtual memory, it can reserve and commit the memory simultaneously, or it can simply reserve the memory, committing it only as necessary.

Reserving memory is useful when a thread is creating dynamic data structures. The thread reserves a sequence of virtual addresses that it commits as necessary to contain data. If the data structure needs to grow, the thread can commit additional memory from the reserved region. This strategy guarantees that no other thread running within the process (a library package, for example) or another process (such as a Win32 subsystem thread) can use the contiguous virtual addresses that the data structure might need for expansion. A thread can select the starting virtual address of a reserved region, or it can allow the VM manager to find a place for it in the process's virtual address space.

The VM manager deducts from a process's paging file quota for committed memory but not for reserved memory. This dual level of semantics allows a thread to reserve a large region of virtual memory but avoid being charged quota for it until the memory is actually needed. It also helps to keep the paging file free for virtual memory pages that are actually being used. When a particular range of addresses is not being used, a thread can "decommit" them, thus freeing space in the paging file and restoring the process's paging file quota. (See Chapter 4, "Processes and Threads," for more information regarding process quotas.)

For time-critical applications and those with other performance requirements, the VM manager allows a user-mode subsystem or other process with special privileges to lock selected virtual pages in memory. This ensures that a critical page will not be removed from memory while any thread in the process is running. For example, a database application that uses a tree structure to maintain its data might choose to lock the root of the tree in memory so that accessing the database doesn't result in unnecessary page faults.

Like other NT services, the VM services allow the caller to supply a process handle to indicate a process whose virtual memory is to be manipulated. The caller can manipulate its own virtual memory or that of another process. This capability is powerful because it allows one user-mode process to manage the address space of another. For example, one process can create another process, giving itself the right to manipulate the new process's virtual memory. Thereafter, the first process can allocate and free and read and write memory on behalf of the second process by calling virtual memory services and passing in the second process's handle. This feature is used by subsystems to manage the memory of their client processes.

Win32 applications have access to many of these VM manager capabilities through the Win32 API. They can allocate and free virtual memory, read and write virtual memory, flush virtual pages to disk, get information about a range of virtual pages, lock virtual pages in memory, and protect specified pages. None of these API routines allow a Win32 program to tweak the virtual memory of another process, however, with the exception of the ReadProcessMemory() routine and the WriteProcessMemory() routine. These are intended for use by user-mode debuggers to establish breakpoints and maintain instance data for a process being debugged.

6.2.2 Sharing Memory

An important task of any memory management system is to allow processes to share memory when they require it or when sharing would make the operating system more efficient. For example, if two processes compile C programs, memory usage can be minimized if only one copy of the C compiler is loaded into memory. (Of course, each process must also retain private memory areas in which private code and data are stored.)

Virtual memory provides a convenient mechanism for sharing memory. Because each process has a separate virtual address space, the operating system can load the compiler into memory once, and when another process invokes the compiler, the VM manager can simply map the second process's virtual addresses to the physical page frames already occupied by the compiler, as illustrated in Figure 6-4.

Similarly, if two cooperating processes create a shared memory buffer, the virtual address space of each can be mapped to the same physical page frames occupied by the buffer. In the compiler example, the VM manager allows neither process to modify the pages occupied by the compiler. The virtual pages in both processes are designated read-only. In the case of the buffer, however, threads in both processes might need to write to the shared buffer. Therefore, the pages are designated read/write. Of course, when sharing a data structure in this way, the threads using it must synchronize their access to the shared memory to prevent simultaneous access and corrupted data. (Memory protection is described in Section 6.2.3.)

The Win32 subsystem makes the NT executive's memory-sharing capabilities available to Win32 applications through its file-mapping API routines, a topic described in the next subsection.

6.2.2.1 Sections, Views, and Mapped Files

Like all other components of Windows NT, the VM manager is fully parallel. It runs simultaneously on all processors in a multiprocessor computer and must share its data structures among threads running on different processors. Therefore, it was important to create an efficient and secure solution for sharing memory in Windows NT, not only for user-mode programs but also for the system itself.

Shared memory can be defined as memory that is visible from more than one process or that is present in more than one virtual address space. Windows NT's approach to sharing resources is to implement them as protected objects, and memory is no exception. The *section object,* which the Win32 subsystem makes available as a *file-mapping object,* represents a block of memory

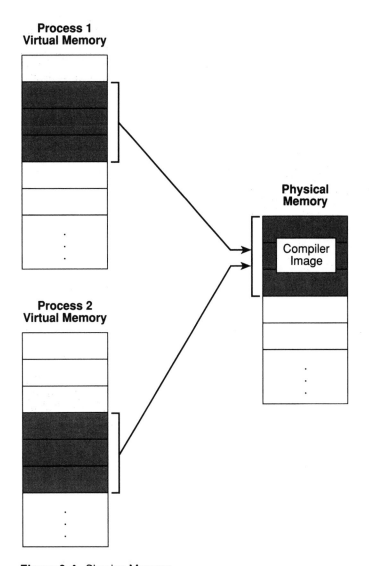

Figure 6-4. Sharing Memory

that two or more processes can share. A thread in one process creates a section object and gives it a name so that threads in other processes can open handles to it. After opening a handle to a section object, a thread can map the section or parts of the section into their own (or another process's) virtual address space.

An NT section object can be quite large, spanning tens, hundreds, or even thousands of pages. To conserve its virtual address space, a process need map only the portion of the section object that it requires; the portion it maps is called a *view* of the section. A view provides a window into the shared memory region, and different processes can map different or even multiple views of a section, as shown in Figure 6-5.

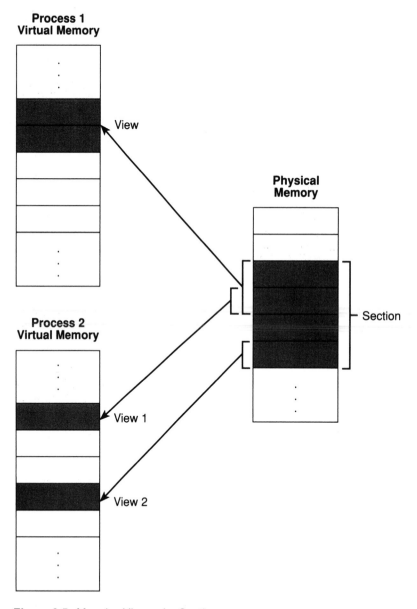

Figure 6-5. Mapping Views of a Section

Mapping views of a section allows a process to access large blocks of memory that it otherwise might not have enough virtual address space to map. For example, a company might have a large database containing information about its employees. The database program creates a section object to contain the entire employee database. When a user queries the database, the program maps a view of the database section into its virtual address space, gets data from it, unmaps the view, and then maps another view of the section to get more information. In effect, it "windows" through this large section object a region at a time, getting data from every part of the database, without running out of virtual address space.

Like private memory, the contents of shared memory are paged to disk when demand for memory is high. The VM manager writes most pages, both private and shared, to the paging file when it removes them from memory. However, the VM manager also allows section objects to be paged to a *mapped file*. The corporate employee database is an example of a mapped file. The database program uses the section object to bring the contents of the database file into virtual memory. The program can then access the file as a large array by mapping different views of the section object and reading or writing to memory rather than to the file (an activity called *mapped file I/O*). When the program accesses an invalid page (one not in physical memory), a page fault occurs, and the VM manager automatically brings the page into memory from the mapped file. If the application modifies the page, the VM manager writes the changes back to the file during its normal paging operations.

The NT executive uses mapped files to load executable images into memory, and the system's cache manager uses mapped files to read and write cached pages. NT's I/O system uses memory-mapped files to carry out I/O requests, allowing the VM manager to page any changes to disk as part of its normal paging operations.

Win32 applications can use mapped files to conveniently perform random I/O (in addition to sequential I/O) to large files. The application creates a Win32 file-mapping object (which corresponds to an NT section object) to contain the file, and then reads or writes to random locations in the file. The VM manager pages in the needed portions of the file automatically and writes any changes back to disk.

6.2.2.2 Section Object

Section objects, like other objects, are allocated and deallocated by the object manager. The object manager creates and initializes an object header, which it uses to manage the objects; the VM manager defines the body of the section object. The VM manager also implements services that user-mode threads can call to retrieve and change the attributes stored in the body of section objects. The section object is shown in Figure 6-6.

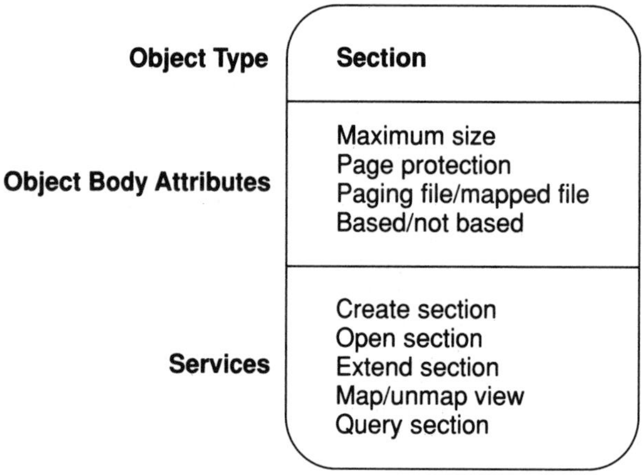

Object Type	**Section**
Object Body Attributes	Maximum size Page protection Paging file/mapped file Based/not based
Services	Create section Open section Extend section Map/unmap view Query section

Figure 6-6. Section Object

The following table summarizes the unique attributes stored in section objects:

Attribute	Purpose
Maximum size	The largest size to which the section can grow in bytes; if mapping a file, it is the size of the file.
Page protection	Page-based memory protection assigned to all pages in the section when it is created.
Paging file/ mapped file	Indicates whether the section is created empty (backed by the paging file) or loaded with a file (backed by the mapped file).
Based/not based	Indicates whether a section is a based section, which must appear at the same virtual address for all processes sharing it, or a nonbased section, which can appear at different virtual addresses for different processes.

Table 6-1. Section Object Attributes

Mapping a view of a section object makes a portion of the section visible in a process's virtual address space. Likewise, unmapping a view of a section removes it from the process's virtual address space.

Sharing occurs when two processes map portions of the same section object into their address spaces. When two processes share memory in this way, they must synchronize their access to it to avoid changing data at the same time. Events, semaphores, or even hardware-dependent locks can be used to synchronize access to a shared section. Section objects themselves are not defined as synchronization objects; that is, a thread cannot synchronize its execution by waiting on a handle to a section object. Win32 applications can use mutexes, events, critical sections, or semaphores to synchronize their access to the file-mapping object—their equivalent of a section object.

To map a view of a section, a process must first acquire a handle to it. The process that creates the section object always has a handle. Other processes (those with appropriate access rights) can open handles to the section object if the section has a name. Alternatively, a process can be given a handle to a section object through process inheritance or when another process duplicates its section handle and passes the duplicate handle to the recipient process. Memory sharing occurs in all of these cases. If a shared section is created as a temporary object, the object manager deletes the shared memory when the last reference to the section object is released. Permanent section objects are not deleted.

6.2.3 Protecting Memory

Memory protection in Windows NT is provided in four forms. The first three are common to most modern operating systems:

- A separate address space for each process. The hardware disallows any thread from accessing the virtual addresses of another process.

- Two modes of operation: kernel mode, which allows threads access to system code and data; and user mode, which doesn't.

- A page-based protection mechanism. Each virtual page has a set of flags associated with it that determines the types of access allowed in user mode and in kernel mode.

And the following mechanism, unique to Windows NT, provides one more form of memory protection:

- Object-based memory protection. Each time a process opens a handle to a section object or maps a view to it, the Windows NT security reference monitor checks whether the process attempting the operation is allowed access to the object.

The following subsections focus on the two types of memory protection that these mechanisms support—process-private memory protection and shared memory protection.

6.2.3.1 Process-Private Memory

Each time a thread uses an address, the NT executive's VM manager, along with hardware, intervenes and translates the virtual address into a physical address. A virtual memory system, by controlling the translation of virtual addresses, can ensure that threads in one process do not access a page frame of memory belonging to another process.

In addition to the implicit protection offered by virtual-to-physical address translation, every processor that supports virtual memory provides some form of hardware-controlled memory protection. The protections they provide and their hardware implementations vary, however. Often, hardware protection is minimal and must be supplemented with mechanisms provided by the virtual memory software. This fact makes the VM manager in Windows NT subject to hardware differences more than other parts of the operating system are.

Hardware-based page protection takes effect each time a thread accesses memory. On the MIPS R4000 processor, for example, each page of a process's virtual memory is designated as either a user-mode page (low 2 GB) or a kernel-mode page (high 2 GB) and either a read-only or a read/write page. If the executing thread is running in kernel mode, the processor allows it to read any valid page of memory and write valid pages with the read/write designation. If the thread is running in user mode, it can read only valid user pages and can write only those valid user pages with the read/write designation. The MIPS R4000 issues a page fault if the accessed page is invalid (not in memory). It issues an address-error exception (access violation) if a thread attempts to read or write a valid page in violation of the rules.

The hardware can perform its protection checks only on valid pages—those that are present in memory. If a thread accesses an invalid page (one that is not in memory), the MIPS R4000 issues a page fault, and the VM manager's paging software takes over the page protection task.

The VM manager provides the same page protections that the MIPS R4000 supplies for valid pages:

- Read-only
- Read/write

The VM manager supplements these basic protections with a few of its own:

- Execute-only (if the hardware supports it)
- Guard-page
- No-access
- Copy-on-write

Using native virtual memory services, an environment subsystem can control the page-level protection on private virtual pages. Controlling page-level protection can lead to more reliable programs by ensuring that threads do not write to pages that should be read-only. This capability is also useful, for example, in debugging a multithreaded program in which one thread is erroneously writing to memory. By temporarily changing the protection of that page to read-only or no-access, the debugger can catch the thread in action and find the error.

A thread can neither read from nor write to a page with execute-only access, but it can jump to an address within the page and begin executing. This type of protection is appropriate for shared application software, such as an editor or a compiler. All threads should be able to run the software, but none should be allowed to read from or write to the executable image. (Note that neither the MIPS R4000 nor the Intel 386 or 486 support execute-only protection. Therefore, on these processors, execute access is equivalent to read-only access.)

The VM manager provides guard-page protection to facilitate automatic bounds checking on stacks, but this type of page protection can be used to demarcate other data structures as well. When a thread accesses a guard page, the VM manager generates a guard-page exception and the caller receives a message that the guard page was touched. The VM manager then allows the operation to continue. If a subsystem or other native application places a guard page at the end of a dynamic array, for example, the subsystem will receive a warning from the VM manager when it accesses the guard page, and it can extend the array dynamically.

No-access page protection is used to prevent any thread from reading from or writing to a particular page. The VM manager issues an exception if an address in the page is accessed. Virtual pages that have not been allocated at all or those that have been reserved but not committed are assigned the no-access page protection by the VM manager. No-access page protection is used primarily by debuggers.

The Win32 subsystem makes the VM manager's page protection visible to Win32 applications through its VirtualProtect() routine. This routine allows applications to designate individual virtual pages as read-only, read/write, or no-access. Guard-page, execute-only, and copy-on-write protection are not provided.

6.2.3.2 Shared Memory

The *copy-on-write* page protection, mentioned in the previous subsection, is an optimization the VM manager uses to save memory. When two processes want to read and write the same memory contents (but not share them), the VM manager assigns the copy-on-write page protection to the memory region. It then shares the physical memory between the processes as long as neither of them writes to it. If a thread in one of the processes writes to a page, the VM manager copies the physical page frame to another location in memory, updates the process's virtual address space to point to the copy, and sets the new page's protection to read/write. As shown in Figure 6-7, the copied page is not

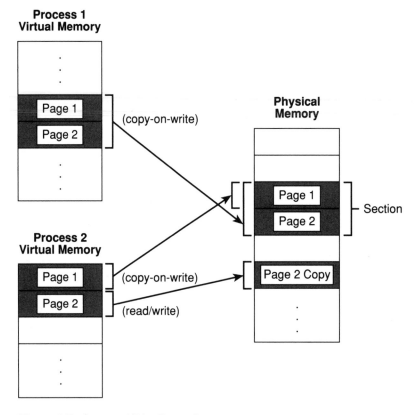

Figure 6-7. Copy-on-Write Protection

visible to threads in other processes. Hence, the thread can write to its copy of the page without affecting other processes that are using the page.

Copy-on-write protection is useful for pages containing code; it ensures that only the process whose thread modifies the image is affected by the change. For example, code pages start out as execute-only pages. However, if a programmer sets a breakpoint while debugging a program, the debugger must add a breakpoint instruction to the code. To do so, it first changes the protection on the page to copy-on-write. The VM manager immediately creates a private copy of the code page for the process whose thread set the breakpoint. Other processes continue using the unmodified code. The Win32 subsystem does not make copy-on-write page protection directly available to Win32 applications, but it indirectly uses copy-on-write protection to implement per-process instance data in its dynamic-link libraries (DLLs) and elsewhere.

Copy-on-write page protection is one example of an optimization technique called *lazy evaluation* that the VM manager uses whenever possible. Lazy-evaluation algorithms avoid performing an expensive operation until it is absolutely required. If the operation is never required, then no time is wasted on it. The POSIX subsystem is one component that takes great advantage of this optimization. Typically, when a process calls the fork() API routine to create another process on a POSIX system, the operating system copies the address space of the first process to the second—a time-consuming operation. The new application frequently calls the exec() API routine immediately, which reinitializes the address space with an executable program, rendering the first copy operation superfluous. The VM manager's lazy-evaluation algorithm, in contrast, simply marks the parent's pages with the copy-on-write page protection designation and shares the parent's pages with the child. If the child (or parent) process never writes to its address space, the two processes continue sharing and no copying is done. If one of them does write, the VM manager copies only the pages the process has written to, rather than copying the entire address space.

All the memory protection mechanisms described so far are implemented in either hardware or low-level memory management software that is invoked each time a thread uses an address. The Windows NT object architecture provides an additional layer of protection for memory shared between two processes. The security subsystem protects section objects in the same way it protects other executive objects—by using access control lists (ACLs). (See Chapter 3, "The Object Manager and Object Security.") A thread can create a section object whose ACL specifies which users or groups of users can read, write, get information about, or extend the size of the section.

The security reference monitor checks the protection on a section object whenever a thread tries to open a handle to a section or to map a view of it. If the ACL doesn't allow the operation, the object manager rejects the call. Once a thread has successfully opened a handle to a section, its actions are still subject to the page-based protections previously described.

A thread can change the page-level protection on virtual pages in a section if the change doesn't violate the ACL on the section object. For example, the VM manager allows a thread to change the pages of a read-only section to have copy-on-write access but not to have read/write access. The change to copy-on-write access is allowed because it has no effect on other processes sharing the data.

Security also comes into play when a thread creates a section to contain a mapped file. To do so, the thread must have access to the underlying file object. For example, a thread that creates a section object to map a file must have at least read access to the file, or the operation will fail. Once a file is loaded into a section, the thread can change the ACL on the section object, but only within the bounds set by the ACL on the file that was mapped.

6.3   Virtual Memory Implementation

Thus far, this chapter has focused on general virtual memory principles and the user-mode features provided in the NT executive's VM manager. The following subsections delve into internal matters—data structures and algorithms that are not visible to user-mode code but that affect the operation and performance of virtual memory. The layout of a process's virtual address space is described first, followed by an explanation of paging mechanisms and policies governing a process's use of memory. A brief description of the two primary data structures in the virtual memory component follow. Finally, the higher-level issues of multiprocessing and portability of the virtual memory system are addressed.

6.3.1 Address Space

Each native NT process has a large virtual address space of 4 GB, 2 GB of which are reserved for system use.[5] The lower half of the virtual address space is accessible to user-mode and kernel-mode threads and is unique for each process. The upper half of the virtual address space is accessible only to

---

5. The MIPS R4000 dictates that 2 GB of address space be reserved for system use. Other processors require less, but to ensure the system's portability, 2 GB are always reserved.

kernel-mode threads and is the same for every process. A process's virtual address space is illustrated in Figure 6-8.

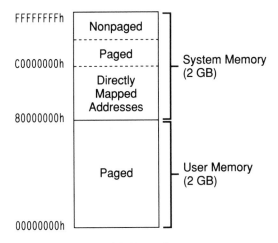

Figure 6-8. Virtual Address Space

Kernel code and data reside in the lower portion of system memory (from 80000000 through BFFFFFFFh on the MIPS R4000), and they are never paged out of memory. On the MIPS R4000, this region of memory is directly mapped by the hardware. That is, the processor zeroes out the three most significant bits of any virtual address in this range and uses the remaining bits as a physical address (which has the effect of placing the data in low physical memory). Because the addresses in this range are translated by the hardware and are never invalid, data access from this region of memory is extremely fast. It is used for portions of the kernel that rely on maximum performance, such as the code that dispatches threads for execution on a processor.

The upper portion of system memory is controlled by the VM manager and is used to store other system code and data. A part of this area is reserved for code and data that can be paged to disk, and another part is reserved for system code that can never be paged out of memory (the code that does the paging, for example).

When you create a new process, you can specify that the VM manager initialize its virtual address space by duplicating the virtual address space of another process or by mapping a file into its virtual address space. For instance, the POSIX subsystem uses the former tactic when one of its clients creates a child process. The child process's address space is a replica of its

POSIX parent process. (Actually, the parent and child share copy-on-write pages, so no copying takes place immediately.) The latter tactic is used when a new process is created to run an executable program. For example, when a user runs the chkdsk utility, the NT process manager creates a process and the VM manager initializes its address space with the chkdsk image, which is then executed.

Environment subsystems can present to their client processes views of memory that do not correspond to the virtual address space of a native NT process. Win32 applications use an address space that is identical to the native address space, but the 16-bit OS/2 subsystem and the virtual DOS machines (VDM) subsystem present altered views of memory to their clients.

6.3.2 Paging

The design of an operating system component often reveals itself when you ask two important questions:

- What mechanisms does the component use to do its work?

- What policies govern the mechanisms?

Virtual memory mechanisms include the way in which the VM manager translates virtual addresses into physical addresses and the way in which it brings pages into physical memory. Virtual memory policies, in contrast, determine when to bring a page into memory and where to place it, for example.

Often the processor provides primitive paging mechanisms, which the virtual memory system augments. The *pager,* the VM manager's code that transfers pages to and from disk, is an important intermediary between hardware mechanisms and software policies:

- It makes an invalid page valid when a page fault occurs (for example, by loading a page into memory from disk).

- It provides page-based protection for invalid pages and enhances the protections that the hardware provides for valid pages.

- It updates and maintains memory management data structures.

In addition, the pager enforces the paging policies set by the VM manager. The next subsection describes the virtual memory mechanisms supplied by the MIPS R4000. The subsection that follows it summarizes the paging policies of the VM manager.

6.3.2.1 Paging Mechanisms

Every processor that supports virtual memory does so differently. Therefore, code that directly interfaces with virtual memory hardware is not portable and must be modified for each new hardware platform. In the best of circumstances, as in Windows NT, such code is small and well isolated.

The information in this section is specific to the MIPS R4000 and provides one example of how the VM manager interoperates with a processor. Much of this information is also applicable to the Intel CISC processors, but for simplicity, the Intel processors are not discussed at length here.

The MIPS R4000 contains two modules: the 32-bit RISC processing unit (called CP1) and a separate on-chip module (called CP0) that handles address translation and exception handling. CP0 automatically captures each address that a program generates and translates it into a physical address. If the page containing the address is valid (present in memory), CP0 locates it and retrieves the information. If the page is invalid (not present in memory), CP0 generates a page fault, and the VM manager's pager is invoked.

To ensure fast memory access, the MIPS R4000 (as well as the Intel processors) provides an array of associative memory called the *translation lookaside buffer* (TLB). Associative memory, such as the TLB, is a vector whose cells can be read simultaneously and compared to a target value. In the case of the TLB, the vector contains the virtual-to-physical page mappings of the most recently used pages and the type of page protection applied to each page. Figure 6-9 is a simplified depiction of the TLB.

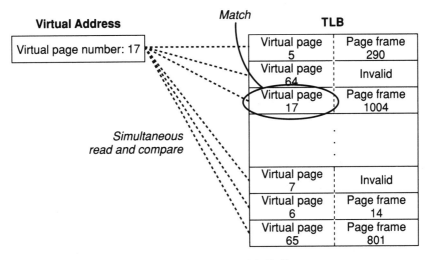

Figure 6-9. Accessing the Translation Lookaside Buffer

Virtual addresses that are used frequently are likely to have entries in the TLB, which provides extremely fast virtual-to-physical address translation and, therefore, memory access. If a virtual address is not present in the TLB, it might still be in memory, but virtual memory software, rather than hardware, must find it, in which case access time is slightly slower. If a virtual page has been paged out of memory, the virtual memory system makes its TLB entry invalid. If a process accesses it again, a page fault occurs, and the VM manager brings the page back into memory and re-creates an entry for it in the TLB.

The kernel and the VM manager use software-created *page tables* to find pages that are not present in the TLB. Page tables are found on most virtual memory systems; sometimes they are implemented by the hardware and sometimes by the software. Conceptually, a page table resembles the data structure shown in Figure 6-10.

A *page table entry* (PTE) contains all the information necessary for the virtual memory system to locate a page when a thread uses an address. In a simple virtual memory system, an invalid entry in a page table means that the page is not in physical memory and must be loaded from disk. A page fault exception occurs, and the paging software loads the requested page into

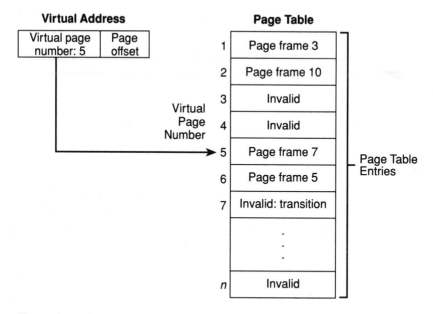

Figure 6-10. Conceptual Page Table

memory and updates the page table. The processor reissues the instruction that generated the page fault. This time, however, the page table entry is valid and the data is successfully retrieved from memory.

The MIPS R4000 has 32-bit addresses, or 2^{32} possible virtual addresses for each process. It organizes these virtual addresses into pages 2^{12} bytes (4 KB) long, which yields 2^{20}, or 1,048,576, pages per address space. If page table entries are 4 bytes wide, it takes 1024 page frames of storage (2^{20} times 2^2 divided by 2^{12}) to map all of virtual memory. And that takes care of only one address space! Each process has a separate address space. To avoid consuming all the memory just for page tables, the VM manager pages the tables in and out of memory as they are needed.

The MIPS R4000 processor allows the operating system to structure page tables in whatever format is most convenient. In contrast, the Intel 386 processor establishes a page table format in hardware. To provide maximum portability from MIPS to Intel processors, the VM manager adopts a two-level page table structure that mimics the Intel format. The first-level table, called a *page directory,* points to pages in a second-level page table. The second-level page table points to actual page frames, as shown in Figure 6-11 on the next page.

When locating a page table entry, the VM manager (and the NT kernel) translates a MIPS-style virtual address into an Intel-style address using different portions of it as offsets into the page table structure. In addition, one entry in the TLB always contains the virtual base address of the page directory for the currently executing process. (This is the reason that one user process cannot "see" the address space of another. They have different page directories, which point to different page tables.)

Entries in a process's page directory and page tables can be either valid or invalid. If an entry in the page directory is invalid, a page fault occurs to load the directory page and locate a page table page. After the page table page has been made valid, the appropriate entry in the page table is checked. If the page table entry is also invalid, another page fault occurs to locate the code or data page.

The page table entries in these NT-defined page tables are an improvement over the conceptual page table shown earlier. Each page table entry (and each page directory entry) has a transition flag. If the page table entry is marked invalid and the transition flag is set, the page is slated to be reused, but its contents are still valid. Making a transitional page valid is a very fast operation because the VM manager doesn't need to read the page into memory from disk. The page table entries also contain flags that record the page-level protections that the VM manager applies to each page.

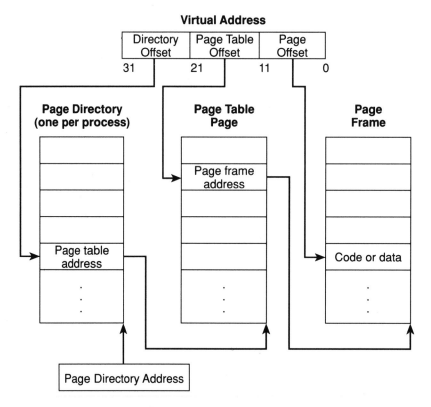

Figure 6-11. Page Table Structure on the Intel 386 and the MIPS R4000[6]

When a page frame is shared between two processes, the VM manager inserts a level of indirection into its page tables, as Figure 6-12 illustrates. The data structure it inserts is called a *prototype page table entry* (prototype PTE).

The prototype PTE, a 32-bit structure that looks similar to a normal page table entry, allows the VM manager to manage shared pages without needing to update the page tables of each process sharing the page. For example, a shared code or data page might be paged out to disk at some point. When the VM manager retrieves the page from disk (pages it in), it needs only to update the pointer stored in the prototype PTE to point to the page's new physical location. Each sharing process's page table remains the same. Prototype PTEs are allocated from paged system space, so, like page table entries, they can be paged if necessary.

6. This figure is based on Figure 5-9 in the *Intel 80386 Processor Reference Manual* (Intel Corporation, 1988), 5–8.

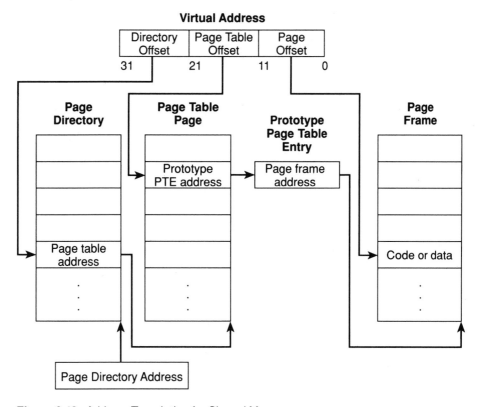

Figure 6-12. Address Translation for Shared Memory

6.3.2.2 Paging Policies and Working Sets

Virtual memory systems generally define three policies that dictate how (or when) paging is performed: a fetch policy, a placement policy, and a replacement policy.

A *fetch policy* determines when the pager brings a page from disk into memory. One type of fetch policy attempts to load the pages a process will need before it asks for them. Other fetch policies, called *demand paging policies,* load a page into physical memory only when a page fault occurs. In a demand paging system, a process incurs many page faults when its threads first begin executing, as they reference the initial set of pages they need to get going. Once this set of pages is loaded into memory, the paging activity of the process decreases.

NT's VM manager uses a demand paging algorithm with "clustering" to load pages into memory. When a thread gets a page fault, the VM manager

191

loads into memory the faulted page plus a small number of pages surrounding it. This strategy attempts to minimize the number of page faults a thread will incur. Because programs, especially large ones, tend to execute in small regions of their address space at any given time, loading clusters of virtual pages reduces the number of page faults.

When a thread receives a page fault, the memory management system must also determine where in physical memory to put the virtual page. The set of rules it uses is called a *placement policy*. Placement policies, although frequently complicated for segmented memory architectures, are usually simple for linear architectures, which require only that a free page frame be found. In NT, if memory is not full, the VM manager simply selects the first page frame on a list of free page frames. If the list is empty, it traverses a series of other page frame lists that it maintains; the order of traversal depends upon the type of page fault that occurred. (More information about page frame lists appears in Section 6.3.3.)

If physical memory is full when a page fault occurs, a *replacement policy* is used to determine which virtual page must be removed from memory to make room for the new page. Common replacement policies include *least recently used* (LRU) and *first in, first out* (FIFO). The LRU algorithm requires the virtual memory system to track when a page in memory is used. When a new page frame is required, the page that has not been used for the greatest amount of time is paged to disk, and its frame is freed to satisfy the page fault. The FIFO algorithm is somewhat simpler; it removes the page that has been in physical memory for the greatest amount of time, regardless of how often it has been used.

Replacement policies can be further characterized as either global or local. A *local replacement policy* allocates a fixed (or, as in NT, a dynamically adjustable) number of page frames to each process. When a process uses all of its allotment, the virtual memory software frees (that is, removes from physical memory) one of its pages for every new page fault it incurs. A global replacement policy allows a page fault to be satisfied by any page frame, whether or not that frame is owned by another process. For example, a global replacement policy using the FIFO algorithm would locate the page that has been in memory the longest and would free it to satisfy a page fault; a local replacement policy would limit its search for the oldest page to the set of pages already owned by the process that incurred the page fault.

Global replacement policies have a number of problems. First, they make processes vulnerable to the behavior of other processes. For example, if one or more processes in the system are using large amounts of memory, an executing application is more likely to incur heavy paging. Execution time will increase. Second, an ill-behaved application can undermine the entire operating system by inducing excessive paging activity in all processes. In Windows NT, it is important that the environment subsystems not compete with other processes for their fair share of memory. They must keep a certain number of pages in memory in order to execute efficiently and support their client applications adequately. For these reasons, the VM manager uses a local FIFO replacement policy. This approach requires the VM manager to keep track of the pages currently in memory for each process. This set of pages is called the *process's working set*.[7]

When created, each process is assigned a minimum working-set size, which is the number of pages the process is guaranteed to have in memory while it is running. If memory is not overly full, the VM manager allows the process to have as many pages as its working-set maximum.[8] If the process requires more pages, the VM manager removes one of the process's pages for each new page fault the process generates.

To determine which page to remove from a process's working set, the VM manager employs a simple FIFO algorithm, removing pages that have been in memory the longest. (Because replaced working-set pages actually remain in physical memory for a period of time after the replacement, they can be brought back into the working set quickly without requiring a disk read operation. See Section 6.3.3.)

When physical memory runs low, the VM manager uses a technique called *automatic working-set trimming* to increase the amount of free memory available in the system. It examines each process in memory, comparing the current size of its working set to its minimum working-set value. When it finds processes using more than their minimums, it removes pages from their working sets, making the pages available for other uses. If the amount of free memory is still too low, the VM manager continues removing pages from processes' working sets until each process reaches its working-set minimum.

Once a process drops to its working-set minimum, the VM manager tracks the number of page faults the process incurs. If the process generates page faults and memory is not overly full, the VM manager increases the size

---

7. P. J. Denning, who published his seminal paper on virtual memory in 1970, used the term *working set* to refer to the minimum number of pages a process must have in physical memory before its execution can progress. A process with less than its working set is susceptible to thrashing (continuous page faulting). Our definition, "the set of pages in memory at any given time for a process," is slightly different from Denning's definition, and the two should not be confused.

8. The VM manager can also allow a process to exceed its maximum if ample memory is available.

of the process's working set. If, however, the process incurs no page faults for a period of time, either the code the process's threads are executing fits comfortably within the process's minimum working set or none of the process's threads are executing. For example, the Windows NT logon process simply waits for a user to log on. Once the user is logged on, the process waits for the user to log off. For the logon process, and for other processes that remain idle much of the time, the VM manager continues lowering the process's working set until the process incurs a page fault. The page fault indicates either that the process's threads have awakened or that the process has reached the lower limit of memory its threads need in order to execute.

A process can change its working-set minimum and maximum by calling a process object service, but the security system's local policy database sets an absolute minimum and maximum for each user-mode process. Although this capability is provided, it is largely unnecessary for individual processes to modify their working-set values. The memory manager is designed, through its use of the local replacement policy and automatic working-set trimming, to track the load on memory and to adjust memory usage accordingly. It attempts to provide the best possible performance for each process without requiring system tuning by individual users or an administrator.

6.3.3 Page Frame Database

A process's page tables track where in physical memory a virtual page is stored. The VM manager also needs a data structure to track the state of physical memory. For example, it needs to record whether a page frame is free, and if not, who is using it. The *page frame database* fills this need. It is an array of entries numbered from 0 through the number of page frames of memory in the system (minus 1). Each entry contains information about the corresponding page frame. The page frame database and its relationship to page tables is depicted in Figure 6-13. As this figure shows, valid page table entries point to entries in the page frame database, and the page frame database entries point back to the page table that is using them. The VM manager uses the forward pointer when a process accesses a valid virtual address. It follows the pointer to locate the physical page corresponding to a virtual address.

Some invalid page table entries also refer to entries in the page frame database. These "transitional" page table entries refer to page frames that are eligible for reuse but have not yet been reused and, therefore, are still intact in memory. If the process accesses one of these pages before it is reused by another process, the VM manager can recover the contents quickly.

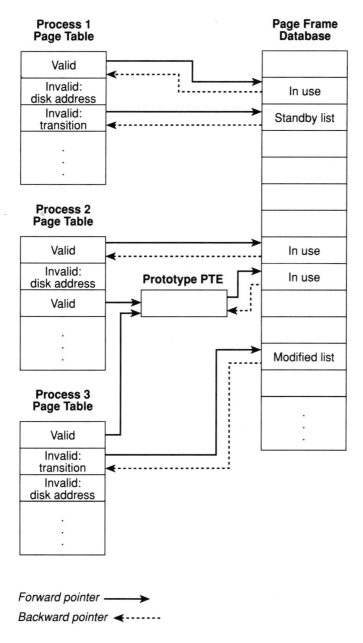

Forward pointer ——————▶
Backward pointer ◀-------

Figure 6-13. Page Tables and the Page Frame Database

Other invalid page table entries contain the disk address where the page is stored. When a process accesses one of these pages, a page fault occurs and the VM manager reads the page from the disk.

Page frames can be in one of six states at any given time:

■ Valid. The page frame is in use by a process, and a valid page table entry points to it.

■ Zeroed. The page frame is free and has been initialized with zeros.

■ Free. The page frame is free but is not initialized.

■ Standby. A process was using the page frame, but the page frame was removed from the process's working set. The page table entry for it is invalid but marked with a transition flag.

■ Modified. This state is the same as the standby state except that the process that used the page also wrote to it, and the contents have not yet been written to disk. The page table entry for it is invalid but marked with a transition flag.

■ Bad. The page frame has generated parity or other hardware errors and cannot be used.

Of the page frames that are not in use, the page frame database links together all those that are in the same state, thus creating five separate lists: the zeroed list, the free list, the standby list, the modified list, and the bad page list. The relationship between the page frame database and the page lists is shown in Figure 6-14.

As shown in the figure, these lists account for every page frame in the computer that is not in use. Those that are in use by a process are pointed to by that process's page table. When a process finishes with a page frame or when the VM manager pages its contents to disk, the page frame becomes free and the VM manager places it back in one of its page frame lists.

When the VM manager needs an initialized page frame (one containing all zeros) to service a page fault, it attempts to get the first one in the zeroed page list; if the list is empty, it gets one from the free list and zeroes it.[9] When the VM manager doesn't require a zeroed page, it uses the first one in the free list; if the free list is empty, it uses one from the zeroed list. In either of these cases, the VM manager uses the standby list if both of the other lists are empty. Whenever the number of pages in the zeroed, free, and standby lists

---

9. The U.S. Department of Defense specifies that, for C2-level security, user-mode processes must be given initialized page frames to prevent them from reading a previous process's memory contents. Therefore, the VM manager gives user-mode processes zeroed page frames unless the process is loading data from a disk file, such as an executable image. In the latter case, the VM manager uses nonzeroed page frames, initializing them with the disk image.

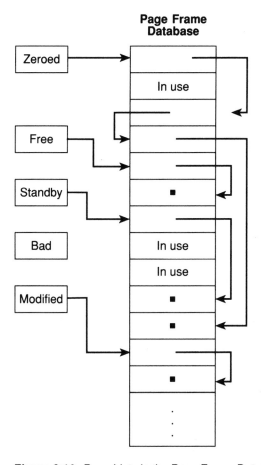

Figure 6-14. Page Lists in the Page Frame Database

shrinks below a minimum threshold, a thread called the *modified page writer* "wakes up," writes the contents of the modified pages to disk, and then moves them to the standby list for reuse.

If even the modified page list becomes too short, the VM manager begins trimming each process's working set to its minimum working-set size. The newly freed pages are placed on the modified or standby list to be reused on demand. A state diagram of page frame transitions is shown in Figure 6-15 on the next page.

Before the VM manager can use a page frame from the standby or modified list, it must first backtrack and update the invalid page table entry (or prototype PTE) that still points to the page frame. Referring back to Figure 6-13, you can see that entries in the page frame database contain pointers back

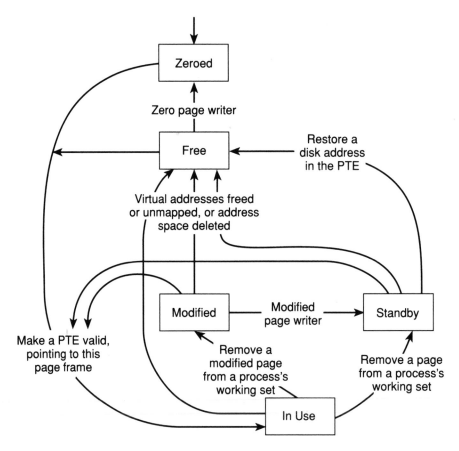

Figure 6-15. State Diagram for Page Frames

to the previous user's page table (or to a prototype PTE for shared pages), which allows this updating to occur.

6.3.4 Virtual Address Descriptors

An earlier section of this chapter described the paging policies the VM manager uses to determine when to bring a page into memory, where to put it, and which pages to remove when memory gets full.

The VM manager uses a demand-paging algorithm to know when to load pages into memory. It waits until some thread uses an address and incurs a page fault before it gets a page from disk. Demand paging such as this is a form of lazy evaluation. Lazy-evaluation algorithms avoid performing an expensive operation, such as paging, until it is absolutely required.

The VM manager uses lazy evaluation in another area, that of constructing page tables. For example, when a thread allocates a large region of virtual memory, the VM manager could immediately construct the page tables required to access the entire range of allocated memory. However, if the application doesn't use all the allocated memory, constructing the page tables is a wasted effort. Therefore, the VM manager waits to do so until a thread incurs a page fault. Using lazy evaluation in this way yields a significant performance gain for applications that reserve a lot of memory but use (commit) it sparsely.

Allocating memory, even large blocks of it, is extremely fast with the lazy-evaluation algorithm. The performance gain is not without its trade-offs, however. When a thread allocates memory, the VM manager must respond with a range of virtual addresses for the thread to use. However, because the VM manager doesn't load the process's page table until the thread actually accesses the memory, it can't look at the page table to determine which virtual addresses are free. Therefore, the VM manager must maintain another set of data structures to keep track of the virtual addresses that have already been allocated in the process's address space and those that have not. Virtual address descriptors fill this need.

For each process, the VM manager maintains a set of virtual address descriptors that describes the status of the process's virtual address space. See Figure 6-16.

When a process allocates memory (or maps a view of shared memory), the VM manager creates a virtual address descriptor in which to store any information supplied in the allocation request, such as the range of addresses

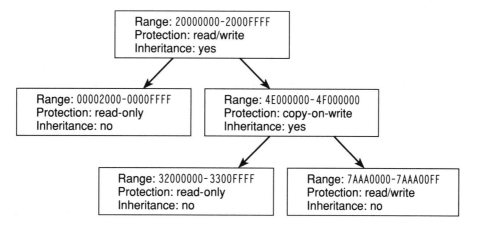

Figure 6-16. Virtual Address Descriptors

being allocated, whether the range will be shared or private memory, whether a child process can inherit the contents of the range, and the page protection applied to pages in the range. It then inserts the virtual address descriptor into a process-specific splay tree (a self-balancing binary tree) to speed the process of locating it.

When a thread first accesses an address, the VM manager must create a page table entry for the page that contains the address. To do so, the VM manager finds the virtual address descriptor whose address range also contains the accessed address and uses the information it finds to fill in the page table entry. If the address falls outside the range covered by the virtual address descriptor, the VM manager knows that the thread did not allocate this memory address before using it; an access violation has occurred.

6.3.5 Multiprocessing Considerations

Any code that can be run on more than one processor at the same time is subject to some coding constraints. The code must be reentrant, it must allow only one thread to access shared data structures at one time, and it must not permit two threads to acquire resources in such a way that they block each other's execution (a condition known as deadlock). In addition, performance considerations arise in multiprocessor systems that do not occur in single-processor systems.

The VM manager is reentrant, so preventing data corruption and deadlock and achieving good performance were the most important concerns for its multiprocessor execution.

The VM manager uses a spin lock to protect its most important data structure—the page frame database. Whenever a page fault occurs, the pager takes control of the faulting thread to resolve the page fault and update the database. Before accessing the database, the thread must gain ownership of the database spin lock. While the thread owns this spin lock, no other thread can read from or write to the page frame database. Therefore, when two page faults occur simultaneously on Windows NT, one thread might be held up momentarily until the page frame database is free.

Delaying a thread's access to the page frame database is an example of the trade-off between speed and the needs of multiprocessing systems. The VM manager could have allowed separate threads to access different parts of the database simultaneously by carving the database into several data structures and guarding each piece with a separate lock. However, acquiring and releasing locks is an expensive operation, so page faults would take longer if a thread had to acquire three locks instead of one to access the database. In balancing this trade-off, Lou Perazzoli, the VM manager's designer, gave preference to fast page faults over increased parallelism in the pager. He chose to use a single lock to protect the database, assuming that with the lower overhead, a thread would enter and exit the database more quickly, thus freeing it for other threads.

Using a single database lock means that the page frame database can become a performance bottleneck when paging activity is high. To avoid this problem, the VM manager attempts to minimize page faulting in Windows NT. It does the following to keep the number of page faults low:

- It gives each process enough pages in its working set to prevent excessive faulting.

- It automatically trims processes' working sets to make their unused or excess pages available for other processes.

6.3.6 Portability Considerations

The VM manager depends on certain hardware features. The following are processor requirements for the VM manager:

- 32-bit addresses. (64-bit addresses are supported, but they require some redesign in the VM manager.)

- Virtual memory and paging support. The processor must provide the ability to map virtual addresses to physical addresses, and it must supply paging mechanisms.

- Transparent, coherent hardware caches for multiprocessor systems. When a thread on one processor updates data in its cache, all other processors must be notified that the data in their caches is no longer correct.

- Virtual address aliasing. The processor must allow two page table entries in the same process to map to the same page frame. The operating system often shares a page with a user process by mapping a second page table entry.

Certain parts of the VM manager are dependent on the features of the processor on which the operating system runs. The parts of the memory manager listed at the top of the next page must be modified for each hardware platform to which it is ported.

- Page table entries. When a page table entry is valid, the processor divides the 32 bits into fields and sets them accordingly. When a page table entry is invalid, the VM manager uses the remaining 31 bits as it chooses. The format it selects is based on the virtual memory facilities the processor provides.

- Page size. Different processors use different page sizes. The VM manager allocates virtual memory on 64-KB boundaries, which ensures that it can support any page size from 4 KB to 64 KB. Page sizes smaller than 4 KB are not supported.

- Page-based protection. The way in which the VM manager manipulates the hardware-based page protection to perform additional software-based page protection is hardware dependent.

- Virtual address translation. The algorithm the VM manager uses to translate a virtual address to a page table entry is hardware dependent.

6.4   In Conclusion

Windows NT's VM manager implements a sophisticated virtual memory system. It gives each process access to a large number of virtual addresses, protecting one process's memory from another's but allowing processes to share memory efficiently and with a great degree of control. With appropriate access rights, a process can also manage the address space of other processes, a feature exploited by the environment subsystems. Advanced capabilities are also available, such as mapped files and the ability to sparsely allocate memory. The Win32 environment subsystem makes many of the NT virtual memory capabilities available to applications in its 32-bit API.

The VM manager implements page-based memory protection that augments the protection processors provide. Shared memory regions are implemented as objects, and their use is thus controlled and monitored by the security mechanisms that protect all objects. Additionally, a process can add page-based protections to selected portions of shared memory.

The VM manager's implementation relies on lazy-evaluation techniques whenever possible to avoid performing unnecessary and time-consuming operations unless they are required. This is one of several optimizations the VM manager uses to ensure fast and efficient memory access.

The next chapter takes a step inward and downward to the NT kernel, the true center of Windows NT.

CHAPTER SEVEN

THE KERNEL

The developers of the NT executive sometimes describe its kernel component as "the bottom of the food chain." The metaphor, although imperfect, is correct in at least one regard: An operating system, like any large body of software, consists of layer upon layer of code. Higher layers of code rely on more primitive (but in this case, more powerful) functions and data structures provided by lower layers. Another metaphor, perhaps more apt, likens the kernel to the hub of a wheel. It is the center of the operating system around which everything else revolves.

The kernel performs the most fundamental operations in Windows NT, determining how the operating system uses the processor or processors and ensuring that they are used prudently. Thus, the success of the entire operating system rides on the kernel's correct and efficient operation.

With this challenge, it was essential that the NT kernel rest in capable hands. Dave Cutler, director of the Windows NT development group and primary architect of the system, designed and implemented the NT kernel. Dave, a former senior corporate consultant at Digital Equipment Corporation (DEC), was instrumental in designing several successful DEC operating systems, among them the VAX/VMS operating system and the RSX-11M operating system for the PDP-11 machine.

Dave's overriding goal for the NT kernel was to provide a low-level base of well-defined, predictable operating system primitives and mechanisms that would allow higher-level components of the NT executive to do what they need to do. Using kernel primitives, the NT executive can build higher-level abstractions of an infinite variety. It doesn't need to resort to backdoor interfaces, undocumented side effects, or direct hardware manipulation. The kernel separates itself from the rest of the executive by implementing operating system mechanisms and avoiding policy-making. It leaves nearly all policy decisions to the NT executive.[1]

By providing a rich set of controlled, uniform mechanisms, the NT kernel enables Windows NT to grow and change over time, but in a predictable, orderly way. Richard Rashid, in discussing why he and his colleagues created the Mach operating system (a client/server version of UNIX) stated that "...the UNIX kernel has become a 'dumping ground' for virtually every new feature or facility....Abstractions have become mixed and information has been jumbled."[2] This is a common fate of popular operating systems during their multi-decade lifetimes. They are pushed to their architectural limits, extended, and then pushed again. The NT kernel, by relying on simple, extensible primitives and by rejecting policies that might become outdated, seeks to shield the NT executive from an eventual "dumping ground" fate.

7.1 Overview

Separating the operating system's mechanisms from its policies is an important principle in Windows NT. Mechanisms refer to the way in which tasks are performed in a system, as exemplified by algorithms and code. Policies determine which tasks should be performed and when, or even whether certain tasks should be performed at all. Operating system code that maintains a strict line between mechanisms and policies helps the operating system remain flexible. Policies can be changed over time without causing a ripple of changes throughout the system or forcing the mechanisms to change too.

The principle of separating policies from mechanisms exists at several levels in Windows NT. At the highest level, each environment subsystem establishes a layer of operating system policies that differs from that of the other subsystems. Beneath the subsystems, the NT executive establishes another, more basic layer of policies that accommodates all the subsystems. At the lowest layer of the operating system, the kernel avoids policy-making altogether. Instead, it serves as a layer between the rest of the operating system and the processor. Forcing all processor-related operations to be channeled through the kernel results in greater portability and predictability. The executive exerts only limited control over these operations by calling kernel functions.

---

1. The kernel is a component of the executive, but its nature is different. For convenience, this chapter frequently uses the term *executive* to refer to all kernel-mode components of the operating system except the kernel.

2. Richard Rashid, "Threads of a New System," *UNIX Review*, August 1986.

In addition to the functions it provides to the NT executive, the kernel performs four main tasks:

- Schedules threads for execution
- Transfers control to handler routines when interrupts and exceptions occur
- Performs low-level multiprocessor synchronization
- Implements system recovery procedures after a power failure occurs

The kernel is different from the rest of the executive in several ways. Unlike other parts of the executive, the kernel is never paged out of memory. Similarly, although it can be interrupted to execute an interrupt service routine (see Chapter 8, "The I/O System"), its execution is never preempted. In other words, multitasking ceases for short periods of time while the kernel runs. The kernel always runs in kernel mode, Windows NT's privileged processor mode, and is designed to be small, compact, and as portable as performance and differences in processor architectures allow. The kernel code is written primarily in C, with assembly code reserved for those tasks that require the fastest possible code or that rely heavily on the capabilities of the processor.

Outside the kernel, the executive represents threads and other shareable resources as objects. These objects require some policy overhead, such as object handles to manipulate them, security checks to protect them, resource quotas to be deducted when they are created, and the prosaic mechanics of allocating and deallocating memory to hold them. This overhead is eliminated in the kernel, which implements a set of simpler objects, called *kernel objects*, that helps the kernel control central processing and supports the creation of executive objects. Most executive-level objects encapsulate one or more kernel objects, incorporating their powerful, kernel-defined attributes.

One set of kernel objects, called *control objects*, establishes semantics for controlling various operating system functions. This set includes the kernel process object, the *asynchronous procedure call* (APC) object, the *deferred procedure call* (DPC) object, and several objects used by the I/O system, including the interrupt object, the power notify object, and the power status object. Another set of kernel objects, known as *dispatcher objects*, incorporates synchronization capabilities and alters or affects thread scheduling. The dispatcher objects include the kernel thread, kernel mutex, kernel mutant, kernel event, kernel event pair, kernel semaphore, and kernel timer. The executive uses kernel functions to create instances of kernel objects, to manipulate them, and to construct the more complex objects it provides to user mode. The kernel objects are discussed in more detail throughout this and the following chapter.

Describing the kernel's design presents a chicken-and-egg problem. There is no particularly appropriate starting point because each part of the kernel relies on the other parts. Therefore, topics in this chapter proceed in order of general interest or significance to the operating system's functioning. Thread scheduling and dispatching are discussed first, followed by interrupt and exception handling. Multiprocessor synchronization is described next, followed by power failure recovery, a topic closely related to Chapter 8's topic—the I/O system.

7.2 Thread Scheduling and Dispatching

A thread is an executable entity that runs in the address space of a process, using resources allocated to the process. One of the NT kernel's jobs is to keep track of the threads that are ready to execute and to select the order in which they will run, a task known as *thread scheduling.* When conditions are right, the kernel selects a new thread to run and performs a context switch to it. A *context switch* is the procedure of saving the volatile machine state associated with a running thread, loading another thread's volatile state, and starting the new thread's execution. The module that performs these duties is the kernel's *dispatcher.*[3]

This section begins with some background information about how the kernel represents threads and processes, followed by a discussion about the dispatcher's duties: scheduling and context switching.

7.2.1 Kernel Process and Thread Objects

The dispatcher's job is to ensure that of all the threads waiting to execute, the processors are always executing the most appropriate ones. When system events that change the status of some thread occur, the dispatcher examines the list of waiting threads and performs a context switch to a new thread if a change is required.

Although the dispatcher manipulates threads, it does not share the same view of threads as user-mode programs do or as the rest of the operating system does. The kernel works with a pared-down version of the thread object,

---

3. The term *dispatch* means to transfer control. In this context, it refers to thread dispatching, or transferring control to a thread. It can also mean transferring control to an appropriate handler routine when an interrupt or exception occurs.

called the *kernel thread object*. A kernel thread object is contained within an executive thread object and represents only the information the kernel needs in order to dispatch the thread for execution. Similarly, the kernel implements a minimal version of a process object, called a *kernel process object*. Figure 7-1 illustrates the relationship between kernel process and kernel thread objects and their higher-level, executive counterparts.

As shown in Figure 7-2 on the next page, the kernel process object contains a pointer to a list of kernel threads. (The kernel has no knowledge of handles, so it bypasses the object table.) The kernel process object also points to the process's page table directory (used to keep track of the process's virtual address space), the total time the process's threads have executed, the process's default base scheduling priority, and the default set of processors on which the threads can run (called their *processor affinity*). The kernel maintains control over the information stored in the kernel process object. The rest of the executive can read or alter the information only by calling a kernel function.

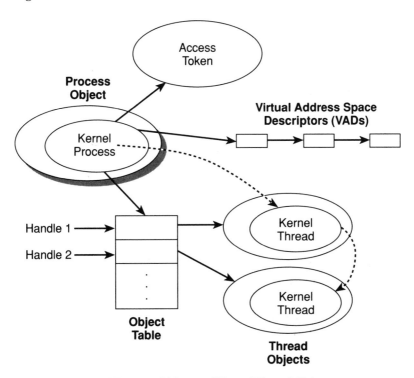

Figure 7-1. Kernel Process Object and Kernel Thread Objects

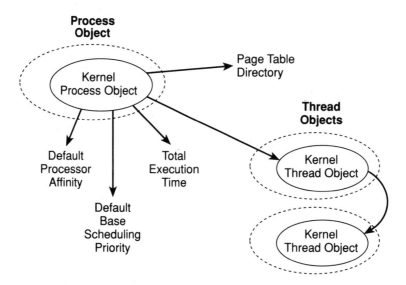

Figure 7-2. Kernel Process Object

The kernel thread object is more complicated than the kernel process object. It contains some obvious information, such as a thread's processor affinity (a nonproper subset of the process's default setting) and the total amount of time the thread has executed. It also includes the thread's base scheduling priority (which can differ from the default base scheduling priority assigned to its process) and the thread's current priority. A particularly important bit of data that the kernel thread object contains is the dispatcher state of a thread. A thread can be in any of six states at any given time, only one of which makes the thread eligible for execution. The dispatcher states of a thread are illustrated in Figure 7-3 on page 210.

A thread's "life cycle" starts when a program creates a new thread. The request filters down to the NT executive, where the process manager allocates space for a thread object and calls the kernel to initialize the kernel thread object contained within it. Once initialized, the thread progresses through the following states:

- Ready. When looking for a thread to execute, the dispatcher considers only the pool of threads in the ready state. These threads are simply waiting to execute.

- Standby. A thread in the standby state has been selected to run next on a particular processor. When the correct conditions exist, the dispatcher performs a context switch to this thread. Only one thread can be in the standby state for each processor on the system.

- Running. Once the dispatcher performs a context switch to a thread, the thread enters the running state and executes. The thread's execution continues until either the kernel preempts it to run a higher priority thread, its time quantum ends, it terminates, or it voluntarily enters the waiting state.

- Waiting. A thread can enter the waiting state in several ways: A thread can voluntarily wait on an object to synchronize its execution; the operating system (the I/O system, for example) can wait on the thread's behalf; or an environment subsystem can direct the thread to suspend itself. When the thread's wait ends, the thread moves back to the ready state to be rescheduled.

- Transition. A thread enters the transition state if it is ready for execution but the resources it needs are not available. For example, the thread's kernel stack might be paged out of memory. Once its resources are available, the thread enters the ready state.

- Terminated. When a thread finishes executing, it enters the terminated state. Once terminated, a thread object might or might not be deleted. (The object manager sets policy regarding when to delete the object.) If the executive has a pointer to the thread object, it can reinitialize the thread object and use it again.

The waiting state bears a little more discussion. A thread is in the waiting state when it is waiting for an object or a group of objects to be set to the signaled state. As discussed in Chapter 4, "Processes and Threads," executive objects that support synchronization are always in one of two states: either signaled or nonsignaled. Objects remain in the nonsignaled state until some significant event takes place. A thread, for example, is set to the signaled state when it terminates. Any user threads that waited on the terminated thread's handle are released and can continue executing. Similarly, a file object is set to the signaled state when a requested I/O operation completes. A thread waiting on the file handle is released from its wait state and can continue executing.

It is, in fact, the kernel that implements Windows NT's wait and signal semantics (not to be confused with POSIX signals, which are more closely akin to NT exceptions). Every synchronization object visible to user mode incorporates one or more of the kernel's dispatcher objects. For example, a thread object contains a kernel thread, an event object contains a kernel event, and a file object contains a kernel event. The kernel is responsible for setting dispatcher objects to the signaled state according to well-defined

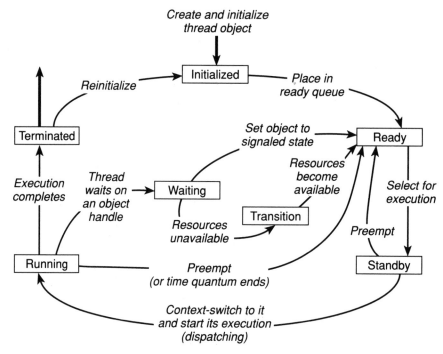

Figure 7-3. Thread States

rules; when it does, it releases threads that were waiting on those objects by changing their dispatcher state from waiting to ready. This in turn prompts the dispatcher to initiate thread scheduling, the topic of the next section. This chapter later revisits the subject of kernel dispatcher objects and synchronization.

7.2.2 Scheduling Priorities

The kernel's dispatcher uses a priority scheme to determine the order in which threads should execute, scheduling higher-priority threads before those with lower priorities. The kernel even discontinues, or *preempts*, a thread's execution if a higher-priority thread becomes ready to execute.

Initially, a thread gets its priority from the process in which it is created. For example, when an environment subsystem creates a process, it assigns a default base priority to the process (a system default or a number set by a system administrator). The thread inherits that base priority and can alter it to be either slightly higher or slightly lower. This is the scheduling priority at which the thread begins executing. The thread's priority might then vary from that base as it executes.

In order to make thread-scheduling decisions, the kernel maintains a set of data structures known collectively as the *dispatcher database*. The dispatcher database keeps track of which threads are waiting to execute and which processors are executing which threads. The most important structure in the dispatcher database is called the *dispatcher ready queue*. This queue is really a series of queues, one queue for each scheduling priority. The queues, shown in Figure 7-4 on the next page, contain threads that are in the ready state, waiting to be scheduled for execution.

As the figure illustrates, the NT executive supports 32 priority levels, divided into two classes: real-time and variable-priority. Real-time threads, those with priorities 16 through 31, are high-priority threads used by time-critical programs—such as an instrument-monitoring application—that require immediate attention from the processor.

When the dispatcher reschedules a processor, it starts at the highest-priority queue and works its way down until it finds a thread; thus, it schedules all real-time threads before scheduling any variable-priority threads. Most threads in the system fall into the variable-priority class, with priorities ranging from 1 to 15. (Priority 0 is reserved for system use.) These threads are called *variable priority* because the dispatcher adjusts their priorities as they execute to optimize system response time. For instance, because Windows NT is a preemptive multitasking system, the dispatcher interrupts a thread after it has executed for a full time quantum. If the interrupted thread is a variable-priority thread, the dispatcher lowers the thread's priority. Thus, the priority of a compute-bound thread gradually decays (down to its base priority).

In contrast, the dispatcher raises a thread's priority after releasing it from a wait operation. Executive code outside the kernel usually determines the size of a thread's priority boost, but the boost size follows a pattern based on what the thread was waiting for. For example, a thread waiting for keyboard input receives a larger boost than one that was waiting for disk I/O to complete. Overall, interactive threads tend to run at a high variable priority, I/O-bound threads at an intermediate priority, and compute-bound threads at a low priority. (A variable-priority thread cannot have its priority boosted into the real-time class.)

A thread's processor affinity also plays a role in deciding the order in which threads execute. The kernel selects a thread based on its priority, and then it checks which processors the thread can run on. If the thread's processor affinity does not allow it to run on any available processor, then the kernel selects the next-higher-priority thread.

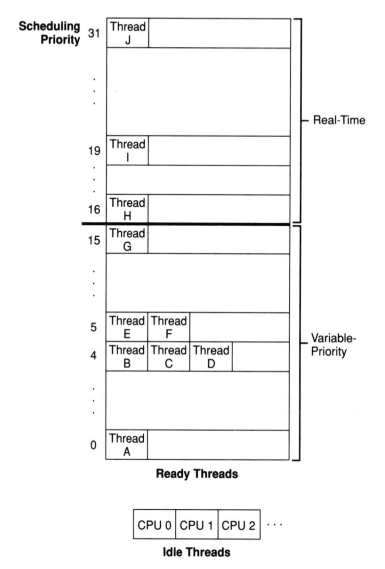

Figure 7-4. Dispatcher Ready Queue

When nothing is happening in the system, the kernel supplies one thread (per processor) that can always execute. These threads are called *idle threads,* and the dispatcher treats them as if their priority were below that of all other threads. An idle thread simply loops, checking whether another thread has entered the standby state and is ready to execute on its processor.

When it detects a thread, the idle thread initiates a context switch to that thread. The idle thread also checks whether there are any deferred procedure call (DPC) routines to be executed. (DPCs are described in Section 7.3.2.3.)

7.2.3 Context Switching

After a thread executes for a complete time quantum, the kernel preempts it and reschedules the processor. Time quantum expiration is not the only thing that initiates thread scheduling, however. Scheduling is event driven, triggered when the thread that is running can't continue or when the status of a thread changes and the executing thread is no longer the highest-priority thread. Some examples of conditions that cause rescheduling are listed below:

- When a thread becomes ready to execute—for instance, a newly initialized thread or one just released from the waiting state

- When a thread's time quantum ends, when it terminates, or when it enters the waiting state

- When the dispatcher or the executive (perhaps at the request of an application program) changes a thread's priority

- When the executive or an application program changes the processor affinity of a thread that is running

The purpose of rescheduling is to select the thread to execute next on a particular processor and put it into the standby state. Simply finding the thread is not enough, however. The dispatcher must also start its execution.

If the thread that was running has terminated or otherwise cannot continue executing, the dispatcher simply performs a context switch to the new thread. Otherwise, the dispatcher needs to do more. For example, if a high-priority, real-time thread becomes ready to execute but a lower priority thread is still running, the dispatcher must preempt the executing thread. To preempt a thread, the dispatcher requests a software interrupt to initiate a context switch, as shown in Figure 7-5 on the next page.

When rescheduling threads, the kernel uses the dispatcher database to quickly determine which processors are busy, which are idle (running their idle thread), and what priority of thread each processor is executing. In this example, the kernel (running on Processor A) determines that Processor B is running a thread with a lower priority than that of the newly ready thread. The kernel requests a dispatch interrupt to preempt the thread running on Processor B. The kernel running on Processor B responds to the

Time

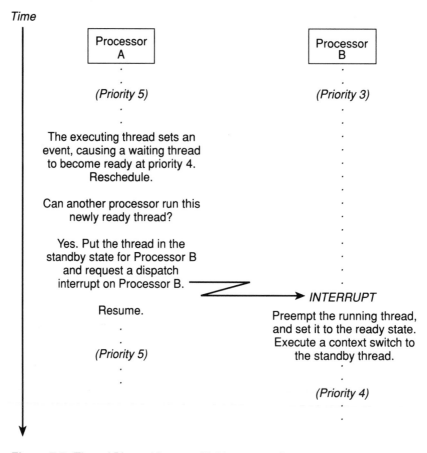

Figure 7-5. Thread Dispatching on a Multiprocessor System

interrupt by rescheduling, that is, initiating a context switch from the priority 3 thread it is running to the new thread. The preempted thread is reset to the ready state and returned to the dispatcher ready queue to be scheduled later, perhaps on a different processor. Although most threads are placed at the end of the queue for their priority, a preempted thread is given the benefit of being placed in the first position of the queue.

A thread's context and the procedure for context switching varies depending on the architecture of a processor. A typical context switch requires saving and reloading the following data:

- Program counter
- Processor status register

- Other register contents

- User and kernel stack pointers

- A pointer to the address space in which the thread runs (the process's page table directory)

To make a context switch, the kernel saves this information by pushing it onto the current thread's kernel-mode stack and updating the stack pointer. The kernel loads the new thread's context and, if the new thread is in a different process, loads the address of its page table directory so that its address space is available. After the kernel does some cleanup, control passes to the new thread's restored program counter and the thread begins executing.

It is worth repeating here that although a thread running NT executive code can be preempted by a higher-priority thread, a thread running kernel code cannot be preempted. When the kernel runs, it effectively runs at a priority higher than that of any other thread in the system. (Actually, it temporarily disables thread dispatching.) Although it can't be preempted, most of the kernel can be interrupted by high-level interrupts, a topic described later in this chapter.

7.3 Interrupt and Exception Handling

Interrupts and exceptions are operating system conditions that divert the processor to code outside the normal flow of control. They can be detected by either hardware or software. When an interrupt or an exception is detected, the processor stops what it is doing and transfers control (dispatches) to a special location in memory, the address of the code that deals with the condition. In NT, this code is called the *trap handler.*

The NT kernel distinguishes between interrupts and exceptions in the following way. An *interrupt* is an asynchronous event, one that can occur at any time, unrelated to what the processor is executing. Interrupts are generated primarily by I/O devices, processor clocks, or timers, and they can be enabled (turned on) or disabled (turned off).

An *exception,* in contrast, is a synchronous condition, resulting from the execution of a particular instruction. Exceptions can be reproduced by running the same program with the same data under the same conditions. Examples of exceptions include memory access violations, certain debugger instructions, and divide-by-zero errors. The NT kernel also regards system service calls as exceptions (although technically, they are system traps).

The following discussion focuses on interrupt and exception handling as it is implemented on the MIPS R4000 processor. Implementations of

Windows NT on other architectures might work differently because of variations in the support supplied by the processor.

7.3.1 Trap Handler

The term *trap* refers to a processor's mechanism for capturing an executing thread when an exception or interrupt occurs, switching from user mode into kernel mode, and transferring control to a fixed location in the operating system. In Windows NT, the processor transfers control to the NT kernel's trap handler, a module that acts as a switchboard by fielding exceptions and interrupts detected by the processor and transfering control to code that handles the condition.

Exceptions and interrupts can be generated by either hardware or software. For example, a bus error exception is caused by a hardware problem, whereas a divide-by-zero exception is caused by a software bug. Likewise, an I/O device can generate an interrupt, or the kernel itself can issue a software interrupt. Figure 7-6 illustrates some of the conditions that activate the trap handler and the modules the trap handler calls to service them.

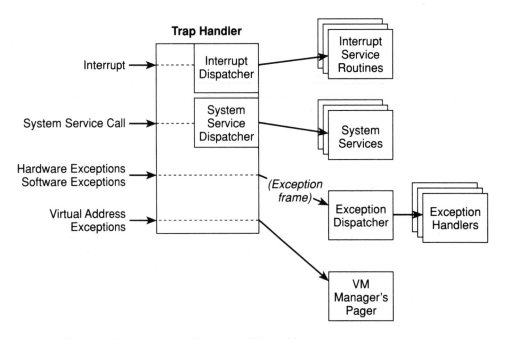

Figure 7-6. Interrupt and Exception Dispatching

When invoked, the trap handler disables interrupts briefly while it records the machine state (information that would be wiped out if another interrupt or exception occurred). It creates a *trap frame* in which it stores the execution state of the interrupted thread. This information allows the kernel to resume execution of the thread after handling the interrupt or the exception. The trap frame is usually a subset of a thread's complete context. As mentioned in the previous section, a thread's context varies with the architecture of the processor.

The trap handler resolves some problems itself, such as some virtual address exceptions, but in most cases, it determines the condition that occurred and transfers control to other kernel or executive modules. For example, if the condition was a device interrupt, the kernel transfers control to the *interrupt service routine* (ISR) provided by the device driver for the interrupting device. If the condition was caused by a call to a system service, the trap handler transfers control to the system service code in the NT executive. The remaining exceptions are fielded by the kernel's own exception dispatcher. The following sections describe interrupt dispatching, system-service dispatching, and exception handling in greater detail.

7.3.2 Interrupt Dispatching

Hardware-generated interrupts typically originate from I/O devices that must notify the processor when they need service. Interrupt-driven devices allow the operating system to get the maximum use of the processor by overlapping central processing with I/O operations. The processor starts an I/O transfer to or from a device and then executes other threads while the device completes the transfer. When the device is finished, it interrupts the processor for service. Pointing devices, printers, keyboards, disk drives, and network cards are generally interrupt driven.

System software can also generate interrupts. For example, the kernel can issue a software interrupt to initiate thread dispatching and to asynchronously break into the execution of a thread. The kernel can disable interrupts so that the processor does not receive them, but it does so only infrequently—at critical moments while processing an interrupt or dispatching an exception, for example.

A submodule of the kernel's trap handler, called the *interrupt dispatcher*, responds to interrupts. It determines the source of an interrupt and transfers control either to an external routine that handles the interrupt, called an interrupt service routine (ISR), or to an internal kernel routine that responds to the interrupt. Device drivers supply ISRs to service device interrupts, and the kernel provides interrupt handling routines for other types of interrupts.

The following subsection begins by describing the types of interrupts that the NT kernel supports. More details about interrupt processing follow, including a brief discussion about the way device drivers interact with the kernel. The last subsection describes the software interrupts that the kernel recognizes and the kernel objects that are used to implement them.

7.3.2.1 Interrupt Types and Priorities

Different processors are capable of recognizing different numbers and types of interrupts. The interrupt dispatcher maps hardware-interrupt levels onto a standard set of *interrupt request levels* (IRQLs) recognized by the operating system.

IRQLs rank interrupts by priority. IRQL priorities are different from the scheduling priorities described earlier. A scheduling priority is an attribute of a thread, whereas an IRQL is an attribute of an interrupt source, such as a keyboard or a mouse. In addition, each processor has an IRQL setting that changes as operating system code executes. A thread running in kernel mode can raise or lower the IRQL setting of the processor on which it is running to mask or unmask lower-level interrupts.

The kernel defines a set of portable IRQLs, which it can augment if a processor has special interrupt-related features (a second clock, for example). Interrupts are serviced in priority order, and a higher-priority interrupt preempts the servicing of a lower-priority interrupt. The portable IRQLs are shown in Table 7-1, from highest to lowest priority.

The IRQLs from high level down to device level 1 are reserved for hardware interrupts, and dispatch/DPC level and APC level interrupts are software interrupts that the kernel generates. The low IRQL is not really an interrupt level at all; it is the setting at which normal thread execution takes place and all interrupts are allowed to occur.

Each processor's IRQL setting determines which interrupts that processor can receive. As a kernel-mode thread runs, it raises or lowers the processor's IRQL. As Figure 7-7 illustrates, interrupts from a source with an IRQL above the current setting interrupt the processor, whereas interrupts from sources with IRQLs equal to or below the current level are blocked, or *masked*, until an executing thread lowers the IRQL.

A kernel-mode thread raises and lowers the IRQL of the processor on which it is running, depending on what it is trying to do. For example, when an interrupt occurs, the trap handler (or perhaps the processor) raises the processor's IRQL to the assigned IRQL of the interrupt source. This blocks all

IRQL	Type of Interrupt
High level	Machine check or bus error[4]
Power level	Power failure
Interprocessor interrupt level	Work request from another processor
Clock level	Interval clock
Device level n	Highest-priority I/O device
⋮	⋮
Device level 1	Lowest-priority I/O device
Dispatch/DPC level	Thread dispatching and deferred procedure call (DPC) processing
APC level	Asynchronous procedure call (APC) processing
Low level	Normal thread execution

Table 7-1. Interrupt Request Levels (IRQLs)

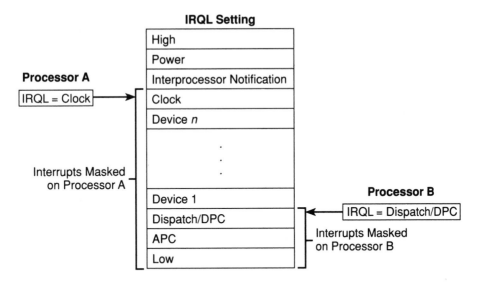

Figure 7-7. Masking Interrupts

---

4. These catastrophic hardware errors actually generate exceptions rather than interrupts. However, when a machine check or bus occurs, the kernel raises the processor's IRQL to high level to mask all interrupts so that it can shut down the system immediately, preventing damage.

interrupts at and below that IRQL (on that processor only), which ensures that the processor servicing the interrupt is not waylaid by a less-important interrupt. The masked interrupts are either handled by another processor or held back until the IRQL drops. Changing a processor's IRQL is a powerful operation that must be performed with great care. User-mode threads cannot change the processor's IRQL.

Each interrupt level has a specific purpose. The processor issues a power level interrupt when it detects a drop in voltage from the power source. A power level interrupt causes the operating system to shut itself down, recording critical information about the system's state before it does so that it can restart when the power returns and continue where it left off. (See Section 7.5 for more information.) The kernel issues an interprocessor interrupt (IPI) to request that another processor perform an action, such as dispatching a particular thread for execution or updating its translation lookaside buffer (TLB) cache. The system clock generates an interrupt at regular intervals, and the kernel responds by updating the clock and measuring thread execution time. If a processor supports two clocks, the kernel adds another clock interrupt level for performance measurement. The kernel provides a number of interrupt levels for use by interrupt-driven devices; the exact number varies with the processor and system configuration. The kernel uses software interrupts at dispatch/DPC and APC IRQLs to initiate thread scheduling and to asynchronously break into a thread's execution. Software interrupts are described in Section 7.3.2.3.

7.3.2.2 Interrupt Processing

When an interrupt occurs, the trap handler saves the machine's state and then calls the interrupt dispatcher. The interrupt dispatcher immediately raises the processor's IRQL to the level of the interrupt source to mask interrupts at and below that level while interrupt servicing is in progress.

Like many operating systems, NT uses an *interrupt dispatch table* (IDT) to locate the routine to handle a particular interrupt. The IRQL of the interrupting source serves as a table index, and table entries point to the interrupt-handling routines, as shown in Figure 7-8.

After the service routine executes, the interrupt dispatcher lowers the processor's IRQL to where it was before the interrupt occurred and then loads the saved machine state. The interrupted thread resumes executing where it left off. When the kernel lowers the IRQL, lower-priority interrupts that were blocked might materialize. If this happens, the kernel repeats the process to handle the new interrupt.

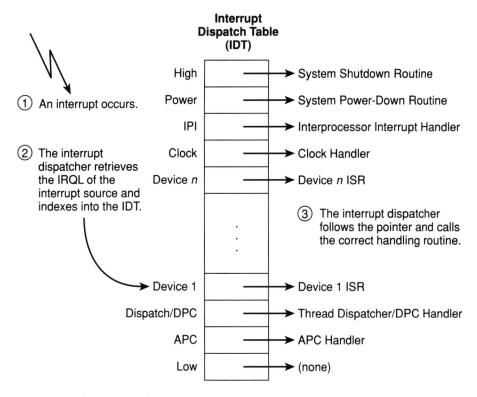

Interrupt Dispatch Table (IDT)

① An interrupt occurs.

② The interrupt dispatcher retrieves the IRQL of the interrupt source and indexes into the IDT.

High	→	System Shutdown Routine
Power	→	System Power-Down Routine
IPI	→	Interprocessor Interrupt Handler
Clock	→	Clock Handler
Device *n*	→	Device *n* ISR

③ The interrupt dispatcher follows the pointer and calls the correct handling routine.

Device 1	→	Device 1 ISR
Dispatch/DPC	→	Thread Dispatcher/DPC Handler
APC	→	APC Handler
Low	→	(none)

Figure 7-8. Servicing an Interrupt

Each processor has a separate interrupt dispatch table so that different processors can run different ISRs, if appropriate. For example, in a multiprocessor system, each processor receives the clock interrupt but only one processor updates the system clock in response to this interrupt. However, all the processors use the interrupt to measure time quantum and to initiate rescheduling when a thread's time quantum ends. Similarly, some system configurations might require that certain device interrupts be handled by a particular processor.

Most of the routines that handle interrupts reside in the kernel. The kernel updates the clock time, for example, and shuts down the system when a power level interrupt occurs. However, many interrupts are generated by external devices, such as keyboards, pointing devices, and disk drives. Therefore, device drivers need a way to tell the kernel which routine to call when a device interrupt occurs.

The kernel provides a portable mechanism—a kernel control object called an *interrupt object*—that allows device drivers to register ISRs for their devices. An interrupt object contains all the information the kernel needs to associate a device ISR with a particular level of interrupt, including the address of the ISR, the IRQL at which the device interrupts, and the entry in the kernel's IDT with which the ISR should be associated.

Associating an ISR with a particular level of interrupt is called *connecting an interrupt object,* and dissociating an ISR from an IDT entry is called *disconnecting an interrupt object.* These operations, accomplished by calling a kernel function, allow a device driver to "turn on" an ISR when the driver is loaded into the system and to "turn it off" again if the driver is unloaded.

Using the interrupt object to register an ISR prevents device drivers from fiddling directly with interrupt hardware, which differs among processor architectures, and from needing to know any details about the interrupt dispatch table. This kernel feature aids in creating portable device drivers because it eliminates the need to code in assembly language or to reflect processor differences in device drivers.

Interrupt objects provide other benefits as well. By using the interrupt object, the kernel can synchronize the execution of the ISR with other parts of a device driver that might share data with the ISR. (See Chapter 8, "The I/O System," for more information.) Furthermore, interrupt objects allow the kernel to easily call more than one ISR for any interrupt level. If multiple device drivers create interrupt objects and connect them to the same IDT entry, the interrupt dispatcher calls each routine when an interrupt occurs at that level. This allows the kernel to easily support "daisy-chain" configurations, in which several devices interrupt at the same priority.

7.3.2.3 Software Interrupts

Although hardware generates most interrupts, the NT kernel also generates software interrupts for a variety of tasks:

- Initiating thread dispatching
- Handling timer expiration
- Asynchronously executing a procedure in the context of a particular thread
- Supporting asynchronous I/O operations

Descriptions of these tasks follow.

Dispatch Interrupts You've already seen one place in which the kernel uses software interrupts—in the thread dispatcher. When a thread can no longer continue executing, perhaps because it has terminated or because it waits on an object handle, the kernel calls the dispatcher directly to effect an immediate context switch. However, sometimes the kernel detects that rescheduling should occur when it is deep within many layers of code. In this situation, the ideal solution is to request dispatching but defer its occurrence until the kernel completes its current activity. Using a software interrupt is a convenient way to achieve this.

For synchronization purposes (see Section 7.4), the kernel always raises the processor's IRQL to dispatch/DPC level or above when it runs, which masks software interrupts (and disables thread dispatching). When the kernel detects that dispatching should occur, it requests a dispatch/DPC level interrupt, but because the IRQL is at or above that level, the processor holds the interrupt in check. When the kernel completes its current activity, it lowers the IRQL below dispatch/DPC level, and the dispatch interrupt surfaces.

Deferred Procedure Call (DPC) Interrupts Activating the dispatcher by using a software interrupt is a way to defer dispatching until conditions are right. NT uses software interrupts to defer other types of processing as well.

Dispatching takes place at the dispatch/DPC IRQL. Interrupts that occur at this level pass through the trap handler to the dispatcher, which performs thread scheduling. En route, the kernel also processes deferred procedure calls (DPCs). A DPC is a function that performs a system task, one that is less important than the current task. The functions are called "deferred" because they might not execute immediately. Similar to dispatch interrupts, DPCs execute only after the kernel (or, often, the I/O system) finishes more important work and lowers the processor's IRQL below dispatch/DPC level.

DPCs provide the operating system with the capability to generate an interrupt and execute a system function in kernel mode. The kernel uses DPCs to process timer expiration (and release threads waiting on the timers) and to reschedule the processor after a thread's time quantum expires. Device drivers use DPCs to complete I/O requests. (See Chapter 8, "The I/O System," for more information.)

A DPC is represented by a *DPC object,* a kernel control object that is not visible to user-mode programs but is visible to device drivers and other system code. The most important piece of information the DPC object contains is the address of the system function that the kernel will call when it processes the DPC interrupt. DPC routines that are waiting to execute are stored in a kernel-managed queue called the *DPC queue.* To request a DPC, system code calls the kernel to initialize a DPC object and then places it in the DPC queue.

Placing a DPC in the DPC queue prompts the kernel to request a software interrupt at dispatch/DPC level. Because DPCs are generally queued by software running at a higher IRQL, the requested interrupt does not surface until the kernel lowers the IRQL to APC level or low level. DPC processing is depicted in Figure 7-9.

DPC routines execute "under the covers"; that is, when the IRQL drops, they execute without regard to what thread is running. Because user-mode threads execute at low IRQL, the chances are good that a DPC will interrupt the execution of an ordinary user's thread. This means, for example, that a DPC might execute in your address space with access to your resources, without your knowing it. Because of this and because they execute at dispatch/DPC IRQL, DPCs cannot acquire system resources or modify the borrowed thread's virtual memory. They can call kernel functions but cannot call system services, generate page faults, or create or wait on objects. Fortunately, only system code can queue a DPC, and the operating system

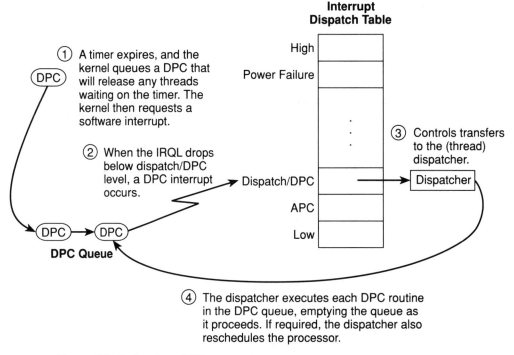

Figure 7-9. Delivering a DPC

guarantees that its DPCs behave correctly. (Device drivers must be sure to use them properly as well.)

DPCs are provided primarily for device drivers, but the kernel uses them too. The kernel most frequently uses a DPC to handle time-quantum expiration. At every tick of the system clock, an interrupt occurs at clock IRQL. The clock interrupt handler (running at clock IRQL) updates the system time and then decrements a counter that tracks how long the current thread has run. When the counter reaches zero, the thread's time quantum has expired and the kernel might need to reschedule the processor, a lower-priority task that should be done at dispatch/DPC IRQL. The clock interrupt handler queues a DPC to initiate thread dispatching and then finishes its work and lowers the processor's IRQL. Because the DPC interrupt has a lower priority than do device interrupts, any pending device interrupts that surface are handled before the DPC interrupt occurs.

Asynchronous Procedure Call (APC) Interrupts When the kernel queues a DPC object, the ensuing DPC interrupt breaks into the execution of whatever thread is running. Sometimes it is also handy to be able to interrupt a specific thread and direct it to execute a procedure.

The kernel provides the means to do that with what is called an asynchronous procedure call (APC). Both system code and user-mode code can queue an APC, although kernel-mode APCs are more powerful. Like the DPC, an APC executes asynchronously when conditions are right. For user-mode APCs, the conditions imposed are as follows:

- The thread that is to execute the APC must be running.

- The processor's IRQL must be at low level.

- The thread that is the target of the user-mode APC must have declared itself to be alertable (a topic discussed shortly).

Kernel-mode APCs do not require "permission" from a target thread to run in that thread's context, as user-mode APCs do. Kernel-mode APCs can interrupt a thread and execute a procedure without the thread's intervention or consent.

A program queues an APC to a particular thread by calling the kernel, either directly (for system code) or indirectly (for user-mode code). The kernel, in turn, requests a software interrupt at APC level, and when all the conditions listed above are met, the targeted thread is interrupted, and it executes the APC.

Like DPCs, APCs are described by a kernel control object, called an *APC object*. APCs waiting to execute reside in a kernel-managed *APC queue*. Unlike the DPC queue, which is system-wide, the APC queue is thread-specific—each thread has its own APC queue. When asked to queue an APC, the kernel inserts it into the queue belonging to the thread that will execute the APC routine.

Because an APC executes in the context of a particular thread and because it executes at a lower IRQL, it does not operate under the same restrictions as a DPC. It can acquire resources (objects), wait on object handles, incur page faults, and call system services. This makes APCs useful even for user-mode code.

Although user-mode code cannot create or queue an APC object directly, certain native NT services accept a user-mode APC routine as a parameter. For example, a subsystem or DLL can specify an APC routine when it sets a timer. When the timer goes off, the kernel queues the APC back to the subsystem, which executes it. If a subsystem makes NT's APC capability available to client applications, an application could, for example, use APCs to perform garbage collection at regular intervals. Similarly, native I/O services take an optional APC as a parameter, which allows a caller to perform a routine based on the outcome of an I/O operation. (Although the Win32 subsystem doesn't export NT APCs directly in its API, it does provide APC capabilities in its ReadFileEx() and WriteFileEx() API routines.)

Although it can't block kernel-mode APCs, a thread can block delivery of user-mode APCs. In fact, a thread must explicitly indicate its willingness to accept a user-mode APC interrupt by declaring itself to be *alertable*. It can do this either by waiting on an object handle and specifying that its wait is alertable or by testing directly whether it has a pending APC. In both cases, if a user-mode APC is pending, the kernel interrupts (alerts) the thread, transfers control to the APC routine, and resumes the thread's execution when the APC routine completes.

The NT executive uses kernel-mode APCs to perform operating system work that must be completed within the address space (in the context) of a particular thread. It can use kernel-mode APCs to direct a thread to stop executing an interruptible system service, for example, or to record the results of an asynchronous I/O operation in a thread's address space. Environment subsystems use kernel-mode APCs to make a thread suspend or terminate itself or to get or set its user-mode execution context. Chapter 8, "The I/O System," revisits the topic of APCs because they are used extensively in NT I/O processing.

7.3.3 Exception Dispatching

In contrast to interrupts, which can occur at any time, exceptions are conditions that result directly from the execution of the program that is running. Microsoft C defines a software architecture known as structured exception handling, which allows applications to respond to exceptions uniformly. Chapter 2, "System Overview," introduced the basic concepts behind structured exception handling. This subsection examines it from another point of view—how the kernel sees an exception and what it does when one occurs.

All exceptions, except those simple enough to be resolved by the trap handler, are serviced by a kernel module called the *exception dispatcher*. (Refer to Figure 7-6.) This kernel module is dependent on the processor architecture, but it is written in C. The exception dispatcher's job is to find an exception handler that can "dispose of" the exception. The following are architecture-independent exceptions that the kernel defines:

Memory access violation	Integer divide by zero
Integer overflow	Floating-point overflow/underflow
Floating point divide by zero	Floating-point reserved operand
Debugger breakpoint	Data-type misalignment
Illegal instruction	Privileged instruction
Debugger single step	Guard page violation
Page read error	Paging file quota exceeded

The NT kernel traps and handles some of these exceptions, unbeknownst to user programs. For example, encountering a debugger breakpoint while executing a program being debugged generates an exception, which the kernel handles by calling the debugger. The kernel handles certain other exceptions by returning an unsuccessful status code to the caller.

A few exceptions are allowed to filter back, untouched, to user mode. For example, a memory access violation or an arithmetic overflow generates an exception that the operating system does not handle. An environment subsystem or a native application can establish *frame-based exception handlers* to deal with these exceptions by using high-level language statements designed specifically for exception handling. Microsoft C is the first Microsoft language to support structured exception handling but Windows NT's exception handling capabilities are not language-specific.

The term *frame-based* refers to an exception handler's association with a particular procedure activation. When a procedure is invoked, a stack frame representing that activation of the procedure is pushed onto the stack. A stack frame can have one or more exception handlers associated with it, each of which protects a particular block of code in the source program. When an exception occurs, the kernel searches for an exception handler associated with the current stack frame. If none exists, the kernel searches for an exception handler associated with the previous stack frame, and so on, until it finds a frame-based exception handler. If no exception handler is found, the kernel calls its own default exception handlers. (Note that exception handling is implemented differently on different processors. The Intel *x*86 implementation uses a stack-frame approach, whereas the MIPS R4000 implementation uses a table-based approach.)

When an exception occurs, whether it is explicitly raised by software or implicitly raised by hardware, a chain of events begins in the kernel. Control transfers to the trap handler, which creates a trap frame (as it does when an interrupt occurs). The trap frame will allow the system to resume where it left off if the exception is resolved. The trap handler also creates an exception record that contains the reason for the exception and other pertinent information.

If the exception occurred in kernel mode, the exception dispatcher simply calls a routine to locate a frame-based exception handler that will handle the exception. Because unhandled kernel-mode exceptions are considered fatal operating system errors, you can assume that the dispatcher always finds an exception handler.

If the exception occurred in user mode, the exception dispatcher does something more elaborate. You might recall from Chapter 4, "Processes and Threads," that an environment subsystem can establish a debugger port and an exception port for each process it creates. The kernel uses these in its default exception handling, as illustrated in Figure 7-10.

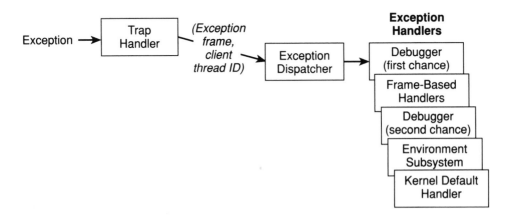

Figure 7-10. Dispatching an Exception

Debugger breakpoints are common sources of exceptions. Therefore, the first action the exception dispatcher takes is to send a message (via LPC) to the debugger port associated with the process that incurred the exception. This allows a user to manipulate data structures and issue debugger commands.

If no debugger port is registered or if the debugger doesn't handle the exception, the exception dispatcher switches into user mode and calls a routine to find a frame-based exception handler. If none is found or if none handles the exception, the exception dispatcher switches back into kernel mode and calls the debugger again to allow the user to do more debugging.

If the debugger isn't running and no frame-based handlers are found, the kernel sends a message to the exception port associated with the thread's process. This exception port, if one exists, was registered by the environment subsystem that controls this thread. The exception port gives the environment subsystem, which presumably is listening at the port, the opportunity to translate the NT exception into an environment-specific signal or exception. For example, when POSIX gets a message from the kernel that one of its threads generated an exception, the POSIX subsystem sends a POSIX-style signal to the thread that caused the exception.

Although by default the POSIX subsystem associates an exception port with each of its processes, other subsystems might not supply a port or might not take action when the kernel informs them of an unhandled exception in one of their processes. If the kernel progresses this far in processing the exception and the subsystem doesn't handle the exception, the kernel executes a default exception handler that simply terminates the process whose thread caused the exception.

7.3.4 System Service Dispatching

As Figure 7-6 illustrated, the NT kernel's trap handler dispatches interrupts, exceptions, and system service calls. The previous sections described interrupt and exception handling, and this section looks briefly at system services. System service calls, which generate traps that are treated as exceptions in Windows NT, are interesting from the viewpoint of system extensibility. The way in which the kernel implements system services allows new services to be added dynamically to the operating system in future releases.

Whenever a user-mode thread calls a system service, the thread is suddenly allowed to run privileged operating system code. Ordinarily, this is anathema to an operating system. A user-mode thread could tamper with system data structures or move things around in memory, wreaking havoc on the system or on other users. For this reason, processors generally provide a special instruction only for system services. The instruction—*syscall* on MIPS processors and *int 2Eh* on Intel *x86* processors—is generated when a user-mode thread calls a system service. The hardware issues a trap and switches from user-mode to kernel-mode execution. When this happens, the kernel copies the caller's arguments from the thread's user-mode stack to its kernel-mode stack (so that the user can't change the arguments willy-nilly), and then executes the system service.

As Figure 7-11 illustrates, the kernel uses a system-service dispatch table to find system services. This table is similar to the interrupt dispatch table described earlier except that each entry contains a pointer to a system service rather than to an interrupt handling routine.

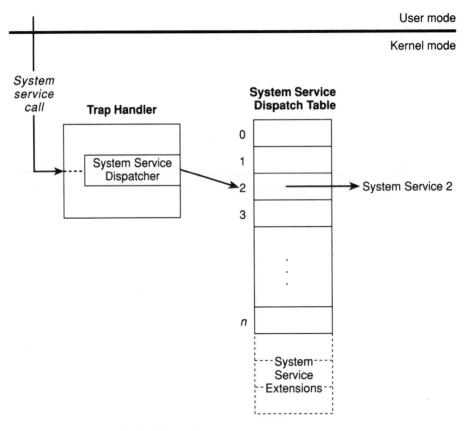

Figure 7-11. System Service Exceptions

Using a system-service dispatch table provides an opportunity to make native NT services extensible. The kernel can support new system services simply by expanding the table, without requiring changes to the system or to applications. After code is written for a new service, a system administrator could simply run a utility program that dynamically creates a new dispatch table. The new table would contain another entry that points to the new system service. Although neither this capability nor its user interface is present in the first release of Windows NT, it could be added at a later time.

7.4 Multiprocessor Synchronization

The concept of *mutual exclusion* is a crucial one in operating systems development. It refers to the guarantee that one, and only one, thread can access a particular resource at a time. Mutual exclusion is necessary when a resource does not lend itself to shared access or when sharing would result in an unpredictable outcome. For instance, if two threads copy a file to a printer port at the same time, their output could be interspersed. Similarly, if one thread reads a memory location while another one writes to it, the first thread will receive unpredictable data. In general, "writable" resources cannot be shared without restrictions, whereas resources that are not subject to modification can be shared. Figure 7-12 illustrates what happens when two threads running on different processors both write data to a circular queue.

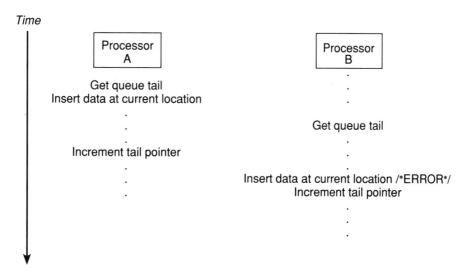

Figure 7-12. Incorrect Sharing of Memory

Because the second thread got the value of the queue tail pointer before the first thread had updated it, the second thread inserted its data into the same location that the first thread had used, overwriting data and leaving one queue location empty. Note that although this figure illustrates what could happen on a multiprocessor system, the same error could occur on a single-processor system if the operating system were to perform a context switch to the second thread before the first thread updated the queue tail pointer.

Sections of code that access a nonshareable resource are called *critical sections*. To ensure correct code, only one thread at a time can execute in a critical section. While one thread is writing to a file, updating a database, or modifying a shared variable, no other thread can be allowed to access the same resource. The code shown in Figure 7-12 is a critical section that incorrectly accesses a shared data structure without mutual exclusion.

The issue of mutual exclusion, although important for all operating systems, is especially important (and intricate) for a *tightly-coupled, symmetric multiprocessing* (SMP) operating system such as Windows NT, in which the same system code runs simultaneously on more than one processor, sharing certain data structures stored in global memory. In Windows NT, it is the kernel's job to provide mechanisms that system code can use to prevent two threads from modifying the same structure at the same time. The kernel provides mutual-exclusion primitives that it and the rest of the executive use to synchronize their access to global data structures.

The following subsection describes how the kernel uses mutual exclusion to protect its global data structures. The next section focuses on the mutual-exclusion and synchronization mechanisms the kernel provides to the executive and which it, in turn, provides to user mode.

7.4.1 Kernel Synchronization

At various stages during its execution, the kernel must guarantee that one, and only one, processor at a time is executing within a critical section. Kernel critical sections are the code segments that modify a global data structure such as the kernel's dispatcher database or its DPC queue. The operating system cannot function correctly unless the kernel can guarantee that threads access these data structures in a mutually exclusive manner.

The biggest area for concern is interrupts. For example, the kernel might be updating a global data structure when an interrupt occurs whose interrupt-handling routine also modifies the structure. Simple single-processor operating systems sometimes prevent such a scenario by disabling all interrupts each time they access global data, but the NT kernel has a more sophisticated solution. Before using a global resource, the kernel temporarily masks those interrupts whose interrupt handlers also use the resource. It does so by raising the processor's IRQL to the highest level used by any potential interrupt source that accesses the global data. For example, an interrupt at dispatch/DPC level causes the dispatcher, which uses the dispatcher database, to run. Therefore, any other part of the kernel that uses the dispatcher database raises the IRQL to dispatch/DPC level, masking dispatch/DPC level interrupts before using the dispatcher database.

This strategy is fine for a single-processor system, but it is inadequate for a multiprocessor configuration. Raising the IRQL on one processor does not prevent an interrupt from occurring on another processor. The kernel also needs to guarantee mutually exclusive access across several processors.

The mechanism the kernel uses to achieve multiprocessor mutual exclusion is called a *spin lock*. A spin lock is a locking mechanism associated with a global data structure, such as the DPC queue, shown in Figure 7-13.

Before entering either critical section shown in the figure, the kernel must acquire the spin lock associated with the protected DPC queue. If the spin lock is not free, the kernel keeps trying to acquire the lock until it succeeds. The spin lock is called a "spin lock" because the kernel (and thus, the processor) is held in limbo, "spinning," until it gets the lock.

Spin locks, like the data structures they protect, reside in global memory. The code to acquire and release a spin lock is written in assembly language for speed and to exploit whatever locking mechanism the underlying

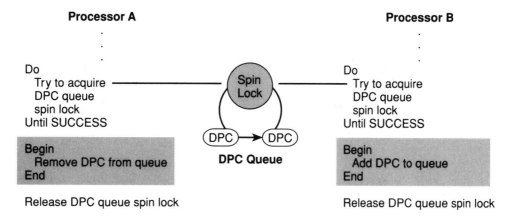

Figure 7-13. Using a Spin Lock

processor architecture provides. On many architectures, spin locks are implemented with a hardware-supported test-and-set operation, which tests the value of a lock variable and acquires the lock in one atomic instruction. Testing and acquiring the lock in one instruction prevents a second thread from grabbing the lock between the time when the first thread tests the variable and the time when it acquires the lock.

When a thread is trying to acquire a spin lock, all other activity ceases on that processor. Therefore, a thread that holds a spin lock is never preempted but is allowed to continue executing so that it will release the lock quickly. The kernel uses spin locks with great care, minimizing the number of instructions it executes while it holds a spin lock.

The kernel makes spin locks available to other parts of the executive through a set of kernel functions. Device drivers, for example, require spin locks in order to guarantee that device registers and other global data structures are accessed by only one part of a device driver (and from only one processor) at a time. This topic is revisited in Chapter 8, "The I/O System."

7.4.2 Executive Synchronization

Executive software outside the kernel also needs to synchronize access to global data structures in a multiprocessor environment. For example, the VM manager has only one page frame database, which it accesses as a global data structure, and device drivers need to ensure that they can gain exclusive access to their devices. By calling kernel functions, the executive can create a spin lock, acquire it, and release it.

Spin locks only partially fill the executive's needs for synchronization mechanisms, however. Because waiting on a spin lock literally stalls a processor, spin locks can be used only under the following strictly limited circumstances:

- The protected resource must be accessed quickly and without complicated interactions with other code.

- The critical section code cannot be paged out of memory, cannot make references to pageable data, cannot call external procedures (including system services), and cannot generate interrupts or exceptions.

These restrictions are confining and cannot be met under all circumstances. Furthermore, the executive needs to perform other types of synchronization in addition to mutual exclusion and it must also provide synchronization mechanisms to user mode.

The kernel furnishes additional synchronization mechanisms to the executive in the form of kernel objects, known collectively as dispatcher objects. A thread can synchronize with a dispatcher object by waiting on the object's handle. Doing so causes the kernel to suspend the thread and change its dispatcher state from running to waiting, as highlighted in Figure 7-14. The kernel removes the thread from the dispatcher ready queue and no longer considers it for execution.

A thread cannot resume its execution until the kernel changes its dispatcher state from waiting to ready. This change occurs when the dispatcher object whose handle the thread is waiting on also undergoes a state change, from the nonsignaled state to the signaled state (when a thread sets an event object, for example). The kernel is responsible for both types of transitions. Some of the kernel dispatcher objects and the system events that induce their state changes are illustrated in Figure 7-15 on the next page.

Each type of dispatcher object provides a specialized type of synchronization capability. For example, mutex objects provide mutual exclusion, whereas semaphores act as a gate through which a variable number of threads can pass—useful when a number of identical resources are available. Events can be used either to announce that some action has occurred or to implement mutual exclusion. Event pairs are the the kernel's means of supporting

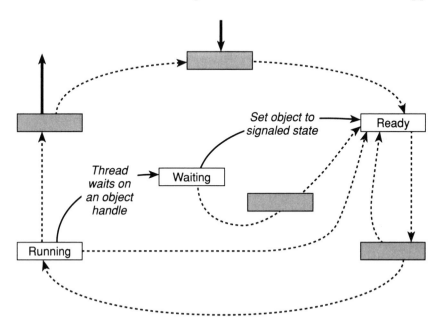

Figure 7-14. Waiting on a Dispatcher Object

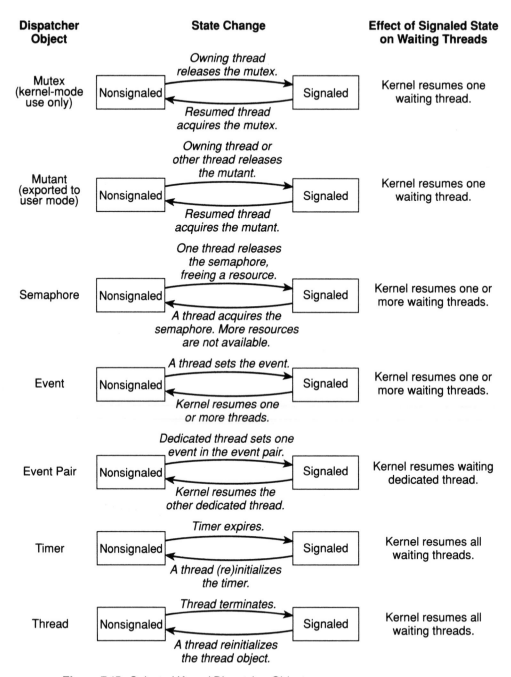

Figure 7-15. Selected Kernel Dispatcher Objects

quick LPC, the optimized form of message passing used by the Win32 subsystem. Timers "go off" when a set amount of clock time has passed. A thread can wait on another thread to terminate, which is useful for synchronizing the activities of two cooperating threads. Together the kernel dispatcher objects provide the executive with great flexibility in synchronizing its execution.

The user-visible synchronization objects described in Chapter 4, "Processes and Threads," acquire their synchronization capabilities from kernel dispatcher objects. Each user-visible object that supports synchronization encapsulates at least one kernel dispatcher object. The following example of setting an event illustrates how synchronization interacts with thread dispatching:

1. A user-mode thread waits on an event object's handle.

2. The kernel changes the thread's scheduling state from ready to waiting and then adds the thread to a list of threads waiting for the event.

3. Another thread sets the event.

4. The kernel marches down the list of threads waiting on the event. If a thread's conditions for waiting are satisfied,[5] the kernel changes the thread's state from waiting to ready. If it is a variable-priority thread, the kernel might also boost its execution priority.

5. Because a new thread has become ready to execute, the dispatcher reschedules. If it finds a running thread with a lower priority than that of the newly ready thread, it preempts the lower-priority thread, issuing a software interrupt to initiate a context switch to the higher-priority thread.

6. If no processor can be preempted, the dispatcher places the ready thread in the dispatcher ready queue to be scheduled later.

7.5 Power Failure Recovery

A major goal in designing Windows NT was to make it a robust, reliable operating system. One might ask, then, how far should reliability go? Although the exception-handling architecture helps to protect the system's reliability from the inside, what happens when external conditions intrude and threaten an operating system's integrity? One form of external threat is that of lawless users who attempt to bypass system security measures.

---

5. Some threads might be waiting for more than one object, so they continue waiting.

Another potential threat are programs that run amok and exhaust system resources. The Windows NT security architecture addresses the first concern, and resource quota limits help to thwart the second problem. However, another area of vulnerability remains: power failure.

The NT kernel reserves the second-highest interrupt priority for power failure. A power failure interrupt notifies the operating system when a change in the power supply occurs so that it can shut down as gracefully as possible. If the operating system didn't shut down, all processing in progress would be lost when the power failed. Executing programs might or might not complete and might or might not leave the persistent resources they use, such as files, in a recoverable state.

When power fails, an operating system has just enough time to initiate an orderly shutdown of the system. If the computer is equipped with a backup battery for memory, data can be restored from memory when power returns. Jobs that were in progress can be either restarted or continued, depending on their state when the power failed. (Of course, if no battery backup exists, this sort of recovery is not possible.)

Reloading volatile registers and resuming execution is not sufficient for full system recovery. Because I/O devices work independently from the rest of the operating system, they require the following kernel support to recover from a power failure:

- They must be reinitialized when the power returns after an outage.

- They must be able to determine whether the power has failed.

Two kernel control objects provide these capabilities. The *power notify object* allows device drivers to register a power recovery routine that the kernel calls when the power returns. The driver decides what the routine should do, but in general, it performs operations such as reinitializing a device and restarting I/O operations that were interrupted.

To register a power recovery routine, a driver creates a power notify object, calling the kernel to initialize it with a pointer to the power recovery routine, and then calls the kernel again to insert the object into a kernel-managed queue. When the power returns, the kernel traverses the queue, calling each power recovery routine in order.

The kernel supplies another control object used by device drivers, called a *power status object*. By creating a power status object and inserting it into another kernel-defined queue, a device driver can determine, before it performs uninterruptible operations (such as storing data in a device register), whether the power has already failed. If it has, the driver does not proceed with the operation. Chapter 8 provides more information on these I/O-related topics.

7.6   In Conclusion

The NT kernel is the hub of all activity in Windows NT. It maintains control over the processor by scheduling and dispatching threads for execution, responding to interrupts and exceptions, and implementing low-level synchronization mechanisms for use by itself and by other parts of the executive. The rest of the NT executive relies on kernel-provided functions and primitives upon which it builds its operating system policies and makes capabilities available to user mode.

Kernel primitives include a series of objects that executive objects encapsulate. The kernel control objects enable a variety of special operating system functions, whereas the kernel dispatcher objects are primitives with built-in synchronization capabilities. Synchronization, both inside and outside the kernel, is critical to the correct functioning of the operating system. The task is particularly challenging when the operating system runs on multiprocessor computers. The kernel synchronizes its own execution to work correctly, and the mechanisms it provides allow the rest of the executive to do the same.

Among its other duties, the kernel lends special assistance to the I/O system. It provides objects and functions that device drivers use to synchronize their execution across multiple processors and to recover I/O operations after power failures occur. The I/O system and its connection to the NT kernel are topics explored more fully in the following chapter.

CHAPTER EIGHT

THE I/O SYSTEM

In his book, *Fundamentals of Operating Systems*, A. M. Lister wrote, "Traditionally, I/O is regarded as one of the more sordid areas of operating system design in that it is a field in which generalisation is difficult and *ad hoc* methods abound."[1] Indeed, it is the sheer number and wildly different natures of I/O devices an operating system must support that creates the difficulty. The challenge facing an I/O system designer lies in creating a virtual interface to I/O devices that allows programmers to simply retrieve or store data without concern for the idiosyncrasies of individual devices.

An I/O system that can condense the vast array of devices into a single model must be comprehensive. It must accommodate the needs of existing devices, from a simple mouse to keyboards, printers, graphics display terminals, disk drives, CD-ROM drives, and even networks. It must consider future storage and input technologies as well. The NT I/O system, which provides a uniform, high-level interface for executive-level I/O operations, protects application programs from differences among physical devices. It also shields the rest of the operating system from the details of device manipulation and thus minimizes and isolates hardware-dependent code.

Darryl Havens, who has designed and implemented operating system components for more than 12 years, designed the I/O manager, which is the unifying component of the I/O system. I/O on Windows NT borrows some of its characteristics from other systems Darryl has worked on—in particular DEC's VAX/VMS and VAX ELN operating systems. Supporting Win32, OS/2, and POSIX also posed some requirements that influenced the I/O design.

---

1. A. M. Lister, *Fundamentals of Operating Systems* (New York: Springer-Verlag, 1984), 63.

The design goals for the I/O system include the following:

- Provide support for multiple *installable file systems* including the FAT file system; the high-performance file system (HPFS); the CD-ROM file system (CDFS); and the NT file system (NTFS), a new, fully recoverable file system.

- Provide services to make device-driver development as easy as possible yet workable on multiprocessor systems.

- Allow a system administrator to add drivers to the system or remove them from the system dynamically.

- Make I/O processing fast, yet allow drivers to be written in a high-level language.

- Provide mapped file I/O capabilities for image activation, file caching, and application use.

In addition to these specific goals, the I/O system must also fulfill the requirements of the operating system as a whole. For example, it must be portable; it must protect its shareable resources by using objects; it must provide capabilities to support Win32, OS/2, and POSIX I/O interfaces; and it must work correctly on multiprocessor systems.

This chapter first examines the structure and design features of the I/O system and then looks at how I/O requests are processed as they move through the system. It concludes by examining the layered model used to create drivers.

8.1 An Overview of NT I/O

The NT executive's I/O system is a collection of operating system code that accepts I/O requests from user-mode and kernel-mode processes and delivers them, in a different form, to I/O devices. Between the user-mode services and the mechanics of I/O hardware lie several discrete system components, including full-blown file systems, numerous device drivers, and one or more network transport drivers.

The overview of NT I/O begins by identifying the components of the I/O system and how they fit together. Following is a discussion that highlights the I/O system design: its use of objects, its uniform model for file system drivers and device drivers, its asynchronous operation, and its provisions for mapped file I/O.

8.1.1 I/O System Components

To understand the design of the NT I/O system, one must first become familiar with its various pieces. Figure 8-1 provides a simplified view of the I/O system structure.

The I/O system is *packet driven*, which means that every I/O request is represented by an *I/O request packet* (IRP) as it travels from one I/O system component to another. An IRP is a data structure that controls how the I/O operation is processed at each stage along the way.

The component called the *I/O manager* defines an orderly framework— a model—within which I/O requests are delivered to file systems and device drivers. The I/O manager doesn't actually manage I/O processing. Its job is to create an IRP that represents each I/O operation, pass the IRP to the correct driver, and dispose of the packet when the I/O operation is complete. In contrast, a driver receives an IRP, performs the operation the IRP specifies,

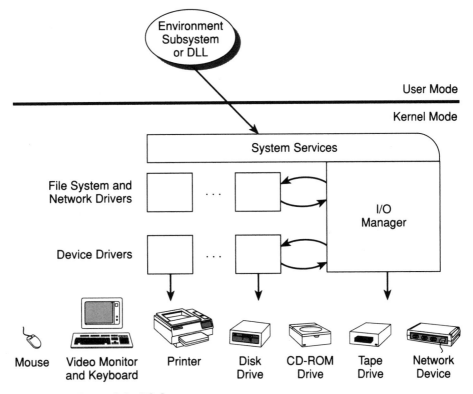

Figure 8-1. Parts of the I/O System

and either passes it back to the I/O manager for completion or passes it on to another driver (via the I/O manager) for further processing.

In the NT I/O system, the term *driver* takes on a broader meaning than the more common term *device driver*. File systems in NT are simply sophisticated "device" drivers that accept I/O requests to files and satisfy the requests by issuing their own, more explicit, requests to physical device drivers. File system drivers and device drivers communicate by passing IRPs.

In addition to creating and disposing of IRPs, the I/O manager supplies code that is common to different drivers and that the drivers call to carry out their I/O processing. By consolidating common tasks in the I/O manager, individual drivers become simpler and more compact. For example, the I/O manager provides a function that allows one driver to call other drivers. It also manages buffers for I/O requests, provides time-out support for drivers, and records which installable file systems are loaded into the operating system.

The I/O manager also provides flexible I/O facilities that allow environment subsystems, such as Win32 and POSIX, to implement their respective I/O APIs. The services that the I/O manager provides are rich in functionality so that they can support different user-mode I/O requirements.

8.1.2 Design Features

The structure of the NT I/O system is a result of both long-standing tradition and forward-looking goals. When creating a new operating system, backward compatibility is an important consideration. Unless one is creating a revolutionary new system with no history—a rare event—the system must be compatible with, or at least able to interoperate with, existing systems. Backward compatibility is a particularly prominent issue in an I/O system. Computer users generally upgrade software more frequently than they buy new hardware. Although a new operating system might require a user to add memory or disk storage, only rarely should it require the user to buy a new hard disk model or to upgrade a video monitor. This means that an I/O system must perpetually support outdated, and even antiquated, I/O devices.

Nevertheless, Windows NT is an operating system designed to run on state-of-the-art processors using 1990s technology. Shaping a hodgepodge of archaic I/O requirements into a coherent, unifying model was one of the challenges in designing the I/O system. Another challenge was to design a model that did not represent the lowest common denominator of outdated technology but that would provide for future needs and mesh with the rest of the operating system. The following sections introduce some of the defining characteristics of the NT I/O model.

8.1.2.1 NT Object Model

When it was originally developed, the UNIX operating system defined a new, simplified view of I/O. All data that is read or written is regarded as a simple stream of bytes directed to virtual files, which are represented by file descriptors. A *virtual file* refers to any source or destination for I/O that is treated as if it were a file. The operating system determines whether the "file" is a console terminal, a pipe, or a true file located on a disk, and it directs data to the proper location at runtime.

In Windows NT, programs also perform I/O on virtual files, manipulating them by using *file handles*. The concept of a file handle is not new, but within the NT executive, a file handle actually refers to an executive *file object*. All potential sources or destinations for I/O are represented by file objects. User-mode threads call native NT file object services to read from a file, write to a file, and perform other operations. The I/O manager dynamically directs these virtual file requests to real files, to file directories, to physical devices, to pipes, to networks, to mailslots, and to any destinations that are supported in the future.

As in other operating systems, an application opens a file by using a standard library function in a programming language such as C. Returned to the application, in one form or another however, is a handle to an NT executive file object. For example, when a Win32 application calls the fopen() function, the C runtime library calls the Win32 CreateFile() API routine, which in turn calls an NT I/O object service. The I/O manager opens a file object and returns an object handle to the C runtime library, which returns it to the application program, as shown in Figure 8-2 on the following page.

The sources and destinations for I/O take the form of objects because they fit the criteria for objects in Windows NT: They are system resources that can be shared by threads in two or more user-mode processes. File objects, like other objects, have hierarchical names, are protected by object-based security, support synchronization, and are manipulated by object services.

When opening a file, a user supplies the file's name and the type of access required—usually read, write, append, or delete access. The request passes to an environment subsystem (or DLL), which calls an NT system service. This launches an object name lookup in the object manager. As described in Chapter 3, the object manager begins searching its object namespace and then turns over control to the I/O manager to find the file object.

Like other executive objects, file objects are protected by a security descriptor that contains an access control list (ACL). When a thread opens a file,

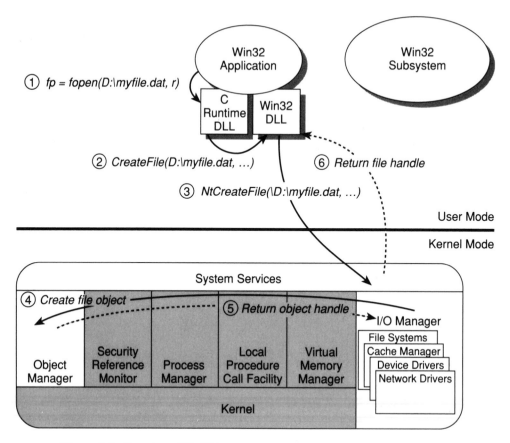

Figure 8-2. Opening a File Object

the I/O manager consults the security subsystem to determine whether the file's ACL allows the process to access the file in the way its thread is requesting. If so, the object manager grants the access and associates the granted access rights with the file handle that it returns. If this thread or another thread in the process needs to perform additional operations not specified in the original request, it must open another handle, which prompts another security check. (See Chapter 3, "The Object Manager and Object Security," for more information about object protection.)

File objects are also used for synchronization. After issuing an I/O request, a thread can wait on a file handle to synchronize its execution with the disk drive or other device's completion of the data transfer. This synchronization capability is related to another important feature of the I/O system—asynchronous I/O operations.

8.1.2.2 Uniform Driver Model

A second characteristic of the I/O system is the uniform structure of its drivers and its broad definition of what constitutes a driver. In the NT executive, a device driver and a file system are built in the same way and present an identical face to the rest of the operating system. Furthermore, named pipes and network redirectors (software that directs file requests over various networks) are viewed as "file systems" and are implemented as file system drivers. Each driver is a self-contained component that can be added to or removed from the operating system dynamically.

The I/O manager defines a model around which drivers are constructed. The chief characteristics of the driver model include the following:

- Drivers are portable and are written in a high-level language. They are designed to require few or no changes from one processor architecture to another. Top-level drivers, such as file systems, require no changes at all.

- I/O operations are packet driven, organized around the transmission of IRPs from one driver to another. IRPs can be reused as they pass through various layers of the I/O system.

- The I/O system can dynamically assign drivers to control additional or different devices if the system configuration changes.

- Drivers must synchronize their access to global driver data. The execution of a driver can be preempted by higher-priority threads or can be interrupted by high-priority interrupts. This fact, as well as NT's ability to run driver code simultaneously on more than one processor in a multiprocessor computer, requires careful attention to synchronization.

- Drivers should recover gracefully after a power failure and restart interrupted I/O operations.[2]

The uniform, modular interface that drivers present allows the I/O manager to call any driver "blindly," without requiring any special knowledge of its structure or internal details. Drivers can also call each other (via the I/O manager) to achieve layered, independent processing of an I/O request.

---

2. This feature is not expected to appear in NT's first-release drivers but will be added in a subsequent release.

Consider the following example. A file system accepts a request to read characters from a particular file. It translates the request into a request to begin reading from the disk at a particular "logical" location and continue reading for a certain number of bytes. It passes this request to a simple disk driver. The disk driver, in turn, translates the request into a cylinder/track/sector location on the disk and manipulates the disk heads to retrieve the data. The ability to layer drivers one on top of another in this way allows drivers to be modular and increases the reusability of driver code.

The layered I/O model can accommodate an arbitrary number of drivers. With a single-layered driver, an I/O request passes to the I/O manager and then to the device driver, which communicates directly with the device, as shown in Figure 8-3.

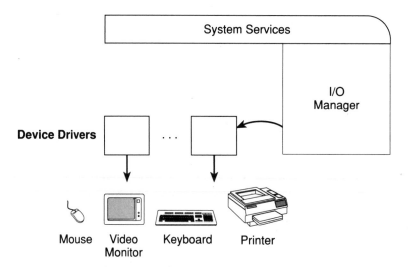

Figure 8-3. I/O to a Single-Layered Driver

Figure 8-4 shows an example of a multilayered driver, in which a request passes through two or more drivers during its processing. In this example, the two layers are a file system driver and a device driver. Note that a higher-level driver does not call a lower-level driver directly; instead, it calls the I/O manager, which calls the lower-level driver.

Multilayered drivers are more common than single-layered drivers, although some simple, byte-oriented devices, such as serial or parallel devices, can be accessed using a single-layered device driver.

Mass-storage devices are always accessed using multilayered drivers. A request first passes through a file system driver and then through a device

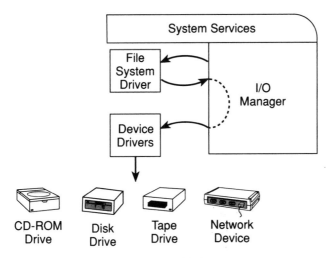

Figure 8-4. I/O to a Multilayered Driver

driver. More complicated sets of layered drivers can also be constructed. For example, a computer might have multiple devices, such as disk or tape drives, attached to a SCSI ("scuzzy," which stands for Small Computer System Interface) bus. An I/O request to such a disk drive would travel through the following drivers:

- A file system driver

- A disk class driver that issues SCSI requests

- A SCSI port driver that sends the requests to the disk using the SCSI bus protocol

Each of these drivers is modular so that all can be used in other configurations as well.

8.1.2.3 Asynchronous Operation

A third feature of the NT I/O system is its asynchronous nature. *Asynchronous I/O* is defined most easily by first describing its opposite: *synchronous I/O.* Most programmers are familiar with synchronous I/O. You call an I/O service; a device completes the data transfer and then returns a status code to your program; the program can access the transferred data immediately. When used in their simplest form, the Win32 ReadFile() and WriteFile() API routines, for example, are executed synchronously. They complete an I/O operation before returning control to the caller, as illustrated in Figure 8-5 on the following page.

Synchronous I/O is standard on most operating systems and is adequate in many circumstances. However, modern processors are incredibly fast—much faster than most I/O devices. While a device processes a single I/O request, the processor could execute thousands of lines of code. Ideally, an application should be able to use the processor while a device is transferring data. For this reason, the NT I/O manager also provides asynchronous I/O capabilities. A subsystem elects to use either synchronous or asynchronous I/O itself and, depending on how its API operates, it can provide either type of I/O to its client applications. The Win32 subsystem provides file-access API routines that can be executed either synchronously or asynchronously.

Asynchronous services allow an application to issue an I/O request and then continue executing while the device transfers the data, as shown in Figure 8-6.

Asynchronous I/O provides an important advantage over synchronous I/O: the potential for improving an application's execution speed. While the device is busy transferring data, the application continues with other work. For example, the application can write an image to the video screen while a

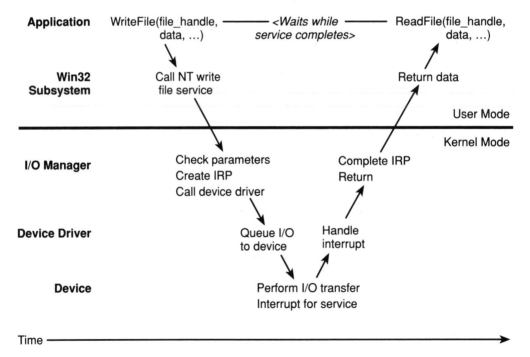

Figure 8-5. Synchronous I/O

device driver is filling a buffer with data from a disk file. To use asynchronous I/O, the thread must specify asynchronous I/O ("overlapped," in Win32 terminology) when it opens a handle. After issuing asynchronous I/O operations, the thread must be careful not to access any data from the I/O operation until the device driver has finished the data transfer. In other words, the thread must synchronize its execution with the completion of the I/O request by waiting on a handle, as shown in Figure 8-6.

Approximately one-third of the native NT services the I/O manager provides to subsystems and DLLs are asynchronous by default. The asynchronous services are those likely to be lengthy operations or those of unpredictable length—for example, reading or writing a file or enumerating the contents of a file directory. A thread that calls these services must synchronize its execution with their completion. Alternatively, a caller can force all NT services to behave synchronously by specifying synchronous I/O when opening a file handle.

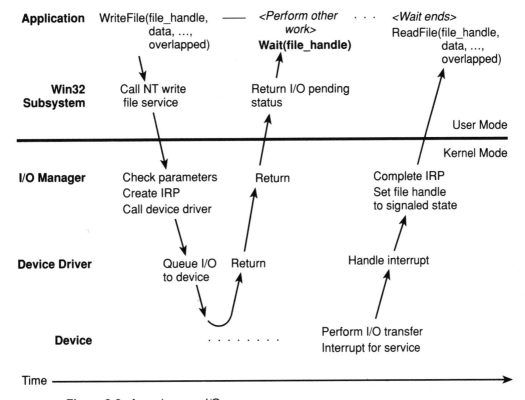

Figure 8-6. Asynchronous I/O

A distinction exists between how a service appears to behave to its caller and how the NT I/O system actually implements it. Although some services behave synchronously and some behave asynchronously, the I/O system works completely asynchronously—from interrupt processing to passing results back to user mode to starting I/O requests on a device. Working asynchronously gives the I/O system maximum flexibility to perform other tasks while the relatively slow devices transfer data. Asynchronous procedure calls (APCs), another feature of NT and Win32 asynchronous I/O, are described in Section 8.2.2.3.

8.1.2.4 Mapped File I/O and File Caching

Mapped file I/O is an important feature of the I/O system, one produced jointly by the I/O system and the virtual memory (VM) manager. Within the operating system, mapped file I/O is used for important functions such as file caching and image activation (loading and running executable programs). The VM manager also makes mapped file I/O available to user mode through native services. Environment subsystems can use the services to provide mapped file capabilities to client applications.

Mapped file I/O refers to the ability to view a file residing on disk as part of a process's virtual memory. A program can access the file as a large array without buffering data or performing disk I/O. The program accesses memory, and the VM manager uses its paging mechanism to load the correct page from the disk file. If the application writes to its virtual address space, the VM manager writes the changes back to the file as part of normal paging.

Applications that perform a lot of file I/O or that access portions of many different files can potentially speed their execution by using mapped I/O because writing to memory is much faster than writing to a device. Also, the VM manager optimizes its disk accesses, so mapped I/O allows applications to take advantage of its expertise.

A component of the I/O system called the *cache manager* uses mapped I/O to administer its memory-based cache. File systems and the Windows NT network server use the cache to place frequently accessed file data in memory in order to provide better response time for I/O-bound programs. While most caching systems allocate a fixed number of bytes for caching files in memory, the NT cache grows or shrinks depending on how much memory is available. When a thread opens and uses a file, the file system tells the cache manager to create an unnamed section object and maps the caller's file into it.[3] As the

---

3. NT's cache thus consists of a series of section objects. The cache manager uses internal data structures to track the various section objects and to locate data in the cache.

caller uses the file, the VM manager brings accessed pages into the section object from disk and flushes them back to disk during paging. The pager automatically expands the size of the cache (using normal working-set mechanisms) when plenty of memory is available and shrinks the cache when it needs free pages. By taking advantage of the VM manager's paging system, the cache manager avoids duplicating the work that the VM manager already performs.

8.2   I/O Processing

The previous section described the NT I/O system from the exterior, focusing on its broad design features. The next step in understanding executive-level I/O is to tour the interior of the I/O system. Because IRPs do precisely that, this section "hitches a ride" with several IRPs as they travel through the system.

I/O requests pass through several predictable stages of processing. The stages vary depending on whether the request is destined for a device operated by a single-layered driver or a device reached through a multilayered driver. Processing varies further depending on whether the caller specified synchronous or asynchronous I/O.

Most I/O requests begin the same way. After opening a file handle, an application calls an I/O routine. The routine is ordinarily one supplied by a language library or an environment subsystem. A Win32 programmer, for example, can call the C function read() or it can call the Win32 ReadFile() API routine. In either case, the Win32 subsystem (or DLL) calls a native I/O system service.

Although environment subsystems can represent file handles in many different ways, most user-mode file handles have as their core an NT object handle. Files in NT are represented as objects, and the NT I/O system supplies object services to manipulate them. The following tour through the I/O system begins by describing NT file objects and native file object services. The second section describes what happens when the NT I/O system is invoked, using as an example a request to an interrupt-driven device controlled by a single-layered driver. The third section expands the discussion to multilayered drivers and shows an I/O request passing through more than one driver before it is complete. The final section discusses programming issues surrounding the use of asynchronous I/O services.

8.2.1   File Objects

Although most shared resources in Windows NT are memory-based resources, most of those that the I/O system manages are either located on or are physical devices. Despite this difference, shared resources in the I/O system, like those in other components of the NT executive, are manipulated as objects.

Objects managed by the I/O system require special handling because the NT object manager doesn't know much about file system directory structures and knows even less about on-disk structure or the format of data stored on a tape. Because of these and other complications introduced by physical devices, one of the chief difficulties in creating the I/O system is to integrate it cleanly into the object system.

File objects are the intermediary. They provide a memory-based representation of shareable physical resources.[4] When a caller opens a file or a simple device, the I/O manager returns a handle to an NT file object. The NT object manager treats file objects like other objects until it needs to retrieve some information from a device or store information on a device, at which time the object manager calls the I/O manager for assistance in accessing the device. (See Chapter 3, "The Object Manager and Object Security," for more information.) Figure 8-7 summarizes the contents of file objects and the services that operate on them (and consequently, on the open files or devices they represent). Table 8-1 describes the attributes of the file object.

Because a file object is a memory-based representation of a shareable resource and not the resource itself, it is different from other executive objects. A file object contains only data that is unique to an object handle, whereas the file itself contains the data or text to be shared. Each time a thread opens a file handle, a new file object is created with a new set of handle-specific attributes. For example, the attribute byte offset refers to the location in the file where the next read or write operation using that handle will occur. Each thread that opens a handle to a file has a private byte offset even though the underlying file is shared. In fact, you can think of file object attributes as being specific to a single handle, as illustrated in Figure 8-8 on page 256.

Although a file handle is unique to a process, the underlying physical resource is not.[5] Therefore, as when using any shared resource, threads must synchronize their access to shareable files, file directories, or devices. If a thread is writing to a file, for example, it should specify exclusive write access when opening the file handle to prevent other threads from writing to the file at the same time. Alternatively, it could lock portions of the file while writing to it.

---

4. A few shareable resources in the I/O system, such as named pipes and mailslots, are memory-based rather than physical resources. These resources are also represented by file objects in the NT I/O system.

5. A file object is also unique to a process, except when a process duplicates a file handle to another process or when a child process inherits a file handle from a parent process. In these situations, the two processes have separate handles that refer to the same file object.

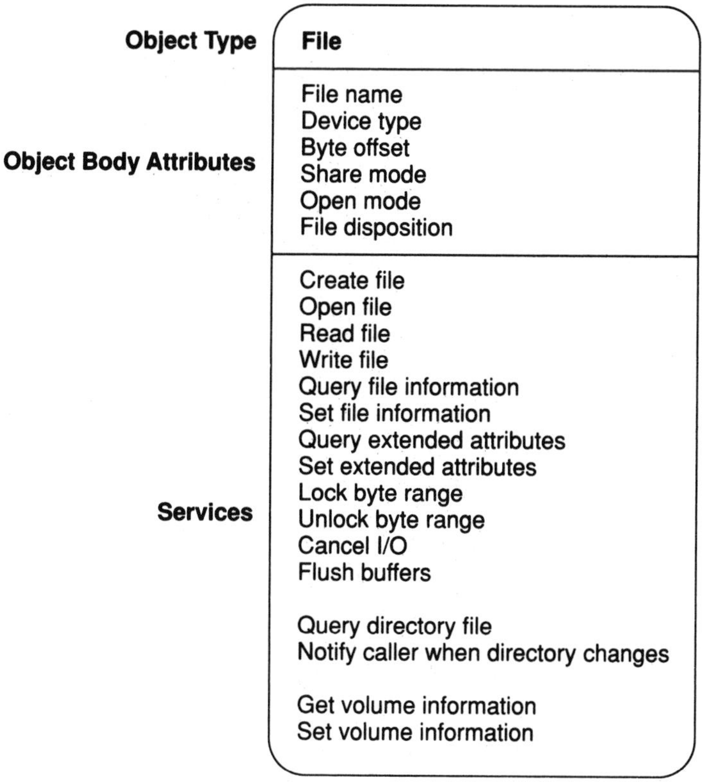

Object Type

> **File**
>
> **Object Body Attributes**
>
> File name
> Device type
> Byte offset
> Share mode
> Open mode
> File disposition
>
> Create file
> Open file
> Read file
> Write file
> Query file information
> Set file information
> Query extended attributes
> Set extended attributes
> Lock byte range
> **Services**   Unlock byte range
> Cancel I/O
> Flush buffers
>
> Query directory file
> Notify caller when directory changes
>
> Get volume information
> Set volume information

Figure 8-7. File Object

Attribute	Purpose
File name	Identifies the physical file that the file object refers to
Device type	Indicates the type of device on which the file resides
Byte offset	Identifies the current location in the file (valid only for synchronous I/O)
Share mode	Indicates whether other callers can open the file for read, write, or delete operations while this caller is using it
Open mode	Indicates whether I/O will be synchronous or asynchronous, cached or noncached, sequential or random, and so on
File disposition	Indicates whether to delete the file after closing it

Table 8-1. File Object Attributes

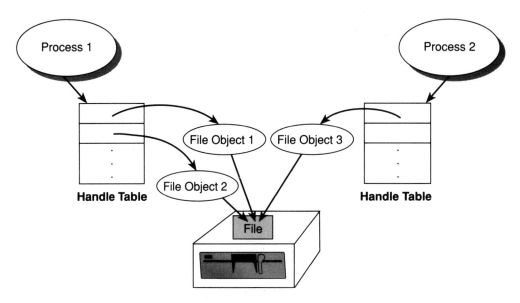

Figure 8-8. Sharing a File

When a file handle refers to a physical file (as opposed to a device or pipe or other "file"), a thread can use the file handle to retrieve information that is stored either in the file object or in the file itself. Table 8-2 lists some of the information stored in a file (or a file directory, where appropriate) in addition to the data that resides in a file object. This information varies with different file systems. The NTFS and the HPFS define extended attributes as well.

Attribute	Purpose
Time of creation	Indicates the date and time when the file was created
Time of last access	Indicates the date and time when the file was last read or written
Time of last write	Indicates the date and time when the file was last changed
Time of last time change	Indicates the date and time when the time was last changed
File characteristics	Indicates whether the file is a read-only file, a system file, a hidden file, an archive file, or a control file
Allocation size	Indicates the allocated size of the file in bytes
End of file	Marks the offset of the first free byte in the file

Table 8-2. File Attributes

8.2.2 I/O Request to a Single-Layered Driver

The I/O manager's job is to accept an I/O request, use the supplied file handle to process the I/O request, and send the result back to the caller. To illustrate the processing of I/O requests in the NT executive, this section examines the path of an IRP into and out of the I/O system. In the first example that follows, a user-mode caller, such as an environment subsystem or a DLL, issues a synchronous request to a simple, interrupt-driven device. The device is controlled by a single-layered driver.

The processing of a synchronous request progresses in three stages:

1. The I/O manager sends the request in the form of an IRP to the driver (a device driver, in this case), and the driver starts the I/O operation.

2. The device completes the operation and interrupts, and the device driver services the interrupt.

3. The I/O manager completes the I/O request.

In the second example that follows, the user-mode caller issues an asynchronous I/O request. Processing an asynchronous request differs from processing a synchronous request primarily in one regard. The asynchronous call adds a step between steps 1 and 2, in which the I/O manager returns control to the caller. The caller can then continue with other work while steps 2 and 3 proceed, but it must synchronize with the completion of step 3 in order to know when the data has been transferred. The three stages of processing for both synchronous and asynchronous I/O requests are presented in detail in the following sections.

8.2.2.1 Queuing an I/O Request

To begin with a simple example, assume that an application synchronously writes a buffer of characters to a printer. The printer is attached to the computer's parallel port and is operated by a single-layered parallel port driver. (Ordinarily, printer requests are spooled to disk first, but for simplicity's sake, this example ignores that step.)

In Windows NT, the printer request first passes through an environment subsystem or DLL, which in turn calls the I/O manager's NtWriteFile() service. The first parameter of the NtWriteFile() service is a handle to a file object, which represents the destination of the I/O request. Because the destination is the parallel port, the subsystem must have previously opened a handle to the port (a virtual file known as *\Device\Parallel0*) and specified synchronous I/O.

The I/O manager creates an IRP in which it stores a pointer to the file object and a function code that tells the parallel port driver which operation to perform—a write operation in this case. The I/O manager locates the driver and then calls it, passing the IRP to the driver. Figure 8-9 illustrates the path the IRP takes from there.

In Figure 8-9, steps 1 through 3 represent the queuing of the synchronous I/O request. Step 5, servicing the interrupt, and step 6, completing the I/O request, are shown in abbreviated form to illustrate the flow of the IRP. They are described in more detail in subsequent sections.

An asynchronous I/O request proceeds in a slightly different fashion, as illustrated in Figure 8-10.

In Figure 8-10, the printer is busy with several requests waiting. The new request must wait its turn. The device driver places the IRP in a device-specific

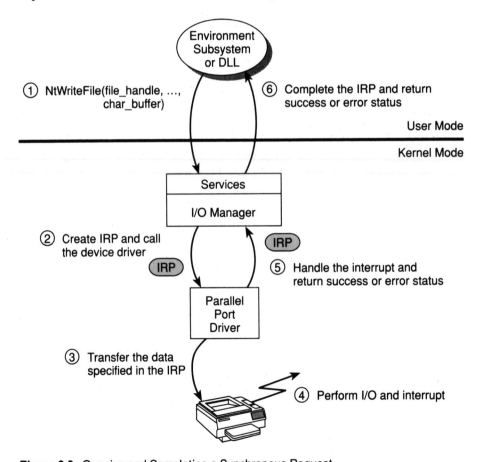

Figure 8-9. Queuing and Completing a Synchronous Request

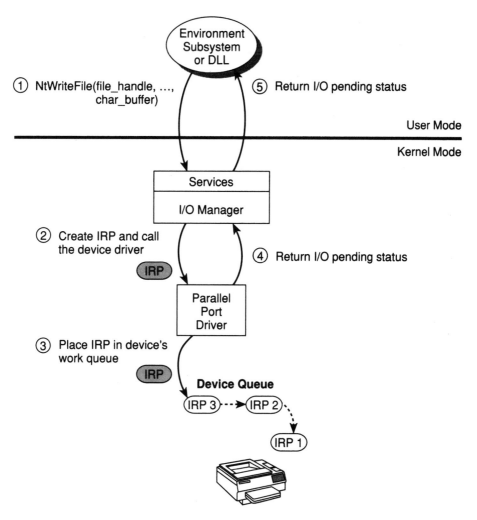

Figure 8-10. Queuing an Asynchronous Request

queue and immediately returns the status "I/O pending," which filters back
to the caller. The application (or subsystem) can continue its work while the
printer plods along. For example, the application might prepare more data to
print.[6] Because this is asynchronous I/O, the application thread must not
overwrite the contents of the print buffer until the printer has completed the
first I/O request. Therefore, before the thread refills the buffer with new data,

---

6. Asynchronous I/O requests return immediately to the caller even if there are no IRPs in the device queue.

it waits on the file handle it used when issuing the request. After the I/O operation is complete, the NT kernel sets the file handle to the signaled state, and the waiting thread continues executing, perhaps refilling the buffer.

8.2.2.2 Servicing an Interrupt

The second stage of processing an I/O request directed to an interrupt-driven device is the servicing of the device's interrupt. After the I/O device completes a data transfer, it interrupts for service, and the device driver, the NT kernel, and the I/O manager are called into action. Figure 8-11 illustrates the first phase of the process. (The device driver is described in more detail in Section 8.3.1.)

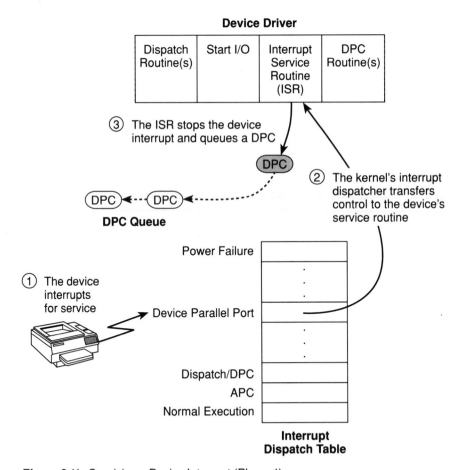

Figure 8-11. Servicing a Device Interrupt (Phase 1)

When a device interrupt occurs, the processor that accepts the interrupt[7] transfers control to the kernel, which indexes into its interrupt dispatch table to locate the *interrupt service routine* (ISR) for the device. (Device drivers for interrupt-driven devices must supply an ISR, a driver routine that stops the device's interrupt and processes the interrupt request.)

Device interrupts are high-priority interrupts on most operating systems, and the operating system generally blocks lower-priority interrupts, or perhaps all interrupts, until the ISR finishes servicing the device. In Windows NT, however, ISRs handle device interrupts in two steps. Device interrupts occur at a high interrupt request level (IRQL), but the ISR remains at this level only long enough to stop the device's interrupt. The thread then lowers the processor's IRQL and completes interrupt processing. This technique ensures that software interrupts and lower-level device interrupts are blocked no longer than necessary.

NT device drivers use deferred procedure calls (DPCs), described in Chapter 7, to accomplish their two-level interrupt processing. For example, when a printer interrupt occurs, the ISR stops the interrupt immediately. Depending on the device, it can do this simply by reading a device status register. The ISR then saves any device state it will need later, queues a DPC, and exits. The DPC contains the rest of the code for processing the interrupt.

After the ISR exits, NT kernel code lowers the processor's IRQL to the level it was at before the interrupt occurred. As mentioned in Chapter 7, placing a DPC in one of the kernel's DPC queues causes a software interrupt to occur the next time the processor's IRQL drops below dispatch/DPC level. Figure 8-12 on the following page illustrates the second phase of interrupt servicing. (Figure 8-12 is a continuation of Figure 8-11.)

Like other interrupts, the DPC interrupt causes the kernel's interrupt dispatcher to gain control. The interrupt dispatcher handles this interrupt by calling the device driver's DPC routine. The printer's DPC routine might, among other things, start the next I/O request that is waiting in the printer queue and then record the status of the just-completed I/O operation. After finishing its work, the DPC calls the I/O manager to complete the I/O and dispose of the IRP.

The advantage of using a DPC to perform most of the device servicing is that any blocked interrupt whose priority lies between the device IRQL and the dispatch/DPC IRQL is allowed to occur before the lower-priority

---

7. Depending on the processor's architecture, software might or might not be able to control which processor actually accepts the interrupt.

DPC interrupt occurs. Intermediate-level interrupts are thus serviced more promptly than they otherwise would be.

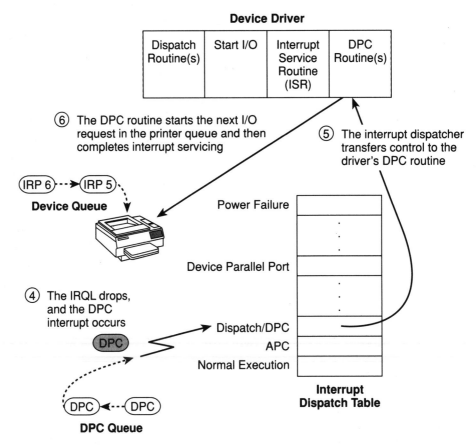

Figure 8-12. Servicing a Device Interrupt (Phase 2)

8.2.2.3 Completing an I/O Request

After a device driver's DPC routine has executed, some work remains before the I/O request can be considered finished. This third stage of I/O processing is called *I/O completion,* and what it entails varies with different I/O operations. For example, all the I/O services record the outcome of the operation in an *I/O status block,* a data structure supplied by the caller. Similarly, some services that perform buffered I/O require the I/O system to return data to the calling thread.

In both cases, the I/O system must copy some data that is stored in system memory into the caller's virtual address space. To gain access to the caller's virtual address space, the I/O manager must transfer the data "in the context of the caller's thread," that is, while the caller's thread is executing. It does so by queuing a kernel-mode APC to the thread, as shown in Figure 8-13. (Figure 8-13 is a continuation of Figure 8-12.)

An APC bears some resemblance to a DPC, except that an APC must execute in the context of a particular thread, whereas a DPC can execute in any thread's context. Furthermore, both APCs and DPCs trigger software interrupts, but APC interrupts occur at a lower IRQL than do DPC interrupts.

System code (such as the I/O manager) queues a kernel-mode APC to a specific thread by calling a kernel routine. The next time that thread begins to execute at low IRQL, a software interrupt occurs. Figure 8-14 on the next page illustrates the second stage of I/O completion. (Figure 8-14 is a continuation of Figure 8-13.)

When the APC interrupt occurs, the kernel transfers control to the I/O manager's APC routine, which copies the data (if any) and the return status into the original caller's address space, deletes the IRP representing the I/O operation, and sets the caller's file handle (or caller-supplied event, as explained later) to the signaled state. The I/O is complete. The original caller

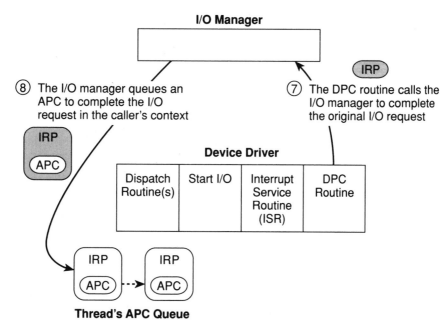

Figure 8-13. Completing an I/O Request (Phase 1)

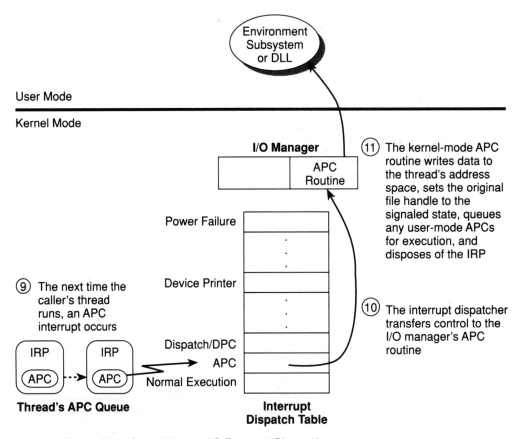

Figure 8-14. Completing an I/O Request (Phase 2)

or any other threads that are waiting on the file handle (the handle to the parallel port in the original example) are released from their waiting state and resume execution.

A final note about I/O completion: The asynchronous I/O services allow a caller to supply a user-mode APC as a parameter. If the caller does so, the I/O manager queues this APC to the caller as the last step of I/O completion. This feature allows a caller to specify in advance an operation it wants to perform when an I/O request is complete. For example, a thread in an environment subsystem might perform a read operation on behalf of a client thread. The subsystem thread issues an asynchronous I/O request to read from a file and specifies a user-mode APC routine. It is then free to service other clients' requests. When the I/O is complete, the I/O manager queues the subsystem's APC back to the subsystem thread, and the processor interrupts the thread. The subsystem is thus prompted to execute the APC routine, which in this example sends the results of the read operation back to the client. The NT kernel then restores the subsystem thread's context, and the subsystem continues executing where it left off before it received the APC interrupt. (NT's user-mode APCs are made visible to Win32 programmers as "completion routines" in the ReadFileEx() and WriteFileEx() API routines.)

8.2.3 I/O Requests to Layered Drivers

The previous examples were based on I/O requests to a simple device controlled by a single device driver. I/O processing for file-based devices or for requests to other layered drivers is much the same. The major difference is, of course, that one or more additional layers of processing are added to the model. Figure 8-15 on the following page shows how an asynchronous I/O request travels through layered drivers. It uses an example of a disk controlled by a file system.

Once again, the I/O manager receives the request and creates an I/O request packet to represent it. This time, however, it delivers the packet to a file system driver. The file system driver exercises great control over the I/O operation at that point. Depending on the type of request the caller made, the file system can send the same IRP to the device driver, or it can generate additional I/O request packets and send them separately to the device driver.

The file system is most likely to reuse an IRP if the request it receives translates into a single straightforward request to a device. For example, if an application issues a read request for the first 512 bytes in a file stored on a floppy disk, the FAT file system would simply call the disk driver, asking it to read one sector from the floppy disk, beginning at the file's starting location.

To accommodate its reuse by multiple drivers in a request to layered drivers, an IRP contains a series of *IRP stack locations,* as shown in Figure 8-15. These data areas, one for every driver that will be called, contain the information that each driver needs in order to execute its part of the request—for example, function code, parameters, and driver context information. As Figure 8-15 illustrates, additional stack locations are filled in as the IRP passes from one driver to the next. You can think of an IRP as being similar to a stack in the way data is added to it and removed from it during its lifetime. However, an IRP is not associated with any particular process, and its allocated size does not grow and shrink. The I/O manager allocates an IRP from nonpaged system memory at the beginning of the I/O operation.

After the disk driver finishes a data transfer, the disk interrupts, and the I/O completes, as shown in Figure 8-16. (Figure 8-16 is a continuation of Figure 8-15.)

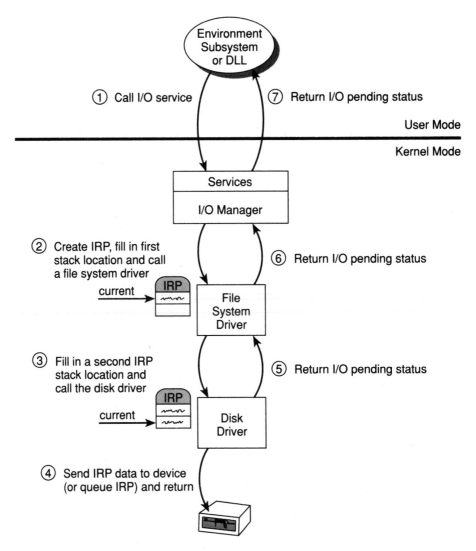

Figure 8-15. Queuing an Asynchronous Request to Layered Drivers

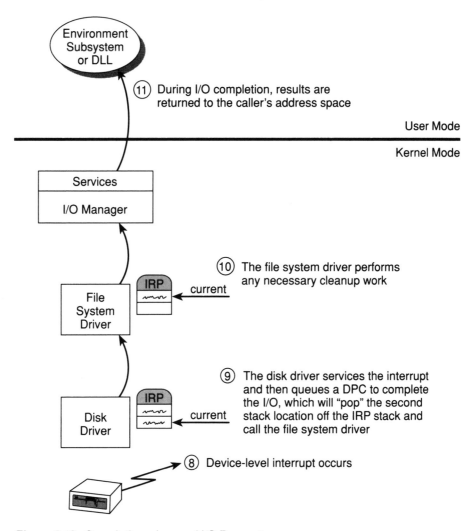

Figure 8-16. Completing a Layered I/O Request

As an alternative to reusing a single IRP, a file system can establish a group of *associated IRPs* that work in parallel on a single I/O request. For example, if the data to be read from a file is dispersed across the disk, the file system driver might create several IRPs, each of which reads some portion of the request from a different sector. Figure 8-17 on the next page illustrates.

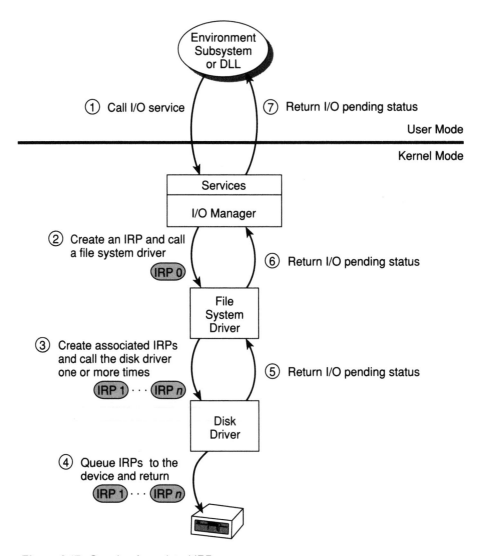

Figure 8-17. Queuing Associated IRPs

The file system driver delivers the associated IRPs to the device driver, which queues them to the device. They are processed one at a time, and the file system driver keeps track of the returned data. When all the associated IRPs complete, the I/O system completes the original IRP and returns to the caller, as shown in Figure 8-18. (Figure 8-18 is a continuation of Figure 8-17.)

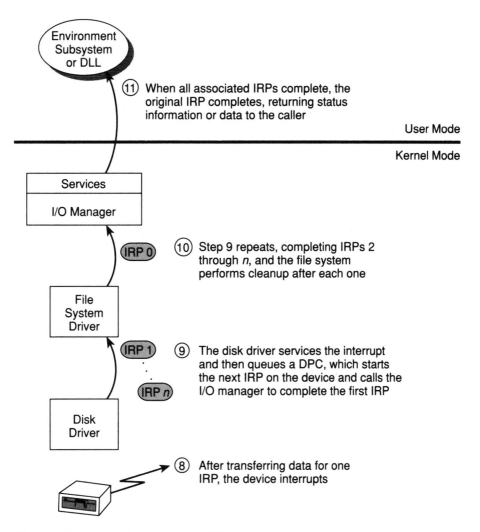

Figure 8-18. Completing Associated IRPs

8.2.4 Considerations in Using Asynchronous I/O

When calling NT I/O services, a developer must choose whether to call them synchronously or asynchronously. For fast operations, or for those of a predictable duration, using synchronous I/O is efficient, so the I/O system only supplies synchronous operation for those services. Asynchronous I/O is most beneficial for operations whose time to completion is either long or highly variable. For example, the number of files stored in a directory can greatly affect the speed of enumerating its files. Thus, the query directory file service

269

is asynchronous by default, as are read file, write file, notify caller when directory changes, and several other services.

Asynchronous I/O can be characterized as requiring a little more programming in exchange for more control over I/O operations and a potentially large increase in efficiency. The thread using asynchronous I/O is not delayed during a data transfer. However, the thread must synchronize its use of any transferred data with the device's completion of the transfer.

When performing asynchronous I/O, user-mode code can use one of several executive objects to synchronize its continuation with the completion of the I/O transfer. File objects support synchronization, so the easiest way for a thread to synchronize is to wait on the file handle at some point after issuing an I/O request. When the data transfer is complete, the I/O manager sets the file handle to the signaled state, and the waiting thread continues executing.

Figure 8-19 illustrates a problem that can occur with this approach if the caller has more than one outstanding I/O request in progress. Suppose a

Server Thread 1	Server Thread 2	I/O Manager	Device
buffer1 = read(file_handle, record_3) wait(file_handle)			
<Thread 1 waits>	buffer2 = read(file_handle, record_12) wait(file_handle)		
	<Thread 2 waits>		
			Perform buffer1 transfer
		Complete I/O for buffer1	
		Set file_handle to signaled state	
<Wait is satisfied>	<Wait is satisfied>		
Return buffer1 data	Return buffer2 data		
			Perform buffer2 transfer

Figure 8-19. Erroneous Use of a File Handle

native NT database server receives a client request to read a record from the database. While this operation is in progress, another client thread requests the server to read a record from the database. The server, which opened the database file only once, uses the same handle to refer to the opened file.

In this example, two threads issue I/O requests using the same file handle, and then both wait on the handle. As Figure 8-19 shows, one of the I/O operations completes. When it does, the I/O manager sets the file handle to the signaled state, which releases both threads from their wait operations, and they continue executing.

Unfortunately, due to the variability involved in scheduling threads on a processor and the fact that a thread can be preempted by another thread at any time, it is impossible to know which of the I/O operations actually completed. Asynchronous I/O requests do not necessarily finish in the order in which they are submitted. In Figure 8-19, only one data transfer is complete, but both threads return data to their clients. Therefore, one client receives erroneous data.

One solution to this problem is to avoid synchronizing with a file handle when more than one thread is issuing requests using the same handle. Instead, each thread can wait on separate executive event objects, using one for each I/O request. Appropriately, all the asynchronous NT I/O services allow the caller to supply a handle to an event object for this purpose. Alternatively, the caller can specify an APC that will execute a function after a particular I/O request completes (a function that returns data to the client, for example).

Another solution is to specify that all I/O services be performed synchronously (to ensure that only one I/O is in progress at a time). When the I/O manager performs synchronous I/O, it also serializes multiple I/O requests. That is, if two threads request I/O using the same file handle, the I/O manager ensures that the second thread stalls until the first thread's I/O operation is complete. (NT's OS/2 subsystem, which always serializes multiple I/O requests, uses this feature extensively.)

8.3   Layered Driver Model

The preceding sections focused primarily on the design features of the I/O system and the way in which an I/O request passes from one place to another during its processing. This section describes the structure of drivers, the relationship between the I/O manager and the drivers it calls, and how one driver communicates with another in the layered driver model. The section concludes with a discussion of two important system features that affect drivers and the people who develop them.

8.3.1 Structure of a Driver

A floppy disk drive, a hard disk drive attached to a SCSI bus, a graphics monitor, the FAT file system, and a network device are radically different I/O "devices," but they are practically interchangeable to the I/O manager. Each NT driver has the following standard set (or subset) of components:

- An initialization routine. The I/O manager executes a driver's initialization routine when it loads the driver into the operating system. The routine creates system objects that the I/O manager uses to recognize and access the driver.

- A set of dispatch routines. Dispatch routines are the main functions that a device driver provides. Some examples are read or write functions and any other capabilities the device, file system, or network supports. When called on to perform an I/O operation, the I/O manager generates an IRP and calls a driver through one of the driver's dispatch routines.

- A start I/O routine. The driver uses a start I/O routine to initiate a data transfer to or from a device.

- An ISR. When a device interrupts, the kernel's interrupt dispatcher transfers control to this routine. In the NT I/O model, interrupt service routines run at a high IRQL, so they perform as little work as possible in order to avoid blocking lower-level interrupts unnecessarily. An ISR queues a DPC, which runs at a lower IRQL, to execute the remainder of interrupt processing. (Note that only drivers for interrupt-driven devices have ISRs. A file system, for example, doesn't have one.)

- An interrupt-servicing DPC routine. A DPC routine performs most of the work involved in handling a device interrupt after the ISR executes. It executes at an IRQL that is lower than that of the ISR to avoid blocking other interrupts unnecessarily. A DPC routine initiates I/O completion and starts the next queued I/O operation on a device.

- A completion routine. A layered driver can create a completion routine that will notify it when a lower-level driver finishes processing an IRP. For example, the I/O manager calls a file system's completion routine after a device driver finishes transferring data to or from a file. The completion routine notifies the file system about the operation's success, failure, or cancellation, and it allows the file system to perform cleanup operations.

- A cancel I/O routine. If an I/O operation can be cancelled, a driver can define one or more cancel I/O routines. The cancel routine that the I/O manager calls can vary depending on how far along the operation has progressed when it is cancelled. The IRP records which cancel I/O routine is active at any given time.

- An unload routine. The unload routine releases any system resources a driver is using so that the I/O manager can remove it from memory. A driver can be loaded and unloaded while the system is running.

- Error logging routines. When unexpected errors occur (for example, when a disk block goes bad), a driver's error logging routines note the occurrence and notify the I/O manager. The I/O manager writes this information to an error log file.

In its simplest form, a device driver has an initialization routine that loads the driver into the system and an unload routine that removes it. It has one dispatch routine for each operation it supports (or one dispatch routine that handles all operations). Device drivers for interrupt-driven devices also have an optional routine that starts an I/O operation, an interrupt service routine that stops a device's interrupt, and a DPC routine to perform lower-priority interrupt processing. In addition, a high-level, layered driver usually has a completion routine.

8.3.2 Driver Object and Device Object

When a thread opens a handle to a file object, the I/O manager must determine from the file object's name which driver (or drivers) it should call to process the request. Furthermore, the I/O manager must be able to locate this information the next time a thread uses the same file handle. The following system objects fill this need:

- A *driver object*, which represents an individual driver in the system and records for the I/O manager the address of each of the driver's dispatch routines (entry points).

- A *device object*, which represents a physical, logical, or virtual device on the system and describes its characteristics, such as the alignment it requires for buffers and the location of its device queue to hold incoming I/O request packets.

The I/O manager creates a driver object when a driver is loaded into the system, and then it calls the driver's initialization routine, which fills in the object with the driver's entry points. The initialization routine also creates one device object for each device to be operated by this driver. It hangs the device objects off the driver object, as shown in Figure 8-20.

Recall from Chapter 3 that when a caller opens a handle to a file object, the caller supplies a filename. Within this name is the name of the device object on which the file resides. For example, the name \Device\Floppy0\myfile.dat refers to the file called *myfile.dat* on the floppy disk drive A. The substring \Device\Floppy0 is the name of the NT device object representing that floppy disk drive. When opening *myfile.dat*, the I/O manager creates a file object and stores a pointer to the *Floppy0* device object in the file object and then returns a file handle to the caller. Thereafter, when the caller uses the file handle, the I/O manager can find the *Floppy0* device object directly.

As Figure 8-20 illustrates, a device object points back to its driver object, which is how the I/O manager knows which driver routine to call when it receives an I/O request. It uses the device object to find the driver object representing the driver that services the device. It then indexes into the driver object using the function code supplied in the original request; each function code corresponds to a driver entry point.

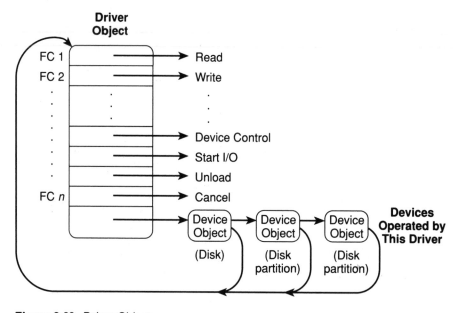

Figure 8-20. Driver Object

A driver object often has multiple device objects associated with it. The list of device objects represents the physical, logical, and virtual devices that the driver controls. For example, each partition of a hard disk has a separate device object that contains partition-specific information. However, the same hard disk driver is used to access all partitions. When a driver is unloaded from the system, the I/O manager uses the queue of device objects to determine which devices will be affected by the removal of the driver.

Using objects to record information about drivers prevents the I/O manager from needing to know details about individual drivers. The I/O manager merely follows a pointer to locate a driver, which provides a layer of portability and allows new drivers to be loaded easily. Representing devices and drivers with different objects also makes it easy for the I/O system to assign drivers to control additional or different devices if the system configuration changes.

8.3.3 I/O Request Packet

The IRP is where the I/O system stores information it needs to process an I/O request. When a thread calls an I/O service, the I/O manager constructs an IRP to represent the operation as it progresses through the I/O system. The I/O manager stores a pointer to the caller's file object in the IRP. Figure 8-21 on the following page shows the relationship between an IRP and I/O system objects.

An IRP consists of two parts: a fixed portion (called a header) and one or more stack locations. The fixed portion contains information such as the type and size of the request, whether the request is synchronous or asynchronous, a pointer to a buffer for buffered I/O, and state information that changes as the request progresses. An IRP stack location contains a function code, function-specific parameters, and a pointer to the caller's file object. In Figure 8-21, the IRP stack location contains the WRITE function code.

While active, each IRP is stored in an IRP queue associated with the thread that requested the I/O. This allows the I/O system to find and delete any outstanding IRPs if a thread terminates or is terminated with outstanding I/O requests.

8.3.4 Adding Layered Drivers

Figure 8-21 illustrated how the I/O manager calls a single-layered device driver. The I/O manager uses the caller's file handle to locate device and driver objects and then calls the device driver. Most I/O operations are not this direct, however. Usually more than one driver must be called to process an I/O request.

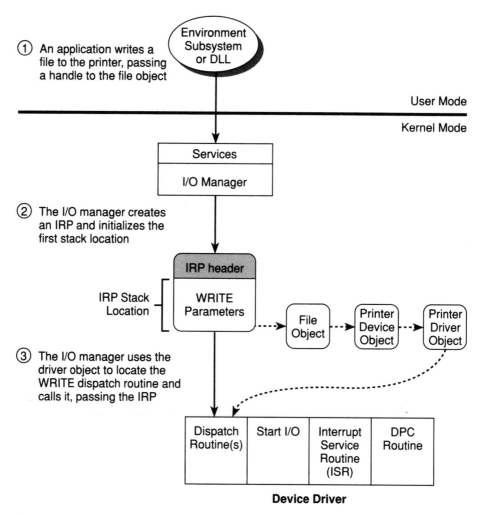

Figure 8-21. Calling a Driver

The design of the I/O system allows one driver to be layered on top of another; that is, one driver performs an action based on information stored in the first stack location of the IRP and then passes the request to another driver, storing the information the second driver requires in a second IRP stack location. For example, writing data to a file on a hard disk requires at least two driver layers, as shown in Figure 8-22.

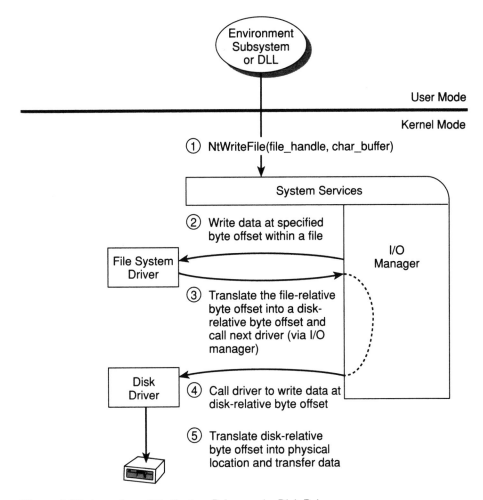

Figure 8-22. Layering a File System Driver and a Disk Driver

This figure illustrates the division of labor between two layered drivers. The I/O manager receives a write request that is relative to the beginning of a particular file. The I/O manager passes the request to the file system driver, which translates the write operation from a file-relative operation to a starting location (a sector boundary on the disk) and a number of bytes to read. The file system driver calls the I/O manager to pass the request to the disk driver, which translates the request to a physical disk location and transfers the data.

Because all drivers—both device drivers and file system drivers—present the same framework to the operating system, another driver can be easily inserted into the hierarchy without altering the existing drivers or the I/O system. For instance, several disks can be made to seem like a very large single disk by adding a driver. Such a driver actually exists in Windows NT to provide fault tolerant disk support. This logical, multivolume driver is located between the file system and disk drivers, as shown in Figure 8-23.

Notice in this example that adding another driver in the hierarchy does not affect either the file system driver or the disk driver. They perform the same actions as they did previously. The I/O manager uses internal data structures that are created when a driver is loaded and subsequently mounted to determine which drivers to call and in which sequence order to access a device.

8.3.5 Issues in Driver Development

Two special features of Windows NT—multiprocessing and power failure recovery—require some extra consideration when creating a driver. A multiprocessing environment is one in which an interrupt can occur on one processor while the same type of interrupt is being serviced on another, causing the driver to execute on two processors at once. This environment forces a driver to use a different model for its operation than the models used in the MS-DOS and OS/2 operating systems, for example.

Windows NT also provides the capability to recover after a power failure occurs. With most operating systems, when the power fails while they are running, the systems generally crash, losing any I/O operations that are in progress. In contrast, if a Windows NT system is equipped with an *uninterruptible power supply* (UPS), it warns users about imminent power failures well in advance and then shuts the system down in a controlled fashion. If the computer is equipped with a battery backup for memory, Windows NT provides a "warm boot" capability that allows the I/O system to recover I/O operations that were in progress when the failure occurred.[8] This section describes some driver design considerations resulting from NT's multiprocessing and power failure recovery capabilities.

8.3.5.1 Multiprocessing

A symmetrical multiprocessing environment is one in which the same system code can run simultaneously on more than one processor. Although the operating system as a whole must concern itself with functioning properly on

---

8. This feature might not be available in the first release of the system.

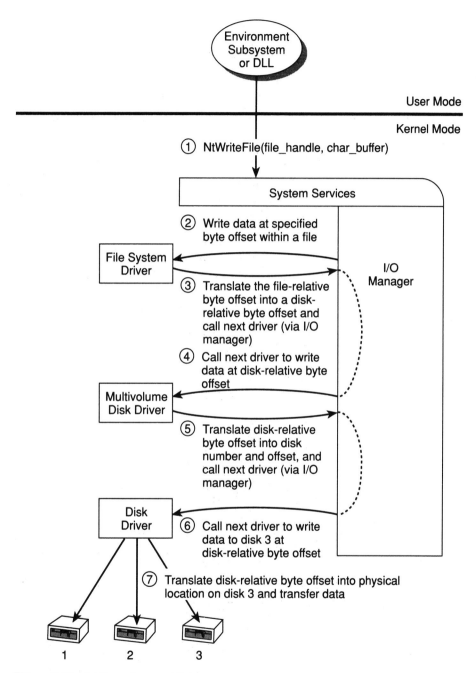

Figure 8-23. Adding a Layered Driver

multiprocessor computers, nowhere are multiprocessing considerations more evident than in the I/O system, particularly in device drivers.

The central requirement for making code work in a multiprocessing environment is to protect shared resources from being used by two threads of execution at the same time. Like other system components, a driver can execute on two or more processors at once, and therefore it must synchronize its access to driver data by using a kernel-defined spin lock. In the I/O system, shared resources include not only device driver data structures but also single-user devices. For example, if two threads attempt to write to a printer at the same time, their output should not be interspersed.

Handling device interrupts correctly on a multiprocessor system is a unique area of concern in the I/O system. Much device driver code runs at the IRQL in effect when a caller initiates an I/O operation. For normal user-mode threads, this is the lowest IRQL available (low level, or normal operation). Device driver interrupts, on the other hand, occur at high IRQLs. Therefore, a device can generate an interrupt and cause its ISR to execute while its own device driver is already running. If the device driver was modifying data that its ISR also modifies, such as device registers, heap storage, or static data, the data can become corrupted when the ISR executes. Figure 8-24 illustrates.

This scenario is not limited to multiprocessor operating systems. A variation of the problem can also occur in single-processor operating systems. To prevent the problem, device drivers in OS/2 and MS-DOS, for example, typically disable interrupts (using the CLI instruction on Intel's *x*86 hardware) while accessing device registers or other data shared in an ISR. This blocks

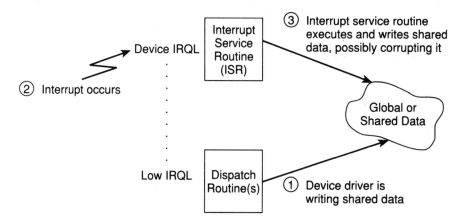

Figure 8-24. Data Corruption in a Device Driver

interrupts and allows the device driver to execute without the possibility that the ISR might break in and access the same data.

This strategy is effective on single-processor systems. On multiprocessor systems, however, disabling interrupts on one processor does not prevent an interrupt from occurring and being serviced on another processor. For example, suppose a thread running on Processor 1 disables interrupts and then begins writing data to the parallel port. While the thread is writing data to the port's buffer, the printer attached to the port interrupts for service. Processor 2, on which interrupts are not disabled, takes the interrupt and begins executing the ISR for the parallel port. This ISR writes data to the port buffer. The buffer is now in an unknown state.

To avoid this situation, a device driver written for NT must synchronize its access to any data that the device driver shares with its ISR. Before attempting to update shared data, the device driver must lock out all other threads to prevent them from updating the same data structure. Furthermore, the lock it uses must be stored in memory global to all processors. The NT kernel provides special synchronization routines that device drivers must call when they access data that their ISRs also access. These kernel synchronization routines keep the ISR from executing while the shared data is being accessed.

It should be apparent after this discussion that, although ISRs require special attention, any data that a device driver uses is subject to being accessed by the same device driver running on another processor. Therefore, it is critical for device driver code to synchronize its use of any global or shared data. If that data is used by the ISR, the device driver must use kernel synchronization routines; otherwise, the device driver can use a kernel spin lock.

8.3.5.2 Power Failure Recovery

When a power failure occurs, even if the power is restored so quickly that the outage is imperceptible to people, electronic components—and I/O devices, in particular—are likely to notice the disruption. Any data stored in a device register, for example, can be corrupted, and the device itself can be knocked offline or can be reset to a random state.

Because device drivers execute in kernel mode with access to system memory, a power failure that affects device operation can cause serious problems in an operating system. To prevent these problems in Windows NT, each device driver must know when the power has failed, however momentarily, and must reset the device it operates to a known state after the failure. Also, any I/O operation that was interrupted should be restarted, but if that is not possible, at least the I/O manager should be notified that an I/O operation failed so that an error condition can be returned to the caller.

The I/O manager, together with the NT kernel, provides a capability that allows device drivers to handle power failure interrupts gracefully. When the power fails, a power failure interrupt occurs, and the operating system has a brief period of time in which to prepare for the outage. The kernel quickly copies into memory all important system registers, including the program counter. If the computer's memory is equipped with a battery backup, this information is saved, and when the power returns, the kernel and the I/O system can use the saved information to restart execution where they left off. The I/O system can restart or terminate I/O operations that were interrupted.

In NT, each device driver can perform several tasks to help it recover from power failures. First, each device driver can create and register a power recovery routine that resets its device to a known state after a power outage. After the power is restored, the kernel locates and executes each driver's power recovery routine.

Second, each driver ensures that a power failure interrupt cannot occur while the driver is writing sequences of critical data to its device. This is important because, when power is restored, the processor will resume its execution at the program counter at which it was interrupted. Any device operation that was in progress might or might not have completed correctly and should be restarted from the beginning. Before writing any critical data to hardware registers, each device driver first ensures that the power hasn't already failed and then momentarily blocks power failure interrupts by raising its processor's IRQL to power level. After writing its data, each device driver immediately lowers the IRQL (actually, restores the previous IRQL). If a power failure occurs in the meantime, the interrupt is postponed briefly until the program counter has advanced past the critical operation. This ensures that when the system restarts, the device driver will not jump into the middle of a critical operation, assuming erroneously that a preceding, important step succeeded.

8.4   In Conclusion

The NT I/O system comprises a number of software modules, including the I/O manager and a series of components falling under the broad classification of "driver." The I/O manager defines NT's model of I/O processing and performs functions that are common to, or required by, more than one driver. Its chief responsibility is to create IRPs representing I/O requests and to shepherd the packets through various drivers, returning results to the caller when an I/O is complete.

Drivers include not only traditional device drivers, but also file system, network, named pipe, and other drivers. All drivers adopt a common structure and communicate with one another and the I/O manager by using the same mechanisms. The I/O manager accepts I/O requests and locates various drivers by using I/O system objects, including driver and device objects. Because drivers present a common structure to the operating system, they can be layered one on top of another to achieve modularity and reduce duplication between drivers. Internally, the NT I/O system operates asynchronously to achieve high performance and provides both synchronous and asynchronous I/O capabilities to user-mode subsystems.

Designing drivers for NT is different from designing drivers for other operating systems because the drivers must work correctly on multiprocessor systems and can participate in NT's power failure recovery procedures. However, all drivers are written in a high-level language to lessen development time and to enhance their portability. The following chapter examines networking in Windows NT, a topic that includes two special NT drivers: the redirector and the Windows NT server.

NETWORKING

During Windows NT's development, one could walk through the hallways occupied by the development team and see perhaps half the people wearing one or another of the many t-shirts given to Microsoft employees at one meeting or another, or for achieving one milestone or another. In the networking group's hallway, the most frequently observed t-shirt carried this image:[1]

We're building it in.

Until recently, personal computer networks were generally added to existing operating systems when the need for intercomputer communication arose. For example, Microsoft LAN Manager is sometimes referred to as a "network operating system," but it's actually a set of sophisticated applications and drivers that add networking capabilities to existing operating systems—in particular, MS-DOS, OS/2, and UNIX. It supplies facilities such as user accounts, resource security, and intercomputer communication mechanisms, including named pipes and mailslots. Although earlier versions of

---

1. Reproduced from a logo designed by Joe Belfiore and David Tuniman.

LAN Manager still perform those crucial functions for other operating systems, on Windows NT, networking software is no longer implemented as an add-on layer to the operating system. Instead, it is an integral part of the NT executive, with the capabilities listed above included in the operating system.

So what does built-in networking mean? This question has several answers, but the most basic is that peer-to-peer (also called workgroup) networking software is included in the Windows NT product. The system is equipped to support file copying, electronic mail, and remote printing without requiring the user to install special server software on any of the machines. Because networking is an integral part of the operating system, the network software can exploit the internal operating system interfaces used by other components of the NT executive to optimize its performance. This topic is covered in detail later in this chapter.

In addition to building networking capabilities into the operating system, the overriding goal of the NT networking architecture, as described by Dave Thompson, development manager for the NT network team, was to give network software and network hardware manufacturers the ability to "plug 'n' play" with NT. By this he means that existing networks, network drivers, and network servers (such as Novell NetWare, Banyan VINES, and Sun NFS) are able to interact and exchange data with Windows NT systems easily. With so many network protocols, cards, and drivers to support, Microsoft must rely on other vendors to help produce various parts of Windows NT's network software. This task is made easier because Windows NT contains mechanisms that enable its built-in network software to be loaded into and out of the operating system; the same mechanisms can be used to load other network software into and out of the operating system.

In addition to allowing the loading (and unloading) of network software, Windows NT networking goals include the following:

- Interoperate with existing versions of LAN Manager running on other operating systems.

- Allow applications to access non-Microsoft file systems on networks other than LAN Manager without modifying their code.

- Provide the proper facilities to construct distributed and "you bet your business" applications, such as Microsoft SQL Server, transaction processing applications, and so forth.

This chapter introduces some of the features that make Windows NT networking unique. The first section describes the major networking components and their connections to early Microsoft networking products. The second section elaborates on the meaning of "built-in networking." The third section examines Windows NT's open network design, which allows LAN Manager, NetWare, and other network components to be loaded into the operating system dynamically. The fourth section describes some of the ways in which Windows NT is equipped to support distributed applications through its named pipes, mailslots, and remote procedure call (RPC) facilities. The final section describes Windows NT's advanced networking and distributed security facilities, which support the needs of large, corporation-wide computer networks.

9.1   Background

Networking is a complicated topic, steeped in historical footnotes and awash in acronyms—even though the entire history of computer networking is only about two decades old. In its infancy, networking simply meant connecting two computers with a wire and allowing files to be transferred from one computer to the other across the wire. Over time, computer manufacturers developed unique network architectures that worked within their own systems but didn't work across different types of systems. Nowadays, however, it is common for individuals or businesses to own a mishmash of computer hardware, all of which must communicate.

In some ways, the challenge of intermingling different network architectures resembles the problem posed by the sundry I/O devices that operating systems must support. Incompatibilities abound, and one must establish a model into which the different components fit. In Windows NT, networking software is largely implemented as a series of sophisticated extensions to the NT I/O system. This makes sense if you view networking as the means by which users and applications can access not only local resources but also remote resources such as files and devices and, ultimately, processors.

Before examining the Windows NT networking software, the following two sections look first at the precursors to some of the Windows NT networking components and then at how those components fit into the standard model of networking.

9.1.1 History[2]

Microsoft's history in the networking business dates back to MS-DOS version 3.1. This version of MS-DOS added to the FAT file system necessary file-locking and record-locking extensions, which allowed more than one user to access MS-DOS files. With the release of MS-DOS version 3.1 in 1984, Microsoft also released a product called Microsoft Networks, which was informally referred to as "MS-NET."

MS-NET established some traditions that carried over into LAN Manager and now into Windows NT. For example, when a user or an application issued an I/O request destined for a remote file, directory, or printer, MS-DOS detected the network reference and passed it to a component of the MS-NET software called the *redirector*. The MS-NET redirector accepted the request and sent it, or "redirected" it, to a remote server. Although completely redesigned and much more sophisticated, Windows NT networking also includes a redirector. In fact, it can incorporate multiple redirectors, each of which directs I/O requests to remote file systems or devices.

Another piece of MS-NET that has carried over into Windows NT is its *server message block* (SMB) protocol. Simply stated, a *protocol* is the set of rules and conventions by which two entities—and in this case, computers—communicate. Networking software generally consists of multiple levels of protocols layered one on top of another. Depending on which computers a system talks to, it might support (as Windows NT does) several different protocols at different levels in the hierarchy. MS-NET's SMB protocol is a high-level specification for formatting messages to be sent across the network. An API called the *NetBIOS interface* was used to pass I/O requests structured in the SMB format to a remote computer. Both the SMB protocol and the NetBIOS API subsequently were adopted in numerous industry networking products and appear in Windows NT as well.

A final carryover from MS-NET is the *network server*. MS-NET's network server was software that resided on the remote computer, transforming it into a dedicated file and print server. The software simply monitored the network connection and waited for SMBs to arrive. It then unpackaged them, determined what they were requesting, performed the operation (such as reading data from a file), and then sent the results back in another SMB message. The term *server* is often used in the context of networking to mean a computer

---

2. Steve Kanzler provided source material for portions of this section and the following section.

that is set up to accept requests from a remote computer. However, you can think of a network server as functionally equivalent to a local server (a protected subsystem, in Windows NT terminology) that accepts requests from a process on another machine rather than from a process on the same machine.

Windows NT's built-in networking software includes a basic peer-to-peer network server that speaks the SMB protocol (making it compatible with MS-NET and LAN Manager). In addition, Windows NT can load other network servers and run them alongside its built-in server. For high-end or large networked enterprises, an additional product, tentatively called LAN Manager for Windows NT, will be available. It will transform a peer-to-peer networked workstation into an advanced domain server. A domain server has the ability to share user accounts and security information with multiple associated systems grouped together in a *network domain* and with other trusted network domains. It also supplies facilities to enable fault tolerant disks and other advanced features. These capabilities allow Windows NT to support the needs of large, corporation-wide networks.

Incidentally, MS-NET also included a set of utilities and a command syntax for accessing remote disks and printers. As you might have guessed, it included the NET USE X: \\SERVER\SHARE nomenclature. Names prefixed with the string \\ still indicate resource names on the network and are called *uniform naming convention* (UNC) names.

9.1.2 OSI Reference Model

In his classic book titled *Computer Networks*, Andrew Tanenbaum defines a computer network as "an *interconnected* collection of *autonomous* computers."[3] That is, each computer is physically separate and runs its own operating system. This is the environment for which the Windows NT network architecture was designed.

The goal of network software is to take a request (usually an I/O request) from an application on one machine, pass it to another machine, execute the request on the remote machine, and return the results to the first machine. To accomplish this requires transforming the request several times along the way. A high-level request such as "read x number of bytes from file y on machine z" requires software to determine how to get to machine z and what

---

3. Andrew S. Tanenbaum, *Computer Networks*, 2d ed. (Englewood Cliffs, N.J.: Prentice-Hall, 1989), 2.

communication software that machine understands. Then the request must be altered for transmission across a network—for example, divided into short packets of information. When the request reaches the other side, it must be checked for completeness, decoded, and sent to the correct operating system component to execute the request. Finally, the reply must be coded for sending back across the network.

To help different computer manufacturers standardize and integrate their networking software, the International Standards Organization defined a software model for sending messages between machines. The result is the *Open Systems Interconnection* (OSI) *reference model.* The model defines seven layers of software, as shown in Figure 9-1.

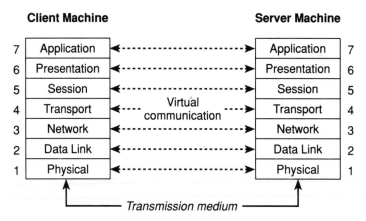

Figure 9-1. OSI Reference Model

The OSI reference model is an idealized scheme that few systems implement precisely, but it is often used to frame discussions of networking principles. Each layer on one machine assumes that it is "talking to" the same layer on the other machine. Both machines "speak" the same language, or protocol, at the same level. In reality, however, a network transmission must pass down each layer on the client machine, be transmitted across the network, and then pass up the layers on the destination machine until it reaches a layer that can understand and implement the request.

The purpose of each layer in the model is to provide services to higher layers and to abstract how the services are implemented at lower layers. Detailing the purpose of each layer is beyond the scope of this book, but here are some brief descriptions:

- Application layer. Handles information transfer between two network applications, including functions such as security checks, identification of the participating machines, and initiation of the data exchange.

- Presentation layer. Handles data formatting, including issues such as whether lines end in carriage return/line feed (CR/LF) or just carriage return (CR), whether data is to be compressed or encoded, and so forth.

- Session layer. Manages the connection between cooperating applications, including high-level synchronization and monitoring of which application is "talking" and which is "listening."

- Transport layer. Divides messages into packets and assigns them sequence numbers to ensure that they are all received in the proper order. It also shields the session layer from the effects of changes in hardware.

- Network layer. Handles routing, congestion control, and internetworking. It is the highest layer that understands the network's *topology*, that is, the physical configuration of the machines in the network, the type of cabling used to tie them together, and any limitations in bandwidth, length of cables that can be used, and so forth.

- Data-link layer. Transmits low-level data frames, waits for acknowledgment that they were received, and retransmits frames that were lost over unreliable lines.

- Physical layer. Passes bits to the network cable or other physical transmission medium.

The dashed lines in Figure 9-1 represent protocols used in transmitting a request to a remote machine. As stated earlier, each layer of the hierarchy assumes that it is speaking to the same layer on another machine and uses a common protocol. The collection of actual protocols through which a request passes on its way down and back up the layers of the network is called a *protocol stack*.

Figure 9-2 on the next page previews the components of Windows NT networking, how they fit into the OSI reference model, and which protocols they use between layers. The various components are described later in this chapter.

As the figure shows, the OSI layers do not correspond to actual software. Transport software, for example, frequently crosses several boundaries. In fact, people often refer to the bottom four layers of software collectively as the "transport." Software components residing in the upper three layers are referred to as "users of the transport."

The remainder of this chapter examines the networking components shown in Figure 9-2 (as well as others not shown in the figure), how they fit together, and how they relate to Windows NT as a whole.

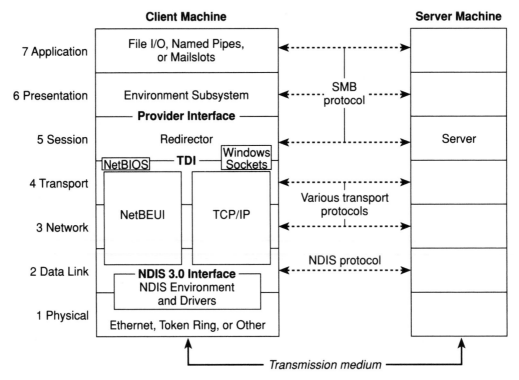

Figure 9-2. OSI Model and Windows NT Networking Components

9.2 Built-In Networking

The previous section showed how some of Windows NT's networking components correspond to the OSI reference model. Figure 9-3 shows how they fit into Windows NT.

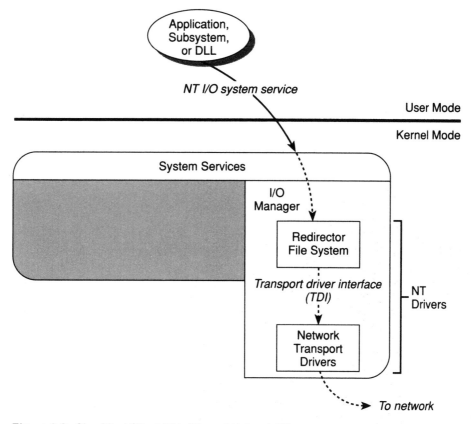

Figure 9-3. Simplified Client-Side View of Network I/O

User-mode software (the Win32 I/O API, for example) issues a remote I/O request by calling native NT I/O services. After some initial processing (described later), the I/O manager creates an I/O request packet (IRP) and passes the request to one of its registered file system drivers, in this case the Windows NT redirector. The redirector forwards the IRP to lower-layer drivers (the transport drivers), which process it and place it on the network.

When the request arrives at a Windows NT destination, it is received by the transport drivers and then passes through several more drivers. Figure 9-4 on the next page illustrates the receipt of a network write request. A read operation would follow the same path to the server, with the data returned through the reverse path. Details about the redirector, server, and transport drivers are presented later in this chapter.

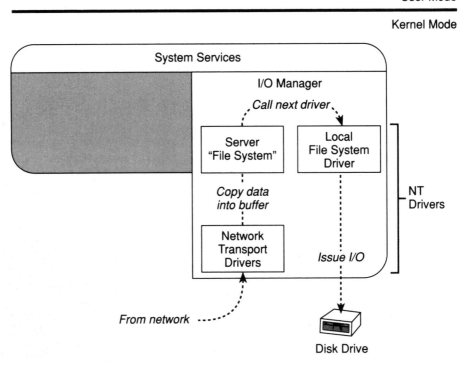

Figure 9-4. Simplified Server-Side View of Network I/O

9.2.1 Network APIs

Consider how an application might access the network. Windows NT supplies several means:

- Win32 I/O API. The I/O routines perform standard open, close, read, write, and other functions. They pass across the network only when the file or named pipe to be accessed exists on a remote machine. Generally this means that the filename is a UNC name or that the name starts with a drive letter that refers to a remote machine.

- Win32 network (WNet) API. These routines are useful for applications, such as the Windows File Manager, that connect to and browse remote file systems. The WNet routines can be used to browse Microsoft or other file systems over a LAN Manager, NetWare, VINES, or other network.

- Win32 named pipe and mailslot APIs. Named pipes provide a high-level interface for passing data between two processes, regardless of whether the recipient process is local or remote. Mailslots are similar, except that instead of providing a one-to-one communication path between the sender and receiver, mailslots provide one-to-many and many-to-one communication mechanisms. Mailslots are useful for broadcasting messages to any number of processes.

- NetBIOS API. This API provides backward compatibility for those MS-DOS, 16-bit Windows, and OS/2 applications that pass streams of data directly across the network. A new 32-bit version is also supplied.

- Windows Sockets API. This new API provides 16-bit and 32-bit sockets, a standard UNIX-style interface for networking. Windows NT also provides lower layers of code that support UNIX applications and allow Windows NT to easily participate in the wide-area Internet network.

- Remote procedure call (RPC) facility. This runtime library and the compiler allow programmers to easily write distributed applications. (See Section 9.4.1 for more information.)

Each API finds its way to the network through a different route. Figure 9-5 on the next page shows Win32 I/O routines that the Win32 subsystem implements by calling NT I/O system services.[4] The I/O manager then issues IRPs to the redirector. The Windows Sockets API and the NetBIOS API, in contrast, are DLLs that call NT I/O services, and the I/O manager issues IRPs to the Windows Sockets and NetBIOS drivers, respectively.

As Figure 9-5 shows, calls to the WNet API (implemented as a DLL) detour through a networking component called the *workstation service*. In networking lingo, the term *service* refers to a server process that provides a specific function (meaning a job) and perhaps exports an API to support that function. The service functions include the following:

- Administering the built-in redirector (the workstation service) and the server (the *server service*)

- Sending alert messages to logged-on users (the *alerter service*) — for example, when the hard disk becomes full

---

4. Note that most Win32 API functions are optimized in a client-side DLL and do not actually pass through the Win32 subsystem. See Chapter 5, "Windows and the Protected Subsystems," for more information.

■ Receiving messages from other systems (the *messenger service*), such as notification when a print job is completed

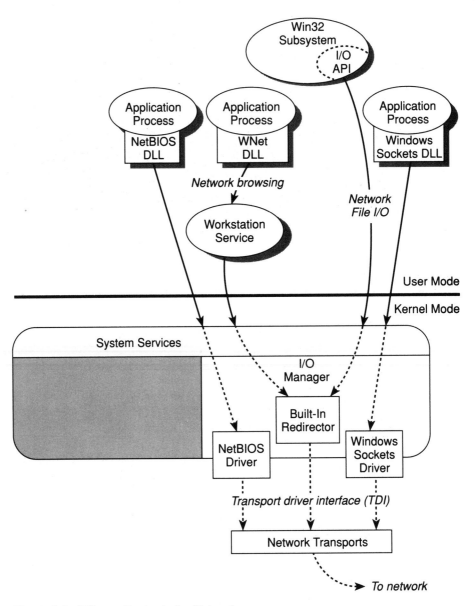

Figure 9-5. Different Routes to the Network

A service is a process similar to a Windows NT protected subsystem. Some services simply run in the background, whereas others provide APIs that other processes' threads can call by sending messages to the service. Unlike the protected subsystems, services that supply APIs generally use the RPC message-passing facility rather than the LPC facility to communicate with clients. Using RPC makes the services available to processes on remote machines as well as to local processes. (See Section 9.4.1 for more information.)

The workstation service is essentially a user-mode "wrapper" for the Windows NT redirector. It performs work to support the WNet API, provides configuration functions for the redirector, and contains user-mode code for returning redirector statistics. When an application calls a WNet API function, the call passes first to the workstation service before going to the NT I/O manager and on to the redirector.

A component called the *service controller* is responsible for loading and starting Windows NT services. It is also the means by which those drivers that are not loaded at boot time are loaded into and unloaded from the system. Many of the networking components are implemented as drivers and are therefore loaded into the system (or removed from it) by the service controller.

9.2.2 Built-In Networking Components

Although many software components are involved in Windows NT networking, two of the most important are those with the longest history at Microsoft: the redirector and the network server. As in the original MS-NET software, the redirector steers locally issued I/O requests to a remote server, and the server receives and processes such requests.

Of course, except for the names, little else about the redirector or server resembles the early software. The originals were written in assembly language and entwined around existing MS-DOS system software. Although the new redirector and server are built into Windows NT, they have no dependencies on the hardware architecture that the operating system is running on. They are written in C and implemented as loadable file system drivers, which can be loaded or unloaded from the system at any time. They can also coexist with other vendors' redirectors and servers.

Implementing the redirector and server as file system drivers makes them a part of the NT executive. As such, they have access to the specialized interfaces that the I/O manager provides for drivers. These interfaces, in turn, were designed with the needs of the network components in mind. This access to driver interfaces, plus the ability to call cache manager functions directly, contributes greatly to the performance of the redirector and server.

297

The I/O manager's layered driver model mimics the natural layering of network protocols. Because the redirector and server are drivers, they can be layered on top of as many transport protocol drivers as necessary. This structure makes the network components modular and creates efficient transitions from the redirector or server layer down to the transport and physical layers of the network.

9.2.2.1 Redirector

A network redirector provides the facilities necessary for one Windows NT–based machine to access resources on other machines on a network. The Windows NT redirector can access remote files, named pipes, and printers. Because it implements the SMB protocol, it works with existing MS-NET and LAN Manager servers, allowing access to MS-DOS, Windows, and OS/2 systems from Windows NT. Security mechanisms ensure that the Windows NT data shared on the network connection is protected from unauthorized access.

As a file system driver, the redirector operates like other drivers. When it is loaded into the system, its initialization routine creates a device object (called \Device\Redirector) to represent it. The initialization routine also establishes function codes that represent the operations it handles and records the driver entry points (dispatch routines) for those operations. When the I/O manager receives a network I/O request, it creates an IRP and calls a dispatch routine in the redirector, passing along the IRP. After the redirector processes the request (by accessing the network), the IRP is completed, and results are returned to the caller.

Between sending a request and receiving a reply, the redirector has one primary task: to provide a "file system" that behaves like a local file system although it operates over an inherently unreliable medium (a network). The physical link from one computer to another simply fails much more often than that between a computer and its hard disk or floppy disk drive. When the link does fail, the redirector is responsible for recovering the connection, where possible, or for failing gracefully so that applications can retry the operation. The redirector uses various techniques to accomplish this. For example, it quietly reconnects to a server when a connection is lost. It also remembers which files were open and reopens them under certain circumstances. (Beneath the redirector, the transport layer ensures reliability for bit-level data transmissions.)

Like other file system drivers, the redirector must work within the asynchronous I/O model, supporting asynchronous I/O operations when they are issued. When a user-mode request is issued asynchronously (as described in Chapter 8, "The I/O System"), the network redirector must return immediately whether or not the remote I/O operation is finished. In most cases, an asynchronous network I/O request doesn't finish immediately, so the redirector must wait for its completion after returning control to the caller. Paradoxically, driver code is always activated by a calling thread, within that thread's context. It has no address space of its own or any threads. How can the driver call a routine to wait?

This problem is not unique to redirectors; most file system drivers have the same dilemma. In the original I/O system design, file system drivers that needed to perform processing in their own context simply created a kernel-mode process associated with the driver and used its threads to perform asynchronous processing. However, this solution was a costly one in terms of system memory usage. Therefore, a new solution was devised.

Windows NT has a special system process for initializing the operating system when it is booted. This process has several worker threads that loop, waiting to execute requests on behalf of drivers and other executive components that perform asynchronous work. If a file system driver needs a thread to perform asynchronous work, it queues a work item to this special process before returning control and a status code to the original caller. A thread in the system process is awakened and performs the operations necessary to process the I/O request and complete the original caller's IRP.

The redirector sends and receives SMBs to perform its work. Although for simplicity Figure 9-2 depicted the redirector and server as session-layer components in the OSI model of networking, the SMB protocol is really an application-layer protocol, as illustrated in Figure 9-6 on the next page.

The interface over which the redirector sends its SMBs is called the *transport driver interface* (TDI). The redirector calls TDI routines to transmit SMBs to the various transport drivers loaded into Windows NT. In order to call TDI functions, the redirector must open a channel called a *virtual circuit* to the destination machine and then send its SMBs over that virtual circuit. The redirector maintains one virtual circuit for each server to which Windows NT is connected and multiplexes requests destined for that server across the same virtual circuit. The transport layer below the redirector determines how to actually implement the virtual circuit and send the data across the network connection.

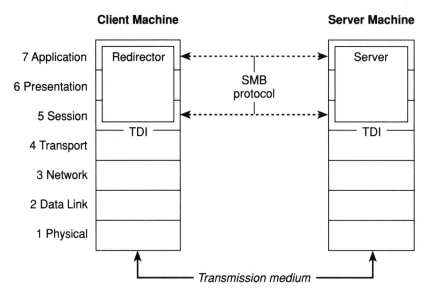

Figure 9-6. Using the SMB Protocol

Larry Osterman, the developer who transformed the MS-NET redirector into the MS-DOS LAN Manager 1.0 redirector and subsequently rewrote it for LAN Manager 2.0, also designed the Windows NT redirector. In addition to improving reliability, he was required to provide 100 percent compatibility with the existing SMB protocol. To accomplish this, he used the same protocol to pass messages to "down-level" (existing MS-NET and LAN Manager) servers. Maintaining this core protocol allows Windows NT to interact with Windows, OS/2, or MS-DOS servers running LAN Manager. For transmissions between Windows NT systems, Larry enhanced the core SMB protocol to support operations common in the NT I/O system. For example, the enhanced protocol can accommodate NT-specific operations such as opening a file for delete access, opening a directory, placing access control lists (ACLs) on files for security purposes, and performing query operations to retrieve information about files. In addition, the new SMB protocol passes text strings as Unicode characters to ensure correct transmission of characters from international character sets.

9.2.2.2 Server

Like the redirector, the Windows NT server is written for 100 percent compatibility with existing MS-NET and LAN Manager SMB protocols. This complete compatibility allows the server to process requests that originate not only from other Windows NT systems but also from other systems running

LAN Manager software. Like the redirector, the server is implemented as a file system driver.

One might wonder why something named a "server" is not implemented as a server process. It could reasonably be expected that a network server would function like a protected subsystem—a process whose threads wait for requests to arrive from the network, execute them, and then return the results over the network. This approach was the most obvious choice, and Chuck Lenzmeier considered it carefully when he began designing the Windows NT server. Chuck, the primary developer of the server, with seven years of VAX/VMS-based networking and RPC experience behind him, decided instead to implement the server as a file system driver. Although the server isn't a driver in the usual sense and although it doesn't manage a file system, using the driver model provides advantages over implementing the server as a process.

The main advantage is that as a driver the server exists within the NT executive and can call the NT cache manager directly to optimize its data transfers. For example, if the server receives a request to read a large amount of data, it calls the cache manager to locate the data in the cache (or to load the data into the cache if it isn't already there) and to lock the data in memory. The server then transfers the data directly from the cache to the network, thus avoiding unnecessary disk accesses or data copying. Similarly, if asked to write data, the server calls the cache manager to reserve space for the incoming data and to be assigned a cache location for it. The server then writes the data directly into the cache. By writing to the cache rather than to disk, the server can return control to the client more quickly; the cache manager then writes the data to disk in the background (using the VM manager's paging software).

When calling the cache manager, the server is, in effect, assuming some of the responsibilities of the I/O manager to achieve more streamlined processing. Another way in which the server assumes this role is in formatting its own IRPs and passing them directly to the NTFS, FAT, and HPFS drivers. It can also choose to copy data into and out of the cache directly instead of creating IRPs. If it were a user-mode (or even a kernel-mode) subsystem, it would instead call NT I/O services to process incoming requests, which would require a little more overhead.

As a file system driver, the server also has a bit more flexibility than it would as a process. For example, it can register an I/O completion routine, which allows it to be called immediately after lower-layer drivers finish their processing, so that it can perform any postprocessing needed. Although the Windows NT server is implemented as a file system driver, other servers can be implemented either as drivers or as server processes.

Like the redirector, the server uses the initial system process to handle asynchronous I/O operations and those occasionally used, high-overhead operations that don't require optimal speed, such as opening a file. Operations that require utmost speed, such as reading and writing, are executed directly in the driver whenever possible in order to avoid the overhead of a context switch. Although it requires a context switch, using the initial system process to perform network operations allows the server to wait on object handles when necessary or to take page faults, neither of which it can do when executing in another thread's context at a raised IRQL. The ability to take page faults means that less of the server code must remain memory-resident.

When Windows NT is booted, the I/O manager loads those drivers that are required early in the boot sequence (such as the file system and disk drivers, the video driver, and the mouse and keyboard drivers). After the boot sequence progresses far enough to switch from kernel mode to user mode, the service controller is invoked to load the remaining drivers, including the redirector, the server, and the network transport drivers. The service controller loads these drivers by calling I/O system services, which copy them into memory and execute their initialization routines. Each driver's initialization routine creates a device object and inserts it into the object manager namespace. The service controller can also be invoked at any time after the system is running to load or unload network servers or to stop or start network services.

9.2.3 Name Resolution

One of the main objectives Windows NT accomplishes is to extend the reach of the local I/O system to include remote resources. Because all such resources are objects, the networking software must work within the local object structure in order to access those resources. When an application opens a file, it actually opens a handle to an NT file object. The file object contains data specific to that "opened instance" of the file—for example, data such as the share mode and the file pointer. Processing is the same when the file to be opened is located on a remote computer. The object manager gets involved by creating a file object and opening a handle to it.

As with local files, the remote filename that the application opens must be resolved; that is, the operating system must determine which device the file is on, which file system is used on the device, and where the file is located within the file system. For remote files, the operating system must also ascertain what machine the file is stored on and how to send a request to that machine.

Suppose the user has assigned a drive letter to a remote server by issuing the command NET USE T: \\TOOLSERV\TOOLS. The workstation service creates a symbolic link object called *T:* in the NT object manager namespace, as shown in Figure 9-7.

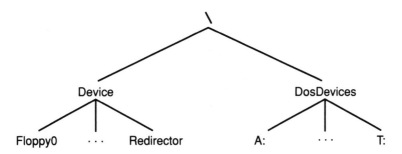

Figure 9-7. Object Manager Namespace

Later a Win32 application opens the remote file *T:\editor.exe*. The Win32 subsystem translates the name into an NT object, *\DosDevices\T:\editor.exe*, and calls the NT executive to open the file. During processing, the object manager discovers that *\DosDevices\T:* is a symbolic link object and substitutes the specified name for *\DosDevices\T:*. As shown in Figure 9-8, *\Device\Redirector* is the name of the device object representing the Windows NT redirector, and *T:* refers to a remote LAN Manager share that the redirector will locate.

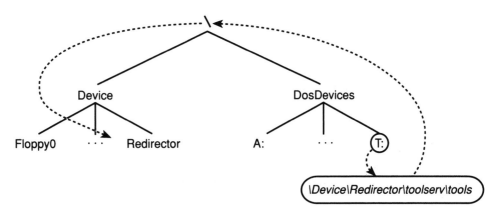

Figure 9-8. Resolving a Network Filename

Device objects are used in NT as a launching point into an object namespace that is not controlled by the NT object manager. When parsing an object name, if the object manager finds a device object in the path, it calls the parse method associated with the device object. In this case, the method is an I/O manager routine that calls the redirector. The redirector builds SMBs and passes them via a transport driver to a remote SMB server, which opens the file \editor.exe on \\TOOLSERV\TOOLS. The NT object manager creates a local file object to represent the opened file and returns an object handle to the caller. Thereafter, any operation on the object handle passes directly to the Windows NT redirector.

A similar object namespace exists on the Windows NT destination system. The remote object namespace contains the name \Device\Server, which refers to the file system driver that implements Windows NT's built-in server functions. This device object is not used when the server receives a request, however; it is used only when a system administrator refers to the server by name while managing it.

9.3 Open Architecture

Because the network server is built into Windows NT, it might seem that the server is "hard-wired" and there to stay—but it isn't. Dave Thompson's "plug 'n' play" objective dictated that Windows NT be able to link to a variety of networks. Therefore, not only can the redirector, server, and transport drivers be loaded and unloaded dynamically, but a variety of such components can coexist. Windows NT supports networks other than LAN Manager in several ways:

- It provides access to non-Microsoft file systems for resource connection and network browsing and for remote file and device I/O through a common Win32 API (the WNet API).

- It allows multiple network transport protocol drivers to be loaded at the same time and allows redirectors to call a single, common interface to access them.

- It supplies an interface and environment (NDIS 3.0) for network card drivers to access Windows NT transport drivers and to gain portability to future MS-DOS systems.

The following sections examine each of these capabilities and the software used to implement them.

9.3.1 User-Mode Access to Remote File Systems

As stated in Section 9.2.1, the Win32 WNet and I/O APIs provide two ways for user-mode applications to access files (and other resources) on remote systems. Both of these APIs use the capabilities of the redirector to find their way to the network. Although the earlier discussion focused on the built-in network software, additional redirectors can be loaded into the system to access different types of networks. This section expands on the original example by examining the software that decides which redirector to invoke when remote I/O requests are issued. The responsible components are these:

- *Multiple provider router* (MPR). A DLL that determines which network to access when an application uses the Win32 WNet API for browsing remote file systems

- *Multiple UNC provider* (MUP). A driver that determines which network to access when an application uses the Win32 I/O API to open remote files

9.3.1.1 Multiple Provider Router for the WNet API

The Win32 WNet functions allow applications (including the Windows File Manager) to connect to network resources, such as file servers and printers, and to browse the contents of any type of remote file system. Because the API can be called to work across different networks using different transport protocols, software must be present to send the request correctly over the network and to understand the results that the remote server returns. Figure 9-9 on the next page shows the software responsible for this task.

A *provider* is software that establishes Windows NT as a client of a remote network server. Some of the operations performed by a WNet provider include making and breaking network connections, printing remotely, and transferring data. The built-in WNet provider includes a DLL, the workstation service, and the built-in redirector. Other network vendors need only supply a DLL and a redirector.

When an application calls a WNet routine, the call passes directly to the multiple provider router (MPR) DLL, a networking component designed by Chuck Chan. The MPR takes the call and determines which WNet provider recognizes the resource being accessed. Each provider DLL beneath the MPR supplies a set of standard functions collectively called the *provider interface*. This interface allows the MPR to determine which network the application is trying to access and to direct the request to the appropriate WNet provider software.

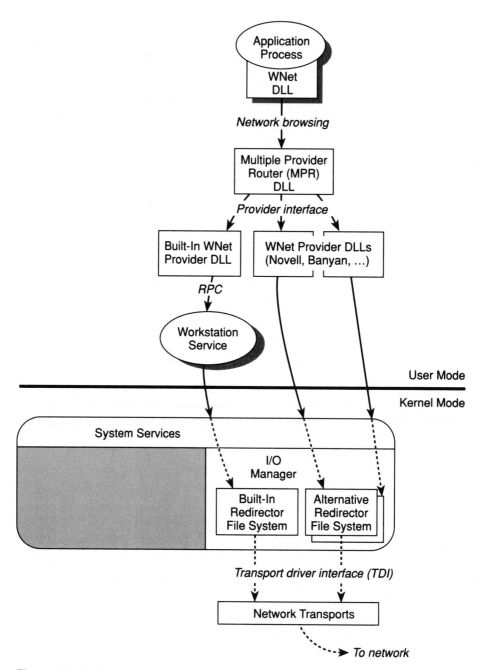

Figure 9-9. Multiple Provider Software

When called by the WNetAddConnection() API routine to connect to a remote network resource, the MPR checks the configuration registry to determine which network providers are loaded. It polls them one at a time in the order in which they are listed in the registry until a redirector recognizes the resource or until all available providers have been polled. (The order can also be changed by editing the registry database.)

The WNetAddConnection() routine can also assign a drive letter or device name to a remote resource. When called to do so, WNetAddConnection() routes the call to the appropriate network provider. The provider, in turn, creates an NT symbolic-link object that maps the drive letter being defined to the redirector (that is, the remote file system driver) for that network. Figure 9-10 illustrates how network resource names fit into the NT object manager namespace.

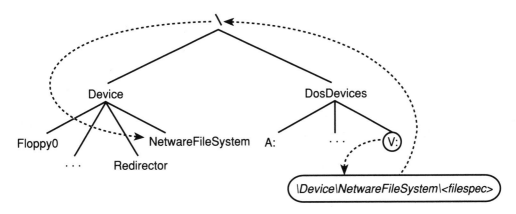

Figure 9-10. Resolving a Network Resource Name

Like the built-in redirector, other redirectors create a device object in the object manager namespace when they are loaded into the system and initialized. Then, when the WNet or other API calls the object manager to open a resource on a different network, the object manager uses the device object as a jumping-off point into the remote file system. It calls an I/O manager parse method associated with the device object to locate the redirector file system driver that can handle the request. (See Chapter 8, "The I/O System," for more information.)

9.3.1.2 Multiple UNC Provider for Win32 File I/O

The multiple UNC provider (MUP), designed by Manny Weiser, is a networking component similar to the MPR. It fields I/O requests destined for a file or a device that has a UNC name (names beginning with the characters \\, indicating that the resource exists on the network). The MUP takes such requests and, like the MPR, determines which local redirector recognizes the remote resource.

Unlike the MPR, the MUP is an NT driver (loaded at system boot time) that issues I/O requests to lower-layer drivers, in this case to redirectors, as shown in Figure 9-11.

The MUP driver is activated when an application first attempts to open a remote file or device, specifying a UNC name (instead of a redirected drive letter, as described earlier in this chapter). When the Win32 subsystem receives such a request, the subsystem appends the UNC name to the string *\DosDevices\UNC* and then calls the NT I/O manager to open the file. This object name is the name of a symbolic link that resolves to *\Device\Mup*, a device object that represents the MUP driver, as shown in Figure 9-12.

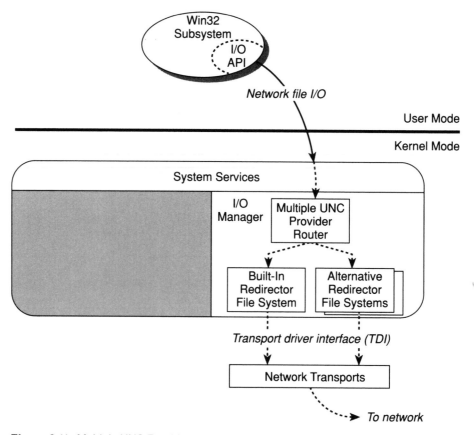

Figure 9-11. Multiple UNC Provider (MUP)

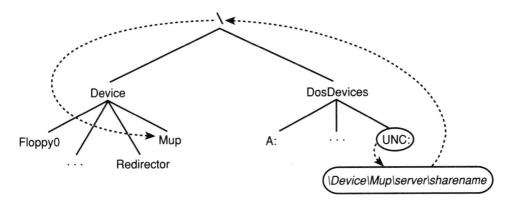

Figure 9-12. Resolving a UNC Name

The MUP driver receives the request and sends an IRP asynchronously to each registered redirector. Then, it waits for one of them to recognize the resource name and reply. When a redirector recognizes the name, it indicates how much of the name is unique to it. For example, if the name is *\\HELENC\PUBLIC\inside\scoop.doc*, the Windows NT redirector recognizes it and claims the string *\\HELENC\PUBLIC* as its own. The MUP driver caches this information and thereafter sends requests beginning with that string directly to the Windows NT redirector, skipping the "polling" operation. The MUP driver's cache has a timeout feature, so that after a period of disuse, the string's association with a particular redirector expires.

If more than one redirector claims a particular resource, the MUP driver uses the configuration registry's list of loaded redirectors to determine which redirector takes precedence. The list of redirectors can be reordered by editing the registry database.

9.3.2 Transport Protocols

After a network-bound request reaches a redirector, the request must be delivered to the network. During the last decade, many different protocols for transmitting information across networks have evolved. Windows NT doesn't provide all the protocols, but it must at least allow them to be provided. And the easier it is to do, the better.

In Windows NT, transport protocols are implemented as drivers, which, like redirectors and servers, can be loaded into and out of the system. In a traditional networking model, a redirector that uses a particular transport protocol must know which type of input that protocol driver expects and send requests to it in that format. The lower layers of the redirector must be rewritten to support different data-passing mechanisms for each transport used.

Windows NT avoids this problem by providing a single programming interface—called the *transport driver interface* (TDI)—for redirectors and other high-level network drivers. TDI allows redirectors and servers to remain independent from transports. Thus, a single version of a redirector or a server can use any available transport mechanism, as shown in Figure 9-13.

TDI is an asynchronous, transport-independent interface that implements a generic addressing mechanism and a variety of services and libraries. Each transport driver provides the interface in its uppermost layer so that redirectors (and servers on remote Windows NT machines) can call it without regard to what transport is in use beneath the interface. To send a request, the

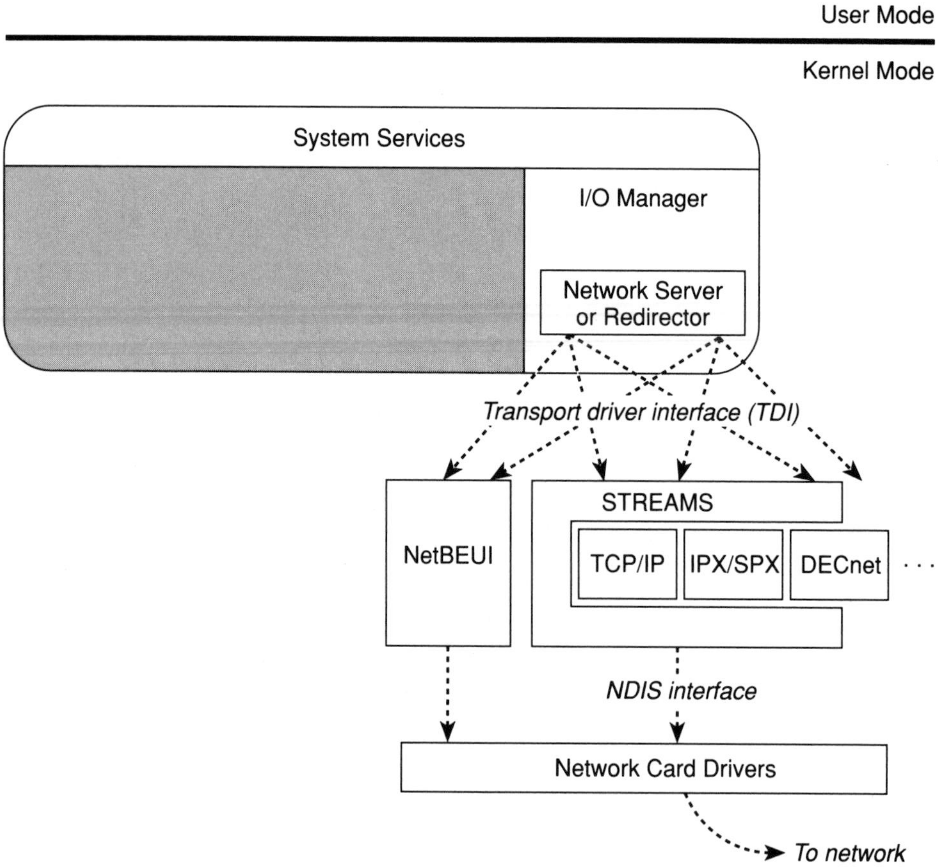

Figure 9-13. Transport Driver Interface (TDI)

I/O manager calls a redirector, passing it an IRP to process. The built-in redirector handles such a request by passing SMBs across a virtual circuit connection to a remote server. Other redirectors can use different means to communicate with remote servers.

TDI provides a set of functions that redirectors can use to send any type of data across a transport. The TDI supports both connection-based (virtual circuit) transmissions and connectionless (datagram) transmissions. Although LAN Manager uses connection-based communication, Novell's IPX software is an example of a network that uses connectionless communications. Microsoft initially supplies the following transports:

■ *NetBEUI* (NetBIOS Extended User Interface) *transport*. NetBEUI is a local-area transport protocol developed by IBM to operate underneath Microsoft's NetBIOS network interface.

■ *TCP/IP* (Transmission Control Protocol/Internet Protocol) *transport*. TCP/IP is a protocol developed for the U.S. Department of Defense to connect heterogenous systems on a wide-area network. TCP/IP is commonly used in UNIX-based networks and allows Windows NT to participate in popular UNIX-based bulletin board, news, and electronic mail services. The TCP/IP transport operates in a *STREAMS*-compatible environment.

Other transports that exist or that are in development by Microsoft or other vendors include:

■ IPX/SPX (Internet Packet Exchange/Sequenced Packet Exchange). IPX/SPX is a set of transport protocols used by Novell Corporation's NetWare software.

■ DECnet transport. DECnet is a proprietary protocol used by Digital Equipment Corporation that is supplied to link Windows NT systems to DECnet-based networks.

■ AppleTalk. A protocol developed by Apple Computer, Inc., that allows Apple Macintosh systems to communicate with Windows NT.

■ XNS (Xerox Network Systems) transport. XNS is a transport protocol developed by Xerox Corporation that was used in early Ethernet networks.

The STREAMS environment is worthy of further mention. It is a driver-development environment in UNIX System V that allows transport drivers to achieve a high degree of portability from one operating system to another. The STREAMS environment (which maps to TDI at its upper boundary and to NDIS 3.0 at its lower boundary) allows the many STREAMS-based transport drivers that already exist to be plugged into Windows NT with little or no modification. Transport drivers such as IPX/SPX, DECnet, and others can be implemented either as STREAMS-based drivers or as monolithic drivers (such as NetBEUI).

9.3.3 NDIS Environment for Network Drivers

The protocol drivers described in the previous section don't place actual bits onto the network. The cable connection is provided by a network card or chip that either is built in or slides into an add-on slot in the back of a machine. Each network card (sometimes called a network adapter) is capable of communicating over a particular type of cable, using a particular network topology.[5]

Network cards come with network drivers, which in the past often implemented a specific network protocol—XNS or TCP/IP, for example. Because Windows NT allows many different protocol drivers to be loaded, each network card vendor using this approach might want to rewrite its drivers to support several protocols—not an ideal strategy. To help vendors avoid this unnecessary work, Windows NT provides an interface and an environment, called the *network driver interface specification* (NDIS), which shields network drivers from the details of various transport protocols, and vice versa. Figure 9-14 illustrates.

Instead of writing a transport-specific driver for Windows NT, network vendors provide the NDIS interface as the uppermost layer of a single network driver. Doing so allows any protocol driver to direct its network requests to the network card by calling this interface. Thus, a user can communicate over a TCP/IP network and a NetBEUI (or DECnet, NetWare, VINES, and so forth) network using one network card and a single network driver.

---

5. This discussion assumes an old-fashioned network connected by a series of cables or perhaps telephone lines. However, modern network hardware also includes high-tech media such as fiber-optic cables, satellite links, and microwave transmitters.

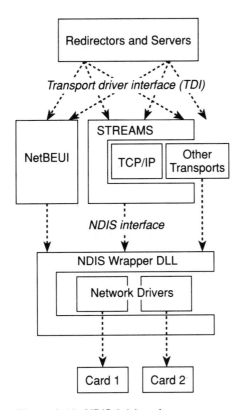

Figure 9-14. NDIS 3.0 Interface

The NDIS interface has been available in LAN Manager but is updated in Windows NT to NDIS version 3.0.[6] Version 3.0 is portable (written in C), is updated to use 32-bit addresses instead of 16-bit addresses, and is multiprocessor enabled. Like earlier versions, it can handle multiple independent network connections and multiple, simultaneously loaded transport protocols.

Each NDIS network driver is responsible for sending and receiving packets over its network connection and for managing the physical card on behalf of the operating system. At its lowest boundary, the NDIS driver communicates directly with the card or cards it services, using NDIS routines to access them. The NDIS driver starts I/O on the cards and receives interrupts from them. It calls upward to protocol drivers to indicate that it has received data and to notify them of its completion of an outbound data transfer.

---

6. 3Com Corporation and Microsoft jointly developed NDIS versions 1.0 and 2.0.

NDIS allows network drivers to be portable without containing embedded knowledge of the processor or operating system upon which they are running. The network drivers can call NDIS routines to shield themselves from platform-specific information so that they can move easily from one Windows NT system to another or from Windows NT to future MS-DOS/Windows systems. In Windows NT, the NDIS software calls NT kernel routines to acquire and release spin locks (for multiprocessor-safe operation) and calls I/O manager routines to connect interrupt objects to the appropriate IRQL in the kernel's dispatch table. These are only two examples of tasks that the network card driver would need to do for itself if it were written as an NT-specific driver. By calling NDIS routines instead, NDIS drivers written for Windows NT move easily to the Windows virtual device driver environment.

9.4   Distributed Application Environment

In contrast to his definition of a computer network, Andrew Tanenbaum defines a distributed system as one in which "the existence of multiple autonomous computers is transparent (i.e., not visible) to the user."[7] That is, a single operating system controls several networked computers and schedules their processors. Windows NT is not a distributed operating system. It runs on multiprocessor computers, scheduling all processors, but it requires the processors to share memory.

Although it isn't a distributed operating system, Windows NT provides facilities to create and run distributed applications. Distributed processing used to mean that a user could print from one of several computers by sending a print job to a remote print server. Similarly, it was not uncommon for an entire computer to be used simply as a place to store shareable files, which users could retrieve and copy to local machines for processing. Now distributed processing is more sophisticated. Instead of storing large database files on a remote machine and copying them to a local machine every time a user wants to query the database, applications such as Microsoft SQL Server allow the user to submit a query request that is filled by searching and sorting operations on the remote machine. When processing is complete, only the results are returned to the user's machine. This type of client/server computing minimizes the load on the part of the system that has the smallest capacity to handle it—the network—and offloads the work to a remote processor,

---

7. Andrew S. Tanenbaum, *Computer Networks*, 2d ed. (Englewood Cliffs, N.J.: Prentice-Hall, 1989), 2.

leaving the local processor free. The advantage of such applications is that they extend the computing capacity of a single-user workstation by exploiting the processor cycles of remote, often more powerful, computers.

This type of computing is an extension of the client/server model presented in Chapter 5, in which a client process sends a request to a server process for execution. The difference here is that the server process runs on a different computer. In Windows NT's local client/server model, the two processes use a message-passing facility called local procedure call (LPC) to communicate across their address spaces. For distributed processing, a more generic message-passing facility is needed. Assumptions about which process the message will be sent to and which computer the process is running on need to be removed from the facility. Also, because the client and the server processes are unlikely to share memory (unless they happen to be running on the same computer), the facility must assume that all data will be copied from one discrete address space to another over a network.

Client/server computing represents an application (rather than an operating system) approach to distributed processing, but it cannot succeed without proper operating system support. The operating system must supply the following to successfully implement networked client/server computing:

- A way to create and run parts of an application on both local and remote computers

- Application-level mechanisms for passing information between local and remote processes

- Support for network operations, including transport facilities

Much of this chapter has been devoted to describing the third capability. The following subsections examine the first two.

9.4.1 Remote Procedure Call[8]

A *remote procedure call* (RPC) facility is one that allows a programmer to create an application consisting of any number of procedures, some that execute locally and others that execute on remote computers via a network. It provides a procedural view of networked operations rather than a transport-centered view, thus simplifying the development of distributed applications.

---

8. Some information in this section is based on material in Microsoft's *Remote Procedure Call Programmer's Guide and Reference*, portions of which are provided under license from Digital Equipment Corporation. The document was modified at Microsoft by John Murray. The figures in this section were developed by Paul Leach of Microsoft.

Networking software is traditionally structured around an I/O model of processing. In Windows NT, for example, a network operation is initiated when an application issues a remote I/O request. The operating system processes it accordingly by forwarding it to a redirector, which acts as a remote file system. After the remote system fills the request and returns the results, the local network card interrupts. The kernel handles the interrupt, and the original I/O operation completes, returning results to the caller.

RPC takes a different approach altogether. RPC applications are like other structured applications with a main program that calls procedures or procedure libraries to perform specific tasks, as Figure 9-15 illustrates.

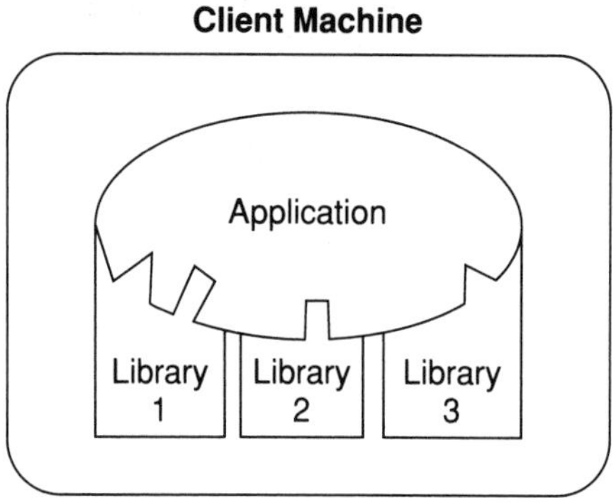

Client Machine

Figure 9-15. Application Using Libraries

The difference between RPC applications and regular applications, however, is that some of the procedure libraries in an RPC application execute on remote computers, whereas others execute locally, as shown in Figure 9-16.

To the RPC application, all the procedures appear to execute locally. In other words, instead of making a programmer actively write code to transmit computational or I/O-related requests across a network, handle network protocols, deal with network errors, wait for results, and so forth, RPC software handles these tasks automatically. And Windows NT's RPC facility can operate over any available transports loaded into the system.

To write an RPC application, the programmer decides which procedures will execute locally and which will execute remotely. For example, suppose an ordinary workstation has a network connection to a Cray supercomputer or to a machine designed specifically for high-speed vector operations. If the programmer were writing an application that manipulated large matrices, it would make sense performance-wise to offload the mathematical calculations to the remote computer by writing the program as an RPC application.

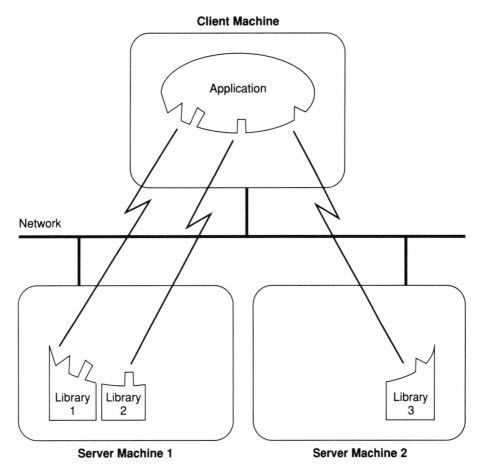

Figure 9-16. RPC Application Using Libraries

RPC applications work like this: As an application runs, it calls local procedures as well as procedures that are not present on the local machine. To handle the latter case, the application is linked to a local DLL that contains *stub procedures,* one for each remote procedure. The stub procedures have the same name and use the same interface as the remote procedures, but instead of performing the required operations, the stub takes the parameters passed to it and *marshals* them for transmission across the network. Marshaling parameters means ordering and packaging them in a particular way to suit a network link, such as resolving references and picking up a copy of any data structures that a pointer refers to.

The stub then calls RPC runtime procedures that locate the computer where the remote procedure resides, determine which transport mechanisms that computer uses, and send the request to it using local transport software. When the remote server receives the RPC request, it unmarshals the parameters (the reverse of marshaling them), reconstructs the original procedure call, and calls the procedure. When the server finishes, it performs the reverse sequence to return results to the caller. The RPC runtime is illustrated in Figure 9-17.

In addition to the RPC runtime, Microsoft's RPC facility includes a compiler, called the *Microsoft Interface Definition Language* (MIDL) compiler. The MIDL compiler simplifies creation of an RPC application. The programmer

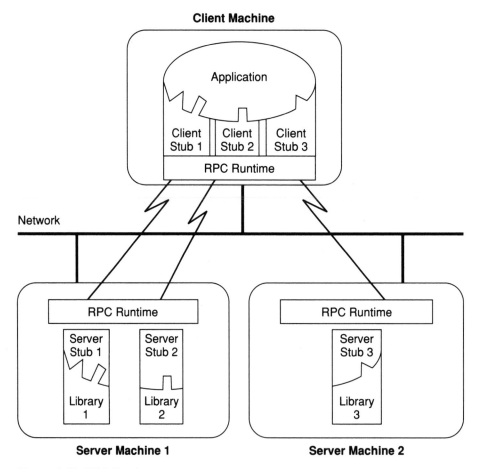

Figure 9-17. RPC Runtime

writes a series of ordinary function prototypes (assuming a C or C++ application) that describes the remote routines, and then places the routines in a file. He then adds to these prototypes some additional information, such as a network-unique identifier for the package of routines and a version number, plus attributes that specify whether the parameters are input, output, or both. The embellished prototypes form the developer's *interface definition language* (IDL) file.

Once the IDL file is created, the programmer compiles it with the MIDL compiler, which produces both client-side and server-side stub routines as well as header files to be included in the application. When the client-side application is linked to the stub routines file, all remote procedure references are resolved. The remote procedures are then installed, using a similar process, on the server machine. A programmer who wants to call an existing RPC application need only write the client side of the software and link the application to the local RPC runtime facility.

The RPC runtime uses a generic *RPC transport provider interface* to talk to a transport protocol. The provider interface acts as a thin layer between the RPC facility and the transport, mapping RPC operations onto the functions provided by the transport. Windows NT's RPC facility implements transport provider DLLs for named pipes, NetBIOS, TCP/IP, and DECnet. Additional transports can be supported by writing new provider DLLs. In a similar fashion, the RPC facility is designed to work with different network security facilities. Like the transport provider DLLs, security DLLs can be added between the RPC facility and the network. In the absence of other security DLLs, Windows NT's RPC software uses the built-in security of named pipes. (Section 9.4.2 describes named pipes in further detail.)

In order for one RPC facility to interoperate with RPC applications on other machines, both must use the same RPC conventions. Microsoft's RPC facility conforms to the RPC standard defined by the Open Software Foundation (OSF) in its distributed computing environment (DCE) specification. Thus, applications written using Microsoft's RPC facility can call remote procedures made available on other systems that use the DCE standard.

Most of the Windows NT networking services are RPC applications, which means that they can be called by both local processes and processes on remote computers. Thus, a remote client computer can call your server service to list shares, open files, print queues, or active users on your server, or it can call your messenger service to direct messages to you (all subject to security constraints, of course). Chuck Lenzmeier, who developed the Windows NT server, regards RPC-enabled services as one of the most noteworthy and useful features of Windows NT networking.

9.4.2 Named Pipes

Named pipes were originally conceived by Microsoft as a high-level interface to NetBIOS. NetBIOS did for networking applications what BIOS did for MS-DOS—it abstracted the hardware. Thus, it adopted a low-level view of network communications. Named pipes provide a more abstract (and pleasant) interface to the network. Rather than be concerned with routing, data transmission, and so forth, a programmer using named pipes can simply open a pipe and place data into it. A user of the pipe opens it and reads data from it. The cross-computer delivery is handled automatically, and one named pipe call is equivalent to many transport-level operations.

Named pipes are implemented in Windows NT by the named pipe file system driver, a pseudo–file system that stores pipe data in memory and retrieves it on demand. It acts like an ordinary file system when processing local named pipe requests or when receiving a named pipe request from a remote computer.

When a local program uses a named pipe that has a UNC (network) name, processing proceeds as for any other remote "file" request. The MUP driver intercepts the request and sends it to the redirector responsible for that network. Figure 9-18 illustrates both local and remote named pipe processing.

Named pipes, like files, are represented as file objects in Windows NT and operate under the same security mechanisms as other NT executive objects. When a local thread attempts to open a named pipe, the thread's desired access is checked against the ACL on the named pipe's file object. If no match occurs, access is denied. The named pipe facility, therefore, has built-in security. In addition, it allows one process to adopt the security context of another, a capability called *impersonation*. This capability allows a subsystem to take on the identity of a client process when opening a remote named pipe, for example.

Because they can exist on either local or remote computers, named pipes provide a means for client and server processes in a distributed application to communicate and share data. This interprocess communication facility hides the intermachine communication from the application. Underneath its API, the named pipe facility uses one of the lower-level transports to transmit its data. In contrast to RPC, the named pipe facility operates on an I/O-centered model and is useful for sending streams of data from one process to another.

The RPC facility can run over multiple transports using different types of security mechanisms. However, when operating over the LAN Manager network, the RPC facility uses named pipes as its network transport. By doing so, RPC operations take advantage of the built-in security that Windows NT applies to named pipes.

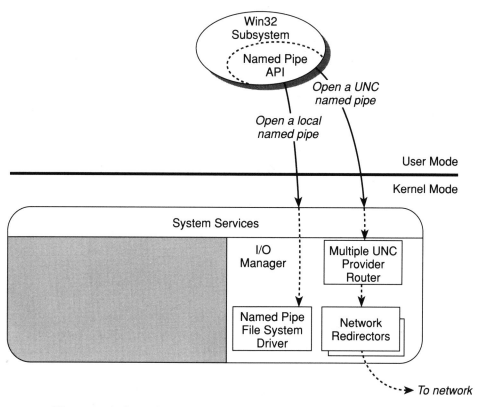

Figure 9-18. Client-Side Named Pipe Processing

9.5 Corporation-Wide Networking and Distributed Security

The standard Windows NT system comes with server capabilities built into it. The server enables workgroup operations, such as copying files between two systems or setting up a printer that several workstations can share. This type of small-scale networking is useful for small offices, home networks, or individual workstations that connect to networks over phone lines. In larger offices or labs, however, more facilities might be needed.

Earlier chapters of this book have described various facets of Windows NT security. Security is an important part of any network operation, necessary for protecting one user's data from being accessed by other users, a company's records from being tampered with by outsiders, and so on. Security, however, has some administration associated with it. For example, Chapter 5, "Windows and the Protected Subsystems," describes how users must log onto

Windows NT and how their logon information is authenticated by the operating system. For a user to be recognized by the operating system, a system administrator must set up an account for the user on the system she wants to access. Windows NT stores account names and passwords in a database called the *security accounts manager* (SAM) *database.*

When a user attempts to log onto her own workstation, Windows NT checks the SAM database associated with her workstation to authenticate her password. In a small network of systems, each user operates a Windows NT workstation and each workstation has its own private database of user accounts, as Figure 9-19 illustrates.

Network

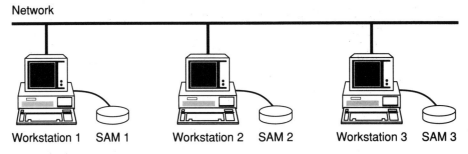

Figure 9-19. Small Network Configuration

If a particular user wants to access files (or devices) on each of the workstations, she must have a separate account on each machine. In practical terms, this means that if she changes her password and wants to keep the same one on each machine she accesses, she must update her password separately on each system.

This type of system maintenance is a nuisance for large business or corporate network installations. As the number of workstations increases, the task of administering them increases proportionally. To accommodate the needs of business networks, Cliff Van Dyke, Jim Kelly, and Jim Horne designed enhancements to Windows NT's built-in network software. Tentatively called LAN Manager for Windows NT, this software adds capabilities to the peer-to-peer networking support that exists in the Windows NT workstation.[9] It allows the creation of *network domains* (a more primitive version appears in LAN Manager 2.*x*) for simplifying the task of system administration. Figure 9-20 illustrates a sample network domain.

---

9. As this book goes to press, Microsoft plans to ship this product separately from the operating system. The product is expected to contain the advanced networking capabilities described in the remainder of this section.

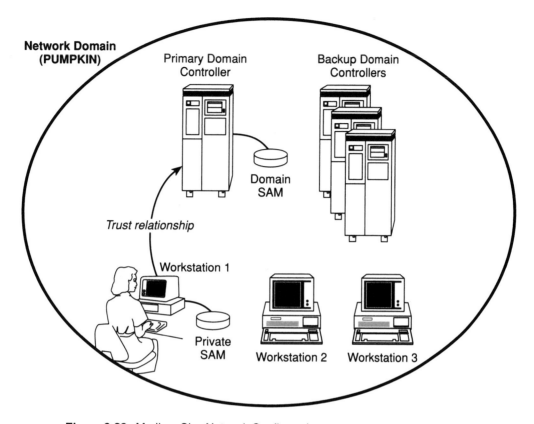

Figure 9-20. Medium-Size Network Configuration

In this figure, the large circle represents a network domain in which all the computers are linked. The domain includes several workstations and several server machines; the latter are called *domain controllers.* When a user logs on, she selects whether to log onto an account defined at her own workstation or onto an account located in her *primary domain,* the domain to which her machine belongs.

If the user logs onto an account on her workstation, the local authentication software uses the information stored in the workstation's SAM database to authenticate her logon. In contrast, if the user logs onto the domain, the local authentication software sends the logon request to the domain for authentication. The primary domain controller has a SAM database that applies to the entire domain, and the backup domain controllers maintain replicated copies of the database. This convenience frees the user from acquiring accounts on each server and improves fault tolerance. If a particular domain controller goes down, the system can dynamically direct a logon request to a different server.

In Figure 9-20, the line between the workstation and the primary domain controller represents a *trust relationship,* a security term meaning that the workstation "trusts" the domain to determine whether the user's logon is legitimate. A trust relationship allows Windows NT to set up a secure channel between the two systems and to access resources on the domain.

A side effect of establishing a domain is that the user can also log onto the domain from any other workstation (or server) in the domain and access her own workstation remotely. For example, if a group has established a development or testing lab of Windows NT systems, and those systems are grouped together into a domain, a user who has an account on the domain can log onto her account from any system in the lab.

The ability to create a network domain is convenient for medium-size network installations in which several servers are used by a large number of workstations. In even larger installations, such as corporation-wide networks, domains become even more valuable; they allow a company to divide its resources into several discrete units (domains) and to manage those units in a flexible manner. Figure 9-21 shows a large network configuration.

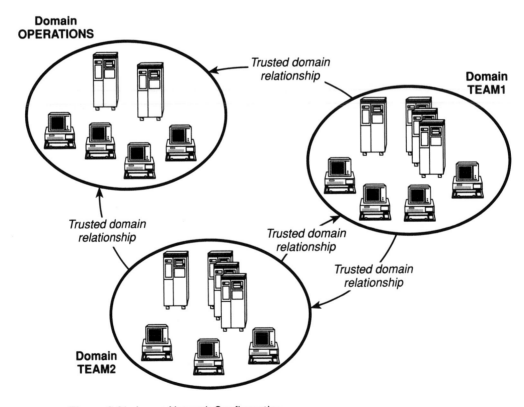

Figure 9-21. Large Network Configuration

This network contains three different domains: two for development groups (named TEAM1 and TEAM2) and one for system administrative staff (named OPERATIONS). *Trusted domain relationships* exist between both development domains and between the development domains and the operations domain. This structure allows a developer from TEAM1 to log onto her primary domain from a machine in the TEAM2 domain, for example. More interestingly, however, this structure allows a member of the operations group to log onto his normal account and transparently access resources in both the TEAM1 and TEAM2 domains as if they belonged to the OPERATIONS domain. Earlier LAN Manager products required operations staff to obtain an account on each domain it needed to administer, but LAN Manager for Windows NT removes this requirement. In this example, after a system administrator logs on, he can access resources on the other domains. When he connects to the TEAM1 domain, the TEAM1 security software checks whether it has a trust relationship with the OPERATIONS domain. The trust relationship exists, so the TEAM1 domain uses its secure channel to pass an implicit logon request to the OPERATIONS domain, which authenticates the user by accessing the OPERATIONS domain's SAM database. If the authentication succeeds, the system administrator can install software, perform backups, and complete other maintenance activities. This type of distributed security allows even a large organization with multiple domains to manage its resources easily while providing access to all network resources from anywhere in the network.

Although the medium and large network configurations allow users flexibility in accessing resources, each user can set up his own machine to limit others' access to it in the following ways:

- By applying access control lists (ACLs) to files and other local resources that permit or deny access to individual users or groups of users

- By assigning (or not assigning) privileges to individual users or groups of users

- By explicitly allowing individuals or groups to log on in specific ways, such as one or more of these:

  □ Interactive. Logging on from the keyboard

  □ Network. Logging on across a network connection

  □ Services. Logging on as a service (such as the messenger service or the alerter service)

By denying privileges to an individual or a group of individuals, by assigning ACLs to local objects, and by limiting which users can log onto an individual workstation, a user maintains control over his environment. If the user wants to, he can deny everybody but himself the ability to access his machine for any reason. Reflecting its versatility, the developers sometimes refer to Windows NT's administration software as "FlexAdmin."

In addition to domains, trusted domains, and distributed security, the LAN Manager for NT software provides disk mirroring and striping, file replication, and graphical server administration tools.

9.6 In Conclusion

The proliferation of large computer networks and the need for users to communicate and share centralized databases of information have elevated networking software from the realm of usefulness to the realm of necessity. By participating in one or more networks, an operating system can increase its processing power and storage capabilities, allow users to communicate and share data, and provide a richer set of capabilities to its applications than it could alone. To provide these advantages in an efficient way, Windows NT's networking software is built in, operating on an equal basis with the rest of the NT executive. Although built in, network components are not hard-wired into the system. Windows NT's flexible DLL and I/O system models allow network software to be added to and removed from the operating system dynamically.

Windows NT provides several network interfaces that allow it to be linked to different types of networks and to interact with different kinds of computer systems. The provider interface allows non-Microsoft network vendors to link to Win32 browsing and file I/O APIs; the TDI layer allows network redirectors and servers to access and use any available transport driver without modifying their code; and the NDIS layer allows transport drivers to access any vendor's network card and will give network drivers portability from Windows NT systems to the Windows virtual device driver environment.

Distributed application facilities, including RPC and interprocess communication mechanisms, allow application developers to exploit networked computers by offloading compute-intensive work to other machines or by accessing remote resources as if they were local. In addition, the LAN Manager for Windows NT product extends the networking capabilities of the standard Windows NT system to accommodate large businesswide networks with distributed security and administration facilities. With its extensive networking capabilities, Windows NT can transform a simple desktop workstation into an expansive web of computing resources.

EPILOGUE

Windows NT was designed as an extensible operating system—one that could evolve in a consistent, modular way over time. Indeed, it has already begun to evolve in directions not highlighted in this book.

The *configuration manager,* for example, is only briefly mentioned but represents the demise of the AUTOEXEC.BAT file, the CONFIG.SYS file, and all the INI files that users have become accustomed to seeing, fiddling with, and sometimes breaking. Designed primarily by Bryan Willman and Keith Logan, the configuration manager consists of several components, the most important of which is the *configuration registry.* The configuration registry is a repository for all information about the computer hardware the operating system is running on, the software installed on the system, and the person or persons using the system.

The purpose of the registry and its associated software is, first and foremost, to make systems easy for people to manage. It does so by examining the hardware and learning what it can at boot time, by configuring as much of the system automatically as possible, by asking the user a minimum number of questions when the operating system is installed, and by storing all the information it gleans in the registry so that the user never has to be bothered twice for the same information. Device drivers, applications, and users can also place information in the registry, and they can query the registry to retrieve the information they need. The user can view, update, or modify configuration information by using the graphical Registry Editor. Information in the configuration registry is stored in *key objects,* which are subject to the security mechanisms and other semantics applied to NT executive objects. This design allows Windows NT to maintain a unified storage facility for this seemingly random information and, at the same time, to make it available in a distributed but secure manner on networked systems.

An important component of *fault tolerance* also made it into the first release of Windows NT thanks to the Herculean efforts of Bob Rinne and Mike Glass. Their fault tolerant disk driver is an intermediate driver layered between a file system driver and a disk driver. According to Bob, it provides "disk data protection through partition redundancy." This means that a disk partition can be dynamically duplicated in one of several ways, so that if the disk fails, a copy of the data is still accessible. *Disk mirroring* refers to duplicating a disk partition on another disk and, if possible, on a disk attached to a different controller so that the data remains safe if either the disk or the disk controller fails. *Disk striping* refers to combining a set of same-sized disk partitions that reside on different disks into a single volume (or drive letter). Data stored on the volume spans the disks, forming a virtual "stripe" across them, a storage technique that enhances I/O performance by allowing multiple I/O operations on the same volume to proceed concurrently. The enhanced version of disk striping, called *disk striping with parity,* provides disk fault tolerance by maintaining parity information across the disk stripe so that if one partition (that is, disk) fails, the data on that partition can be re-created by performing an exclusive-OR operation across the remaining partitions in the stripe. (Incidentally, all these features are just one part of Windows NT's enhanced volume management capabilities, which allow disk space to be configured logically as well as physically. In addition to supporting disk fault tolerance, volume management allows discontiguous portions of one or more disks to be combined into one logical disk.)

Windows NT's disk fault tolerance, combined with the *uninterruptible power supply* (UPS) features described in Chapter 8, will provide a low-cost way for system administrators to protect and recover data on Windows NT systems. An extra level of fault tolerance is required by certain specialized applications, such as transaction processing software used at banks and other financial institutions. These applications rely on full hardware redundancy support in order to provide continuous system operation. Although continuous operation is used only for high-end software, many of the hooks needed to support it exist in Windows NT. The I/O system, for example, can delete and re-create device objects dynamically to accommodate changes in I/O device configuration. Additional capabilities that would be required include the ability to dynamically reassign drive letters to different physical resources and the ability to reconfigure devices without requiring the user to reboot afterward.

One of the most important projects that still face the Windows NT team is to make the operating system a fully international system. This goal will be the team's primary focus after shipping the first release of Windows NT. A goal for later releases of Windows NT is to provide a single system binary for all the world's markets. Although the NT executive and the Win32 API are fully internationalized, portions of the Win32 shell and system utilities are not yet Unicode-enabled, certain new international features are needed, and the Win32 GDI component needs enhancements to make the system fully usable in Japan and other Asian markets. Some of the required international features include an input method API, a new font architecture with search paths to allow logical combined fonts, the integration of user-defined characters into the font architecture, and enhancements to enable multiscript input.

For the Japanese, Chinese, and Korean versions of the system, additional work must be done. Fonts that support these languages are required, and an input method editor is needed to translate multiple keystrokes into individual characters. In addition, cooperative work with OEM partners is planned to ensure that Windows NT runs well on specialized or proprietary personal computers. For example, NEC has successfully ported Windows NT to their 9800-based personal computer. Because this non-AT–compatible computer is widely used in Japan, it is an important target platform for Windows NT.

Finally, in order to run existing international applications, the 16-bit Windows and MS-DOS environment subsystems must accommodate the double-byte coding scheme traditionally used to represent characters in Japanese and other Asian languages. The MS-DOS environment also must be made backward-compatible with the Japanese version of MS-DOS, which has evolved differently from the MS-DOS used in the U.S. and in European countries. A team of 20 U.S. and Japanese engineers, managed in the U.S. by David McBride, expects to ship the first international update release of Windows NT and Windows NT-J (the Japanese version of the system) six months after the U.S. version ships.

The topic of security is addressed throughout this book—perhaps a fitting choice of structure given the distributed nature of Windows NT security. However, it is a complex topic whose intricacies are only hinted at in discussions of its major components (object security, distributed security, and impersonation). An entire book could be written about the details of security.

Directions for future work in the security arena are quite interesting. The authentication model described briefly in Chapter 5 not only lends itself to supporting new user interfaces, such as bank teller machines or fingerprint or retinal scanners, but also allows for implementing different security architectures on top of Windows NT. For example, the popular Kerberos security model, which issues security "tickets" to entities wishing to communicate or exchange data, is under development as an authentication package and an API on Windows NT. Applications that use the Kerberos model would simply call the Kerberos API, which would be routed through the Windows NT security subsystem and on to a special, loadable Kerberos authentication package. Similarly, industry-specific security models, such as those used by banks, could be added to the system.

Extending Windows NT to handle the U.S. government's B-level security is a topic mentioned briefly in Chapter 3. To move from C-level security to B-level security would require upgrading Windows NT's object architecture and its security reference monitor to recognize security levels (the designation of particular users and their processes as "Secret," "Top Secret," and so on) and to support compartments (groups of users isolated from other groups of users). Mandatory access controls would be used to restrict processes from accessing resources belonging to higher-level processes or to those processes in different compartments.

A description of the NT file system (NTFS) is largely omitted from this book, as are the design details of the NT executive's device, file system, and network drivers. Similarly, the cache manager, a unique component of Windows NT, is left much to the reader's imagination. These topics are worthy of future writings. The ins and outs of the environment subsystems are also much more detailed than the discussions in Chapter 5 imply. Each subsystem has its own structure and philosophy, and although the Win32 subsystem is Windows NT's preeminent user interface, the other subsystems are likely to evolve into fuller-featured environments. I have neglected to describe the user interface of Windows NT, primarily because it is visible and, therefore, more accessible to the system's users than the mostly "invisible" design details that dominate this book. However, Windows NT utilities are likely to evolve along the lines of the Disk Manager utility; that is, they are likely to become more "Windows-native" in their graphical appearance and less reminiscent of MS-DOS applications.

As a portable operating system, Windows NT will undoubtedly migrate to new hardware platforms. Engineers at Digital Equipment Corporation, for example, are porting the system to their 64-bit Alpha APX processor. (Initially Windows NT will run with 32-bit addresses on the Alpha APX, as it does on the MIPS and Intel processors.)

Finally, we've been hearing more and more about object-oriented Windows software that will usher in the age of "Information At Your Fingertips," Bill Gates's vision for personal computing in the coming decades. Internally called Cairo, this software is expected to exist as a set of DLL extensions to Win32 on both Windows NT and MS-DOS. It establishes an object-oriented desktop environment that allows users to create, view, organize, and print resources without respect to the type of resource, its internal format, or its network location.

I intended to end this book with a definitive chapter about the future of Windows NT and perhaps even to pontificate about the future of the desktop. However, this industry is a fast-paced one, and Microsoft is a fast-paced company that responds quickly to changes in the marketplace. Prognostication is, therefore, a risky endeavor. Suffice it to say that Windows NT provides a well-paved road into the future of computing, whatever twists and turns that road may take.

GLOSSARY OF
TERMS AND ACRONYMS

access control entry (ACE) An entry in an access control list (ACL). It contains a security ID (SID) and a set of access rights. A process with a matching SID is either allowed the listed access rights, denied them, or allowed them with auditing. See also *access control list.*

access control list (ACL) The part of a security descriptor that enumerates the protections applied to an object. The owner of an object has discretionary access control of the object and can change the object's ACL to allow or disallow others access to the object. Access control lists are made up of access control entries (ACEs). See also *access control entry, discretionary access control,* and *security descriptor.*

access right A permission granted to a process to manipulate a particular object in a particular way (for example, by calling a service). Different object types support different access rights, which are stored in an object's access control list (ACL). See also *access control entry* and *access control list.*

access token An object that uniquely identifies a user who has logged on. An access token is attached to all the user's processes and contains the user's security ID (SID), the names of any groups to which the user belongs, any privileges the user owns, the default owner of any objects the user's processes create, and the default access control list (ACL) to be applied to any objects the user's processes create. See also *security ID.*

ACE access control entry.

ACL access control list.

address space See *virtual address space.*

alert An asynchronous notification that one thread sends to another. The alert interrupts the recipient thread at well-defined points in its execution and causes it to execute an asynchronous procedure call (APC). See also *alertable thread* and *asynchronous procedure call.*

alertable thread   A thread that has declared itself ready to execute an asynchronous procedure call (APC). A thread becomes alertable either by waiting on an object handle and specifying that its wait is alertable or by testing whether it has a pending APC. See also *alert* and *asynchronous procedure call.*

alerter service   A network service that sends system messages to a user. See also *service.*

alerting a thread   See *alert.*

APC   asynchronous procedure call.

APC object   The kernel's representation of an asynchronous procedure call (APC). It is a control object, containing the address of an APC and a pointer to the thread object that will execute it. See also *asynchronous procedure call* and *APC queue.*

APC queue   A list of asynchronous procedure call (APC) objects to be executed by a particular thread. The presence of an APC object in a thread's APC queue causes a software interrupt to occur at APC interrupt request level (IRQL) the next time the thread executes (if other enabling conditions are present). See also *asynchronous procedure call* and *APC object.*

API   application programming interface.

application programming interface (API)   A set of routines that an application program uses to request and carry out lower-level services performed by an operating system.

ASMP   asymmetric multiprocessing.

associated IRPs   A set of I/O request packets (IRPs) created to process a single I/O request. Each associated IRP causes some part of the request to be fulfilled. When all the associated IRPs are processed, the I/O request completes. See also *I/O request packet.*

asymmetric multiprocessing (ASMP)   A multiprocessing operating system that always selects the same processor to execute operating system code while other processors run only user jobs. See also *multiprocessing* and *symmetric multiprocessing.*

asynchronous   Occurring at any time without regard to the main flow of a program (for example, a device interrupt). Compare *synchronous.*

asynchronous I/O A model for I/O in which an application issues an I/O request and then continues executing while the device transfers the data. The application synchronizes with the completion of the data transfer by waiting on a file handle or an event handle. Compare *synchronous I/O.*

asynchronous procedure call (APC) A function that executes asynchronously in the context of a particular thread. The kernel issues a software interrupt when the thread executes (if other enabling conditions are present) and directs the thread to execute the APC. See also *APC object* and *APC queue.*

attribute caching A technique used in the Win32 subsystem to achieve performance gains when a Win32 application calls drawing functions. The client-side dynamic-link library (DLL) remembers when an application changes some attribute of the screen display and sends the data to the Win32 server only when the application draws something on the screen. See also *batching.*

auditing The ability to detect and record important security-related events, particularly any attempt to create, access, or delete objects. The Windows NT security system uses security IDs (SIDs) to record which process performed the action. See also *security ID.*

authentication Validation of a user's logon information. Performed by an authentication package in conjunction with the Windows NT security subsystem. See also *authentication package.*

authentication package A software module that can be plugged into the Windows NT security system to authenticate user logons for various input devices. See also *authentication.*

automatic working set trimming A technique used by the NT virtual memory (VM) manager to increase the amount of free memory available in the system. It decreases each process's working-set size when free memory runs low. See also *working set.*

backing store A storage medium, such as a disk, that serves as backup "memory" for paging when physical memory becomes full. See also *paging.*

batching A technique used in the Win32 subsystem to achieve performance gains when a Win32 application calls drawing functions. The client-side dynamic-link library (DLL) stores drawing application programming interface (API) calls in a queue, sending them in a single message to the server when the queue gets full or when the user enters input. See also *attribute caching.*

cache manager   A component in the I/O system that provides file-caching services to file systems and the Windows NT redirector. It uses the paging mechanisms of the virtual memory (VM) manager to bring pages into memory from disk and to write cached pages back to disk.

callback   A request message that a server sends to a client in response to a request from the client. A server sends a callback to a client to get more information about a client request. See also *local procedure call.*

CDFS   CD-ROM file system.

child process   A process created by another process that is called a parent process. The child process inherits some or all of the parent process's resources. Compare *parent process.*

CISC   complex instruction set computer.

client   A process whose threads call services provided by either a local or a remote server process. In Windows NT, communication between a client and a server occurs through the local procedure call (LPC) or remote procedure call (RPC) facilities. See also *client/server model, local procedure call,* and *remote procedure call.*

client/server model   A model for structuring applications or operating systems. The system is divided into processes (servers), each of which provides a set of specialized services to other processes (clients). Client processes request service by sending messages to server processes, and servers return results through another message. Systems built on a strict client/server model are appropriate for distributed computing environments in which servers can run on different computers.

code set   The binary codes used to represent the characters of a particular language.

committed memory   Virtual memory for which space in the paging file has been set aside. The process that commits the memory is charged paging file quota at that time. See also *reserved memory.*

complex instruction set computer (CISC)   A processor that employs powerful, often elaborate, machine instructions. Because of the instructions' complexity, each can take several clock cycles to complete. Compare *reduced instruction set computer.*

concurrent application An application that can execute in two or more locations. In Windows NT, a concurrent application is one that has created more than one thread of execution, either within a single process or in separate processes. See also *process* and *thread.*

configuration manager A set of software components that simplifies storage and retrieval of system configuration information. It includes the configuration registry, the graphical Registry Editor, and hardware recognizer firmware/software. See also *configuration registry.*

configuration registry A database repository for information about a computer's configuration—for example, the computer hardware, the software installed on the system, and environment settings and other information entered by the person or persons using the system. See also *key object.*

connecting an interrupt object Associating an interrupt service routine (ISR) with a particular interrupt request level (IRQL). A device driver calls the system to connect an interrupt object, which "turns on" interrupt handling for the device. See also *disconnecting an interrupt object, interrupt object,* and *interrupt service routine.*

console A text-based window managed by the Win32 subsystem. Environment subsystems direct the output of character-mode applications to consoles.

context See *thread context.*

context switching Saving the context of an executing thread, loading another thread's context, and transferring control to the new thread. Context switching is performed by the kernel's dispatcher. See also *dispatcher* and *thread context.*

control object A kernel object that provides a portable method for controlling various system tasks. The set of control objects includes the asynchronous procedure call (APC) object, the deferred procedure call (DPC) object, the kernel process object, and several objects used by the I/O system. See also *kernel object.*

copy-on-write Page-based (as opposed to object-based) memory protection that allows two processes to share a page until one of them writes to it. At that time, the process whose thread modified the page is given a private copy of the page in its virtual address space.

critical section   A block of code that accesses a nonshareable resource. To ensure correct code, only one thread can execute in a critical section at a time. See also *mutual exclusion.*

deferred procedure call (DPC)   A function that executes asynchronously, interrupting the execution of the thread that is currently running. DPCs perform system tasks that have been deferred until the processor's interrupt request level (IRQL) drops below dispatch IRQL. See also *DPC object* and *DPC queue.*

demand paging   A fetch policy for paging that postpones loading pages into physical memory until a page fault occurs. See also *fetch policy.*

desired access rights   The set of access rights a thread requests when opening a handle to an object. See also *granted access rights.*

device object   A system object that represents a physical, logical, or virtual device and describes its characteristics. A device object is associated with a driver object. See also *driver object.*

disconnecting an interrupt object   Dissociating an interrupt service routine (ISR) from a particular interrupt request level (IRQL). A device driver calls the system to disconnect an interrupt object, which "turns off" interrupt handling for the device. See also *connecting an interrupt object, interrupt object,* and *interrupt service routine.*

discretionary access control   The protection the owner of an object applies to the object by assigning various access rights to various users or groups of users. Discretionary protections can be limited by mandatory access controls applied to the object. See also *mandatory access control.*

disk mirroring   The procedure of duplicating a disk partition on two or more disks, preferably on disks attached to separate disk controllers so that data remains accessible if either a disk or a disk controller fails. See also *fault tolerance.*

disk striping   The procedure of combining a set of same-size disk partitions that reside on separate disks into a single volume, forming a virtual "stripe" across the disks. This technique enables multiple I/O operations in the same volume to proceed concurrently. See also *disk striping with parity.*

disk striping with parity   The procedure of maintaining parity information across a disk stripe so that if one disk partition fails, the data on that disk can be recreated by performing an exclusive-OR operation across the remaining partitions in the disk stripe. See also *disk striping* and *fault tolerance.*

dispatcher   A kernel module that keeps track of threads that are ready to execute, selects the order in which they will run, and initiates context switching from one thread to another. See also *context switching*.

dispatcher database   A set of global data structures that the kernel uses to keep track of which threads are ready to execute and which processors are executing which threads. The database includes the dispatcher ready queue. See also *dispatcher* and *dispatcher ready queue*.

dispatcher object   A kernel object that supports synchronization. The kernel's dispatcher implements the signaled and nonsignaled synchronization semantics. See also *kernel object, signaled state,* and *nonsignaled state*.

dispatcher ready queue   The data structure in the dispatcher database that tracks threads that are ready to execute. It is a series of queues, one queue for each scheduling priority. See also *dispatcher* and *dispatcher database*.

domain controller   A server in a network domain that accepts user logons and initiates their authentication. See also *authentication*.

DPC   deferred procedure call.

DPC object   A kernel object used to asynchronously execute a system function. It is a control object that contains the address of a deferred procedure call (DPC) to execute. The kernel places DPC objects in a global DPC queue to await execution. See also *deferred procedure call* and *DPC queue*.

DPC queue   A kernel-managed data structure that contains deferred procedure calls (DPCs) waiting to execute. The presence of a DPC object in the DPC queue causes the kernel to issue a software interrupt at dispatch/DPC interrupt request level (IRQL). The processor that takes the interrupt transfers control to the kernel, which executes all the DPCs in the queue. See also *deferred procedure call* and *DPC object*.

driver object   A system object that represents an individual driver on the system and tells the I/O manager the address of the driver's entry points. A driver object can be associated with multiple device objects (each one representing a device the driver operates). See also *device object*.

dynamic-link library (DLL)   An application programming interface (API) routine that user-mode applications access through ordinary procedure calls. The code for the API routine is not included in the user's executable image. Instead, the operating system automatically modifies the executable image to point to DLL procedures at runtime.

environment subsystem   A protected subsystem (server) that provides an application programming interface (API) and environment—such as Win32, MS-DOS, POSIX, or OS/2—on Windows NT. The subsystem captures API calls and implements them by calling native Windows NT services. See also *integral subsystem* and *protected subsystem*.

exception   A synchronous error condition resulting from the execution of a particular machine instruction. Exceptions can be either hardware-detected errors, such as division by zero, or software-detected errors, such as a guard page violation. See also *exception handler, structured exception handling,* and *trap handler*.

exception dispatcher   A kernel module that fields exceptions, transferring control to caller-supplied exception handlers or, if none are present, executing system default exception handlers. See also *exception* and *exception handler*.

exception handler   Code that responds to exceptions. The two types are frame-based exception handlers (including termination handlers) and system default exception handlers. See also *exception, structured exception handling,* and *termination handler*.

executive   See *NT executive*.

executive object   An NT object made visible to user mode by a component of the NT executive. The NT executive exports object services, which are used to manipulate executive objects.

FAT   file allocation table.

FAT file system   The file system traditionally used on MS-DOS systems.

fault tolerance   A computer and operating system's ability to respond gracefully to catastrophic events such as power outage or hardware failure. Usually, fault tolerance implies the ability either to continue the system's operation without loss of data or to shut the system down and restart it, recovering all processing that was in progress when the fault occurred.

fetch policy   The algorithm a virtual memory system uses to determine when the pager should bring a page from disk into memory. Windows NT uses a modified demand paging algorithm. See also *demand paging*.

file handle   A handle to a file object. See also *file object*.

file-mapping object   The Win32 subsystem's version of an NT section object that is backed by a mapped file.

file object   An executive object that represents an open file, a directory, a volume, or a device. See also *executive object*.

frame-based exception handler   An exception handler that is associated with a particular procedure or part of a procedure. The kernel invokes a frame-based exception handler when an exception occurs within that block of code. A frame-based exception handler can either resolve the exception, resignal the exception to a higher layer of code, or ignore the exception and resume the program's execution. See also *exception, structured exception handling,* and *termination handler*.

granted access rights   The set of access rights the security system gives a thread that opens a handle to an object. The granted access rights are a nonproper subset of the requester's desired access. The object manager stores granted access rights in the object handle it returns. See also *desired access rights*.

HAL   hardware abstraction layer.

handle   See *object handle*.

hardware abstraction layer (HAL)   A dynamic-link library (DLL) that protects the NT executive from variations in different vendors' hardware platforms in order to maximize the operating system's portability. The HAL implements functions that abstract I/O interfaces, the interrupt controller, hardware caches, multiprocessor communication mechanisms, and so forth.

high performance file system (HPFS)   A file system designed for OS/2, version 1.2, which was created to address the limitations of the file allocation table (FAT) file system used by MS-DOS. It added features such as longer filenames, the ability to associate attributes with a file, faster searching for files, and other optimizations.

HPFS   high performance file system.

idle thread   A system thread that executes when no other thread is ready to execute. The idle thread executes deferred procedure calls (DPCs) and initiates context switching when another thread becomes ready to execute. One idle thread exists for each processor in a multiprocessor system.

IDT   interrupt dispatch table.

IFS   installable file system.

impersonation   The ability of a thread in one process to take on the security identity of a thread in another process and perform operations on the thread's behalf. Used by environment subsystems and network services when accessing remote resources for client applications.

installable file system (IFS)   A file system that can be loaded into the operating system dynamically. Windows NT can support multiple installable file systems at one time, including the file allocation table (FAT) file system, the NT file system (NTFS), the high performance file system (HPFS), and the CD-ROM file system (CDFS). The operating system automatically determines the format of a storage medium and reads and writes files in the correct format.

instruction execution unit   A processor-dependent block of code in a virtual DOS machine (VDM). It acts as a trap handler on Intel processors and as an Intel instruction emulator on the MIPS processors. See also *virtual DOS machine*.

integral subsystem   A protected subsystem (server) that performs an essential operating system task. This group includes network servers and the security subsystem. See also *environment subsystem* and *protected subsystem*.

interrupt   An asynchronous operating system condition that disrupts normal execution and transfers control to an interrupt handler. Interrupts are usually initiated by I/O devices requiring service from the processor. See also *exception* and *trap handler*.

interrupt dispatcher   A submodule of the kernel's trap handler. It determines the source of an interrupt and transfers control to a routine that handles the interrupt. See also *interrupt*.

interrupt dispatch table (IDT)   A per-processor data structure that the kernel uses to locate an interrupt-handling routine when an interrupt occurs. See also *interrupt dispatcher*.

interrupt object   A kernel object that allows a device driver to associate ("connect") an interrupt service routine (ISR) with an interrupt request level (IRQL). It is a control object, containing the address of the ISR, the IRQL at which the device interrupts, and the entry in the kernel's interrupt dispatch table (IDT) with which the ISR should be associated. See also *connecting an interrupt object, interrupt dispatch table, interrupt request level,* and *interrupt service routine*.

interrupt request level (IRQL)   A ranking of interrupts by priority. A processor has an interrupt request level (IRQL) setting that threads can raise or lower. Interrupts that occur at or below the processor's IRQL setting are blocked, or masked, whereas interrupts that occur above the processor's IRQL setting are not masked. See also *masking interrupts*.

interrupt service routine (ISR)   A device driver routine that the kernel's interrupt handler calls when a device issues an interrupt. The routine stops the device from generating interrupts, saves device status information, and then queues a device driver deferred procedure call (DPC) to complete interrupt servicing. See also *deferred procedure call*.

invalid page   A virtual page that causes a page fault if an address from it is referenced. The page is either loaded from disk and made valid or recovered from the standby or modified page list and made valid; otherwise, the reference was an access violation. See also *valid page*.

I/O completion   The final step in the I/O system's processing of an I/O request. Typical operations include deleting internal data structures associated with the request, returning data to the caller, recording the final status of the operation in an I/O status block, setting a file object and/or event to the signaled state, and perhaps queuing an asynchronous procedure call (APC). See also *asynchronous procedure call*.

I/O manager   The Windows NT executive component that unifies the various pieces of the I/O system. It defines an orderly framework within which I/O requests are accepted and delivered to file systems and device drivers. It also provides code that is common to more than one driver.

I/O request packet (IRP)   A data structure used to represent an I/O request and to control its processing. The I/O manager creates the IRP and then passes it to one or more drivers in succession. When the drivers are finished performing the operation, the I/O manager completes the I/O and deletes the IRP. See also *I/O completion*.

IOSB   I/O status block.

I/O status block (IOSB)   A data structure that a caller supplies as a parameter to an I/O service. The I/O manager records the final status of the operation in the I/O status block when processing is complete.

IRP   I/O request packet.

IRP stack location   A data area in an I/O request packet that contains information a particular driver needs to perform its part of an I/O request. Each driver that works on the request has a separate stack location in the IRP. See also *I/O request packet*.

IRQL   interrupt request level.

ISR   interrupt service routine.

kernel   See *NT kernel*.

kernel mode   The privileged processor mode in which Windows NT system code runs. A thread running in kernel mode has access to system memory and to hardware. Compare *user mode*.

kernel object   A runtime instance of a kernel-defined abstract data type. The kernel defines special semantics for the behavior of kernel objects and implements kernel routines that the NT executive can call to manipulate kernel objects. Kernel objects fall into one of two categories: control objects and dispatcher objects. Both types of kernel objects are used as a basis for Windows NT executive objects. See also *control object, dispatcher object,* and *executive object*.

kernel process object   The kernel's representation of a process. It is a control object that contains the information necessary to load the process's address space and to keep track of process resources and default attributes. See also *control object*.

kernel thread object   The kernel's representation of a thread. It is a dispatcher object that contains the elemental information necessary to dispatch the thread for execution. See also *dispatcher object*.

key object   An executive object that represents system configuration information stored in the configuration registry. See also *configuration registry* and *executive object*.

lazy evaluation algorithms   A general category of algorithms that avoid performing an expensive operation until it is required. If the operation is never required, no processing time is wasted. The Windows NT virtual memory (VM) manager uses lazy evaluation algorithms to improve memory performance. Demand paging, copy-on-write page protection, and reserving and committing memory separately are examples. See also *committed memory, copy-on-write, demand paging,* and *reserved memory*.

locale The national and/or cultural environment in which a system or a program is running. The locale determines the language used for messages and menus, the sorting order of strings, the keyboard layout, and date and time formatting conventions.

local procedure call (LPC) facility An optimized message-passing facility that allows one process to communicate with another process on the same machine. Protected subsystems use LPC to communicate with each other and with their client processes. LPC is a variation of the remote procedure call (RPC) message-passing paradigm, optimized for local use. Compare *remote procedure call.*

local replacement policy A page replacement algorithm that allocates a fixed number of page frames to each process. When a process exceeds its allotment, the virtual memory (VM) manager begins transferring pages in the process's working set to disk in order to free space for additional page faults the process generates. See also *replacement policy* and *working set.*

logon process A Windows NT process whose threads detect a user's attempt to log onto the operating system. It verifies the user's logon information with the security system before granting the user access to the system.

LPC local procedure call.

mandatory access control Protection assigned to an object by a system administrator. Mandatory access controls typically label objects with a level, such as "Secret" or "Top Secret." Users wanting to access the objects must be cleared at the appropriate level. Mandatory access control supersedes any discretionary access controls that an owner applies to an object. See also *discretionary access control.*

map To translate a virtual address into a physical address.

mapped file A file that is loaded into a section object in memory. By mapping views of the section into its address space, a process can access the file as a large array stored in virtual memory. The virtual memory (VM) manager automatically pages to and from the file, loading pages from disk when they are used and writing pages to disk when they are modified. See also *map* and *paging file.*

mapped file I/O File I/O performed by reading and writing to virtual memory that is backed by a file. See also *mapped file.*

marshal   To order and package procedure parameters in a particular format for sending across the network. See also *remote procedure call.*

masking interrupts   Raising a processor's interrupt request level (IRQL) to block interrupts at and below the new IRQL.

master/slave system   See *asymmetric multiprocessing.*

messenger service   A network service that receives messages from other systems and displays them. See also *service.*

method   A function associated with an object type that the object manager calls automatically at well-defined points during an object's lifetime. See also *object type.*

MIDL   Microsoft interface definition language.

MIDL compiler   A compiler that takes files written in Microsoft interface definition language and produces stub routines for use in remote procedure call (RPC) applications. See also *remote procedure call* and *stub procedure.*

modified page writer   A thread in the virtual memory (VM) manager that asynchronously writes modified virtual pages to disk, thus increasing the number of available page frames.

MPR   multiple provider router.

multiple provider router (MPR)   A dynamic-link library (DLL) that determines which network (and thus which file system) to access when an application uses the Win32 WNet application programming interface (API) for browsing remote file systems.

multiple UNC provider (MUP)   A driver that determines which network (and thus which file system) to access when an application uses the Win32 I/O application programming interface (API) to open remote files.

multiprocessing   An operating system's simultaneous execution of two or more threads on different processors. Only multiprocessing operating systems can exploit the extra processors in a multiprocessor computer. As a general rule, multiprocessing operating systems also perform multitasking. See also *multitasking.*

multiprogramming   See *multitasking.*

multitasking A processor's execution of more than one thread by context switching from one to the other, providing the illusion that all threads are executing simultaneously. See also *preemptive multitasking*.

multithreading The capability of an application to execute in two or more locations using multiple threads. The term is sometimes used interchangeably with *multitasking* in reference to an operating system that supports threads.

MUP multiple uniform naming convention (UNC) provider.

mutual exclusion Allowing only one thread at a time to access a resource. Mutual exclusion is necessary when a system resource does not lend itself to shared access or when sharing might produce unpredictable results. See also *critical section*.

named pipe An interprocess communication mechanism that allows one process to send data to another local or remote process.

name retention The procedure by which the object manager keeps an object's name in its namespace. When the last handle to the object is closed, the object manager deletes the object's name from its namespace, preventing subsequent open operations on that object. See also *object retention*.

national language support (NLS) An application programming interface (API) that gives applications access to locale-specific information. See also *locale*.

native services System services that the NT executive makes available to user mode for use by environment subsystems, dynamic-link libraries (DLLs), and other system applications.

NDIS network driver interface specification.

NetBEUI transport NetBIOS (Network Basic Input/Output System) Extended User Interface. Windows NT's primary local area network transport protocol. See also *NetBIOS interface*.

NetBIOS interface A programming interface that allows I/O requests to be sent to and received from a remote computer. It hides networking hardware from applications.

network domain A set of workstations and servers that share a security accounts manager (SAM) database and can be administered as a group. A user with an account in a particular network domain can log onto and access his or her account from any system in the domain. See also *SAM database*.

network driver interface specification (NDIS) A Windows NT interface for network card drivers. It provides transport independence for network card vendors because all transport drivers call the NDIS interface to access network cards. Network drivers written to the NDIS interface (NDIS drivers) will be portable to the MS-DOS virtual device driver environment.

network redirector Networking software that accepts I/O requests for remote files, named pipes, or mailslots and sends ("redirects") them to a network server on another machine. Redirectors are implemented as file system drivers in Windows NT. See also *network server*.

network server Network software that responds to I/O or compute requests from a client machine. Windows NT network servers can be implemented either as server processes or as drivers. See also *protected subsystem*.

NLS national language support.

nonpaged pool The portion of system memory that cannot be paged to disk. Compare *paged pool*.

nonprivileged processor mode See *user mode*.

nonsignaled state An attribute of every object whose object type supports synchronization. A thread waiting on an object that is in the nonsignaled state continues to wait until the kernel sets the object to the signaled state. See also *signaled state* and *synchronization*.

NT new technology.

NT executive The portion of the Windows NT operating system that runs in kernel mode. It provides process structure, interprocess communication, memory management, object management, thread scheduling, interrupt processing, I/O capabilities, networking, and object security. Application programming interfaces (APIs) and other features are provided in user-mode protected subsystems. See also *protected subsystem*.

NT file system (NTFS) An advanced file system designed for use specifically with the Windows NT operating system. It supports file system recovery, extremely large storage media, and various features for the POSIX subsystem. It also supports object-oriented applications by treating all files as objects with user-defined and system-defined attributes.

NTFS NT file system.

NT kernel The component of the NT executive that manages the processor. It performs thread scheduling and dispatching, interrupt and exception handling, and multiprocessor synchronization and provides primitive objects that the NT executive uses to create user-mode objects.

object A single runtime instance of an NT-defined object type. It contains data that can be manipulated only by using a set of services provided for objects of its type. See also *object type*.

object attribute A field of data in an object that defines or records the object's state and that can be manipulated by calling an object service.

object class See *object type*.

object directory object An object that stores the names of other objects, much as a file directory stores filenames. It provides the means to support a hierarchical naming structure for Windows NT objects.

object domain A self-contained set of objects that is accessible through the NT object manager's object name hierarchy but is managed by a secondary object manager (such as the NT I/O system).

object handle An index into a process-specific object table. It is used to refer to an opened object and incorporates a set of access rights granted to the process that owns the handle. It also contains an inheritance designation that determines whether the handle is inherited by child processes. Programs use handles to refer to objects when calling object services. See also *object table*.

object manager The component of the NT executive that creates, deletes, and names operating system resources, which are stored as objects.

object model   A model for structuring programs around the data they manipulate. The format of data structures is hidden inside objects, and programs must use specially defined services to manipulate object data. The primary goal of the object model is to maximize the reusability of code. See also *object*.

object retention   The procedure by which the object manager keeps an object in memory. When the last reference to an object is removed, the object manager deletes a temporary object from memory. See also *name retention*.

object service   A user-mode-visible system service for manipulating an object. In Windows NT, an object service generally reads or changes an object's attributes and is used primarily by protected subsystems.

object table   A process-specific data structure that contains handles to all the objects the process's threads have opened. See also *object handle*.

object type   An abstract data type, a set of services that operate on instances of the data type, and a set of object attributes. An object type is defined by using a type object. See also *object attribute* and *type object*.

Open Systems Interconnection (OSI) reference model   A software model defined by the International Standards Organization that standardizes levels of service and types of interaction for networked computers. The OSI reference model defines seven layers of computer communication and what each layer is responsible for.

OSI   Open Systems Interconnection.

page   Blocks of contiguous virtual addresses that the virtual memory (VM) manager copies from memory to disk and back during its paging operation. See also *page frame* and *paging*.

paged pool   The portion of system memory that can be paged to disk. Compare *nonpaged pool*.

page fault   A processor trap that occurs when an executing thread refers to a virtual address that resides on an invalid page. See also *invalid page* and *paging*.

page frame   A block of contiguous physical addresses used to store the contents of a virtual page. Page frame size (and often page size) are dictated by the processor. On most systems, the page size and page frame size are the same. See also *page* and *paging*.

page frame database A data structure that the virtual memory (VM) manager uses to record the status of all physical page frames. See also *page frame.*

pager A component of the virtual memory (VM) manager that performs the paging operation. See also *paging.*

page table A process-specific table that the virtual memory (VM) manager uses to map virtual addresses to physical memory addresses or to disk locations. A page table is made up of page table entries (PTEs). See also *page table entry* and *paging.*

page table entry (PTE) An entry in a process's page table. It contains the information necessary for the virtual memory system to locate a page when a thread uses an invalid address. The size and format of PTEs are processor dependent. See also *invalid page* and *page table.*

paging A virtual memory operation in which memory management software transfers pages from memory to disk when physical memory becomes full. When a thread accesses a page that is not in memory, a page fault occurs and the memory manager uses page tables to locate the required page on disk and load it into memory. See also *invalid page, page fault,* and *page table.*

paging file A system file containing the contents of virtual pages that have been paged out of memory. See also *backing store* and *mapped file.*

parent process A process that has created another process, called a child process. The child process inherits some or all of the parent process's resources. Compare *child process.*

placement policy The algorithm a virtual memory system uses to decide where in physical memory to put data it is paging in from disk. The NT virtual memory (VM) manager uses a series of first in, first out (FIFO) page lists to keep track of free pages and to retrieve a free page when loading information from the disk after a page fault occurs.

port A communication channel through which a client process communicates with a protected subsystem. Ports are implemented as Windows NT objects. See also *local procedure call.*

power notify object A kernel object that allows device drivers to register a power recovery routine with the kernel. It is a control object that contains a pointer to a device driver routine, which the kernel calls when the power returns after a power failure.

power status object   A kernel object that allows device drivers to determine whether the power has failed. It is a control object containing a Boolean variable that a device driver can test before proceeding with an uninterruptible operation. If the power has already failed, the driver does not start the operation.

PPTE   prototype page table entry.

preempt   To interrupt the execution of a thread when a higher-priority thread becomes ready to execute and to context-switch to the higher-priority thread. See *preemptive multitasking*.

preemptive multitasking   A form of multitasking in which the operating system periodically interrupts the execution of a thread and executes other waiting threads. Preemption prevents a thread from monopolizing the processor and allows another thread to run. See also *time quantum*.

primary domain   The network domain with which a particular user account is associated. See also *network domain*.

privileged processor mode   See *kernel mode*.

process   A logical division of labor in an operating system. In Windows NT, it comprises a virtual address space, an executable program, one or more threads of execution, some portion of the user's resource quotas, and the system resources that the operating system has allocated to the process's threads. It is implemented as an object. See also *thread*.

process context   See *thread context*.

processor affinity   The set of processors on which a thread can run.

process tree   A hierarchy of parent and child processes maintained by the POSIX and OS/2 subsystems.

protected subsystem   A server process that performs operating system functions. Each Windows NT protected subsystem operates in user mode with a private address space. See also *environment subsystem* and *integral subsystem*.

protocol   A set of rules and conventions by which two computers pass messages across a network medium. Networking software generally implements multiple levels of protocols layered one on top of another.

protocol stack   The collection and sequence of network protocols used to transmit a network request from one machine to another. See also *protocol*.

prototype page table entry (PPTE) A data structure that looks similar to a normal page table entry (PTE) but points to a page frame shared by more than one process. See also *page table entry* and *section object.*

provider A generic name for software that establishes Windows NT as a client of a remote network server.

provider interface A programming interface that allows network vendors to make their remote file systems available for browsing by applications using Windows' WNet application programming interface (API). See also *multiple provider router.*

PTE page table entry.

quick LPC A form of local procedure call (LPC) used by portions of the Win32 subsystem and its clients. Quick LPC increases the speed of passing a message by bypassing port objects, storing messages in shared memory, and using a built-in synchronization mechanism. See also *local procedure call* and *port.*

quota A resource limit imposed on user accounts. The object manager charges a process some portion of the user's quota each time one of the process's threads creates or opens a handle to an object. When the quota is depleted, the user's processes can no longer create objects or open object handles until the processes release some resources.

raise an exception To deliberately transfer control to an exception handler when an exception occurs. Software raises an exception when errors or unexpected conditions occur. See also *exception* and *exception handler.*

redirector Networking software that accepts I/O requests for remote files, named pipes, or mailslots and sends ("redirects") them to a network server on another machine. Redirectors are implemented as file system drivers in Windows NT. See also *network server.*

reduced instruction set computer (RISC) A processor that employs a small number of simple instructions that are used in conjunction to perform more powerful operations. Because of the instructions' simplicity and their use of large numbers of registers, each generally takes only one clock cycle to execute, and the processor can run at higher clock speeds than can most complex instruction set computers (CISCs). Compare *complex instruction set computer.*

remote procedure call (RPC)   A message-passing facility that allows a distributed application to call services available on various machines in a network without regard to their locations. Remote network operations are handled automatically. RPC provides a procedural view, rather than a transport-centered view, of networked operations. Compare *local procedure call*.

replacement policy   The algorithm used by a virtual memory system to decide which virtual page must be removed from memory to make room for data being paged in from disk. Windows NT adopts a least-recently-used local replacement policy. See also *local replacement policy*.

reserved memory   A set of virtual memory addresses that a thread has allocated. See also *committed memory*.

robustness   The ability of a program to function well or to continue functioning well in unexpected situations.

RPC   remote procedure call.

RPC transport provider interface   A DLL that acts as an interface between the remote procedure call (RPC) facility and network transport software. It allows RPCs to be sent over various transports.

SAM database   A database of security information that includes user account names and passwords. It is administered by the Windows User Manager. See also *security accounts manager*.

script   A system of characters used to write in one or more languages.

section object   An object that represents memory potentially shared by two or more processes. A process can also create an unnamed section object that represents private memory. See also *view*.

secure logon facility   Software in a secure operating system that monitors a particular class of logon devices to ensure that all users enter valid identification before they are allowed access to the system.

security accounts manager (SAM)   A Windows NT protected subsystem that maintains the SAM database and provides an application programming interface (API) for accessing the database. See also *SAM database*.

security descriptor   A data structure attached to an object that protects the object from unauthorized access. It contains an access control list (ACL) and controls auditing on the object. See also *access control list* and *auditing*.

security ID A name, unique across time and space, that identifies a logged-on user to the security system. Security IDs (SIDs) can identify either an individual user or a group of users. An individual security ID usually corresponds to a user's logon identifier.

security reference monitor A component of the NT executive that compares the access token of a process to the access control list (ACL) of an object to determine whether the process's threads should be allowed to open a handle to the object.

security subsystem An integral subsystem that records the security policies in effect for the local computer and participates in logging on users. See also *integral subsystem.*

server A process with one or more threads that accept requests from client processes. It implements a set of services that it makes available to clients running either on the same computer or possibly on various computers in a distributed network. See also *client, local procedure call, network server,* and *remote procedure call.*

server message block (SMB) protocol A network protocol used originally in Microsoft Networks and subsequently adopted in PC networking software. It defines a specific format for packets of data to be transmitted across the network. The Windows NT redirector and built-in server use SMBs to communicate with each other and with computers on LAN Manager networks. See also *network server, protocol,* and *redirector.*

server service A network service that supplies a user-mode application programming interface (API) to manage the Windows NT network server. See also *service.*

service A server process that performs a specific system function and often provides an application programming interface (API) for other processes to call. Windows NT services are RPC-enabled, meaning that their API routines can be called from remote machines.

service controller The networking component that loads and starts Windows NT services. It also loads and unloads many Windows NT drivers, including device drivers and network transport drivers. See also *service.*

SID security ID.

signaled state An attribute of every object whose object type supports synchronization. When the kernel sets an object to the signaled state, threads waiting on the object are released from their waiting states (according to a set of rules) and become eligible for execution. See also *dispatcher object, non-signaled state,* and *synchronization.*

single-byte coding scheme A character encoding scheme (code set), such as Windows ANSI, that uses eight bits to represent each character. See also *Unicode.*

SMB server message block.

SMP symmetric multiprocessing.

spin lock A synchronization mechanism used by the kernel and parts of the executive that guarantees mutually exclusive access to a global system data structure across multiple processors. A thread waiting to acquire a spin lock effectively stalls the processor until it gets the spin lock. See also *mutual exclusion.*

STREAMS A driver-development environment that Windows NT supplies for creating or porting network transport drivers.

structured exception handling A method for capturing unexpected conditions and responding to them consistently throughout the operating system. The operating system (or hardware) issues an exception when an abnormal system event occurs, and the kernel automatically transfers control to an exception handler. See also *exception* and *exception handler.*

stub procedure A procedure in a dynamic-link library (DLL) that serves as an entry point for an application programming interface (API). When a client application calls the API routine, the stub procedure marshals the API parameters it receives into a message and sends them to either a local server (subsystem) or a remote server on the network. See also *local procedure call, marshal,* and *remote procedure call.*

symbolic link object An NT executive object that translates one object name into another.

symmetric multiprocessing (SMP) A multiprocessing operating system that allows operating system code to run on any free processor in a multiprocessor computer. Symmetric multiprocessing systems generally provide better throughput and greater availability than do asymmetric multiprocessing systems. Compare *asymmetric multiprocessing;* see also *multiprocessing.*

synchronization The ability of one thread to pause during execution and wait until another thread performs an operation. In Windows NT, a thread waits for another thread to set a synchronization object to the signaled state. See also *signaled state* and *synchronization objects*.

synchronization objects The collection of user-mode-visible NT executive objects whose object types support synchronization. They include threads, processes, events, event pairs, semaphores, timers, mutants, and files. A thread can wait for a synchronization object to be set to the signaled state by another thread. Each synchronization object contains within it a kernel dispatcher object. See also *dispatcher object, signaled state,* and *synchronization*.

synchronous Occurring at a particular time as a direct result of the execution of a particular machine instruction. Compare *asynchronous*.

synchronous I/O A model for I/O in which an application issues an I/O request and the I/O system does not return control to the application until the I/O request completes. Compare *asynchronous I/O*.

TCP/IP transport Transmission Control Protocol/Internet Protocol. Windows NT's primary wide area network transport protocol. It allows Windows NT to communicate with systems on TCP/IP networks and to participate in popular UNIX-based bulletin board, news, and electronic mail services.

TDI transport driver interface.

termination handler An exception handler that lets an application ensure that a particular block of code always executes, even if the code terminates in an unexpected way. Termination handlers often contain code that frees allocated resources so that if a procedure terminates unexpectedly, the resources are released back to the system. See also *exception handler*.

thread An executable entity that belongs to one (and only one) process. It comprises a program counter, a user-mode stack, a kernel-mode stack, and a set of register values. All threads in a process have equal access to the process's address space, object handles, and other resources. Threads are implemented as objects. See also *process*.

thread context The volatile data associated with the execution of a thread. It includes the contents of system registers and the virtual address space belonging to the thread's process. See also *context switching*.

thread dispatching See *context switching*.

thread object The implementation of a thread in Windows NT. See also *thread.*

thread of execution See *thread.*

thread scheduling The process of examining the queue of threads that are ready to execute and selecting one to run next. This task is performed by the NT kernel's dispatcher module. See also *dispatcher.*

tightly coupled system A multiprocessor computer in which all processors share global memory. The operating system must synchronize its access to data structures stored in global memory.

time quantum A preset amount of time that an operating system kernel allows a thread to execute before preempting it. See also *preempt.*

TLB translation lookaside buffer.

token object See *access token.*

topology The physical configuration of the machines in a network.

translation lookaside buffer (TLB) An array of memory containing the virtual-to-physical address mappings of the pages most recently used system-wide. Both MIPS processors and Intel processors have TLBs, but their structure and operation are hardware dependent.

transport driver interface (TDI) A Windows NT interface for network redirectors and servers to use in sending network-bound requests to transport drivers. The interface provides transport independence for these components by abstracting transport-specific information.

trap A processor's mechanism for capturing an executing thread when an unusual event (such as an exception or interrupt) occurs and transferring control to a fixed location in memory. See also *trap handler.*

trap frame A data structure that the kernel's trap handler creates when an interrupt or exception occurs. It records the state of the processor, which allows the kernel to continue executing the thread that was interrupted after handling the condition. See also *trap handler.*

trap handler A body of code that hardware invokes when an interrupt or exception occurs. It determines the type of condition that occurred and transfers control to a handling routine. See also *trap.*

trusted domain relationship A trust relationship that exists between two network domains. See also *network domain* and *trust relationship*.

trust relationship A security term meaning that one workstation or network server trusts a domain controller to authenticate a user logon on its behalf. One domain controller can also trust a domain controller in another domain to authenticate a logon. See also *domain controller*.

type object An internal system object that defines common attributes for a class of objects. Every object instance contains a pointer to its corresponding type object. See also *object type*.

UNC uniform naming convention.

Unicode A fixed-width, 16-bit character encoding standard capable of representing all the world's scripts. See also *script*.

uniform naming convention (UNC) names Filenames or other resource names that begin with the string \\, indicating that they exist on a remote machine.

uninterruptible power supply (UPS) A backup battery module attached to a computer that allows memory contents to remain intact long enough for the operating system to perform an orderly system shutdown if a power outage occurs.

UPS uninterruptible power supply.

user mode The nonprivileged processor mode in which application code runs. A thread running in user mode can gain access to the system only by calling system services. Compare *kernel mode*.

valid page A virtual page that is in physical memory and immediately available. See also *invalid page* and *page*.

VDM virtual DOS machine.

view The portion of a section object that a process maps into its virtual address space. A process can map multiple, and even overlapping, views of a section. See also *map* and *section object*.

virtual address space The set of addresses available for a process's threads to use. In Windows NT, every process has a unique virtual address space of 2^{32} bytes (4 GB). See also *virtual memory*.

virtual circuit A virtual communication channel between two machines. Multiple network sessions are multiplexed across a single virtual circuit.

virtual DOS machine (VDM) A protected subsystem that supplies a complete MS-DOS environment and a console in which to run an MS-DOS-based application. Any number of VDMs can run simultaneously. See also *console.*

virtual file Any source or destination for I/O that is accessed like a file. In the NT executive, all I/O is performed on virtual files, which are represented by file objects and accessed using file handles. See also *file object.*

virtual memory (VM) A logical view of memory that does not necessarily correspond to memory's physical structure. See also *virtual memory management.*

virtual memory management A memory management system that provides a large address space to each process by mapping the process's virtual addresses onto physical addresses as the process's threads use them. When physical memory becomes full, it swaps selected memory contents to disk, reloading them from disk on demand. Virtual memory management allows programmers to create and run programs that use more memory than is physically present on their computers. Because the placement of data in memory is controlled by the virtual memory system, each process's address space can be separated and protected from the others. See also *map* and *paging.*

virtual memory (VM) manager The NT executive component that implements virtual memory.

VM virtual memory.

Win32 API A 32-bit application programming interface for both MS-DOS/ Windows and Windows NT. It updates earlier versions of the Windows application programming interface (API) with sophisticated operating system capabilities, security, and API routines for displaying text-based applications in a window.

Windows NT The high-end Windows operating system in a family of Windows operating systems. Along with Pen Windows and 16-bit Windows, this system allows Windows applications to run on computers ranging from the smallest notebooks to large multiprocessor workstations and server machines. Windows NT also runs MS-DOS, POSIX, and OS/2 applications by employing user-mode servers called protected subsystems. See also *protected subsystem.*

Windows on Win32 (WOW)   A protected subsystem that runs within a virtual DOS machine (VDM) process. It provides a 16-bit Windows environment capable of running any number of 16-bit Windows applications on Windows NT.

working set   The set of virtual pages that are in physical memory at any moment for a particular process.

workstation service   A network service that supplies user-mode application programming interface (API) routines to manage the Windows NT redirector. See also *service*.

WOW   Windows on Win32.

BIBLIOGRAPHY

The following is a partial list of the published texts and papers I read in preparing to write this book. These works provided background in operating system theory as well as details about specific operating system implementations. This research helped me form a framework for introducing Windows NT's design and gave me a factual basis for comparing it with other operating systems. Because Windows NT represents cutting-edge technology in certain respects, some topics had few or no published sources from which I could draw.

This bibliography includes works used as direct sources and works that provided background information, although it omits design specifications, presentations, notes, code and, most important, individual developers; all of these served as primary sources of information for this book.

Because *Inside Windows NT* took three years to research and write, some of the published sources became outdated along the way. I discovered over the course of the project, however, that at some point one must stop reading and start writing because the reading can go on forever.

Operating Systems, General

Boykin, Joseph, and Susan J. LoVerso. "Recent Developments in Operating Systems." *Computer* (May 1990): 5–6. These authors described the entire history and future of operating systems in two magazine pages, including acknowledgments, references, personal biographies, and even photographs of the authors. Wow.

Dasgupta, Partha. "The Clouds Distributed Operating System." *Computer* (November 1991): 34–44.

Kenah, Lawrence J., Ruth Goldenberg, and Simon F. Bate. *VMS Internals and Data Structures: Version 4.4.* Maynard, Mass.: Digital Press, 1987. Certain parts of Windows NT resemble (sometimes only remotely) certain parts of VMS—for example, exception handling, asynchronous procedure calls, the I/O system, thread scheduling. I also discovered that much of the verbiage the Windows NT developers use to describe NT executive facilities borrows from VMS terminology. With many of the NT executive developers originating from DEC, this is not altogether surprising. (People have noted that if you increment each letter in "HAL," the name of the disembodied computer voice in the film *2001: A Space Odyssey*, you get "IBM." Columnist John Dvorak has also noted that if you take "VMS" and increment each letter you get—you guessed it—"WNT," aka Windows NT. Clever.)

Lister, A. M. *Fundamentals of Operating Systems*, 3d ed. New York: Springer-Verlag, 1984. Although operating systems have been an area of special interest to me for years and although I studied operating systems in college and used quite a few different ones, I never ran across this gem of a book. Mark Lucovsky offhandedly recommended it to me at the beginning of this project when suggesting how my book should end up: short, lucid, and explaining everything in around 150 pages. Although that suggestion is amusing in retrospect, this book is a must-read for anyone who ever wanted to understand the essentials of operating system structure. It was an inspiration.

Myers, Glenford J. *Advances in Computer Architecture*, 2d ed. New York: John Wiley and Sons, 1982.

Naecker, Philip A. "Software Layering on VMS." *DEC Professional* (September 1988): 38–43. This article offers a quick, VMS-specific overview of what layering and modularity mean in an operating system.

Peterson, James L., and Abraham Silberschatz. *Operating System Concepts*, 2d ed. Reading, Mass.: Addison-Wesley Publishing Company, 1985. This was my college text and has held up well over time. There is probably an updated edition by now, but this one served my purposes. It, along with Tanenbaum's operating system design book and Lister's fundamentals, formed the core library that helped me structure the overall presentation of Windows NT.

Pollack, Fred, Kevin Kahn, T. Don Dennis, Gerald Holzhammer, Herman D'Hooge, and Steve Tolopka. "[BiiN:] An Object-Oriented Distributed Operating System." Proceedings, Spring IEEE Compcon, February 1990.

Tanenbaum, Andrew S. *Operating Systems: Design and Implementation*. Englewood Cliffs, N.J.: Prentice-Hall, Inc., 1987. Tanenbaum is unequaled in his ability to write coherently and interestingly on operating system topics. This book was the primary source of information regarding operating system models and the basics of synchronization. Thanks to Ron Burk for recommending it and for loaning me his personal copy for three years.

Watson, Richard W. "The Architecture of Future Operating Systems." Paper presented at Cray Users Group Meeting, Tokyo, September 1988.

Exception Handling

Levin, Roy. "Program Structures for Exceptional Condition Handling." Research paper, Carnegie-Mellon University Computer Science Department, June 1977.

Roberts, Eric S. "Implementing Exceptions in C." Systems Research Center Report, Digital Equipment Corporation, March 1989.

Internationalization and Unicode

Freytag, Asmus. "Program Migration to Unicode." Proceedings of the Unicode Implementer's Workshop, Mountain View, California, August 1991. Asmus generously assisted me with documents and tutoring on internationalization and Unicode issues. The diagram in Chapter 2 illustrating the layout of the Unicode code set first appeared in this publication.

Hall, William S. "Adapt Your Program for Worldwide Use with Windows Internationalization Support." *Microsoft Systems Journal* (November/December 1991): 29–58. This article explains principles that most authors assume everyone understands. It and the Sheldon article are good places to start if you want to learn about writing international software.

Sheldon, Kenneth M. "ASCII Goes Global." *Byte* (July 1991): 108–16.

The Unicode Consortium. *The Unicode Standard: World-Wide Character Encoding*, version 1.0, 2 vols. Reading, Mass.: Addison-Wesley Publishing Company, 1991–92. The Unicode Consortium maintains and promotes this standard and sponsors an ongoing series of implementer's workshops. (The Unicode Consortium, 1965 Charleston Road, Mountain View, California 94043.)

I/O and File Systems

Duncan, Ray. "Design Goals and Implementation of the New High Performance File System." *Microsoft Systems Journal* (September 1989): 1–13. This article, although focused primarily on the HPFS, includes a concise technical explanation of why we've outgrown the FAT file system. It also describes the meaning of "installable file system," a system feature that Windows NT updates.

Mach

When I began this project, I read every Mach document or article I could unearth because Mach was a new client/server operating system with many similarities to Windows NT. I did not update these sources in the last year or two, so there are undoubtedly more-current writings. Rick Rashid joined Microsoft in late 1991 as Director of Research in Microsoft's newly formed research group. Although he graciously agreed to read portions of this book, I regret that I was unable to take full advantage of his expertise because the book was too close to its publication date by the time he arrived. Any errors or inaccuracies in this book related to Mach are entirely my responsibility.

Accetta, M., R. Baron, W. Bolosky, D. Golub, R. Rashid, A. Tevanian, and M. Young. "Mach: A New Kernel Foundation for UNIX Development." Research paper, Carnegie-Mellon University Computer Science Department, April 1986.

Baron, Victor, Richard Rashid, Ellen Siegel, Avadis Tevanian, Jr., and Michael Young. "Mach-1: A Multiprocessor-Oriented Operating System and Environment." Proceedings, New Computing Environments: Parallel, Vector, Systolic, edited by Arthur Wouk. SIAM, 1986.

Rashid, Richard. "From RIG to Accent to Mach: The Evolution of a Network Operating System." Research paper, Carnegie-Mellon University Computer Science Department, August 1987.

——. "Threads of a New System." *UNIX Review* (August 1986): 37–49.

Rashid, Richard, Avadis Tevanian, Jr., Michael Young, David Golub, Robert Baron, David Black, William Bolosky, and Jonathan Chew. "Machine-Independent Virtual Memory Management for Paged Uniprocessor and Multiprocessor Architectures." Proceedings, Second International Conference on Architectural Support for Programming Languages and Operating Systems, IEEE, 1987.

Tevanian, Avadis, Jr. "Architecture-Independent Virtual Memory Management for Parallel and Distributed Environments: The Mach Approach." Ph.D. dissertation, Carnegie-Mellon University, December 1987.

——. "Mach: A New Basis for Future UNIX Development." Proceedings, Autumn EUUG, September 1986.

Tevanian, Avadis, Jr., Richard Rashid, David B. Golub, David L. Black, Eric Cooper, and Michael W. Young. "Mach Threads and the UNIX Kernel: The Battle for Control." Research paper, Carnegie-Mellon University Computer Science Department, August 1987.

Multiprocessing

Multiprocessing was one of those topics that yielded little published information because there weren't many symmetric multiprocessing (SMP) operating systems in existence when I started this book. Someone needs to write a book about the complexities of SMP system design. It's a weighty subject.

Maples, Creve, and Douglas Logan. ''The Advantages of an Adaptive Multiprocessor Architecture.'' Proceedings, New Computing Environments: Parallel, Vector, Systolic, edited by Arthur Wouk. SIAM, 1986.

Oleinick, Peter N. *Parallel Algorithms on a Multiprocessor.* Ann Arbor, Mich.: UMI Research Press, 1982. (Out of print. Provided on microfilm by University Microfilms International.)

William, Tom. ''Real-Time UNIX Develops Multiprocessing Muscle.'' *Computer Design* (March 1991): 126–30. This article provides a quick overview of multiprocessing terms and issues, including symmetric multiprocessing, tightly coupled systems vs. loosely coupled systems, spin locks, and processor affinities.

Networking

Birrell, A. D., and B. J. Nelson. ''Implementing Remote Procedure Calls.'' *ACM Transactions on Computer Systems* (February 1984): 39–59. A classic.

Microsoft Corporation. *Remote Procedure Call Programmer's Guide and Reference,* 1992. A definitive and well-written guide to Microsoft's RPC facility. It is based on an RPC specification written at Digital Equipment Corporation. The spec was modified and adapted at Microsoft by John Murray.

Petrosky, Mary. ''Microsoft's Master Plan.'' *LAN Technology* (April 1991): 71–76. This article was the source of the reference in Chapter 5 to the unflattering name ''many-headed Hydra,'' referring to the fledgling Windows NT system. Because it makes amusing copy, I borrowed the epithet myself. I also found the title of this article…well…amusing.

Ryan, Ralph. *LAN Manager, A Programmer's Guide.* Redmond, Wash.: Microsoft Press, 1990.

Tanenbaum, Andrew S. *Computer Networks,* 2d ed. Englewood Cliffs, N.J.: Prentice-Hall, Inc., 1989. Once again, Tanenbaum lends interest and clarity to an operating system topic. In this case, the topic is dry and dull, but Tanenbaum isn't. I used this book as a reference for the OSI networking model and other networking odds and ends.

Tanenbaum, Andrew S., and Robbert van Renesse. "Distributed Operating Systems." *ACM Computing Surveys* (1985): 419–70.

Objects

Coad, Peter, and Edward Yourdon. *Object-Oriented Analysis.* Englewood Cliffs, N.J.: Prentice-Hall, Inc., 1990. I don't recommend this book for o-o study—only for its concise visual representation of objects. I used a format similar to their most elemental diagrams to illustrate NT executive objects.

Jones, Anita K. "The Object Model: A Conceptual Tool for Structuring Software." In *Lecture Notes in Computer Science,* edited by G. Goos and J. Hartmanis. New York: Springer-Verlag, 1978. This is a lucid description of what objects are and how they relate to operating systems. It also discusses three uses for objects in operating systems: naming, protection, and synchronization. These happen to be three of the major uses of objects in the NT executive. This paper was a real find.

Meyer, Bertrand. *Object-oriented Software Construction.* Hertfordshire, United Kingdom: Prentice-Hall International, 1988. Three years ago, this was the only book I could find that really explained what object-oriented programming was and why you'd ever want to use it. The first four chapters of Meyer's book contain the best introduction to o-o principles I've seen.

OS/2

Iacobucci, Ed. *OS/2 Programmer's Guide.* Berkeley, Calif.: Osborne McGraw-Hill, 1988.

Kogan, M. S., and F. L. Rawson III. "The Design of Operating System/2." *IBM Systems Journal* 27, no. 2 (1988): 90–100.

Letwin, Gordon. *Inside OS/2.* Redmond, Wash.: Microsoft Press, 1988. Although Letwin's book is exceedingly different from this one in form and content, its existence justified my writing this book. We also recycled its name. Thanks, Gordon.

Microsoft Corporation. *Microsoft Operating System/2 Programmer's Reference,* version 1.1, vol. 1, 1989. Written by Brad Hastings, Stan Krute, Donn Morse, Ralph Walden, and Dan Weston.

POSIX/UNIX

Bach, Maurice J. *The Design of the UNIX Operating System.* Englewood Cliffs, N.J.: Prentice-Hall, Inc., 1986.

IEEE. *Portable Operating System Interface for Computer Environments.* IEEE Standard 1003.1-1988, 1988.

Lewine, Donald. *POSIX Programmer's Guide, Writing Portable UNIX Programs.* Newton, Mass.: O'Reilly & Associates, Inc., 1991. This book was bequeathed to me by Ellen Aycock-Wright, formerly Windows NT's POSIX subsystem developer, when she left Microsoft to seek greener pastures. I wish I had had it a year earlier—on cursory reading, it looks like a great book.

Processes, Threads, and Concurrency

Birrell, Andrew D. *An Introduction to Programming with Threads.* Systems Research Center (SRC) Report, Digital Equipment Corporation, January 6, 1989. Finding good sources of information on threads was tough in 1989. Digital's SRC produced several early papers on this topic, this one among them. This document contained an especially useful discussion about alerts. The NT executive's alert and APC capabilities were partially based on work done at SRC.

Birrell, Andrew D., J. V. Guttag, J. J. Horning, and R. Levin. *Synchronization Primitives for a Multiprocessor: A Formal Specification.* Systems Research Center Report, Digital Equipment Corporation, August 20, 1987.

Processors

Hennessy, John L. *VLSI Processor Architecture.* IEEE Transactions on Computers (December 1984). An important work on processor architectures, focusing on different single-processor architectures and their relationship to operating systems. It was useful to me as coherent background on RISC and CISC processors. It also details necessary operating system functions and how processors support those functions.

Intel Corporation. *80386 Programmer's Reference Manual,* 1986.

Intel Corporation. *i486 Microprocessor Programmer's Reference Manual,* 1990.

Kane, Gerry, and Joe Heinrich. *MIPS RISC Architecture.* Englewood Cliffs, N.J.: Prentice-Hall, Inc., 1992.

MIPS R4000 Microprocessor User's Manual. MIPS Computer Systems, Sunnyvale, Calif., 1991.

Security

Department of Defense Trusted Computer System Evaluation Criteria, DoD 5200.28-STD, December 1985. (This is known among security insiders as "the Orange Book." "The Rainbow Collection" is the shorthand name for a series of ancillary documents.)

Reisinger, David A. "Access Control Methods of VAX/VMS." *Information Age* (July 1988): 62–68.

Shannon, Terry C. "An Introduction to VAX/VMS Security Mechanisms and Techniques." *Computer Security Journal* 4, no. 2 (1987): 39–47. Although this article discusses VAX/VMS security, many of the techniques described are also used in Windows NT.

Virtual Memory

Denning, Peter J. "Virtual Memory." *Computing Surveys* (September 1970): 153–189. This paper, a classic in the virtual memory field, was recommended to me by Lou Perazzoli. (As Lou tells it, this work influenced him to specialize in virtual memory and is thus partly responsible for Lou's current status as Windows NT's virtual memory guru.)

————. "The Working Set Model for Program Behavior." *Communications of the ACM* (May 1968): 323–33. This paper is also a classic in the virtual memory field and provides a theoretical foundation for Windows NT's implementation of working sets.

Fitzgerald, Robert, and Richard Rashid. "The Integration of Virtual Memory Management and Interprocess Communication in Accent." *ACM Transactions on Computer Systems* (May 1986): 147–77. Among other things, this article discusses techniques in Accent—specifically, lazy evaluation and copy-on-write—that Windows NT also uses in its virtual memory system.

Series 32000 Databook. National Semiconductor Corporation, Santa Clara, Calif., 1986. This book, recommended to me by Ron Burk when I began writing about virtual memory, was a big surprise. Hidden away in an introduction to the series 32000 architecture is a concise, readable, and relatively complete description of virtual memory principles. This piece helped me form my introductory section for the virtual memory chapter. Unfortunately, the author of this text is not named in the book (a lamentable custom in computer company documentation).

Windows

Petzold, Charles. *Programming Windows.* Redmond, Wash.: Microsoft Press, 1990. Although I mainly paged through Petzold's book rather than reading it from cover to cover, in retrospect I wish I had read more of it. Sprinkled throughout the code fragments and hands-on discussions are bits of lore regarding the design of various pieces of Windows. If I had realized this, I could have saved myself some time in writing the chapter on Windows. As Windows programmers everywhere already know, this book is indispensable in learning about Windows programming. I hope Petzold writes one on Win32 programming.

Microsoft Corporation. *Win32 Application Programming Interface Reference Manual.* 2 vols. Redmond, Wash.: Microsoft Press, 1992.

Index

Italicized page numbers refer to illustrations.

Helen Custer graduated with Highest Distinction from the University of Kansas, earning B.A. degrees in computer science, English, and psychology. Her 8-year professional writing career began when she coauthored *Learning Z-BASIC on the Heath/Zenith Z-100.* Prior to joining the Windows NT team to write *Inside Windows NT,* she worked at Digital Equipment Corporation, writing C language manuals and miscellaneous operating system documentation and developing documentation tools. She has written for the *C User's Journal, Windows/DOS Developer's Journal* (formerly *Tech Specialist*), and *Microsoft Systems Journal.*

The manuscript for this book was prepared and submitted to Microsoft Press in electronic form. Text files were processed and formatted using Microsoft Word.

Principal editorial compositor: Barb Runyan
Principal proofreader/copy editor: Deborah Long
Principal typographer: Katherine Erickson
Interior text designer: Kim Eggleston
Principal illustrator: Connie Little
Cover designer: Rebecca Geisler-Johnson
Cover color separator: Color Service

Text composition by Microsoft Press in New Baskerville with display type in Helvetica Bold, using the Magna composition system and the Linotronic 300 laser imagesetter.

Essential References for the Windows™ Programmer

PROGRAMMING WINDOWS™ 3.1
Charles Petzold
The Classic Guide to Writing Applications for Windows 3.1

"The definitive book on Windows programming is, of course, Charles Petzold's PROGRAMMING WINDOWS." **Dr. Dobb's Journal**

"If you're going to program for Windows, buy this book. It will pay for itself in a matter of hours." **Computer Language**

This new edition of PROGRAMMING WINDOWS—completely updated and revised to highlight version 3.1 capabilities—is once again packed with keen insight, tried-and-true programming techniques, scores of sample programs written in C (on disk too!), and straightforward explanations of the Microsoft Windows operating system. The accompanying disk contains more than 1.2-MB of source code and associated files from the book.

PROGRAMMING WINDOWS 3.1. The most authoritative, example-packed, and thorough resource for programmers writing applications for the Microsoft Windows operating system.

1008 pages, softcover with one 1.44-MB 3.5-inch disk
$49.95 ($67.95 Canada)   ISBN 1-55615-395-3

THE WINDOWS™ INTERFACE:
AN APPLICATION DESIGN GUIDE
Microsoft Corporation
The Microsoft® Guidelines for Designing a User Interface for Windows-based Applications

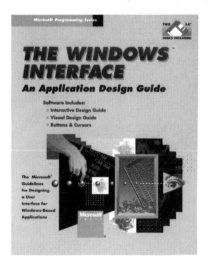

If you're developing for Microsoft Windows, this is *the* guide to designing a world-class user interface. THE WINDOWS INTERFACE is packed with ideas, answers, and options on all aspects of the Windows GUI—including OLE and DDE. This near-definitive set of recommended standards promotes visual and functional consistency within and across Windows-based applications. Compiled by Microsoft, it's an essential reference for developers regardless of experience or tools used.

Bundled with the book are a set of companion disks. They include the following materials:

Interactive Design Guide—A sample application that provides access to an online version of this book.

Visual Design Guide—Descriptions, specifications, and online illustrations of Windows design elements.

Buttons and Cursors—A dynamic link library with standard cursor and toolbar button images—ready to use.

248 pages, softcover with two 1.44-MB 3.5-inch disks
$39.95 ($54.95 Canada)   ISBN 1-55615-439-9

Microsoft Press books are available wherever books and software are sold.
*To order direct, call **1-800-MSPRESS**.* *Refer to campaign **BBK**.*

* In Canada, contact Macmillan Canada, Attn: Microsoft Press Dept., 164 Commander Blvd., Agincourt, Ontario, Canada M1S 3C7, or call (416) 293-8141.
In the U.K., contact Microsoft Press, 27 Wrights Lane, London W8 5TZ.

Register Today!

Return the *Inside Windows NT™* registration form for:

✔ special book upgrade offers
✔ Microsoft Press catalogs featuring
   books on related Microsoft titles
✔ exclusive offers on specially priced books

Please mail the completed form to:

Microsoft Press

Inside Windows NT

PO Box 3019

Bothell, WA   98041-9910

or by fax to:

Microsoft Press

Attn: Marketing Department

Fax #: 206-936-7329

NAME

COMPANY

ADDRESS

CITY   STATE   ZIP

1-55615-481-XA   Type: W1X